Telecourse Study Guide
for
Economics U$A

Seventh Edition

The Components of *ECONOMICS U$A*

ECONOMICS U$A, A Series of Twenty-Eight Television Programs and Twenty-Eight Audio Modules

ECONOMICS U$A, Seventh Edition, By Nariman Behravesh and Edwin Mansfield

TELECOURSE STUDY GUIDE FOR ECONOMICS U$A, Revised by James Sondgeroth

TEXT REVIEW GUIDE FOR ECONOMICS U$A, By Edwin Mansfield, Revised by Deborah Paige

FACULTY MANUAL WITH TEST QUESTIONS FOR ECONOMICS U$A, Prepared by the Southern California Consortium

TEST-ITEM FILE FOR ECONOMICS U$A, By Herbert Gishlick

Telecourse Study Guide for Economics U$A

Seventh Edition

A Television Course Created and Produced by the Educational Film Center

**revised by
James Sondgeroth**

Academic Consultants

Nariman Behravesh
Robert Augur
Ralph Lewis
Sol Kaufler
James Phillips

Writers

Michael D. Hiscox
Vicki Spandel

Problem Set

Edwin Mansfield

Audio Questions and Bibliography

John Peterson

W. W. NORTON & COMPANY, INC.

THE ANNENBERG/CPB PROJECT

Produced by:	The Southern California Consortium
Credits:	This study guide was developed by the Southern California Consortium, incorporating materials from Edwin Mansfield's *Study Guide for Economics*, as part of the *ECONOMICS U$A* telecourse created and produced by the Educational Film Center and Wharton Econometric Forecasting Associates and revised for the Sixth Edition by James Sondegroth. Funds for the preparation of television, audio, and print materials for this telecourse were provided by the Annenberg/CPB Project.
	An Annenberg/CPB Project
Copyright:	Copyright © 2005, 2001, 1998, 1995, 1992, 1989, 1986 by The Corporation for Community College Television, the Educational Film Center, and the Corporation for Public Broadcasting.
	Portions of the Self-Test sections of Chapters 1 through 28 are from Mansfield's *Study Guide for Economics* and are used with permission from W. W. Norton & Company, Inc.

All rights reserved

Printed in the United States of America

ISBN 0-393-92606-0 (pbk.)

W. W. Norton & Company, Inc., 500 Fifth Avenue, New York, N.Y. 10110
www.wwnorton.com

W. W. Norton & Company Ltd., Castle House, 75/76 Wells St., London W1T 3QT

1 2 3 4 5 6 7 8 9 0

CONTENTS

Preface vii

1. Scarce Resources: What Is Economics All About? 1
2. Markets and Prices: Does the Free Market
   Respond to People's Needs? 20
3. U.S. Economic Growth: What Is Gross Domestic Product? 46
4. Booms and Busts: What Causes the Business Cycle? 63
5. John Maynard Keynes: What Did We Learn from the
   Great Depression? 85
6. Fiscal Policy: Can We Control the Economy? 105
7. Inflation: How Did the Spiral Begin? 127
8. The Banking System: Why Must It Be Protected? 146
9. The Federal Reserve: Does Money Matter? 166
10. Stagflation: Why Couldn't Keynesian Policies Beat It? 184
11. Productivity: Can We Get More for Less? 199
12. Federal Deficits: Can We Live with Them? 217
13. Monetary Policy: How Well Does It Work? 235
14. Stabilization Policy: Are We Still in Control? 255
15. The Firm: How Can It Keep Costs Down? 268
16. Supply and Demand: What Sets the Price? 288
17. Perfect Competition and Inelastic Demand: Can the
    Farmer Make a Profit? 308
18. Economic Efficiency: What Price Controls? 327
19. Monopoly: Who Is in Control? 347
20. Oligopolies: Whatever Happened to Price Competition? 365
21. Pollution: How Much Is a Clean Environment Worth? 382
22. Labor and Management: How Do They Come to Terms? 399
23. Profits and Interest: Where Is the Best Return? 416
24. Reducing Poverty: What Have We Done? 432
25. Economic Growth: Can We Keep Up the Pace? 450
26. Public Goods and Responsibilities: How Far Should We Go? 466
27. International Trade: For Whose Benefit? 485
28. Exchange Rates: What in the World Is a Dollar Worth? 501

PREFACE

Economic events and decisions influence our lives, but few Americans have more than a nodding acquaintance with the underlying theories and principles that help explain economic trends. Terms such as *supply and demand, income distribution,* and *resource allocation* punctuate the evening news and financial headlines but have little real meaning for those of us attempting to unravel the day's events.

Economics U$A provides you the opportunity to sit at the feet of leading economists and learn the principles of economics through the absorbing drama of recent historic events.

Description of Course Materials

Should this be your first experience with a telecourse, it is important for you to become familiar with its components, how they interact with each other, and how to use them. As you read the following sections, realize that *Economics U$A* was designed to be offered as *either* a one-semester survey course or a two-semester macro- and microeconomics course. Following your teacher's instructions, use those portions of the course applicable to your situation.

Television Programs

The video portion of *Economics U$A*, developed by the Educational Film Center in Annandale, Virginia, approaches the subject of economics in a journalistic style. Former CBS network correspondent David Schoumacher is the investigative reporter, exploring the causes and effects of the major economic events of the twentieth century. The men and women who participated in many of these events provide a depth of insight rarely offered contemporary television audiences.

In each program, noted economist Dr. Richard Gill, former professor of economics at Harvard University, analyzes and interprets the decisions and consequences that underlie economic events. As a counterpoint to the reportorial, fact-finding Schoumacher, Gill explains the stories that are unfolding in light of specific economic principles. Together, Schoumacher and Gill will provide you a clear explanation of basic economic concepts.

Using television for learning is not like watching a comedy series or sporting events. At first you have to concentrate on active watching. It is easy to slip into the passive, half-viewing stance you usually bring into play when you watch entertainment television. In most instances you have a chance to review the lesson in an alternative time slot or watch videocassettes of the lesson in a learning center on campus.

If you have a VCR available, tape the television program as you view it. This provides an excellent source for review once you have seen the program. Note any questions you have after the program, and contact your teacher on campus during his or her office hours.

Audio Modules

The audio modules are specifically designed to provide greater depth and detail for students enrolled in the two-semester course in macroeconomics and microeconomics. They include expanded interviews with economists who appear in the video portion of the lesson and add the thoughts and insight of other noted authorities.

The audio modules delve deeper into the theory of economics. Within the structure of the 30-minute audio lesson, you have the opportunity to explore the complexities of theoretical applications, such as a cost-benefit analysis in relation to pollution, or product differentiation and monopolistic competition.

If you are enrolled in the one-semester survey course and are interested in learning more about a particular area of study, check with your instructor to see if you can check out or listen to the audio module that accompanies the lesson.

Text

The text *Economics U$A,* Seventh Edition, is a collaborative work written by acclaimed author Edwin Mansfield, who taught at the University of Pennsylvania, and Nariman Behravesh, chief international economist at Global Insight. The case studies presented in the text parallel the video documentaries, linking visual examples to textual content.

The text is an essential part of the course. It establishes a foundation of information, elaborates on concepts introduced in the television segment, and expands ideas through graphs and case studies. Be sure to read each chapter as you go. Economics, like other subjects, builds on the knowledge acquired in previous lessons. If you fall behind, or skip over information you do not understand, subsequent lessons will be more difficult to comprehend.

How can you judge how well you understand the content presented in the video and its companion text chapter? The study guide you are now reading provides a number of opportunities for you to test your knowledge. Each lesson includes an answer key. Once you have completed your study of the video and text chapter and have responded to the questions, check the accuracy of your answers. Use this as a guide to determine which areas need further attention and study. The Lesson Review section of this study guide may assist you in this regard, as will your campus-based instructor.

Study Guide

The Telecourse Study Guide for *Economics U$A* was originally developed by the Southern California Consortium in collaboration with Nariman Behravesh and the project team. James Sondgeroth prepared the current edition.

This study guide is a detailed roadmap to the course. It includes Learning Objectives, Key Terms, Video Questions, Self-Test Questions, and a comprehensive Lesson Review. In addition, two-semester students can utilize the Extended Learning section, which incorporates the audio assignment, more detailed short-answer questions and problem sets, and an annotated bibliography.

You will gain the most from this telecourse by using its components as instructed. Together they provide you an unforgettable learning experience.

LESSON 1. SCARCE RESOURCES: WHAT IS ECONOMICS ALL ABOUT?

INTRODUCTION

Economics—what meaning does the word hold for you? Maybe you think that the study of economics is pretty dry, dull stuff, best left to the president's advisers and other specialists. But have you really stopped to consider the important implications the study of economics has for the way you live your life and the decisions you make every day?

For example, the current state of the economy has direct and significant bearing on

- Whether you are able to get a job.
- Whether you are able to earn more money just by working harder.
- How much you pay for every item or service you purchase.
- What sort of home you can afford.

And that is only the beginning. Economics concerns not only the wages we make and the way we spend them, but our total lifestyle. Ours has been a country of enormous economic growth. And that growth has made possible a lifestyle characterized by (in light of world standards) great luxury and large amounts of leisure time. This is not to say that we do not have serious economic problems. We do. The point is that we have a nation of well-educated, capable workers with the potential to solve many of the problems if we can direct our energies and resources wisely.

An understanding of economics provides the foundation for making important decisions.

- What career to pursue. Twenty years from now, what place will your chosen career occupy in the economy?
- Which political leaders to support. How can you tell whether their arguments and promises make sense or are grounded in a fundamental understanding of basic economics?
- How to be a responsible consumer. Should you buy a domestic or foreign car? Should you support the big companies or smaller businesses? What are monopolies and trusts? How do they work? And are they important?

- Whether to support social welfare programs. Are we doing too little or too much by way of income support programs to help the poor in our country? What about foreign aid? Do those programs really make a difference?

In this and the lessons to come, we consider the ways in which our decisions can influence some of the most significant economic questions of our time:

- What determines the extent of unemployment in the U.S. economy, and what can be done to reduce it? And, in conjunction with this question, what determines the rate of inflation, and how can we reduce it?

- What is the significance of labor productivity? Why did the United States experience a slowdown in productivity growth in the 1970s, 1980s, and the early to mid-1990s? Why were economists worried about this decline? Why did productivity pick up in the late 1990s?

- Why is competition desirable for our economy, and what are some of the ways in which we can preserve a healthy spirit of competition?

- Why does poverty exist in the world, and can anything be done to alleviate it?

In Lesson 1, we lay the foundation for examining these problems in more detail by considering the relationships between resources and technology, and the various factors that determine production—what is produced and how much.

What You Should Learn

You need to acquire several skills to have a good understanding of the discussions that follow. By the end of Lesson 1, you should be prepared to

1. Define *economics*.
2. Define and categorize economic resources.
3. List the four basic questions that economists ask in determining the fundamental characteristics of any economic system.
4. Describe the concept of *opportunity cost,* and explain how it relates to production.
5. Explain how the concept of *opportunity cost* applies to the public policy debates over land use in Alaska and the regulation of the amount of cotton dust allowed in textile mills.
6. Distinguish between *positive economics* and *normative economics.*
7. Explain what a model is.
8. List three important points about models.
9. Describe how *direct* and *inverse* relationships appear on a line graph.
10. Identify Adam Smith, and state when he lived and the title of his masterpiece.

11. State several of Adam Smith's revolutionary ideas.

12. Describe how the *production possibilities curve* is derived and how it is used to explain costs and economic growth.

KEY TERMS

Prologue

labor productivity
unemployment
inflation

emerging markets
poverty

Chapter 1

human wants
resources
free resources
economic resources
capital
technology

opportunity cost
positive economics
normative economics
models
production possibilities curve

VIDEO

Watch

Economics U$A Program 1, "Scarce Resources: What Is Economics All About?"

Illustrative Events

The debate over preservation or development of the wilderness is portrayed in the battle over the Alaska Land Act of 1980, with U.S. Representative Morris Udall supporting the bill and Representative Don Young of Alaska opposing it.

How we mobilized the idle human and material resources during World War II, made vivid through historical footage and discussions with Robert Nathan, then chair of the War Production Board.

Worker health versus the cost of compliance, demonstrated through the ongoing conflict between the textile industry and OSHA, which was seeking to reduce the incidence of brown lung disease.

After Viewing

Answer the following questions.

1. What important economic principle is illustrated through the conflict over the Alaska Lands Act?

2. As a result of World War II, our economy moved from a period of low employment and industrial collapse to a period of economic prosperity and unprecedented growth. What factors contributed to this change, and how do those factors relate to economic choices?

3. How did the passage of the Occupational Safety and Health Act (OSHA) change the nature of the economic choices faced by the textile industry?

Read

Read the Prologue, "Economic Problems: A Sampler," pages 3–9, and Chapter 1, "What Is Economics?" pages 11–26 and 33–35 in your text.

SELF-QUIZ

Multiple Choice

1. Which of the following statements *most* accurately describes our economy from 1930 to the present?

    a. Rates for both unemployment and price level have crept steadily upward.
    b. Unemployment has generally gone up, although in irregular patterns, while price level has remained fairly constant.
    c. Price level has risen substantially; unemployment, after peaking in the 1930s, has gone up and down in irregular cycles.
    d. Unemployment has remained fairly constant since the 1930s, but the price level has tended to decline.

2. Economists today would probably consider all of the following to be among the most pressing economic problems of our time *except*

    a. overabundance of output.
    b. unemployment.
    c. poverty.
    d. labor productivity.

3. According to income distribution figures, about what percent of the U.S. population could be classified as living in poverty?

    a. Fewer than 7 percent
    b. About 11 percent
    c. Between 25 and 35 percent
    d. More than 35 percent

4. The services, goods, and circumstances that people desire are *best* defined as

   a. human wants.
   b. economic resources.
   c. free resources.
   d. capital.

5. A steel mill is an example of

   a. an abundant resource.
   b. a technological resource.
   c. an economic model.
   d. capital.

6. The fact that most resources are limited forces us to constantly

   a. expand output.
   b. raise prices.
   c. develop new technology.
   d. make choices.

7. John had the opportunity to mow Marcy's lawn last Saturday for $15. He could not do it though because he had promised his father that he would work on their own yard for which he was paid $10. John's opportunity cost for working on his own yard was

   a. $15.
   b. $10.
   c. $5.
   d. negative $5.

8. The Labor Department's calculation of the number of people unemployed in the country is an example of

   a. positive economics.
   b. normative economics.
   c. economic theory.
   d. an economic model.

9. According to the text, an economic system does all of the following *except*

   a. determine what and how much society produces.
   b. determine how goods and services are distributed throughout society.
   c. predict the likelihood of future prosperity, given current resources.
   d. define the current growth rate for per-capita income.

10. Suppose we constructed a graph of the production possibilities curve. In a society where half the resources are being employed, the point representing current output appears

    a. on the curve, about midway down.
    b. at the very lowest point on the curve.
    c. somewhere outside the curve.
    d. somewhere inside the curve.

True-False

___ 1. Economics has to do less with the allocation of resources than with the gold reserves and the value of the dollar in international markets.

___ 2. Economic resources include such tangible items as land, labor, machinery, and structures but exclude skills such as technical and managerial knowledge.

___ 3. The test of whether a resource is an economic resource or a free resource is price.

___ 4. The opportunity cost of using a resource to increase the production of one good is the value of what that resource could have produced had it been used in the best alternative way.

___ 5. In attempting to calculate the potential of the economy at the beginning of World War II, Robert Nathan, chair of the War Production Board, determined the number of idle workers and multiplied that number times the average output per worker.

___ 6. The increase in military production during World War II was achieved at the expense of any additional civilian capability.

___ 7. In *normative economics,* the results you get depend on your basic values and preferences; in *positive economics,* the results can be tested by looking at the facts.

___ 8. A model takes a simple situation in the real world and dresses it in the complexities of alternative possibilities. It is less a predictive tool than an intellectual exercise.

___ 9. Because the capacity to produce goods and services is far more limited than human wants, there is the necessity of choice. Economists are concerned with *how* such choices are made in various circumstances and how they *should* be made.

___ 10. Adam Smith doubted that a free, competitive society could function effectively without central planning or government interference.

Discussion Questions

1. Economic moralists are fond of saying, "You cannot get something for nothing." Is this always true? Under what circumstances, if any, is it not true?

2. How do families, as opposed to an entire economy like that of the United States, answer the four basic economic questions?

3. Someone has said that economists study how people make choices and sociologists study why people have no choices to make. What does that statement mean?

4. What is the opportunity cost of (a) spending an evening at a movie and (b) a college education?

Problem Set

1. If the opportunity cost of producing an extra million tons of steel exceeds the value of the extra million tons of steel, should society produce the extra million tons of steel? Why or why not?

2. Suppose that the costs due to crime and the opportunity costs of resources used in law enforcement are as follows:

Proportion of criminals caught and convicted	Costs due to crime	Opportunity costs of resources used in law enforcement (billions of dollars)	Total costs
0.4	60	10	70
0.5	50	—	68
0.6	40	30	—
0.7	30	50	80
0.8	—	80	100

   a. Fill in the three blanks.
   b. What proportion of criminals should society try to catch and convict? Why?
   c. Suppose that each of the figures in the second column of the table (headed "Costs due to crime") were to increase by $5 billion. Would this affect the optimal proportion of criminals that society should try to catch and convict? Why or why not?

3. Mary Minco, a graduate student, has one eight-hour day per week that she can devote to earning extra money. She can write stories for the local newspaper, babysit, or she can divide her time between the two jobs. (For example, she can spend three hours writing stories and five hours babysitting.) If she babysits, she gets $4 per hour. If she spends her day writing stories, it takes her one hour to write the first story, two hours to write the second story, and five hours to write the third story because she runs out of ideas and becomes less productive as time goes on. Assume that she must write an integer number of stories in a day.

   a. If she receives $15 per story, should she do any babysitting if she wants to maximize her income during the day?
   b. If she receives $25 per story, should she do any babysitting if she wants to maximize her income during the day?
   c. What is the lowest price per story that results in her doing no babysitting if she maximizes her income?

4. A metropolitan bus company is faced with the necessity of raising its fares due to increased operating costs. On the basis of estimates drawn from many sources, including other transit systems, the company determines how many tokens it can expect to sell at various prices. In the following table, suppose that the number of tokens sold by the company is Q and the price per token is P.

P (cents)	Q (millions of tokens sold per day)
40	2.0
50	1.9
60	1.8
70	1.7
80	1.6

a. Using these data, plot the relationship between the quantity of tokens sold each day and the price of tokens, or in other words, the demand curve for tokens, on this graph.

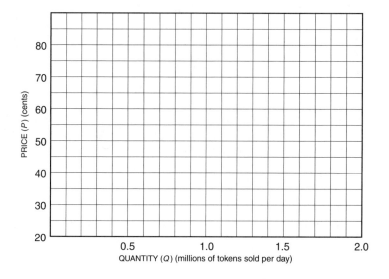

b. Is the relationship between P and Q direct or inverse? Given that this is a demand curve, is it realistic? Why or why not?
c. How many tokens would be sold if the price per token were set at $0.50? How many tokens would be sold if the price were set at $0.60? If the demand curve is a straight line between these two prices ($0.50 and $0.60), how many tokens would be sold if the price were $0.55?

5. A nation's production possibility curve shifts from position 1 to position 2 in the following graph:

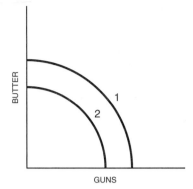

a. Could this shift be due to a war? Why or why not?
b. Could it be due to a natural disaster like an earthquake? Why or why not?
c. Could it be due to technological change? Why or why not?

LESSON REVIEW

If you had difficulty with the Self-Quiz or would like additional assistance, read the following lesson review. It should reinforce and help you understand the content presented in this lesson.

What Is Economics?

Economics is the study of how resources are allocated among alternative uses to satisfy human wants. To make better use of this definition, we must define what we mean by *resources* and *human wants.*

Human wants are material goods, services, and circumstances that people desire. Some of these wants are basic and apply to all persons: the desire for food, clothing, and shelter. Some are highly variable and depend on culture, background, education, and personal preference. For example, some people prefer reading books and gardening to traveling or playing polo. Some like baseball games, some symphonies, and so on. And some wants are, in effect, created by society, largely through advertising. Certain things we see as desirable—luxury cars, expensive homes, stylish clothes—are made appealing to us by the way they are depicted in magazines, on television, and in films.

Resources are the items, substances, and services used to produce whatever satisfies human wants. Economic resources are scarce; free resources, like air, are abundant and may cost nothing. Whether a resource should be classified as economic or free depends entirely on cost. Anything for which we are required to pay—and for most of us these days, that includes practically everything (even water)—is an economic resource, not a free resource.

Economic Resources: Three Categories

Economic resources can be classified into three groups:

1. *Land.* Land is land though sometimes it can include other naturally occurring inputs to the production process such as oceans, seas, rivers, and lakes. Being naturally occurring, it costs nothing to produce, but it is scarce (not free) when the demand for it is greater than the supply of it at zero price. What benefits do we derive from land? Many, including space for housing, commercial and public buildings, factories, recreational centers, and various other facilities and area on which to grow crops and timber, raise livestock, and extract resources like minerals, ores, coal, and oil. Land also provides environmental space that produces scenic and recreational pleasure beyond its contribution to industrial or agricultural output.

2. *Labor.* Labor is typically thought of as physical effort: farming, moving, building, digging, and assembling. But mental efforts are labor too: studying, writing, conducting research, examining, and designing. In 2003, 145 million people were either employed or seeking work in our country.

3. *Capital.* Capital is produced by human labor and inventiveness, and it is often referred to as the *produced means of production.* Capital includes such things as office buildings, factories, facilities, machinery, tools, equipment, and inventories. Oil refineries, blast furnaces, and aircraft plants are all examples of capital resources, but so are pencils, paper, rulers, calculators, and computers.

Technology and Choice

Technology includes the knowledge of scientists, engineers, managers, craftspeople, and others regarding how goods and services can be produced. The state of our current technology sets limits on our production.

Suppose, for example, that engineers at an automobile manufacturing plant determine that it will take 500 hours minimum to build an automobile, given current technology. If that technology expands in some way—say, new methods or materials are used to cut labor time—the number of hours can be shortened and the output increased.

Because resources are limited and current technology sets limits on what can be produced using those resources, our capacity to produce always lags behind our wants. This forces us to make choices.

1. What goods and services are produced? And how much of each is produced?
2. How and with which resources are the goods and services produced?
3. How are the produced goods and services distributed?
4. How is economic growth encouraged and sustained?

Essential Questions and Tasks of an Economic System

To understand the fundamental characteristics of any economic system, economists pose four questions.

1. *What determines the level and composition of society's output?* Within the past few years, particularly, many persons have seriously questioned our spending priorities. Should we be spending as much of our resources as we do on defense? Should we spend more on environmental restoration and protection? More on education? Or should we leave more of the citizens' income in their own hands so they can decide on their own how to spend it? Such questions have important personal and social implications for all of us.

2. *What determines* how *each good and service is produced?* If resources are used wisely and efficiently, our production reflects our true capabilities. If skilled workers are not allowed to use their talents and natural resources are wasted, inefficiency and lower production results.

3. *What determines for* whom *goods and services are produced?* How much should each person receive? Should we continue to base this decision on individuals' skills, knowledge and education, and contributions through labor? Or should we find some other means of dividing goods and services—say, a more egalitarian society in which the amount received by one family of four differs little from what is received by another family of four, regardless of their personal contributions.

4. *What determines the rate of growth of per-capita income?* As a population grows, an adequate economic growth rate becomes essential for economic survival. And it has become a key issue not only in our country but particularly in developing countries throughout Asia, Africa, Latin America, and eastern Europe.

In answering these questions, we need first to define the concept of *opportunity cost.* Imagine for a moment that you live in a "closed" society, one with no access to the outside world, one wholly dependent on its own resources for survival. Now imagine further that this hypothetical society manufactures only two goods: food and clothes. How much of each can it produce? How much should it produce to survive? These are the questions that challenge you and the other inhabitants.

First, you determine what your hypothetical society can do: how much food it can produce if all its resources are devoted to food production; and how much clothing it can produce if all its resources are devoted to clothing production. Then, you determine how much food can be produced at various levels of clothing production and vice versa. The resulting combinations can be charted as shown here:

Possibility	Food produced per year (tons)	Clothing produced per year (tons)
A	0	200
B	100	180
C	200	150
D	300	100
E	400	0

Now you know what is attainable. You know, for instance, that if your society produces 200 tons of clothing per year, it can produce no food at all. On the other hand, if it produces 100 tons of clothing, it can produce 300 tons of food, and so on. These figures give you a realistic basis for making a choice.

Note that, whenever production of one good goes up, production of the other declines. That is because only so many resources are available to devote to production. *The cost of using resources in a certain way is equal to the value of what those same resources could have produced had they been used in the best alternative way.* In other words, this is the opportunity cost—a measure of what is lost by choosing one alternative use of resources over another.

Positive Economics versus Normative Economics

Suppose you read in the paper one day that, if interest rates rise to 10 percent, housing starts are expected to drop by 3 percent. Such a statement merely describes what is and predicts what is likely to occur. It offers no judgment about what should be or whether the drop is good or bad. Such a statement is an example of *positive economics*—statements, propositions, of what is.

If, on the other hand, you read an editorial stating that the president should take steps to lower interest rates because middle-income Americans are being forced out of the housing market, you would be in the world of *normative economics,* statements about what ought to be or what a person, organization, or nation ought to do.

Propositions in positive economics can be tested objectively by appealing to the facts. Sometimes, of course, it is hard to get the facts to work with. If the interest rates suddenly drop, who can say whether the predicted 3 percent drop in housing would have come to pass? Essentially, however, positive economics deals with facts, not value judgments.

Normative economics, by contrast, is a matter of values. One person may feel that the high interest rates serve an important purpose, while another may feel that any benefits gained by such interest rates must be forgone to support the housing industry. These differences cannot be resolved by uncovering more facts. Nevertheless, we must recognize that value judgments are the basis for many economic decisions and policies.

Methodology and Model Building

How do economists make their decisions? How do they look objectively at economic data and make predictions about our future?

One way is through the use of economic models. A model is a simplified way of looking at the world that shows how two (or sometimes more) variables interact. Models are often visually depicted through graphs.

What are the primary characteristics of economic models? Three points are particularly important to remember.

1. *To be useful, a model must simplify the real world.* Models are not meant to replicate reality exactly. In fact, if they did so, they would not be as useful because

they would include too many extraneous variables. Economists use models precisely because the real world is so complex that they need to separate two or more variables and consider them in isolation to see how they interact. Of course, oversimplification is not good either. The trick is to effect a balance: including the most relevant and significant variables and excluding all others.

2. *The purpose of a model is to make predictions about the real world.* The most important test of a model is how well it predicts. This does not mean that the predictions must be right on target every time. That would be unrealistic.

3. *Economists, like weather forecasters, use models that predict the best, even if the best is not absolutely accurate.* The point is that a model capable of predicting events with reasonable accuracy is more useful than one that predicts with far less accuracy.

Models and Graphs

Let us say an economist devises a model that predicts clothing expenditure will rise as income goes up. By collecting data and graphing it, the economist can quantify this model; that is, show how much effect one variable has on another. Without such quantification, most models are much less useful. Almost anyone could guess that people who earn more money would spend more on clothes. So that is not very exciting information. But it might be interesting and useful to know that, for each additional $1,000 in income, the average consumer will spend $60 on clothing. That kind of data would be of particular value to you if you were a clothing manufacturer or retailer.

Direct and Inverse Relationships

Note in the following figure that the line showing the relationship between income and clothing expenditure slopes upward and to the right. That is, the higher is the income, the higher the clothing expenditure. This is a direct relationship between variables.

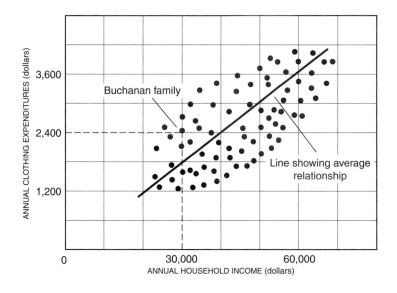

14 | LESSON 1

Now note, by contrast, the next figure, showing the relationship between consumer demand and the price of tennis balls. As the price goes up, consumer demand goes down. Therefore, the line slopes downward to the right. This is an inverse relationship between variables.

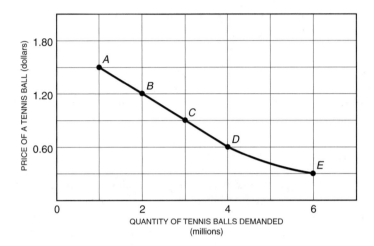

EXTENDED LEARNING

This section of the study guide is specifically designed for the two-semester student.

AUDIO

Before Listening

Read Exploring Further in your text, pages 26–32.

Next

Listen to the audiotape that accompanies Lesson 1.

After Listening

Answer the following questions:

1. Define *opportunity cost,* and explain why, as more and more of a good is produced, the production of yet another unit of this good is likely to entail a larger and larger opportunity cost.

2. Explain how the production possibilities curve sheds light on the basic economic problem of achieving economic growth.

3. In deciding how clean the work environment must be for textile workers, OSHA tries to balance the costs of each level of air cleanliness against the benefits in terms of health risk. The calculation of the benefits of reduced risk often requires some quantification of the value of a worker's life. Why, as the standard of cleanliness increases, do the costs increase more and more rapidly and the additional benefits get smaller and smaller? Is this positive or normative economics or a mixture of both?

4. Which of the following are statements of positive economics and which are of normative economics? Explain.

    a. It would be better to have less unemployment even if it meant inflation would get worse.
    b. If the price of wheat goes up, the amount consumed will fall.
    c. We should improve the distribution of income.
    d. Defense spending should be reduced.
    e. A large part of the defense budget is used to upgrade the skill level of the labor force.

5. "If the United States did not spend money on defense, we would suffer from widespread unemployment." Comment and evaluate.

ADDITIONAL READINGS

Melman, Seymour. *The Permanent War Economy*. New York: Simon & Schuster, 1985.

> Describes the opportunity costs of the U.S. military spending since World War II. No mathematics, simple graphs.

Mundell, Robert A. *Man and Economics*. New York: McGraw-Hill Book Company, 1968.

> The first three brief chapters provide a generalized discussion of the basic concerns of economics. The principles of scarcity, markets, and optimization are presented in a way that builds an intuitive understanding of the material. No mathematics or graphs.

U.S. Civilian Production Administration. *Industrial Mobilization for War,* Vol. 1. Washington, DC: U.S. Government Printing Office, 1947.

> Chapters 4, 5, and 6 detail the war production objectives of the United States in 1942, the problem of achieving a balanced growth of output when the usual market equilibrating mechanisms are not in effect, and the problem of civilian production needs. An interesting account of a command economy facing scarce resources. No mathematics or graphs.

ANSWER KEY

Video Questions

1. The principle at work here is that, in any economic decision, choices must be made. We live in a world where resources are necessarily limited, and even when resources are abundant, our access to them or our capacity to use them is generally limited. We cannot have everything. In the case of the Alaska Lands Act, the choice required value judgments. Would we have wilderness areas and environmental resources to pass on to future generations? Or would we develop mineral and timber resources to boost the economy, create jobs, and free ourselves from a certain degree of foreign dependency? Clearly, such decisions cannot always be made strictly on the basis of profits or losses. This is one reason that such decisions are extraordinarily difficult and why the conflict over the Alaska Lands Act and other similar legislation continues even today.

2. During the Great Depression, industries closed down because they had no market. Consumers could not provide a market for industrial or agricultural goods because they had no jobs and, therefore, no income to spend. There seemed no way out. Suddenly, a market opened. Allies needed equipment and supplies to support the war effort. Steel was in heavy demand, as were aluminum and copper and a number of manufactured goods. Industries geared up. And they needed workers. As consumers went back to work, they boosted markets further, buying goods that had not been demanded in great quantities for years. Both industry and agriculture reaped the benefits. As the war effort accelerated, greater production was required. More people entered the workforce. As citizens were drafted into the war, more housewives, young people, and older people were required to fill jobs that they left. Productive capacity peaked. More goods were produced, and new goods became available.

3. Higher health and safety standards were demanded by OSHA for the textile industry than had previously been demanded. And the industry's response was that if it met the standards satisfactorily, it would cripple its own ability to compete with foreign producers, who had cheap labor and less stringent standards with which to contend. Therefore, the choice was no longer simply one of how to make the best use of resources. It became, rather, a choice between protecting workers, regardless of economic cost or adhering to a profit-oriented philosophy that ignored workers' welfare. Eventually, OSHA won out, and brown lung disease, long the curse of the textile workers, was virtually wiped out but at a cost of over 300,000 jobs. Again a choice had been made. One set of values won out over another, but while this was very much an economic decision, it was at the same time not a choice that could be evaluated in strict financial terms.

Multiple Choice

1. c   Text, 5. Figures 1 and 2.
2. a   Text, 3–9.
3. b   Text, 8.

True-False

1. False   Text, 11.
2. False   Text, 12, 13.
3. True   Text, 12.

4.	a	Text, 11.		4.	True	Text, 16.
5.	d	Text, 12.		5.	True	Video.
6.	d	Text, 13.		6.	False	Text, 29; Video.
7.	a	Text, 14–16.		7.	True	Text, 17.
8.	a	Text, 17.		8.	False	Text, 18–20.
9.	c	Text, 23–25.		9.	True	Text, 13.
10.	d	Text, 28, 29.		10.	False	Text, 26.

Discussion Questions

1. This statement is not always true: In the case of a free good (e.g., air), no price is associated with its consumption, and the consumer is therefore able to have something for nothing. For most goods, however, a price is associated with having or consuming the good. A good is free only if the resources used to produce that good are free.

2. Families, just like entire economies, are constrained by having limited resources and unlimited wants. Scarcity leads to choices, and these choices answer the four basic questions: (1) what to produce, (2) how to produce it, (3) to whom to distribute it, and (4) how to keep output and income growing.
   Answer to question 1. Families allocate their resources to produce the greatest level of satisfaction given the constraints they face. In a family, this is decided by the authority of the parents or some collective decision-making process. In the economy as a whole, governments (national, state, and local) are the authority and through elections decide how to allocate about 25 percent of national output in the United States now. The composition of the rest of the national output is decided by the interplay of the forces of supply and demand.
   Answer to question 2. Families are interested in using their limited resources in the best, most-efficient way; otherwise they would be less well off. The U.S. economy uses the price and the profit/loss signals of the market system to try to achieve the efficient use of resources.
   Answer to question 3. Price and profit/loss signals are also used to determine distributional issues for the economy as a whole, although the government does redistribute about 10 percent of national income. In the family, parental authority or some collective decision process decides the distribution of goods and services among family members.
   Answer to question 4. Families also consider the rate of growth of their "economy": Families recognize that an increase in per-capita income in their family translates into an increase in their command of resources and an expansion of the production possibilities for the family.

3. Economists view decision making in the context of constraints. They see a world where there are limited resources and unlimited wants: This necessarily implies that people constantly make choices about how best to allocate these scarce resources. Sociologists study the development and structure of an organized group of people: They do not focus on scarce resources but instead on the interactions among different people and different groups of people. The quote implies that sociologists tend to view the path humans take as inevitable rather than the result of conscious choices about how best to use their available resources.

4. a. The opportunity cost of spending an evening at a movie includes the cost of the movie and the value of the next-best alternative use of that time available to the individual.
   b. The opportunity cost of a college education includes the costs unique to securing a college education plus the cost of the income forgone by the individual while in college.

Problem Set

1. No, because the forgone output of other goods is more valuable than the extra steel.

2. a. The blank in the second row is 18, the blank in the third row is 70, and the blank in the fifth row is 20.
   b. 50 percent, because this minimizes the total costs to society.
   c. No, because the minimum total costs to society would still be achieved when 50 percent were caught and convicted.

3. a. She has three alternatives.
   (1) She can devote one hour to writing and seven hours to babysitting, which brings in $43.
   (2) She can devote three hours to writing and five hours to babysitting, which brings in $50.
   (3) She can devote eight hours to writing which brings in $45.
   Thus, she should do some babysitting.
   b. The opportunity cost of writing the third story is $20, since this is what she could earn in five hours of babysitting. Since she gets $25 for this story, she is better off writing the story than devoting the five hours to babysitting.
   c. $20.

4. a.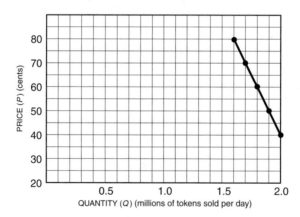

   b. Inverse. Yes. Because one would expect a higher price to result in a smaller number of tokens sold.
   c. 1.9 million. 1.8 million. 1.85 million.

5. a. Yes, since the war could have reduced the nation's resources.
   b. Yes, since this too could have reduced the nation's resources.
   c. No, not so long as technology advanced, not regressed.

Audio/Text Questions

1. The opportunity cost of using resources to produce certain goods is the value of the goods that could have been produced with those same resources if they had been used in the best alternative way. Resources tend to be better suited for one use over another. For example, some land is better for growing wheat, and other land is better for growing cotton. As more and more resources are devoted to one particular good, say, wheat, land not suitable for wheat growing has to be used. The value of the potential cotton production that has to be given up (the opportunity cost), therefore, becomes greater and greater the more the economy tries to specialize in wheat.

2. The trade-off between producing investment goods (machines, factories, etc.) and consumption goods can be shown with a production possibilities curve. A decision to increase the production of investment goods results in greater economic growth of the economy. The production possibilities curve shifts out when there is growth: The more investment goods an economy produces, the larger the shift in the production possibilities curve.

3. The ventilating equipment necessary to reduce the first 10 percent of fibers in the air is much less costly than that required to reduce an additional 10 percent or the last 10 percent of the fibers. Insofar as such analysis quantifies the cost of reducing pollution and balances it against the increased health risk, this is positive economics. There is no objective agreement on the value of good health or a human life, however. Many attempts have been made to calculate this objectively, but value judgements not subject to empirical test still affect the results of the analysis. In this sense, such work is normative economics.

4. Answers a, c, and d are normative statements because they are not descriptive statements subject to a possible test; they are value judgements. The others are statements of positive economics.

5. If we did not spend so much on defense, more money would be available (either in the public sector or, if there were tax cuts, in private hands) to spend on other goods and services. Also, resources currently allocated to producing war material would be freed up for producing other goods.

LESSON 2. MARKETS AND PRICES: DOES THE FREE MARKET RESPOND TO PEOPLE'S NEEDS?

INTRODUCTION

Did you ever put off buying something you really wanted, thinking it was too expensive, only to have the price go up still further? Or maybe you postponed your purchase only to discover later that the item you wanted was no longer carried anywhere, that it was no longer "in demand." If either of these scenarios sounds familiar, you have already experienced firsthand some of the ways in which our price system reflects market demands.

Just what causes prices to move up or down? What creates changes in the market? In this chapter, we look behind the scenes to see how prices are determined by two interacting forces: the demands of consumers and the desire of firms to make a profit. We see that your own income level (among other factors) not only influences the market but is in turn influenced by it. Understanding the influence of the price system on your personal life can help you see the extent to which that system provides a skeletal structure for our entire economy.

Ours is a mixed capitalist system, not a pure capitalist system. This means that government plays a very large role in the economy. Just the same, the price system is the single most powerful force in determining how our economy works. The price system, to a large extent, determines

- What goods and services society produces.
- How those goods and services are produced.
- Who gets what.
- Economic growth of the economy and per-capita income.

In short, it has much to do with the way an economic system fulfills its four primary tasks.

As we shall see, however, the price system, for all the power it has over our lives, has limitations. While most people are unconcerned that income is unequally distributed, many others feel the distribution is unfair and unjust. The people who feel the distribution is unfair think money should be taxed away from the rich so that more assistance can be given to the poor. They usually feel that rewards and penalties are not always equitably distributed through the price system. It is not uncommon, for instance, for many firms within a given field to reap the benefits of another firm's diligent research and technological innovation. Secrets are hard to keep in an open marketplace, and some firms do not know how best to market or are uninterested in exploiting innovations they have come up with.

In addition, many firms and individuals bear the costs of external diseconomies that result from the production or consumption of goods and services by others, for example, the pollution of the air and water. Many people believe the government should intervene in the market process to try to correct these problems.

Finally, public goods would not be produced because of their very nature without government intervention.

In conclusion, many argue that government intervention is necessary to ensure that resources are used efficiently and income distributed fairly. Although government intervention in the affairs of firms and individuals has limitations, we do not consider them here but briefly touch on them in various chapters that follow this one.

As you study this lesson, ask yourself which factors are influenced by the price system and which influence the goods and services available to us and the prices we must pay for them.

What You Should Learn

By the end of Lesson 2, you should feel prepared to

1. Define the terms *consumer* and *firm* and explain their interrelationship.

2. Define the term *market* and offer examples of several markets that exist in today's economy.

3. Describe what is represented by a *market demand curve,* and name four factors that can cause this curve to shift left or right.

4. Distinguish between a *shift in a commodity's demand curve* and a change in the *quantity demanded of the commodity*.

5. Describe what is represented by a *supply curve,* and name two factors that can cause this curve to shift left or right.

6. Distinguish between a *shift in a commodity's supply curve* and a change in the *quantity supplied of the commodity.*

7. Explain the impact on the price level when demand curves or supply curves shift left or right.

8. Define the *equilibrium price*. Describe the effects of *excess supply* and *excess demand* on the *actual price.*

9. Describe the relationship between the *actual price* and the *equilibrium price*.

10. Explain how the price system solves the four primary tasks of our capitalistic economic system.

11. Describe the circular flow of money and products.

12. Name and describe three limitations of the price system.

13. Define external economies and external diseconomies.

14. Explain the effect on equilibrium price and quantity when the demand curve shifts to the right and when it shifts to the left.

15. Explain the effect on equilibrium price and quantity when the supply curve shifts to the right and when it shifts to the left.

KEY TERMS

consumer
firm
market
mixed capitalist system
perfectly competitive
   market
demand curve
supply curve
equilibrium price

actual price
product market
resource market
circular flow of money
   and products
public goods
external economy
external diseconomy

VIDEO

Watch

Economics U$A Program 2, "Markets and Prices: Does the Free Market Respond to People's Needs?"

Illustrative Events

The creative and successful development of Levittown, an example of how the huge postwar demand for low-cost housing was fulfilled, featuring William J. Levitt.

The rise of minimills in the face of foreign competition and hard times for the United States's giant steel industry, featuring steel executive Kenneth Iverson.

The signing of superstar Reggie Jackson by the New York Yankees, and the business judgments that led George Steinbrenner to pay Jackson half a million dollars per year; featuring Bowie Kuhn, former commissioner of baseball.

After Viewing

Answer the following questions:

1. How did William J. Levitt capitalize on the ideas of Henry Ford to take advantage of a strong market for new homes?

2. What role did competition play in changing the structure of the U.S. steel market?

3. What effect did the market have on the salaries of major league baseball players, and what justification do economists offer for the results?

Read

Read Chapter 2, "Markets and Prices," pages 36–56 and 59–62 in your text.

SELF-QUIZ

Multiple Choice

1. Ours has been described as a *mixed* capitalistic system. This means that

    a. not everyone in our country supports a capitalistic form of government.
    b. capitalism, as it exists in our country today, has some benefits and some disadvantages for business.
    c. some goods and services are provided through private enterprise, some through government.
    d. businesses are allowed to operate only within the rules and regulations established by government.

2. Which of the following could *best* be described as a *consumer*?

    a. A small child purchasing a milkshake
    b. A family of six buying a new stationwagon
    c. A teenager visiting a doctor
    d. All of the above.

3. Which of the following is the *best* example of a *firm*?

    a. University of Southern California
    b. Good Samaritan Hospital
    c. IBM
    d. All of the above

4. A *firm* is distinguished from other organizations that provide goods and services by its

    a. profit motivation.

b. size.
c. organizational structure.
d. capacity to create a market.

5. The concept of *market,* properly defined, includes

   a. both buyers and sellers.
   b. just buyers.
   c. just sellers.
   d. buyers, sellers, and resources.

6. The demand curve for a given commodity slopes downward to the right, generally, because

   a. the demand tends to fall as the price rises.
   b. the quantity demanded tends to fall as the price rises.
   c. the consumer tastes and spending power are always in flux.
   d. the supply very rarely equals the demand exactly.

7. Which of the following is *least* likely to create a rapid shift in the demand curve for sports cars?

   a. New technology decreasing the time required to paint the cars
   b. The widespread belief that sports cars get good mileage
   c. A big jump in the average income level among consumers
   d. Large decrease in the average prices of sedans and stationwagons

8. When economists refer to an *increase in demand,* they mean

   a. a leftward shift in the demand curve.
   b. a rightward shift in the demand curve.
   c. a movement upward and to the left along the demand curve.
   d. a movement downward and to the right along the demand curve.

9. Suppose market conditions are such this year that there is an excess supply of wheat in the amount of 400 million bushels. Under these circumstances, forces within the market tend to

   a. hold the price of wheat steady.
   b. cut the price in half.
   c. drive the price up.
   d. push the price down toward equilibrium.

10. An *external diseconomy* exists when

    a. one firm uses the technology of another to boost its own sales.
    b. two or more firms collude to keep prices above ordinary market values.
    c. a firm fails to produce its goods and services in the most cost-efficient manner.
    d. a misuse of resources by one firm results in uncompensated costs for another firm.

True-False

_____ 1. There are two sides to every market: the demand side and the supply side.

_____ 2. When a market contains so many buyers and sellers that none can influence the price, economists call it a supply-side market.

_____ 3. The demand side of the market can be represented by the market demand curve, which almost always slopes upward and to the right.

_____ 4. The position of the demand curve depends on consumer tastes, the number and income of consumers, and the prices of other commodities.

_____ 5. The position of the market supply curve depends on technology and resource prices.

_____ 6. The market system responds to the needs and wants of society as a whole, regardless of how much money individuals have to spend.

_____ 7. The price system controls the ways in which public goods are handled and assures the proper amount of such goods is produced.

_____ 8. Contrary to popular belief, firms that produce goods at minimum cost and respond to what consumers want and buy tend to be less successful than firms with relatively high production costs operating independently of consumer demand.

_____ 9. In a capitalist economy, there are circular flows of money and products.

_____ 10. The equilibrium price and equilibrium quantity of a commodity are given by the intersection of the market demand and market supply curves.

Discussion Questions

1. What will happen to the equilibrium price of corn if the market supply curve shifts to the right? What will happen if it shifts to the left?

2. "The supply curve influences the demand curve, since the more produced of a commodity, the more people want of it (or the more producers convince them they want it)." Do you agree? Why or why not?

3. The tripling of oil prices during 1979 caused fuel prices to increase over 50 percent. Fuel is an important input in the trucking industry, and small, independent truckers were hit particularly hard by these price increases. Independent truckers could not raise their prices enough to cover their costs because of competition from the more efficient railroads and large integrated trucking companies. They faced bankruptcy and joined together in protests. They asked the federal government to bail them out by reducing fuel taxes, releasing oil from government-owned reserves, and even by government-mandated price controls on fuel. Do you think the government should have intervened to save the independent truckers? Why or why not?

4. In recent years, more flexibility in prices for Broadway shows has been achieved by allowing tickets to be sold at less than the stated price if a show is not sold out. If this innovation has worked well for producers and the public, evaluate a

proposal to create even more flexibility by allowing private individuals to come to the Times Square booth and offer to sell their tickets at prices above or below the original purchase price.

5. It is generally agreed that the government should discourage the production of goods and services that entail external diseconomies. What are external diseconomies? Give some examples.

Problem Set

1. Suppose that the market demand curve for corn is as follows:

Price of corn (dollars per bushel)	Quantity of corn demanded (millions of bushels per year)
0.50	100
1	80
2	60
3	40
4	30
5	20

a. Plot the demand curve in this graph. How much corn would be demanded if the price were $0.50?

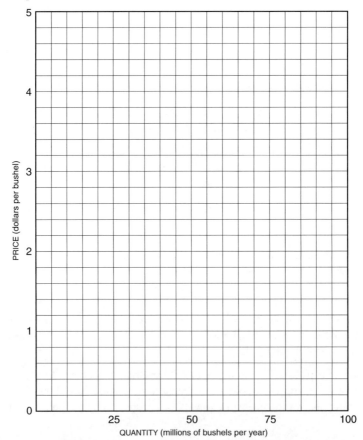

b. Suppose that the market supply curve for corn is as follows:

Price of corn (dollars per bushel)	Quantity of corn supplied (millions of bushels per year)
0.50	10
1	30
2	60
3	70
4	80
5	90

Plot the supply curve in this graph. How much corn would be supplied if the price were $0.50? $2?

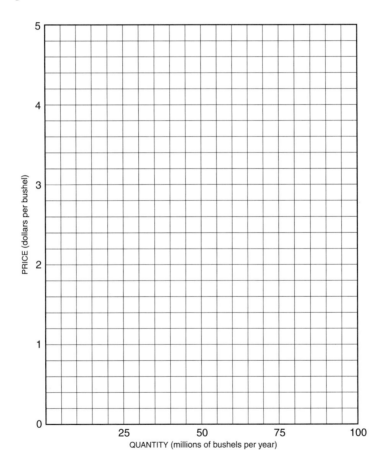

c. Using the data in parts a and b, plot the demand and supply curves. What is the equilibrium price for corn?

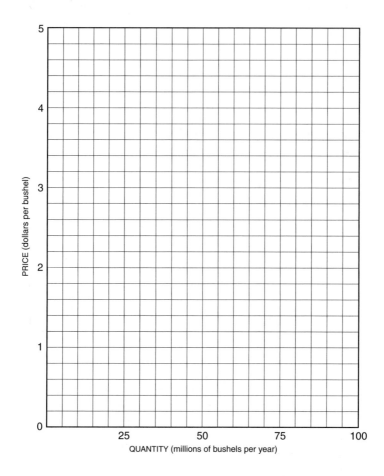

2. Suppose that the demand curve for the tickets to the Metropolitan Opera for a performance of *Carmen* is as follows:

Price of a ticket (dollars)	Quantity demanded
16	3,000
20	2,800
24	2,600
28	2,400
32	2,200
36	2,000
40	1,800

a. If the Metropolitan Opera House has 2,400 seats and sets a price of $32 per ticket, will the house be full? If not, how many seats will be vacant?
b. What is the equilibrium price of a ticket for this performance?
c. What is the shape of the supply curve for tickets?
d. At a price of $32 per ticket is there a shortage or surplus of tickets? In a free market, would the price of a ticket rise or fall?

3. The demand curve for fishing poles is $P = 50 - 10Q$, where P is the price of a fishing pole (in dollars) and Q is the quantity demanded per year (in millions).

   a. If the government orders the producers of fishing poles to produce 1 million fishing poles per year, what is the equilibrium price of a fishing pole?
   b. If the current price of a fishing pole is $60, would you expect the price to rise or fall once the government order occurs?
   c. Suppose that, after it issues the order, the government sets a ceiling of $30 on the price of a fishing pole. Does a surplus or shortage result? How big is it?

4. "When it is said that there are shortages in some market, we know that that market is out of equilibrium. Take natural gas for instance. In the late 1970s, there were shortages. Some people argued that they were due to the government price controls while others claimed that they were due to cold winters combined with the stockpiling of natural gas because firms and individuals feared a shortage might develop. The first group of people worried that releasing the controls would lead to very high prices, while the second group concluded that the shortage would disappear as soon as it warmed up and people became less worried." Explain each side's argument using diagrammatic analysis.

5. Suppose that the demand curve for soybeans is as follows:

Price (dollars per bushel)	Quantity demanded (billions of bushels per year)
4	2.1
5	2.0
6	1.9
7	1.8
8	1.7

The government supports the price of soybeans at $6 per bushel and restricts soybean output to 2.1 billion bushels per year.

   a. How much do farmers receive for their soybean crop under these circumstances?
   b. How much would farmers receive for their soybean crop if the government no longer supported the soybean price and farmers continued to produce 2.1 billion bushels per year?
   c. If the farmers producing soybeans band together and fix the price, which of these prices would they choose? Why?

LESSON REVIEW

If you had difficulty with the Self-Quiz or would like additional assistance, read the following lesson review. It should reinforce and help you understand the content presented in this lesson.

The Price System and the Four Basic Tasks

In a capitalist economy, the price system performs the four basic tasks of the economy.

1. Determining what and how much is produced
2. Determining how goods and services are produced
3. Determining how income is distributed among society's members
4. Determining economic growth and per-capita income

Ours is a *mixed* capitalist system, not a *pure* capitalist system. This simply means that a number of goods and services are provided through the government in addition to those provided through private industry. Nevertheless, the role of the price system in carrying out the four basic economic tasks is critical.

Consumers and Firms

A *consumer* is an individual, group, or household that purchases the goods and services provided through the economic system. When your family buys an automobile, the family as a unit is a consumer. And when you buy a Coke to drink at the park, you are an individual consumer.

A *firm* is an organization that produces a good or service for sale and profit. Over 10 million firms exist in the United States today, and they range from corner delis to industry giants like General Motors. About nine-tenths of the goods and services produced in our country today are provided by firms; the rest are provided by government or nonprofit institutions like schools.

Markets

A *market* is a group of firms and individuals that come together to buy or sell some good or service. Markets are not defined by geography, size, or the buildings in which business transactions occur. Markets are defined by the common interests of buyers and sellers, who want to exchange money for particular goods and services. Although buyers and sellers are the main actors in the marketplace, markets sometimes include third parties like brokers and agents.

Markets vary enormously in the extent to which they are dominated by powerful buyers and sellers who are able to regulate prices. For example, if there were only one automobile manufacturer in the United States, Zippy Autos, and no imports, you would have to buy a car from Zippy or do without one. In such a market, Zippy would set its output and prices to maximize its profits. Its prices would be higher and the quality of its cars would undoubtedly be worse than if it had to compete with other firms to get consumers to buy its products.

By contrast, when a market for a product contains so many buyers and sellers that none of them can influence the price, economists call that a *perfectly competitive market*.

The Demand Side of a Market

Markets have a demand side and a supply side. The demand side is represented by a demand curve, which shows the amount of a given commodity that buyers purchase at various prices. As this figure shows, the demand curve tends to slope downward to the right.

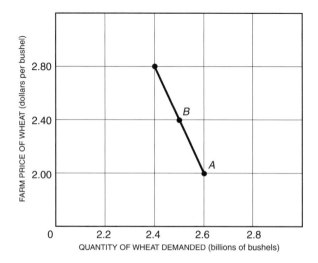

This simply means that, as the price (vertical axis) goes up, the quantity demanded of the commodity (horizontal axis) falls. Relating these principles to the illustration for the wheat market, consumers generally buy more wheat at $2 a bushel than at $3 a bushel, just as we would logically expect.

A Snapshot

Any demand curve represents a snapshot of how things are at a given point in time. In other words, the demand curve for wheat might look quite different tomorrow from the way it looks today. Any demand curve assumes that the tastes and incomes of consumers, the number of consumers, and the prices of other commodities are held constant. For, as we shall see, when these things shift, the demand curve shifts with them.

Shifts in the Demand Curve: What Factors Are Responsible?

Essentially, four factors can cause a commodity's demand curve to shift. We examine each individually.

Factor 1. Consumer tastes. Consumer tastes shift constantly. How many people today own motorcycles who never thought they would get on one? How many people who were intimidated by computers five years ago now use one to earn a living? Did you ever consider a pet alligator, a sports car, or a trip to Tahiti? An advertising campaign somewhere in the future may persuade you to purchase one or all of these. If consumers begin to favor a product like pet alligators, the demand *at a given price* rises. Where previously firms could sell only 1 million alligators annually at a price of $5, suddenly they can sell 5 million at $5. The increased demand pushes the demand curve to the right. Similarly, if consumers become convinced that pet alligators are too hard to train, the demand may fall from 1 million at $5 a head to only 10,000, and the demand curve will shift to the left.

Factor 2. Change in income level. With changes in income, the demand curve for certain products also shifts. For some products, it shifts to the right with a rise in consumer income, while for others it shifts to the left, depending on the product. And, even assuming a shift to the right, the impact of income is much greater for some products than others.

Factor 3. Number of consumers. Obviously, the bigger is the market, the bigger the demand. With some commodities, the market may change drastically only with a shift in population. For example, most of the population consume milk products or wheat products in some form or other. So, unless the population goes up, the market for milk may not expand much.

Factor 4. Level of other prices. The demand curve can shift as prices of other products go up or down. The direction of the shift depends a lot on how the two products are related; that is, whether one is a substitute for the other or complements the other. Take motorcycles, for instance. If the prices of 10-speed bicycles fall drastically, some consumers who were thinking of buying motorcycles may decide to get bicycles instead. The effect is a leftward shift in the demand curve for motorcycles. Suppose, on the other hand, that gasoline prices decline. Since people need gasoline to run their motorcycles, the falling gas prices may well boost motorcycle sales, and then the demand curve shifts to the right.

Changes in Demand versus Changes in the Quantity Demanded

The demand curve reflects the quantity of a commodity demanded at each price. A shift in the demand curve, on the other hand, reflects a *change in demand at each given price*. In other words, a rightward shift in the demand curve for wheat shows that more consumers are willing to purchase wheat at $4 a bushel or at $3 a bushel or at any given price than before. Sales are still higher at $3 than at $4, but the *total demand* is higher at every price level.

When economists refer to an *increase in demand*, they mean a rightward shift in the demand curve. When they refer to a *decrease in demand*, they mean a leftward shift in the demand curve.

A rightward shift spells generally higher prices for a given commodity; a leftward shift spells generally lower prices for a given commodity.

The Supply Side of the Market

The *market supply curve* shows the amount of a given commodity sellers would offer at various market prices. For example, the following figure shows the market supply curve for wheat in the United States in the early 1990s:

Note that this supply curve slopes up to the right. In other words, as prices (vertical axis) rise, suppliers are willing to provide more wheat (horizontal axis). And this is just what we would expect, since the higher is the price, the greater the incentive for sellers to provide more. The supply curve, like the demand curve, is just a "snapshot" of the market situation at a given point in time. It can change. Its constancy is based on the assumption that *technology and input prices* (that is, prices of labor, capital, and land, the factors affecting production costs) are held constant. Let us see what happens to the supply curve when these two factors change.

Factor 1. Technology. Better technology means that products and services can be produced faster and cheaper. For this reason, technological change often causes the supply curve to shift to the right; this means that sellers are willing to offer more of a product or service at a given price because it costs less to offer it. Suppose scientists discover a chemical that enriches the soil at low cost and doubles per acre yield of wheat. Clearly, more wheat can be offered at comparable cost, and the supply curve for wheat shifts to the right.

Factor 2. Input prices. Input prices are the costs of resources—land, labor, and capital—needed to develop a product or service. If land is expensive or the costs of farm machinery rise, sellers offer less wheat at a given price because it costs more to produce it. Therefore, the supply curve for wheat shifts to the left.

When economists refer to an *increase in supply,* they mean a rightward shift in the supply curve. When they refer to a *decrease in supply,* they mean a leftward shift in the supply curve.

As the supply curve shifts right, prices tend to fall. As the supply curve shifts left, prices tend to rise.

Equilibrium Price

The equilibrium price is *the price at which the quantity demanded equals the quantity supplied*. And this is the only price that can be maintained for any extended period.

Where does equilibrium price occur? To find out, we can graph together the demand curve for a commodity and the supply curve for that commodity. The point at which the two curves intersect represents the equilibrium price.

For example, if the price of wheat, according to our figures, were $2.80 per bushel, the demand curve indicates that 2.4 billion bushels of wheat would be demanded; while the supply curve indicates that 2.7 billion bushels would be supplied. In other words, there would be an *excess* supply of 0.3 billion bushels. An excess supply is often referred to as a *surplus*.

On the other hand, if the price were $2.00 per bushel, the demand curve indicates that 2.6 billion bushels would be demanded, while the supply curve tells us that 2.3 billion would be supplied at that price. Hence, there would be an *excess* demand of 0.3 billion bushels. An excess demand is often referred to as a *shortage*.

So long as the quantity supplied exceeds the quantity demanded, there is a resulting *downward pressure* on the price, pushing the price toward equilibrium. So long as quantity demanded exceeds quantity supplied, there is a resulting *upward pressure* on the price, again pushing it toward equilibrium.

Actual Price

Generally, economists assume that actual price is close to equilibrium price, and this assumption makes sense because, as we have just seen, the basic forces within the market tend to push prices steadily toward equilibrium. This movement tends to be slow, however, so that the extent to which actual price really approximates the equilibrium price depends on the length of time involved and the stability of other factors.

What really happens in most cases is that the factors influencing the demand curve and supply curve (new technology, shifts in consumer taste and spending capabilities, and so on) change more rapidly than the prices themselves. As these changes occur, they create a new equilibrium price. It is very difficult to predict just what that equilibrium price will be; but economists can, on the basis of market indicators, attempt to predict with some confidence whether prices for motorcycles, wheat, and alligators will tend to rise or fall.

The Price System and the Four Economic Tasks

In Lesson 1, we considered the four basic tasks performed by any economic system to determine

1. What is produced and in what quantity.
2. How goods and services are produced.
3. How income is distributed.
4. How rates for growth and per-capita income are established.

Basically, the price system performs each of these tasks. We look at them individually to see how.

1. *Determining what is produced.* Every time you make a purchase or decline to make a purchase, you use your power as a consumer to influence what goods and services will be available in the future. Since firms exist to make money, they continue to market only those products and services for which *the amount of money they receive from consumers exceeds the cost of putting the products and services on the market.* This translates into producing what most consumers desire. Producers, of course, are not forced to follow consumer demand. They can offer what they wish. But, generally, those who respond to consumer demand make money, and those who do not eventually go bankrupt.

2. *Determining how goods and services are produced.* Again, to realize a profit, it is in the interest of a firm to produce a good or service at the lowest possible cost. This means using resources efficiently and taking advantage of new relevant technology. If one automobile manufacturer discovers a way to make engine parts at reduced cost, that savings can be passed on to consumers. Other firms that do not take advantage of this technology suffer; either they have to keep their prices high, losing sales, or they have to lower prices more than they can afford to, incurring a loss.

3. *Determining who gets what.* How much people receive in goods and services depends on their money income, which is determined by the price system according to the resources they have. Resources can take many forms. An individual consumer's resources can exist in the form of money or other capital; land; or intelligence, knowledge, and skill—anything that can be exchanged on the market for something else. Money can be used to buy things, but knowledge and skill can be exchanged *for* money if that knowledge and skill are in demand. Some people have numerous resources, and thus great power as consumers, while others have relatively few. The point is that the market determines the value of current resources (regardless of what form those resources take), and the resources in turn determine whether an individual consumer gets a large share of the economy's current output or a relatively small share.

4. *Determining economic growth and per-capita income.* Increase in per-capita income depends on the rate of growth of current resources, and the increase in the efficiency with which they are used. First, the price system controls the amount of new capital goods produced as well as the amount society is willing to invest in educating, training, and upgrading its labor resources. Whether these efforts are profitable depends on current price levels. Second, the price system offers firms a strong incentive to invest in new technology. The firm that has a technological edge stands a better chance of making a profit than one that follows along, copying what others are doing. But staying ahead takes lots of investment since today's technological innovations become tomorrow's common practices.

Circular Flows of Money and Products

People are not consumers all the time. They are consumers sometimes, sellers other times, marketing their own labor, skills and talents to obtain income with which to make more purchases. Therefore, there is a continual flow of money and products between consumers and firms. In the product market, products are bought and sold; in the resource market, resources (including skills) are bought and sold. This flow is represented next.

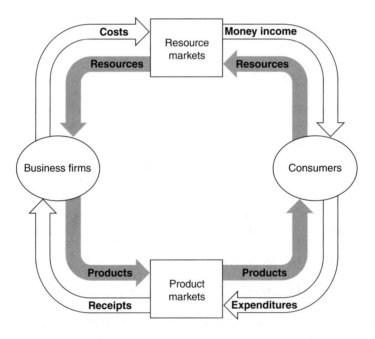

As this model indicates, consumers provide resources to firms, which in turn provide goods and services to consumers. At the same time, firms pay money for resources to consumers, who in turn use that money to buy the goods and services marketed from the firms.

The model is useful in showing how the two kinds of markets keep the money flowing. It does not explain, however, why capitalist economies sometimes experience periods of extensive unemployment, inflation, or both. Also note that the model reflects a pure capitalist system that does not include government. We look at the role played by government in later chapters.

Limitations of the Price System

Although the price system seems to work very well in carrying out the four basic economic tasks, it has severe limitations. These fall, generally, into three categories:

Limitation 1. Distribution of income. Many people feel that the price system does not produce an equitable or fair distribution of income. Citizens and political leaders generally agree that the price system should be altered somewhat to provide help to the poor. The kind of help that should be given and the circumstances under which it should be provided remain, however, subjects of heated controversy.

Limitation 2. Public goods. In our society, many goods and services are provided through government rather than on the open market. This is because, with some goods and services (national defense, for example, or the public highway system), there is no way to exclude citizens from enjoying or consuming the goods and services whether they pay for them or not. Since people do not pay for goods they receive anyway, marketing them in the usual way makes little sense. In addition, such goods are consumed collectively. The number of times you drive over a highway has little to do with how many other people can use the same highway on the same or other occasions. Certain goods and services are hard to divide up into consumable pieces because they can be used by one person without depriving others. Over the years, the number of goods and services provided through government has grown substantially.

Limitation 3. External economies and external diseconomies. The price system does not operate effectively in cases where the production or consumption of a good by one firm or consumer has uncompensated adverse or beneficial effects on other firms or consumers. For example, suppose one firm conducts research that leads to breakthrough technology subsequently adopted by other firms. This situation is given the term *external economy*. Except for the fact that the lead firm may enjoy a short-lived marketing edge, it is not compensated in any way for extra resources it has put into technological research. This lack of compensation results in too few resources being put into technological research.

An *external diseconomy* occurs when consumption or production results in uncompensated costs to another person or firm. For example, if firm A pollutes water needed for production by firm B, then firm B must expend extra resources just to hold the line on output. The market (i.e., the price system) fails to produce the optimal level of firm A's good because the market does not fully adjust for firm A's external diseconomy.

Economists tend to agree that the government should take steps to control external economies and diseconomies, since both are beyond the control of the price system.

EXTENDED LEARNING

This section of the study guide is specifically designed for the two-semester student.

AUDIO

Before Listening

Read Exploring Further in your text, pages 56–59.

Next

Listen to the audiotape that accompanies Lesson 2.

After Listening

Answer the following questions:

1. If both supply and demand in a competitive market increase, one can predict the direction of change of output but not of price. If supply increases but demand decreases, one cannot, without further knowledge, be certain about the direction of either the price or the quantity change. Do you agree with this statement? Explain.

2. When there was an increase in the demand for U.S. wheat from 1972 to 1974, what do you think happened in the corn market? The soybean market? The price of beef?

3. How do you reconcile the hypotheses that *the quantity demanded varies inversely with price* (law of demand) with the statement that *a rise in demand leads to a rise in price, other things equal*?

4. For the market system to function properly, all costs of production should be borne by the producer and all the benefits of consumption should be paid for by the consumer. Why is this necessary for the market system to work well, and what are the general cases in which these requirements are not met?

5. How does the price system, if it functions well, encourage firms to use the resources best suited for producing its goods and avoid using the resources valuable in the production of some other good?

ADDITIONAL READINGS

Freeman, Richard B. "Supply and Salary Adjustments to the Changing Science Manpower Market: Physics, 1948–1973." *American Economic Review* 65 (March 1975): 27–39.

> Examines how the market for physicists responded to the shortage situation in the early 1960s and the surplus of the late 1960s. Details movements of relative salaries and the short- and long-run elasticities of supply. Technical presentation, no mathematics or graphs.

Hayek, F. A. "The Use of Knowledge in Society." *American Economic Review* 35 (September 1945): 519–530.

> A classic article emphasizing the multitude of complex and ever-changing "calculations" the free market and the price system perform and the way the market provides information about the factors that lie behind these calculations. No mathematics or graphs.

Medoff, James L., and Katherine G. Abraham. "Experience, Performance, and Earnings." *Quarterly Journal of Economics* 95 (December 1980): 703–736.

> The authors find that earnings cannot be adequately explained by experience and performance and discuss a variety of other theories that try to account for the discrepancy. Technical discussion, moderately difficult mathematics, no graphs.

ANSWER KEY

Video Questions

1. To support the war effort, it was necessary for the United States to divert resources that might have gone into domestic production into the manufacture of military goods. This meant, among other things, a great slowdown in the housing construction industry. At the same time, with GIs returning from the war, the demand for new, low-cost housing was enormous, at a time when there was virtually no supply. Anyone able to read the signs of this market might have stepped in to take advantage of it, but the man who did so was William J. Levitt. Because Levitt had some experience with mass production of military housing, he reasoned that the same approach could be applied to production of civilian housing: He could use mass production to offer a product at affordable cost. Although he moved teams of workers from construction site to construction site, rather than moving the product to the workers as Henry Ford had done, Levitt's was very much an assemblyline approach. Efficient use of time, supplies, and manpower trimmed costs impressively and put housing within the reach of thousands for the first time. There was a trade-off, of course. Houses

were all alike; they showed no individuality. But what was important was that these mass-produced houses gave many new home buyers a starting point and fed hundreds of thousands of dollars into a depressed market that would consequently expand for some time to come.

2. Thanks to the organizational efforts of entrepreneur J. P. Morgan, competing steel companies in the United States had been organized into one huge U.S. Steel trust. Competition during the first 70 years of the twentieth century was almost unknown in the nation's steel industry. That very lack of competition in turn induced inefficiency, waste, high costs, and careless management of resources. Consequently, foreign competitors saw their chance. They could produce an equivalent product at a lower cost—much lower. They would step in and take the market right out from under U.S. Steel, and that is precisely what they set about to do. Plants closed and workers lost their jobs. It was left to the smaller companies like Allegheny-Ludlum to show the larger companies the way out of this predicament. Allegheny-Ludlum cut costs in several ways. First, it specialized, creating only one product, stainless steel. Second, it trimmed costs wherever it could, downplaying advertising, streamlining management, cutting excess labor. Lack of efficiency had created the problem; a return to efficiency might solve the problem. And to a great extent, it did. Foreign competition could not be totally undercut. But it could be held in check, thanks to the restoration of efficient production methods. The U.S. Steel experience illustrates an important economic lesson: Without competition, efficiency is threatened, and the loss of efficiency may actually spell a company's undoing.

3. The decision to make major league baseball players free agents meant that their salaries would now be determined by the market principles of supply and demand. What impact would that have? For those players with a proven record, it meant an opportunity to secure contracts for unprecedented salaries—hundreds of thousands and later millions of dollars. What would make players worth these immoderate sums of money? The answer was talent, experience, and, above all, the ability to draw fans. More fans meant more tickets sold, television broadcast rights, advertising revenues, and other sources of profit. Thus, a team owner would look on a player's salary as a form of investment, one that could be expected to pay off repeatedly. A player, on the other hand, would look on his salary as a rightful share of the money he would help his employer earn. In economic terms, such a perspective is quite justified. While the players and their employers make the decisions, the relative appropriateness of those decisions is determined by the market, which dictates the parameters of any player's value at a given time.

Multiple Choice

1. c   Text, 36, 53, 54.
2. d   Text, 36.
3. c   Text, 37.
4. a   Text, 37.
5. a   Text, 37–38.

True-False

1. True   Text, 38.
2. False   Text, 38.
3. False   Text, 38, 39.
4. True   Text, 39–41.
5. True   Text, 44, 45.

6. b	Text, 39, 42.	6.	False	Text, 48.
7. a	Text, 38–41.	7.	False	Text, 54.
8. b	Text, 42.	8.	False	Text, 48–50.
9. d	Text, 46.	9.	True	Text, 52–53.
10. d	Text, 54, 56.	10.	True	Text, 45–47.

Discussion Questions

1. If the market supply curve shifts to the right, the equilibrium price of the corn falls. If the market supply curve shifts to the left, the equilibrium price of the corn increases.

2. No. Much confusion can be avoided by not making supply a determinant of the quantity demanded by consumers and not making demand a determinant of the quantity supplied by firms. The market price communicates the strength of demand to suppliers and the availability of supply to consumers. On the basis of this analysis, suppliers could produce more because of an increase in the demand for their commodity. This increase in demand could be due to advertisements that persuade consumers they want to buy more of the commodity at every price, or it could be due to a change in any of the other variables that cause shifts in the demand curve. In any case, the increased strength in demand tends to raise the market price and suppliers respond by producing more as they move up along their supply curve. On the other hand, suppliers could produce more because of cheaper input prices for the resources they use or because of an improvement in the technology they use. In this case, the supply curve shifts to the right, increasing the availability of the commodity. This increased availability tends to push prices down, causing consumers to buy more as they move down along their demand curve.

3. No. While having sympathy for their plight, the independent truckers problem is not one the text lists as a reason for government intervention nor did government policies cause their problem. Indeed, the price system determines how services are produced, and in doing so, it makes sure society gets the most out of its resources. It is impersonal and does not always operate with kid gloves, but this is the way less-efficient production processes are eliminated in favor of more-efficient processes.

4. This proposal attempts to extend the market for tickets to Broadway shows to a greater extent. The proposal will likely result in a wider range of prices for shows. The proposal potentially changes the distribution of income from the shows: If the original sellers do not anticipate accurately the market price, they may lose money when they sell the tickets and the tickets are then resold at a higher price in the new market. This same reasoning applies to the original buyers of the tickets: If they inaccurately predict the ticket price, they may lose money when they resell the tickets at a lower price. The proposal typically already exists in most markets where there is high demand for tickets (e.g., tickets to the big football game of the year): Scalpers buy or sell tickets in order to profit from the ticketing agency's failure to price the ticket accurately given the market demand and supply conditions.

5. External diseconomies occur when the production or consumption of a good or service does not include all the relevant costs. For example, if a factory produces polluted water while manufacturing a good, this polluted water is an externality if the factory does not include the cost of cleaning up the water in its cost of production. An individual who smokes during the consumption of an elegant meal at a restaurant creates an external diseconomy for the individuals at the restaurant who would prefer a smoke-free environment.

Problem Set

1. a. 100 million bushels.

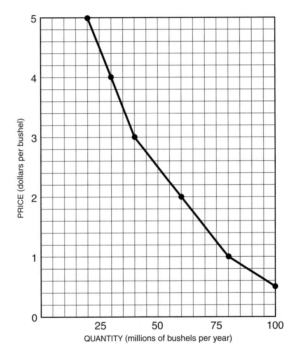

b. 10 million bushels. 60 million bushels.

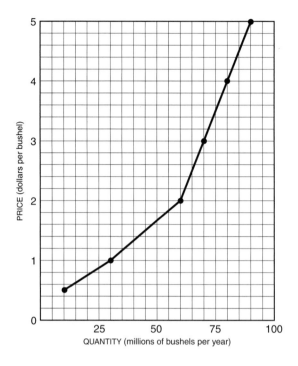

c. $2 a bushel.

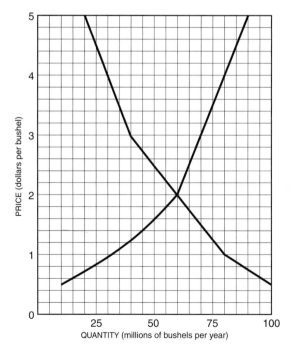

2. a. No. 200 seats
    b. $28.
    c. A vertical line at 2,400 tickets.
    d. Surplus. It would fall.

3. a. Since 50 – 10(1) = 40, the equilibrium price of a fishing pole is $40.
    b. Fall.
    c. Since $Q = 5 - 0.1P$, the quantity demanded equals $5 - 0.1(30) = 2$ million fishing poles when the price is at its ceiling of $30. Since the quantity supplied equals 1 million, there is a shortage of 1 million fishing poles per year.

4. The first group felt that the price P_c was set below the equilibrium price by government controls; the situation is shown here:

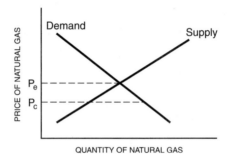

If the controls are released, the price rises to P_e. Thus, government price controls create the shortage.

The second group felt that the demand curve had shifted to the right and the price had not increased, so there was a shortage of $Q_D - Q_S$, as shown next.

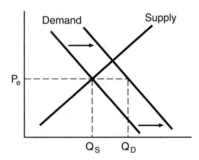

If the demand curve shifts back to its original position when the weather warms up and people become less worried, the shortage disappears. Of course, the price did not increase in the first place because of government price controls.

5. a. $6 × 2.1 billion, or $12.6 billion.
    b. $4 × 2.1 billion, or $8.4 billion.

c. $8, because the amount they received ($8 × 1.7 billion, or $13.6 billion) would be greater than at any lower price, and their costs at this price would be no greater than at lower prices since they would be producing less. Therefore, their profit would be highest at a price of $8.

Audio/Text Questions

1. Yes. If both the supply curve and the demand curve shift to the right, the quantity sold (the level of output) definitely increases, but whether the equilibrium price rises or falls depends on the relative shifts in the curves. If the supply increases a great deal and the demand curve shifts backward only slightly, then the price falls and the quantity sold increases. If the demand falls much more than the supply increases, then the price still falls, but the quantity sold decreases.

2. As the price of wheat rose because of the demand and supply situation in the early 1970s, the demand for corn increased because corn can substitute for some uses of wheat. Therefore, the price of corn rose. Similarly, the price of soybeans rose, and the price of beef increased because the price of feed grains had risen.

3. The first statement refers to movements *along* the demand curve when everything else but price is held constant; that is, incomes, tastes, population, and so on, do not change. The second refers specifically to changes in incomes, tastes, and so on, that cause the demand curve to *shift* to the right. Then, if the position of the supply curve does not change, the price rises.

4. If there are positive or negative externalities to production or consumption, not all the costs and benefits are paid for by the appropriate firm or individual. Pollution is a major external cost of production for which firms often do not pay. Public goods is another general category in which these requirements are not met. It is impossible to exactly apportion the costs of a public good such as national defense. Because many people "consume" national defense at once, the market mechanism breaks down.

5. Since the price of a resource is bid up by the firm that finds that resource most valuable for its purposes, another firm that could use the resource but does not find it as valuable does not use it because it would not be willing to pay such a high price for the good.

LESSON 3. U.S. ECONOMIC GROWTH: WHAT IS GROSS DOMESTIC PRODUCT?

INTRODUCTION

How healthy is the United States's economy? How prosperous are we likely to be a year from now? What factors underlie our present rates of inflation and unemployment?

To answer these and similar questions, economists look very closely at the United States's gross domestic product, or GDP. In the simplest of terms, GDP is *the dollar market value of the total amount of goods and services produced by an economy* in a given year. This figure attempts to measure our productive accomplishments. Knowing GDP helps bankers, economists, government officials, investment specialists, and others make personal, business, and public policy decisions more rationally. Prior to 1934, gauging the country's economic prosperity was far more a matter of guesswork than it is today. But, with economic measures like GDP, we have feedback on how our economy is performing and how well it is likely to do in the near future.

What You Should Learn

You need several important skills to understand gross domestic product and its role in the economy. By the end of the lesson, you should

1. Be able to give a definition of *GDP* and explain why GDP is important to politicians and business executives.

2. Be able to define *price indexing* and calculate a price index given current and constant dollar values.

3. Be able to use a price index to deflate values expressed in current dollars to values expressed in constant dollars.

4. Understand how the following five factors can influence the accuracy with which GDP is calculated:

    - Potential for double counting.

- Valuation at cost.
- Nonmarket transactions and services.
- Nonproductive transactions.
- Sale of secondhand goods.

5. Distinguish between intermediate goods and final goods.
6. Understand how the value of GDP, as a measure of economic well-being, is limited by the following five factors:
   - Population.
   - Leisure.
   - Changes in the quality of goods and services.
   - Value and distribution.
   - Social costs.
7. Be able to explain the expenditure approach to calculating GDP and name and define its components.
8. Be able to explain the income approach to GDP and list its components.

KEY TERMS

gross domestic product
depreciation
final goods
intermediate goods
current dollars
real GDP

base year
constant dollars
price index
value added
expenditures approach
income approach

VIDEO

Watch

Economics U$A Program 3, "U.S. Economic Growth: What Is the Gross National Product?"

Illustrative Events

The development of the GNP,* a tool central to macroeconomics, by the economist Simon Kuznets during the Great Depression, featuring Carol Carson, chief economist for the Commerce Department's Bureau of Economic Analysis.

How GNP figures made it possible for the United States to mobilize the economy during World War II, featuring economist Robert Nathan, a member of the War Planning Board.

The 1960s protests against pollution reveal the failure of GNP measures to take environmental "quality of life" factors into account, examined by Alfred Kahn, former chair of the President's Council of Economic Advisers.

After Viewing

Answer the following questions:

1. What are the strengths and limitations of GNP as a measure of our country's economic growth?
2. Why are intermediate transactions not included in the calculation of GNP?
3. What are some primary economic and social factors influencing GNP?
4. What use of GNP did President Franklin Roosevelt make in coordinating our nation's war effort prior to World War II? How important was the GNP to that effort?
5. Is growth of GNP automatic?

Read

Read Chapter 3, "National Income and Product," pages 69–88 in your text.

SELF-QUIZ

Multiple Choice

1. Which of the following statements about general trends in real GDP is *most* accurate?

    a. Since 1960, the constant dollar value of GDP has remained relatively constant.

---

*The current standard of an economy's output is GDP (gross domestic product), brought into widespread use in the United States beginning in 1991. Prior to 1991, the United States used GNP (gross national product) to measure the economy's output. GDP counts all income produced within the borders of a country, including income earned by resident foreigners. GNP counts only income earned by citizens of the country, including income earned by them outside the country. While the textbook now uses GDP, the video series uses GNP.

b. Real GDP rose significantly through World War II, then began a steady decline.
c. Over the past 40 years, real GDP has risen and fallen unpredictably with an overall declining pattern.
d. Since 1960, real GDP has risen and fallen in irregular cycles with a pronounced overall upward trend.

2. Under which circumstances should the sale of secondhand goods be counted in calculating GDP?

   a. Under no circumstances whatever.
   b. Only when the resale occurs five years or more after the original sale.
   c. Only when the resale involves intermediate goods.
   d. Only when the resale involves final goods.

3. Which of the following *best* describes the difference between GDP and real GDP?

   a. There is no substantive difference.
   b. Real GDP is always lower.
   c. Real GDP is adjusted for changes in price level.
   d. Real GDP accounts for depreciation.

4. Suppose goods that cost $80 in 1995 now cost $100. Using 1995 as a base year, the price index now based on these figures would be

   a. 0.25.
   b. 1.25.
   c. 0.80.
   d. 0.20.

5. The price index can be defined as the ratio of

   a. real GDP to potential GDP.
   b. potential GDP to real GDP.
   c. base year GDP to real GDP.
   d. current dollars to constant dollars.

6. The contribution of a firm or industry to a final product is *best* described as

   a. value added.
   b. quality change.
   c. corporate investment.
   d. proprietors' income.

7. The part of each year's national output devoted to replacing capital goods worn out in the course of production is known as

   a. corporate investment.
   b. depreciation.
   c. value added.
   d. private domestic investment.

8. If one were to add together personal consumption expenditures, gross private domestic investment, government purchases of goods and services, and net exports, the result yields the

   a. measured economic welfare.
   b. net domestic product.
   c. gross domestic product.
   d. net private domestic investment.

9. Which of the following would *not* be used in calculating GDP using the income approach?

   a. Investment
   b. Wages and salaries
   c. Depreciation
   d. Indirect business taxes

10. If one calculated GDP using the expenditures approach, then calculated GDP using the income approach, which of the following results would be *most* likely?

    a. The two methods would yield exactly the same result.
    b. The result from the expenditures approach would tend to be higher.
    c. The result using the income approach would tend to be higher.
    d. It is impossible to make any predictions based on the information given.

True-False

_____ 1. GDP is an ideal measure of total economic output. It is considered the most satisfactory indicator we have to measure the economic well-being of the United States.

_____ 2. Unlike other economic measures, GDP is not affected by price-level changes.

_____ 3. In calculating GDP, it is important to avoid counting the same output more than once but to include the sale of secondhand goods and all financial transactions, even if they do not reflect current production.

_____ 4. To determine GDP using an *income* approach, find the sum of the following categories of income: employee compensation, rent, interest, proprietors' income, and corporate profits plus depreciation and indirect business taxes.

_____ 5. In the United States, the differences between GDP and GNP tend to be quite large.

_____ 6. In a very simple economy, economic transactions can be described by a *circular flow,* with a bottom loop of businesses producing goods and services and selling them to consumers, and a top loop of consumers selling their services to business to create the goods and commodities in the bottom loop.

_____ 7. In the early days of World War II, the concept of GDP was important in convincing depressed industries to expand and determining how much industrial capacity could be diverted to the war effort without jeopardizing civilian needs.

_____ 8. GDP measurements concentrate on goods and services that have market prices rather than on the hidden costs of by-products of growth, such as environmental pollution.

_____ 9. The concept of *value added* refers to the amount of value a firm or industry adds to the total worth of a product.

_____ 10. The ratio of the value of a set of goods and services in *current* dollars to the value of the same set of goods and services in *constant* base-year dollars is a *price index*.

Discussion Questions

1. Does gross domestic product include the value of all goods and services produced? If not, which ones does it include?

2. If each taxpayer hired his or her neighbor to fill out his or her tax return, would this affect gross domestic output? If so, how? Would you favor including in GDP the value of time spent by citizens filling out tax returns? Why or why not?

3. "Aid to the poor is not included in government purchases of goods and services; consequently, it is not included in GDP. Yet such aid is of enormous benefit to the population and the improvement in the income distribution should be regarded as an output of the economic system." Comment in detail.

4. "If you do not subtract depreciation in the calculation of total domestic output, you are making a mistake similar to double counting intermediate goods." In what ways are the two mistakes similar? In what ways are they different?

5. What difficulties would you encounter in trying to compare levels of economic welfare across countries (say, for example, the United States versus Great Britain, India, Sweden, and Mexico) using the gross domestic product as your yardstick?

Problem Set

1. a. Debland is a country where the price level has been rising at a rate of 5 percent per year. GDP in current dollars was 10 percent higher in 2003 than in 2002, and 3 percent higher in 2002 than in 2001. In terms of constant dollars, how much greater was Debland's GDP in 2003 than in 2001?
   b. Debland's largest firm, the Debland Iron Company, sold $3 million worth of iron in 2003. It purchased $1.2 million worth of goods and services from other firms, paid $0.5 million in interest, and paid $0.3 million in excise and property taxes. Since its depreciation allowance was $0.3 million, its profit was $0.7 million. How much was its value added in 2003?

c. In the nation of Debland, government economists have compiled the following data on the economy in 2003 (all figures are in millions of dollars):

Government expenditures on goods and services	300
Gross domestic product	1,000
Personal income	700
National income	800
Net exports of goods and services	1
Net domestic product	900
Personal consumption	500

What is the value of net private investment in 2003?

2. The CIA has collected the following data (in millions of dollars) concerning a foreign country, which shall remain nameless (for security reasons, of course):

Personal consumption expenditures	240
Corporate profits (before taxes)	20
Rental income of persons	10
Proprietors' income	30
Net investment	30
Compensation of employees	200
Indirect business taxes	20
Imports	5
Exports	6
Net interest	60
Depreciation	40

a. The CIA would like to know what GDP is in this country. Can you tell it?
b. On the basis of these data, how much are government purchases of goods and services in this country?

3. In the following table replace the letters with the appropriate numbers.

Year	GDP (billions of current dollars)	GDP (billions of constant dollars)	Price index (2000 = 1.000)	Annual inflation rate (percent)	Annual real GDP growth rate (percent)
1998	8747	9066.9	0.96471782		
1999	9268.4	9470.3	0.978680718	1.447356	4.44915
2000	9817	a	b	c	3.660919
2001	d	e	f	2.373665	0.505246
2002	10480.8	10083	g	h	i
2003	j	10398	1.056732064	k	l

LESSON REVIEW

If you had difficulty with the Self-Quiz or would like additional assistance, read the following lesson review. It should reinforce and help you understand the content presented in this lesson.

How Is GDP Calculated?

Simply defined, GDP is the sum of all the goods and services a country produces. But, in an economy as vast as ours, which produces everything from soybeans to spacecraft, how can we possibly add everything together in a meaningful way? The answer, of course, is to use a common denominator, money, to evaluate everything. In making this calculation, however, we must beware of several pitfalls:

- To avoid double counting, we must calculate only final goods, such as automobiles, not intermediate goods, such as the steel used to make automobiles.

- We must include, as output, intangible services as well as tangible goods.

- We omit certain services, such as the work performed by family members in their home, even though such services are valued and important.

- Because they do not reflect current production, we must also exclude from GDP purely financial transactions, such as the sale of securities (stocks, bonds, T-bills, etc.) and welfare payments.

- We must exclude sales of secondhand goods, because the production of such goods has already been calculated once in determining GDP.

Current Dollars and Constant Dollars

GDP can be expressed in either current dollars (money GDP) or constant dollars (real GDP). Current dollars reflect actual dollar amounts for the present period; constant dollars are figures *deflated* for changes in the price level. Gross domestic product, after being *deflated* for price changes (that is, expressed in constant dollars), is called *real GDP*.

GDP and GNP

GDP is the money value of all final goods and services produced within the borders of a country in a year's time, no matter if it is produced by citizens of the country (or their resources) or citizens of another country (or their resources).

GNP is the money value of all final goods and services produced by citizens of a country (or their resources) in a year's time regardless of whether it is produced within the borders of the country or in other countries.

Using a Price Index to Deflate GDP (or Other Figures) for Price Changes

Economists use price indexes to measure price changes and adjust GDP for those price changes. Economists call GDP figures that have not been adjusted for price changes *current GDP* (GDP in current dollars) or *money GDP;* in other words, the actual figures, for that year as collected. After economists adjust for price changes, deflate, GDP figures are called *constant GDP* (GDP in constant dollars) or *real GDP.* Conceptually, *constant* or *real* GDP is what the value of GDP would have been if the prices that were in effect in the base year had never changed.

How do economists develop an index? First, they narrow the field of goods and services to just a few, the most important. For the consumer price index, or CPI as it is known, only 250 different items are evaluated. These items are important to us, some more important than others. Economists weigh items in the calculation of an index according to how much people spend on the item and how much the quality of an item changes. Then a *price level* is determined, an average price for the 250 selected items for each year. To compare the price levels, economists convert the levels into an index.

An index is the price level of one year compared to the price level of another year. To allow uniform comparisons, a base year is chosen, the year to which all the other years are compared. The base year should be a representative year, one without extraordinary events. The price index for any year is then the price level in that year compared to (that is to say, divided by) the price level in the base year:

$$\text{Price index for any year } X = \frac{\text{price level in year } X}{\text{price level in the base year}}.$$

Note that the price index for the base year would always be equal to 1.0 or 100 (100 percent).

Suppose, for example, that the money GDP in 1939 equaled $90.5 billion and in 1965 it equaled $681.1 billion. Does this mean that GDP increased about seven to eight times during this period? As we have already seen, prices increased substantially between 1939 and 1965. To calculate real GDP for any year, deflate the money GDP by dividing the money GDP for that year by the decimal form of the price index. For any year *X,* real GDP equals

Money GDP for year X ÷ price index for that year (decimal form).

Suppose the implicit price index for 1939 equaled 46.2 and the index for 1965 equaled 105.4, using 1958 as the base year (100.0). Then,

$$\$90.5 \div 0.462 = \text{real GDP for 1939} = \$195.9 \text{ billion}$$
$$\$681.1 \div 1.054 = \text{real GDP for 1965} = \$646.2 \text{ billion}.$$

Note that, in these adjustments, since prices in 1958 (the base year) were higher than in 1939, the 1939 GDP figure was inflated to account for this difference.

Value Added

The process of transforming intermediate products into some final product is described by economists as the concept of value added. In other words, it is the value added to a product or a host of products by a company or manufacturer in creating something finished and ready for purchase; for instance, using glass, steel, bolts, engine parts, aluminum, fiberglass, fabric, plastic, and various other substances to produce an automobile. The sum of the value added at each stage in the manufacturing process of a product equals the value of the output of the final product. And these sums together (that is, the value-added figures for every company within our society) equal the gross domestic product.

GDP: Some Limitations

Economic prosperity is not fully defined by productivity. Many factors go into determining the value of our lives. It is vital, therefore, to realize GDP statistics, although useful indicators of economic productivity, are subject to these limitations:

- *Population.* GDP is meaningful only when we know the population of the society in question, its age distribution, and the percentage of workers. For example, two countries may have approximately the same GDP in dollar figures; but if one country has double the population of the other, the standard of living in the two countries is quite different.

- *Leisure.* The average workweek in the United States is now just over half as long as it was a century ago, and it continues to shrink as people find more efficient ways of completing their work and begin placing a higher value on leisure. Although leisure time does not contribute directly to productivity, it is—for most people—a major factor in determining the quality of life.

- *Quality changes.* The price of a product may go up without an improvement in quality, or conversely, a product may improve significantly without any substantial increase in price, but GDP does not reflect these changes. Economists attempt to assess the quality changes in goods and services produced from year to year and include this in their computation of real GDP, but many economists have questioned their success.

- *Value and distribution.* GDP reflects dollar figures only, not how goods or services are valued. Therefore, a box of candy and a bottle of prescription tablets that sell for the same price contribute equally to GDP, regardless of what relative value one might place on either. Similarly, GDP is calculated for the nation as a whole, with no regard for whether goods and services are consumed by the wealthy few or distributed equally among all members of society.

- *Social costs.* Measured by a "quality of life" index, the costs of increased productivity can be very high. It is no secret that mining, manufacturing, forestry, and countless other productive activities can cause significant harm to the environment through pollution of air, water, and other resources. And what are the psychological effects of widespread computerization of services, a process some consider dehumanizing? GDP, however, is insensitive to these costs and therefore seems to many to overestimate our true economic welfare.

Calculating GDP: Two Approaches

We can measure the market value of any product in one of two ways. Let us say we want to know the market value of a house. The simplest and most straightforward way to determine this is to ask how much a consumer would pay for the house on today's market. There is another, equally valid way to determine the value of the house, however. We can add together all the income generated in the building of the house, such as wages, interest payments, profits, rents, business taxes, and so on. Theoretically, the value of the house is the same regardless of which way we calculate it.

Similarly, we can use two approaches to determining GDP of a society as a whole: the expenditures approach or the income approach. And again, the sum for either equals GDP:

Total spending = GDP = total income.

Precisely what factors go into calculating GDP using these two approaches? We take a closer look at each.

The expenditures approach to GDP. In using this approach, we must add all spending on final goods and services. Economists divide this spending into four broad categories:

- *Personal consumption expenditures.* Personal spending on services, nondurable goods like food, and durable goods like automobiles.

- *Gross private domestic investment.* All final purchases of new plants, tools, equipment, and machinery by companies; all construction expenditures; and any changes in inventories (since GDP reflects the value of all goods and services produced, even if they are not sold in the year of production).

- *Government purchases of goods and services.* All expenditures of federal, state, and local governments for such functions as defense, education, police and fire protection, highway maintenance, health services, and so on. (This does not include transfer payments such as Social Security or veterans' benefits.)

- *Net exports.* The amount spent by other countries on our goods and services less the amount we spend in purchasing their goods and services.

The income approach to GDP. In using this approach, we simply add all income generated by production. Income, in this case, is the sum of these seven factors:

- *Compensation of employees.* This, the largest category of income, includes all wages and salaries paid by employers, as well as benefits and any payments made into public or private pension or welfare funds.

- *Rents.* In this context, *rent* is defined as the payment to households in exchange for the supply of property (nonmonetary) resources.

- *Interest.* Money paid by private businesses to those (including private, individual investors) who lend them money.

- *Proprietors' income.* The net total income (profits) made by unincorporated businesses.

- *Corporate profits.* The total net income made by corporations.
- *Depreciation.* The value of facilities and equipment worn out this year, sometimes termed *capital consumption allowance* because it reflects the value of capital consumed during the year.
- *Indirect business taxes.* Custom duties, sales taxes, and excise taxes imposed on a company's goods or services rather than levied directly on the business.

Although depreciation and indirect business taxes are not income items, they must be added to the sum of the five income items to obtain an accurate GDP. The important point to remember here is that, whether we use the expenditures approach or the income approach, the total (that is, GDP) is the same.

EXTENDED LEARNING

This section of the study guide is specifically designed for the two-semester student.

AUDIO

Listen

Listen to the audiotape that accompanies Lesson 3. There is no specific reading assignment for this lesson.

After Listening

Answer the following questions:

1. Of the following, which is counted in GNP? Should it be counted?

   a. A donation to a charity
   b. The sale of a share of stock on the stock market
   c. Household cleaning services performed by a company
   d. Garage sales
   e. Pollution control equipment
   f. The work of housewives

2. How does NNP differ from GNP? Which is a more accurate measure of gross consumption?

3. The per-capita GNP today is more than three times that of 1900. Does this mean that on average everyone is three times better off than the average person of 1900?

4. How did the national income and product accounts help in national planning during World War II?

5. Do you think the attention paid to GNP has helped or hurt policy making? Has all policy been directed toward improving GNP? If GNP is not used as an indicator, what else could be used?

ADDITIONAL READINGS

Abramovitz, Moses. "The 1971 Nobel Prize for Economics: Simon Kuznets and Economic Growth." *Science* 174 (October 29, 1971): 481–483.

> Contains a biographical sketch of Kuznets and details the early development of the conceptual structure of the national income accounts. No mathematics or graphs.

Boulding, Kenneth E. "Fun and Games with the GNP—The Role of Misleading Indicators in Social Policy." In *The Environmental Crisis*, edited by Harold W. Helfrich, Jr. New Haven, CT: Yale University Press, 1970.

> A lively criticism of the use of GNP as a measure of welfare, stressing the degree to which pollution and wasteful use of resources incur costs not measured by the national income accounts. No mathematics or graphs.

Kendrick, John W. *Economic Accounts and Their Uses.* New York: McGraw-Hill Book Company, 1972.

> Chapters 1 and 2 provide a good overview of the conceptual problems in devising a system of national accounts, and a short history, including efforts in the 1700s, of national income accounts. Simple mathematics, no graphs.

Morgenstern, Oscar. "Does GNP Measure Growth and Welfare?" *Vital Speeches of the Day* 41 (April 1, 1975): 365–370.

> A strong statement against the pervasive use of GNP as a basis for evaluating policy actions and for measuring welfare.

Schultze, Charles L. *National Income Analysis,* 3d ed. Englewood Cliffs, NJ: Prentice-Hall, 1971.

> Chapters 1 and 2 summarize the concepts of the circular flow of economic activity and how GNP is calculated. The relationship between detailed income categories and GNP is clearly explained. Simple mathematics and graphs.

ANSWER KEY

Video Questions

1. Most of us measure our economic well-being informally according to the desired goods and services we can purchase at any given time. Prior to the development of GNP measure, the health of the U.S. economy as a whole was estimated in much this same way; consumers and economists alike had a general idea of whether things were good or bad but no precise measure to validate their perceptions or to tell them whether the economic realities they perceived in their own neighborhoods were applicable throughout the nation.

   GNP provides a reliable and reasonably objective estimate of the true state of the economy as a whole. Calculations of GNP over time tell us the extent to which our production rate is growing or falling. Knowing the difference between the nation's current GNP and the potential GNP is invaluable in planning the funding of major efforts or projects; the space program, for example. In addition, GNP is used by bankers, brokers, and government officials to determine interest rates, as well as investment and tax rates.

   On the other hand, GNP has decided limitations as a measure of our overall well-being. It does not, for instance, take into account the costs of polluting or damaging the environment or even the costs of jeopardizing consumers' health through such pollution (ironically, in fact, health risks may contribute to an increased GNP through greater consumption of health services and products). It must be recognized that GNP is a quantitative measure that can reflect the quality of life only to the extent that we desire and value a production-oriented economy.

2. When Simon Kuznets initiated the economic measure that would later be termed *gross national product,* a chief concern was to make that measure as accurate as possible. Because many producers may contribute to the generation of a given product (particularly one as complex as an automobile or airplane, for instance), Kuznets had to devise a way to avoid double counting. His answer was to consider only final products in production totals. In this way, the steel used in building an automobile would be counted as output once only, at the time it was used in the final product. Kuznets also decided to exclude nonmarket production, primarily the housekeeping and childcare provided by housewives, from his production totals; Kuznets wished to emphasize market production, not work for which people did not receive direct monetary compensation. And in addition, he recognized the extreme difficulty of equitably assigning any dollar figures to such work. Kuznets also excluded all illegal activities from his calculations of GNP.

3. Numerous factors go into determining GNP, and many of these same factors are, in turn, influenced by GNP. These factors include unemployment and underemployment rates, inflation, defense spending, taxes, changes in production sources (whether heaviest production comes from agriculture, communications, or services, for example), and consumer attitudes, consumers' relative faith in the economy and tendencies to spend or invest their disposable income.

4. Franklin Roosevelt made extensive use of GNP data in planning for the war effort. It was used to illustrate what a fully employed economy could accomplish and convince industries like the steel industry to expand. It was used to determine how much of the nation's industrial capacity could be diverted to the war effort without jeopardizing the basic supply of food, clothing, housing, and transportation for the civilian population. GNP was also essential in balancing the military's production needs against that which it was possible to achieve and in reconciling the conflicting demands of the U.S. military and the Allies when the Japanese attacked Pearl Harbor.

5. Continuous growth of GNP was thought by our nation's early economists to be automatic within a capitalist society. Today's economists have a more realistic perspective and recognize that growth of GNP depends on the continuing development of new products and services that reflect the constantly changing needs and values of our society.

Multiple Choice

1. d   Text, 72.
2. a   Text, 71.
3. c   Text, 72.
4. b   Text, 74.
5. d   Text, 74.
6. a   Text, 77.
7. b   Text, 85.
8. c   Text, 81–83.
9. a   Text, 84–86.
10. a   Text, 79–80.

True-False

1. False   Text, 78–79.
2. False   Text, 71–76.
3. False   Text, 70–71.
4. True   Text, 84–86.
5. False   Text, 80.
6. True   Text, 53.
7. True   Text, 80; Video.
8. True   Text, 79; Video.
9. True   Text, 79.
10. True   Text, 74.

Discussion Questions

1. No. It includes the value of the total amount of final goods and services produced by an economy during a particular period of time. GDP avoids double counting, values goods and services produced by government at cost, omits nonmarket transactions, and does not include nonproductive transfers.

2. If each taxpayer hired a neighbor to fill out his or her tax return, this would increase GDP because these services would now represent a marketed good. Time spent in filling out personal tax returns is not included in GDP because it would be extremely difficult to get a reliable estimate of the money value of each individual's service. However, it certainly is true that tax returns do take time to fill out and the resources used to fill out tax returns cannot be used to produce other goods. Government, and the IRS, should be aware of this trade-off and seek to create tax forms and tax rules that do not require an unreasonable amount of time and therefore resources to comply accurately with the law.

3. Although the statement is true, it does not justify the inclusion of these payments in the calculation of GDP. These payments simply represent a redistribution of

income among the individuals in our economy and not an increase in the productive output of the economy.

4. Failure to subtract depreciation in the calculation of total domestic output overlooks the fact that worn-out capital must be replenished for the economy to maintain the same productive capacity. Failure to subtract out depreciation overlooks the fact that some capital expenditure represents replacement. However, even though double counting results in an overstatement of GDP, the failure to subtract out depreciation does not result in an overstatement of GDP.

5. First, GDP does not take into account population differences. It does not take into account leisure, quality changes, output produced within households for their own use, the value of the composition of the output, or the distribution of the nation's output. Also GDP does not include social costs.

Problem Set

1. a. The gross domestic product in *current dollars* in 2003 equals $1.10 \times 1.03 \times \text{GDP}_{01}$, where GDP_{01} = gross domestic product in current dollars in 2001. The price level in 2003 is 10 percent higher than in 2001. To express the gross domestic product in 2001 in 2003 prices, we multiply the gross domestic product in 2001 by 1.10 ($\text{GDP}_{01} \times 1.10$). GDP 2003 in 2003 prices is $1.03 \times 1.10 \times \text{GDP}_{01}$. Since both outputs are expressed in terms of 2003 dollars, the only difference between the two terms is the change in output. Thus, the percent increase in GDP in constant dollars between 2001 and 2003 equals

$$\frac{\text{Change in constant dollar GDP between 2001 and 2003}}{\text{Constant dollar GDP in 2001}}$$

$$= \frac{1.03 \times 1.10 \times \text{GDP}_{01} - 1.10 \times \text{GDP}_{01}}{1.10 \times \text{GDP}_{01}}$$

$$= \frac{1.10 \times \text{GDP}_{01}(1.03 - 1)}{1.10 \times \text{GDP}_{01}} = 0.03 = 3\%.$$

b. $1.8 million.
c. $99 million.

2. a. $20 + 10 + 30 + 200 + 20 + 60 + 40$ million = $380 million for GDP.
b. $380 million (GDP) – [$240 million (personal consumption expenditures) + $30 million (net investment) + $40 million (depreciation) + $6 million (exports) – $5 million (imports)]
= $69 million (government purchases of goods and services).

3. a. 9817.0
b. 1.000
c. 2.178
d. 10100.8
e. 9866.6
f. 1.024
g. 1.039
h. 1.535
i. 2.193
j. 10987.8
k. 1.662367
l. 3.12407

Audio/Text Questions

1. a. Not included, and it should not be included because it is simply a transfer of wealth, not production of a good or a service.
    b. Same as part a.
    c. Yes, and it should be included.
    d. Not included because that would be double counting.
    e. Included, and it should be, although not on a year-to-year basis except insofar as the equipment has an annual operating cost.
    f. Not included because of difficulty in measurement, but it should be included.

2. NNP equals GNP less the value of the goods and services necessary to replace depreciated plant and equipment. NNP is a better measure of output that can be consumed.

3. GNP does not measure the many changes that have affected Americans since 1900. The workweek is shorter, and GNP does not measure leisure time. The enhanced quality of goods such as drugs and automobiles is usually understated in GNP. Increased pollution and the stress of increased population density are not counted either. The increase in the average life span, greater educational opportunities, and so on, may enter GNP only indirectly or at a much lower (or higher) value than the "true" value.

4. National income accounts helped determine the United States's initial productive capacity and pinpointed the industries that could not handle the wartime demand and the industries that would be key to the whole productive process. This facilitated investment and rationing plans and helped forecast personal consumption and target the level of income taxes and bond drives.

5. Not all policy has been directed toward improving GNP. Safety, pollution, and income distribution are among the considerable exceptions. There is no easy substitute for GNP for the economy as a whole, but cost-benefit analysis (in which one can define the costs and benefits more accurately than in GNP) can be used for individual policies, such as safety requirements.

LESSON 4. BOOMS AND BUSTS: WHAT CAUSES THE BUSINESS CYCLE?

INTRODUCTION

Most of us, like the nation as a whole, experience alternate periods of economic prosperity and economic difficulty. Sometimes, saving money and planning for the future seems relatively easy. At other times inflation erodes our purchasing power and sense of security. Many of us also feel the frustration, perhaps despair, of wanting and needing to work in an economy that offers only limited employment opportunities.

To make sense of these fluctuations on a national scale and help explain the causes underlying unemployment and inflation, economists use the concepts of aggregate supply, aggregate demand, and business cycles.

What You Should Learn

By the end of this lesson, you should be able to do the following to better understand business fluctuations:

1. Define *aggregate supply* and *aggregate demand* and recognize the factors that influence each.

2. Offer two reasons why the aggregate demand curve for the nation's total economic output slopes downward and to the right.

3. Explain the classical economists' view of business cycles and state the criticisms of this view.

4. List, in order, the four phases of the business cycle—*trough, expansion, peak,* and *recession*—and explain what each means in relation to the others.

5. Summarize the philosophical contributions offered by

    - The classical economists.
    - Karl Marx.
    - John Maynard Keynes.

6. Identify the three ranges within the short-run aggregate supply curve, and relate these to the general shape of the short-run aggregate supply curve.

7. Describe general trends in our economy from 1962 onward.

8. Explain how the unemployment rate is calculated, the definition of *unemployment,* and the impact unemployment has on GDP.

9. Recognize the impact of various shifts in aggregate demand and aggregate supply on the level of employment and prices.

KEY TERMS

business cycle
real GDP
potential GDP
depression
prosperity
aggregate supply
aggregate demand
Say's law
horizontal range
vertical range
recession
expansion
trough
peak

positively sloped range
equilibrium level
unemployment
frictional unemployment
structural unemployment
cyclical unemployment
full employment
short-run aggregate supply
long-run aggregate supply

VIDEO

Watch

Economics U$A Program 4, "Booms and Busts: What Causes the Business Cycle?"

Illustrative Events

The booms and busts of the early twentieth century help illustrate classical economic theories about the ups and downs of the business cycle; featuring economist Robert L. Heilbroner, author and professor of economics at the New School for Social Research. Richard Gill sums up with a discussion of the classical doctrine, Say's law.

How Karl Marx saw economic fluctuations as evidence of the failure of capitalism while Joseph Schumpeter saw the same as evidence of the system's success, again featuring Robert L. Heilbroner.

The Great Depression and the responses of President Herbert Hoover and Treasury Secretary Andrew Mellon help introduce the theories of British economist John Maynard Keynes, featuring Professor Willard Thorp of Amherst College.

After Viewing

Answer the following questions:

1. During the nineteenth century, people were already noticing economic fluctuations, but no one was trying very hard to explain them. Why?

2. What was the overall impact of World War I on the U.S. economy?

3. What factors contributed to the powerful influence of Karl Marx early in the twentieth century?

4. How did the views of economist Joseph Schumpeter differ from those of Karl Marx?

5. On what basic but critical point did John Maynard Keynes's philosophy of economics differ from what adherents to Say's law believed?

Read

Read Chapter 4, "Business Fluctuations and Unemployment," pages 89–107 and 113–115 in your text.

SELF-QUIZ

Multiple Choice

1. Which of the following statements *best* describes what has happened to real GDP since 1962?

    a. It rose and fell in irregular cycles within an overall strikingly upward trend.
    b. It rose and fell consistently but managed to attain, overall, only slight growth.
    c. It rose sharply through the 1960s, after which, despite several dramatic surges, it tended to fall.
    d. It rose and fell in unpredictable patterns with no definite upward or downward trends.

2. The total amount of goods and services that could be produced if the economy is operating at full capacity is known as

    a. GDP.
    b. real GDP.
    c. potential GDP.
    d. nominal GDP.

3. The *expansion* phase of a business cycle occurs when

    a. output comes closest to achieving its potential.
    b. the economy is first pulling itself out of a trough.
    c. the economy is enjoying a period of prosperity.
    d. the aggregate demand curve shifts to the left.

4. Which of the following *best* characterizes the recessions this country has experienced since World War II?

    a. None of them has been either very long or very deep.
    b. Several have been long and severe enough to be termed *depressions*.
    c. Most have affected only isolated segments of the economy.
    d. Since World War II, the country has not really experienced a true recession.

5. Overall, economic *peaks* tend to be caused by

    a. a dramatic boom in the construction industry.
    b. the positive effects of wartime economy.
    c. the natural tendency of the economy to rejuvenate itself.
    d. widely divergent phenomena that differ from one business cycle to the next.

6. The reasons why the aggregate demand curve slopes downward and to the right have *mostly* to do with the relationship between

    a. real GDP and potential GDP.
    b. interest rates and output.
    c. prosperity and depression.
    d. the horizontal range and the vertical range.

7. Suppose that the aggregate demand curve and short-run aggregate supply curve intersect well within the horizontal range of the short-run aggregate supply curve. If consumers then decide to increase their spending, which of the following describes what is most likely to occur?

    a. The aggregate demand curve shifts outward and to the right; output increases but prices do not.
    b. The aggregate demand curve shifts outward and to the right; prices increase but output does not.
    c. The aggregate demand curve shifts to the left; both output and prices decline.
    d. The aggregate demand curve shifts to the left; output increases but prices fall.

8. When all resources are fully employed and further output is virtually impossible, we can say that the short-run aggregate supply curve is in

    a. the horizontal range.
    b. the positively sloped range.
    c. the vertical range.
    d. none of the above, because the situation described never occurs.

9. If the aggregate demand curve moves to the right and continues moving to the right unchecked, the eventual result is
   a. severe unemployment.
   b. indefinite increase in output.
   c. a sharp decline in domestic investment.
   d. inflation.

10. Which of the following *best* describes the economic loss to our society resulting from unemployment above the 4 percent full-employment unemployment rate?
    a. Although the noneconomic loss is staggering, the economic loss (as measured in dollars) is really inconsequential.
    b. The economic loss even at a 5 percent unemployment rate is significant.
    c. The economic loss is significant only at an unemployment rate of 10 percent or greater.
    d. No one really knows since there is no way to calculate this loss in monetary terms.

True-False

_____ 1. In essence, business cycles are the rise and fall of national output, approaching and moving away from potential full employment.

_____ 2. The four phases of the business cycle (trough, expansion, peak, and recession) are predictable and regular in both length and amplitude.

_____ 3. Until the 1930s, most classical economists were convinced that the price system, left to its own devices, would ensure the maintenance of full employment and supply would create its own demand.

_____ 4. In contrast to most classical economists, John Maynard Keynes felt that the capitalistic system would suffer from increasingly severe unemployment, leading to the system's eventual collapse.

_____ 5. Although Marx and Schumpeter held very different views, they agreed on one point, that crises were a built-in, nonaccidental feature of the capitalistic system.

_____ 6. The gap between actual and potential GDP is a measure of what society loses by tolerating less than full employment.

_____ 7. Aggregate demand is the sum of all the goods and services buyers are willing to purchase at a given price level.

_____ 8. The aggregate supply curve shows the level of real national output supplied at each price level.

_____ 9. According to Keynes, a fall in investment spending might precipitate a fall in consumption spending.

_____ 10. Business cycles are seldom the result of shifts in aggregate demand or total spending.

Discussion Questions

1. Trace the movement of an economy from the expansion phase of a business cycle through one complete cycle (from expansion to peak, from peak to recession, from recession to the trough, and back to expansion).

2. In nation X, output and employment rise, but the price level remains unchanged. Using aggregate demand and supply curves, explain how this combination of events could have occurred. Can you be sure that it was due solely to a shift in one of these curves? If so, can you tell whether the aggregate demand or the aggregate supply curve shifted?

3. President Reagan, in his 1982 *Economic Report of the President,* said, "To spur further business investment and productivity growth, the new [1981] tax law provides faster write-offs for capital investment [that is, depreciation of equipment over shorter periods of time]. . . . Research and development expenditures are encouraged with a new tax credit. Small business tax rates have been reduced." Explain in detail how each of these tax changes might affect the aggregate supply curve. On the basis of what you have learned thus far, can you say anything about the magnitude of their effects?

4. Did Karl Marx believe that there was an automatic tendency toward full employment under capitalism? Why or why not?

Problem Set

1. Use the graph to fill out the table that follows for the given shift in aggregate demand. If the shift causes the specified variable to increase, then write a plus sign (+); to decrease, a negative sign (–); and if there is no change, write a zero (0).

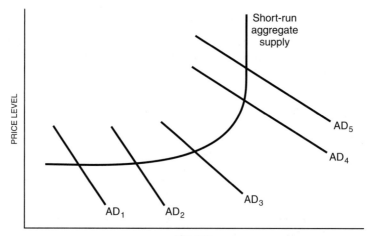

AD shifts		Price level	RGDP	Employment
From	To			
AD_1	AD_2	_____	_____	_____
AD_2	AD_3	_____	_____	_____
AD_3	AD_4	_____	_____	_____
AD_4	AD_5	_____	_____	_____
AD_5	AD_4	_____	_____	_____
AD_3	AD_2	_____	_____	_____

2. a. Given the following aggregate supply–aggregate demand graph, plot the points of equilibrium RGDP associated with different points in time on the second graph, where Q_2 = full employment output.

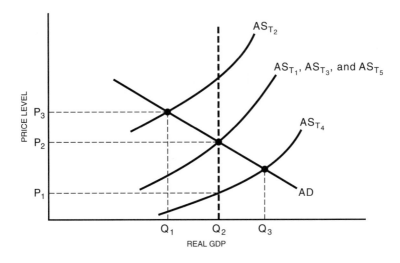

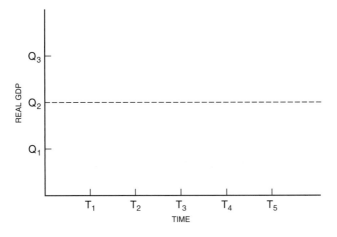

At what point in time is the economy at its peak? At its trough? Between which points in time does the economy experiencing an expansion? Does the price level fluctuates with (coincidental) or is it opposite from (counter-cyclical) fluctuations in RGDP?

b. Given the aggregate supply–aggregate demand that follows, plot the points of equilibrium RGDP associated with different points in time on the second graph, where Q_2 = full employment output.

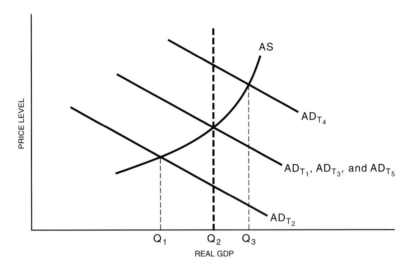

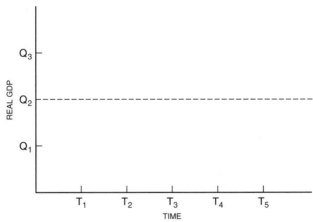

At what time period is the economy at its peak? At its trough? Between which points in time does the economy experience an expansion? Does the price level fluctuate with (coincidental) or is it opposite from (counter-cyclical) fluctuations in RGDP? Is the business cycle you have drawn here in part b the same as the one you drew in part a? If so, how can we determine if shifts in aggregate demand or aggregate supply cause the business cycle?

3. a. Draw a graph of the classical aggregate supply curve, given that classical economists believed that aggregate demand determined only price levels, not output levels ("supply creates its own demand").

b. Draw a graph of the Keynesian aggregate supply curve, where aggregate demand determines output levels but not the price level ("demand creates its own supply").

4. a. Fill in the blanks in the following table. Employment-population ratio = employed/population. Population, not in labor force, unemployed, and employed are in millions.

Year	Population over 16	Not in labor force	Unemployed	Employed	Unemployment rate	Emp-pop ratio
1	80	40	2			
2	100	40	4.5			
3	120	40	8			
4	140	40	7.5			
5	140	30	5.5			

What is the relationship between the unemployment rate and the employment-population ratio here? Is this the relation you were expecting? What do you think is going on here?

b. Fill in the blanks in the following table. Employment-population ratio = employed/population. Population, not in labor force, unemployed, and employed are in millions.

Year	Population over 16	Not in labor force	Unemployed	Employed	Unemployment rate	Emp-pop ratio
1	80	30	2.5			
2	82	35	4.7			
3	84	40	6.6			
4	86	45	8.2			
5	90	45	6.75			

What is the relationship between the unemployment rate and the employment-population ratio here? Is this the relation you were expecting? What do you think is going on here?

LESSON REVIEW

If you had difficulty with the Self-Quiz or would like additional assistance, read the following lesson review. It should reinforce and help you understand the content presented in this lesson.

Business Fluctuations

Overall economic performance can be measured by comparing potential GDP with actual GDP. Potential GDP equals the total amount of goods and services that could be produced if the economy operates at full capacity or full employment. During the prosperous mid-1920s, our country's actual GDP approached this potential; then it fell abysmally below potential GDP during the Depression of the 1930s. Overall, the long-term trend since World War I has been upward, but the climb has been far from steady. The economy rose and fell sporadically in highly irregular fluctuations of GDP, termed *business cycles* (see Figures 4.1 and 4.3 in the text, pages 90 and 92–93).

Business Cycle: The Four Phases

Each business cycle can be divided into four phases: The *trough* is the point at which national output is lowest in comparison to its potential level. The trough is followed by an *expansion* phase, during which national output rises. The *peak* occurs when output hits its highest point relative to the potential level. And *recession* is the phase during which output falls from peak to trough again. It is important to understand that these peaks and troughs are relative (see Figure 4.2 in the text, page 91).

In a *recession*, national output is far below its potential. *Depression* is another term for severe recession. During a recession, unemployment rises. By contrast, *prosperity* is a time when national output comes extremely close to its potential level, and during prosperity, employment is high. Since World War II, we experienced numerous recessions, none very long or deep in comparison to the Great Depression.

Each business cycle may be considered unique. Each one is different in length and each one has slightly different underlying causes.

Aggregate Demand

Aggregate demand is the sum of all goods and services that consumers, firms, and the government are willing and able to purchase at each price level at a given point in time. To avoid confusion, you must not confuse the demand for an individual good with the aggregate demand for all goods and services. The reason that the demand curve for an individual good slopes downward is different from the reason the aggregate demand curve slopes downward and to the right.

How do we explain the slope of the aggregate demand curve? It is the result of two steps.

> *Step 1. Increases in the price level push up interest rates.* In constructing the aggregate demand curve, we assume that the amount of money available within the economy is fixed. So, as prices go up, the money people have does not buy as much as before prices rose. How can people buy as much as they were buying before prices rose? The answer is to either borrow money or sell such assets as government securities. As more people begin to borrow and liquidate assets, interest rates go up.

> *Step 2. The increases in interest rates resulting from step 1 reduce total output.* When interest rates rise, firms cut down on their borrowing for investments in equipment; individual consumers, similarly, stop borrowing money to buy new

homes and automobiles. Less borrowing means less purchasing, and as purchasing declines, the nation's total real output declines.

While these two steps do not explain all the factors influencing the shape of the aggregate demand curve (sloping downward and to the right), they are perhaps the most significant and consistent factors to keep in mind right now.

Aggregate Supply

Aggregate supply is the sum of all goods and services produced by the economy at each price level. We cannot calculate aggregate supply by just adding up all the individual supply curves of the goods and services we produce. Individual supply curves are derived assuming that only the price of the good or service under consideration changes while the prices of other goods and services are held constant, whereas with the aggregate supply curve, the price level (i.e., the average of all prices) changes.

What are the reasons for the short-run aggregate supply curve's shape? To get an upward slope for the aggregate supply curve, economists assume that some prices do not change, at least not in the short run. Specifically, they assume that labor costs are constant in the short run. If the prices for the goods and services businesses produce increase while the labor costs remain constant, then the businesses will earn higher profits. And as profits rise, the businesses have an incentive to increase output, hence the direct relation between the price level and output in the short run.

If *all* prices (costs included) changed by the same percentage, then relative prices (opportunity costs) remain unchanged and output does not change at all. The whole aggregate supply curve is vertical in this case. Most economists believe this is the case in the long run, when all prices including labor costs have a chance to adjust to the new situation.

To better understand the economics of John Maynard Keynes, we must consider the proposition that the short-run aggregate supply curve can be divided into three ranges. The curve not only has the upward-sloping range just discussed but also a horizontal range and a vertical range.

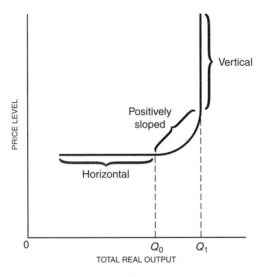

The horizontal range. Within the horizontal or Keynesian range, plenty of unemployed workers and unused productive capacity are available. As aggregate demand increases, output can be easily increased by employing these resources. Since all firms have plenty of excess capacity, if one firm tries to raise its prices, then other firms are more than willing to produce the good or service at the old price. Hence, output and employment increase without price level increases. If aggregate demand does not increase, then the economy could be stuck in this range for a very long time according to Keynes.

The vertical range. Here, all firms produce at their capacity. If aggregate demand increases, there is no way to increase output since all resources are already fully employed. If aggregate demand is greater than aggregate supply at a given price level, then the only thing that can happen is for prices, and hence the price level, to increase. Output and employment do not increase.

The positively sloped range. Within this range, as output increases, shortages of some products develop, and their prices go up. Some firms produce at their capacity; others do not. As more products are affected, this trend eventually has an impact on the price level, the average of all prices of goods and services. Gradually, output increases sufficiently to pull one commodity then another out of the depressed horizontal range. Some areas of the economy reach full employment before others, so the positively sloped range angles to the right a bit at first; then, as more sectors reach full employment, the aggregate supply curve takes a sharp turn upward (as output changes less and price changes more) and eventually shoots straight up into the vertical range of pure price increase.

THE UNITED STATES'S ECONOMY: TWO HISTORIC EXAMPLES

Thousands of books have been written about the U.S. economy. We cannot begin to summarize the effects of the Great Depression and the subsequent war boom in a few short paragraphs, but we can present some highlights that help illustrate what factors can cause the aggregate supply and demand curves to shift.

The Great Crash

Prior to the stock market crash of 1929, the United States was in the midst of a period of general prosperity; real GDP was running very close to its potential. Unemployment was low. The demand for new goods and services was high; prices were relatively stable. After the crash, the picture changed: Real GDP fell far below its potential; unemployment rose to approximately 25 percent of the workforce. Private domestic investment (in new equipment and facilities) also fell, and the money supply shrank, depressing consumer spending even further. The aggregate demand curve shifted markedly to the left, into the horizontal range of the short-run aggregate supply curve. (See Figure 4.7, page 100 of text.)

World War II

Unemployment fell as jobs opened in defense plants and the armed forces expanded. Some 12 million men were drafted into the armed services, and before the war ended, about 50 percent of the nation's entire output was allocated to the war effort. To support the war effort, the government expanded the money supply and spent heavily on military personnel and equipment. As spending increased, the GDP shot upward—with a 75 percent increase from 1939 to 1945. The aggregate demand curve shifted to the right, well into the positively sloped range of the aggregate supply curve. As increased spending pushed military output to its maximum, there was severe upward pressure on the prices of rationed civilian goods. The government countered this pressure for a time with price controls, but once these were lifted, the aggregate demand curve shifted further to the right, into the vertical range of the short-run aggregate supply curve.

UNEMPLOYMENT

Of all economic indicators, none is more closely associated with business fluctuations than unemployment, partly because this is the factor that has potentially the most powerful and immediate effect on our lives.

According to the U.S. government, *any person 16 years old or older who does not have a job and is looking for one is unemployed.* Persons who choose voluntarily not to work are not considered unemployed. Beyond this definition, however, we must recognize that there are different causes of unemployment.

Frictional unemployment occurs because people quit jobs, usually to find better ones, because seasonal workers are temporarily out of jobs, recent graduates are looking for their first jobs, or the number of people do not match the number of jobs available due to technological and institutional factors.

Structural unemployment results when the production of new goods and services calls for different technologies or skills that previous workers have not had time or opportunity to master.

Cyclical unemployment occurs when fluctuations in the business cycle lower production and hence the demand for workers.

How Is the Unemployment Rate Calculated?

Each month, the federal government surveys our population, asking a selected sample of Americans whether they are currently employed and, if not, whether they are actively seeking work. Experts regard these figures as reasonably reliable with certain qualifications:

1. The figures do not reflect the percentage of people who are underemployed. Workers frequently accept temporary or part-time jobs or positions far below their level of skill simply because they cannot find anything else.

2. The figures do not account for persons who have given up looking, even though such persons would gladly accept work if it were offered.

3. The unemployment rate can rise significantly if certain groups of people who were previously not seeking employment decide they want to work; for example, the percentage of married women who work outside the home has risen dramatically in recent years and continues to rise.

How Much Unemployment Is There?

This is a complex question indeed. As we have already seen, our figures for unemployment are approximations at best. Further, since unemployment is figured as a percentage of the civilian workforce, we must recognize that an unemployment rate of 5 percent in the 1950s and an unemployment rate of 5 percent in the 1980s do not, given the growth in the labor force, add up to the same numbers of persons without jobs. Our current labor force is over 100 million; this means that each 1 percent increase in unemployment signifies approximately 1 million workers seeking jobs.

Overall, the unemployment statistics, like all economic indicators, rise and fall in irregular cycles throughout the country's history. Although unemployment has never, since World War II, approached the alarming and tragic levels of the Great Depression, it hit relative peaks (6 percent in 1970 to 1974, 8.5 percent in 1975, 9 percent in 1982) sufficient to worry economists and spell severe hardship for millions of Americans.

Beginning in the 1960s, economists were willing to accept a figure of 4 percent unemployment as constituting, for practical purposes, full employment. In the 1970s and early 1980s, however, they revised that figure to 6 percent. In recent years, the estimate has dropped back to 4 percent. Keep in mind that a zero unemployment figure is not realistically achievable because of our constantly shifting employment patterns: New groups entering the workforce, people changing jobs or seeking additional training for other occupations, high school and college graduates seeking first-time jobs, and so on.

What Are the Costs of Unemployment?

The *noneconomic* costs of unemployment, although not quantifiable, are devastating: loss of self-esteem, loss of a feeling of security, threat to family life, and an increased sense of personal despair and hopelessness. Although these may be the most debilitating costs, in personal terms, they are not the only costs. What is the *economic* loss to our society if we tolerate unemployment above the minimum levels?

In determining this, economists estimate the *potential GDP,* or the level of gross domestic product that could result with full employment. Assume at present most economists accept an unemployment figure of 5 percent as the equivalent of full employment.

Therefore, they would estimate the potential GDP by multiplying 95 percent of the labor force times the normal hours of work per year times the average output per hour of work at the relevant time. Then, *the difference between the actual and potential GDP represents what society loses by tolerating less than full employment.* These economic costs can be significant. For instance, in 1975 (a year of severe recession), the dollar loss to society was about $100 billion.

EXTENDED LEARNING

This section of the study guide is specifically designed for the two-semester student.

AUDIO

Before Listening
Read Exploring Further of Chapter 4, pages 108–113 in your text.

Next
Listen to the audiotape that accompanies Lesson 4.

After Listening
Answer the following questions:

1. What is *potential* GNP? Why isn't it a clearly defined term?
2. What are *frictional, structural,* and *cyclical* unemployment?
3. Some people argue that unemployment compensation increases the unemployment rate. What are their reasons?
4. What are two major problems with the way the government calculates the labor force?
5. Give the reasons for the shape of the short-run aggregate supply curve, and what each section of the curve implies for employment and inflation.

ADDITIONAL READINGS

The History of Economic Thought Website/Business Cycle Theory
<http://cepa.newschool.edu/het/essays/cycle/cyclecont.htm>.

> Essays 1 through 7 give brief but interesting summaries of business cycle theories that preceded Keynes.

The History of Economic Thought Website/After Marx: Structural Change and Steady State <http://cepa.newschool.edu/het/essays/growth/aftermarx.htm>.

> This essay has a summary of Schumpeter's rather interesting theory of business cycles.

Gill, Richard T. *Evolution of Modern Economics.* Englewood Cliffs, NJ: Prentice-Hall, 1967.

> Chapter 3, "Disharmonies and the Marxian Critique," discusses Marx's explanation of business cycles. No mathematics or graphs.

Gordon, Robert A. *Economic Instability and Growth: The American Record.* New York: Harper & Row, 1974.

> Chapters 2 and 3 detail the boom of the 1920s and the depression of the 1930s from the point of view of aggregate demand analysis. The various factors that influenced each component of demand are examined. No mathematics or graphs.

Hansen, Alvin H. *Business Cycles and National Income.* New York: W. W. Norton & Company, 1964.

> Chapters 13 to 16 provide a good survey of the pre-Keynesian theories of the business cycle, including theories regarding aggregate demand that Keynes incorporated in his analysis. No mathematics or graphs.

Lebergott, Stanley. *The Americans: An Economic Record.* New York: W. W. Norton & Company, 1984.

> Chapter 30, "Cycles and Depressions," pp. 388–400, provides a survey of the magnitude and the effects of U.S. business cycles from the Civil War to 1980. Some of the theories of the business cycle are placed in this historical context. No mathematics or graphs.

Peterson, Wallace C. *Income, Employment, and Economic Growth*, 6th ed. New York: W. W. Norton & Company, 1988.

> Chapters 4 and 5 detail the nature of the economy and the policy implications of the theory. The reasons the neoclassical employment theory was attacked by Keynes is also discussed. No mathematics or graphs.

ANSWER KEY

Video Questions

1. For several reasons, Americans during the nineteenth century did not question economic fluctuations much, although many were beginning to notice them. For one thing, the whole country was expanding, building railroads, expanding overseas trade, creating new industries in many forms. With everyone virtually swept up in the tide of general prosperity, few had time or inclination to think of anything else. In addition, while there certainly were slumps, the overall pattern

was overwhelmingly toward growth, so that most people began to accept the fact that periodic setbacks were invariably temporary: Didn't things always turn around?

Furthermore, even though some people may have noticed the contrast between prosperity and decline in a general way, there was little tendency to talk in terms of causes and effects. Economics, as a profession, had not yet come into its own, and it would be years before professional economists had developed cogent theories about how one economic condition precipitated another. Right up through the early years of the twentieth century, business executives still adhered closely to Say's law, believing that the system would be self-maintaining as supply created its own demand and consumers continued to spend their money either to purchase goods and services or invest in industry, stimulating production in another way.

Finally, some economists believe that the nineteenth century economy was simply more resilient than that of today, that its capacity to recover from potential problems was in fact so great that few people had time to notice problems before the economy was in another upswing.

2. In the early twentieth century, in the years just preceding World War I, the U.S. economy was in a severe decline. Business investment was down. Production was down. Unemployment was high. Despite these critical problems, Americans feared government intervention, believing that the business cycle would correct itself given time and that tampering with it might only make things worse.

   Then, in 1914, when Americans began to support the war effort, everything changed. Suddenly, jobs were everywhere. Agriculture had to gear up to produce the food needed; factories opened and expanded. When the United States entered the war in 1917, unemployment declined further as citizens entered the armed services and as production of military weapons and supplies increased. A year and a half later, however, returning soldiers found a different situation. Support for unions, high during the war, shrank to virtually nothing. As products and supplies were no longer needed, factories closed and the agricultural movement slowed. Once again, people were out of work, and production fell heavily. Poverty, violent labor strikes, turmoil, and loss of faith in the capitalist system were but a few of the negative outcomes of this rapid and dramatic business cycle.

3. In the early twentieth century, when workers were struggling against apparently insurmountable odds, Marx's ideas seemed to speak directly to them. His message was simple and direct: The worker gave an economy's goods and services their value, yet the worker was unappreciated, exploited by the capitalist business executives and factory owners. Marx had been the first to speak of a self-generated business cycle in which good times produced bad, then bad produced good. Eventually, Marx said, the capitalist system would not be able to extract itself from the bad times, and it would go under. With production down, millions out of work, and little hope for the future (war seemed to most a heavy price to pay for increased productivity), Marx's words seemed indeed to be forecasting the United States's future.

80 | LESSON 4

4. Both Marx and the young economist Joseph Schumpeter were struck by the boom and bust cycles of economics. To Marx, these cycles signaled the death throes of capitalism. But Schumpeter disagreed totally. Whereas Marx tended to fix on the bust side of the cycle, Schumpeter looked at the boom side and called it "regeneration." Capitalism, Schumpeter said, was dynamic by nature. The boom and bust cycles were but the by-products of a nation in flux, creating and inventing something new continuously and having occasionally to shrug off the old to make way for innovative technology. Without these fluctuations, Schumpeter maintained, the economy would stagnate and real growth would be impossible.

5. Followers of J. B. Say generally held that consumers would use virtually all their income in one of two ways: They would either spend it on products and services or lend it to businesses, which in turn would use the money to rejuvenate and expand. In balance, if consumption demand went up, investment demand would go down; if investment demand went up, consumption demand would go down. But either way, the *total* demand would remain high, and the economy would prosper.

Keynes's view was disarmingly different. Keynes said that a fall in investment spending would not necessarily stimulate an increase in consumer spending; indeed, it might trigger a decline. Further, Keynes argued, once that decline began, it could operate as a sort of self-perpetuating phenomenon, so that *total* demand could fall indefinitely. In brief, Keynes did not believe, as the classical economists had, that a decline would repair itself automatically. He argued instead that the economy was dependent on keeping *demand* levels high, by whatever means. For those opposed to any sort of intervention in the business cycles and those accustomed to believing that economic problems could heal themselves given time, Keynes's ideas were truly revolutionary—and frightening.

Multiple Choice

1. a   Text, 90.
2. c   Text, 90.
3. b   Text, 91.
4. a   Text, 91.
5. d   Text, 91–92.
6. b   Text, 94–95.
7. a   Text, 108.
8. c   Text, 108.
9. d   Text, 100–101.
10. b Text, 106.

True-False

1. True   Text, 90.
2. False   Text, 90–92.
3. True   Text, 103.
4. False   Text, 103, 109.
5. True   Video.
6. True   Text, 106–107.
7. True   Text, 93–95.
8. True   Text, 95–98.
9. True   Video.
10. False Video.

Discussion Questions

1. Expansion is that part of the business cycle when national output increases. The peak occurs when national output is at its highest level relative to its potential level. Recession is that part of the business cycle when national output decreases. The trough occurs when national output is at its lowest level relative to its potential level.

2. An increase in output and employment while prices remain constant occurs only if the aggregate demand curve initially intersects the aggregate supply curve in the horizontal segment of the aggregate supply curve and if the aggregate demand curve then shifts out to the right but continues to intersect the horizontal segment of the aggregate supply curve.

3. All three changes to the tax law result in a rightward shift of the aggregate supply curve. The changes in the tax law affecting write-offs for capital investment encourage businesses to increase their level of investment and hence increase the productivity level in the economy: Businesses are able to produce goods at a lower per-unit cost. Research and development expenditures likewise lead to productivity increases: With the new tax credit businesses have greater incentive to make these expenditures and the economy reaps the benefit in greater productivity and therefore greater potential output. Finally, a reduction in small-business tax rates reduces the cost of producing goods and services so that businesses can produce more output at every price.

4. No, Karl Marx believed that capitalists, by utilizing more labor-saving technology, would increase the level of unemployment in the economy. He did not see the economy as a self-correcting mechanism: Instead Marx felt that capitalism was bound to collapse due to its failure to guarantee full employment.

Problem Set

1. AD shifts

From	To	Price level	RGDP	Employment
AD_1	AD_2	0	+	+
AD_2	AD_3	+	+	+
AD_3	AD_4	+	+	+
AD_4	AD_5	+	0	0
AD_5	AD_4	–	0	0
AD_3	AD_2	–	–	–

2. a.

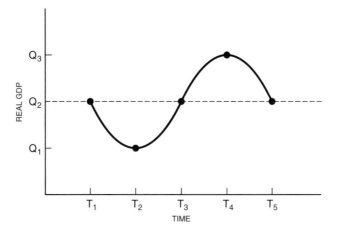

The economy is at its peak at time T_4. It is at its trough at time T_2. It expands between times T_2 and T_4.
The price level fluctuations are countercyclical.

b.

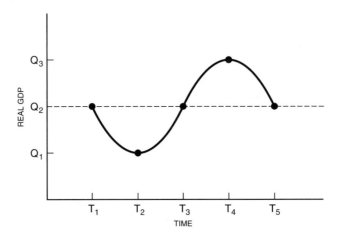

The business cycle looks the same here as in part a. The only difference is that the price level fluctuates with RGDP here, while it fluctuated opposite to RGDP in part a. We can use this to determine if changes in aggregate supply or changes in aggregate demand cause the business cycle.

3. a.

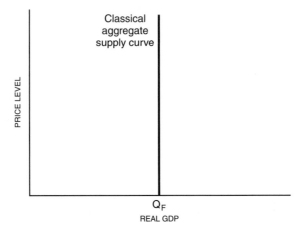

Q_F = full-emplyment output.

b.

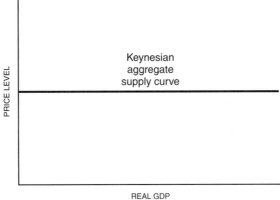

4. a.

Year	Population over 16	Not in labor force	Unemployed	Employed	Unemployment rate	Emp-pop ratio
1	80	40	2	38	5	48
2	100	40	4.5	55.5	7.5	55.5
3	120	40	8	72	10	60
4	140	40	7.5	92.5	7.5	66
5	140	30	5.5	104.5	5	75

The percentage of the population employed is going up at the same time that the unemployment rate is going up. One statistic seems to be saying that the economy is doing fine while the other seems to be saying that it is in trouble. Both the number of unemployed and the number of employed people increase in years 2 and 3. Even though the unemployment rate is rising, real GDP is likely rising also.

b.

Year	Population over 16	Not in labor force	Unemployed	Employed	Unemployment rate	Emp-pop ratio
1	80	30	2.5	47.5	5	59
2	82	35	4.7	42.3	10	52
3	84	40	6.6	37.4	15	45
4	86	45	8.2	32.8	20	38
5	90	45	6.75	38.25	15	43

The percentage of the population employed is going down at the same time that the unemployment rate is going up. That is what one would expect in a recession. Both statistics seem to be saying that the economy is not doing well. The number of unemployed increases and the number of employed people falls in years 2, 3, and 4. Real GDP is likely falling during those years.

Audio/Text Questions

1. Potential GNP is the level of output that would occur if unemployment fell to some specified percentage of the labor force. It is assumed there will always be a certain percentage of unemployment, due to frictional or structual unemployment, but there is no universal agreement about what that percentage is. In the early 1960s, 4 percent was often used, but in the 1980s, some economists used 6 percent. In the 1990s, the estimate has fallen back to a 4 percent unemployment rate again.

2. Frictional unemployment refers to the percentage of the labor force unemployed because of the normal time it takes to search for a job. Some may have voluntarily left their previous job, others may have been laid off because they had seasonal work, and others may be students entering the labor market. Structural unemployment occurs when the mix of job skills required by industry in a certain area does not mesh with the mix of skills of the available workforce. Cyclical unemployment is due to variations in general economic conditions, that is, the fluctuations of the business cycle.

3. Unemployment compensation may enable some to hold out for better job possibilities. It may also cause some to claim to be actively seeking work when in fact they have decided to leave the labor force.

4. It fails to count discouraged workers, those who looked for a long period but gave up trying. These people, who are not actively seeking work, are not considered part of the labor force. Second, it does not take account of those who are underemployed, people who have been forced by hard times to take jobs far below their level of skill.

5. The curve has a horizontal section, a positively sloped section, and a vertical section. The horizontal range reflects a depression, in which there is extensive underutilization of the economy's resources. Unemployment is high, and prices are likely to be stable or falling. In the positively sloped area, unemployment is relatively low, shortages of some goods and labor skills exist, and there is upward price pressure because of these shortages. In the vertical range, essentially all of the economy's productive resources that can be employed are. Any additional stimulus to the economy at this point would lead to an increase only in prices, not output.

LESSON 5. JOHN MAYNARD KEYNES: WHAT DID WE LEARN FROM THE GREAT DEPRESSION?

INTRODUCTION

There is always some level of spending at which GDP hits equilibrium; that is, a point at which GDP equals the intended spending on goods and services. If intended spending exceeds GDP, businesses tend to increase production; if intended spending falls short of GDP, production tends to decline. Whatever intended spending does, it always pushes GDP back toward equilibrium.

The classical economists believed that the market economy would always be moving toward full employment. But, when the Great Depression of the 1930s swept the country, the economist John Maynard Keynes introduced the world to another theory: Consumption and investment, said Keynes, could go down together, and not just temporarily, and the economy would *not* automatically move toward full employment. As the decline began, Keynes pointed out, decreased investment would gradually result in decreased wages and spending power among employed workers, of whom there would be fewer and fewer as the decline gained momentum. Less income means less spending and less money fed back into businesses for investments. Without intervention this self-perpetuating cycle can spell economic disaster. But the reverse can occur as well. As we shall see, investment can spur growth that increases incomes, spending, and investment.

What You Should Learn

By the end of this lesson, you should be prepared to perform the following tasks important to an understanding of national output and the multiplier:

1. Define *consumption function,* and describe its relationship to national output.

2. Distinguish between the *marginal propensity to consume* and the *average propensity to consume.*

3. Define the *saving function* and describe its relationship to national output.

4. Define the *marginal propensity to save*.

5. Identify the primary factors *(expected rate of return and interest rate)* that determine investment; and explain, generally, how businesses make a decision to invest.

6. Describe what is meant by the *equilibrium level* of GDP.

7. Describe the effect on GDP when intended spending is greater than GDP and when it is less than GDP.

8. Define what John Maynard Keynes considered the two basic flaws in the classical view of economics.

9. Give three reasons why investment expenditure tends to be less stable than consumption expenditure.

10. Define the *multiplier effect,* and explain its impact on GDP.

11. Distinguish between *shifts* in the consumption function and *movements along* a given consumption function.

12. Describe the impact of shifts in the consumption function on GDP.

KEY TERMS

consumption function
marginal propensity to consume
average propensity to consume
marginal propensity to save
interest rate
expected rate of return
disposable income
saving function

the equilibrium of GDP
income-expenditure
　analysis
innovation
the multiplier process
the multiplier
autonomous change
induced change

VIDEO

Watch

Economics U$A Program 5, "John Maynard Keynes: What Did We Learn from the Great Depression?"

Illustrative Events

Journalist Eric Sevareid recalls the Great Depression; Robert L. Heilbroner and Robert R. Nathan help David Schoumacher explain why economic policy failed;

Richard Gill introduces Keynes's new idea—that both investment and consumption could go down and stay down.

The conflict between Keynes's *The General Theory of Employment, Interest and Money* and prevailing economic views during the Great Depression, featuring Dr. Lorie Tarshis, a former student of Keynes at Cambridge University, and economist Paul Samuelson, who recalls his own slow conversion to Keynes's ideas.

Franklin Roosevelt's policies during the Great Depression and the economic impact of World War II help illustrate the repercussions of changes in government spending, with New Deal economist Walter Salant.

After Viewing

Answer the following questions:

1. During the early 1930s, when the country was struggling through the Great Depression, President Hoover continued to tell the people of the United States that the economy would soon improve. How could he persist with this message amid the dark economic realities of the time?

2. As a sort of drastic measure in 1932, Hoover was driven to create the Reconstruction Finance Corporation (RFC), a funding agency from which large industries and financial institutions could obtain investment capital. Even though the RFC contributed about $2 billion in investment to the economy, the measure was largely a failure. Why?

3. Economics professor Robert Heilbroner (New York School of Social Research) suggests that, from the classical economists' perspective, the appropriate metaphor to describe our economy might be that of a rocking boat but that, from John Maynard Keynes's perspective, a more accurate metaphor would be that of an elevator. What does Heilbroner mean by this comparison?

4. At one point during the video, the narrator, David Schoumacher, suggests that John Maynard Keynes's economic idea was so revolutionary that it "changed the nature of capitalism forever." To what idea does Schoumacher refer?

5. What economic event finally signaled the end of the Great Depression?

Read

Read Chapter 5, "The Determination of National Output and the Keynesian Multiplier," pages 116–137 and 140–142 in your text. After completing your reading, try the Self-Quiz.

SELF-QUIZ

Multiple Choice

1. Which of the following *best* describes the financial figure at which equilibrium GDP occurs?

    a. It is always higher than $1,000 billion.
    b. It is nearly always lower than $1,000 billion.
    c. It is *exactly* $1,000 billion, since equilibrium can occur at only one point.
    d. It is the one figure where total output is equal to intended spending.

2. A graph of the *consumption function* shows

    a. a direct, predictable relationship between disposable income and consumption spending.
    b. very little relationship between disposable income and consumption spending.
    c. a strong relationship between total income and disposable income.
    d. little relationship between disposable income and investment.

3. An economist would be *most* likely to use the consumption function to do which of the following?

    a. To build a case for economic intervention by the government
    b. To predict how much of their extra income consumers spend or save
    c. To illustrate the real dollar impact of investments on GDP
    d. To show the point at which equilibrium GDP occurs

4. To calculate the *marginal propensity to consume,* we must know

    a. current disposable income and current personal consumption expenditure.
    b. the change in personal consumption expenditure brought about by a change in disposable income.
    c. the average propensity to consume.
    d. current disposable income and total income.

5. Which of the following *best* describes the difference between the *marginal propensity to consume* and the *average propensity to consume?*

    a. They are synonymous terms for the same concept; to know one is to know the other.
    b. The marginal propensity to consume accounts for investment spending, while the average propensity to consume relates only to consumer spending.
    c. The marginal propensity to consume reflects the portion of extra income consumed, while the average propensity to consume reflects the portion of total disposable income consumed.
    d. The average propensity to consume is based on total income before taxes, while the marginal propensity to consume is based on disposable income (after taxes).

6. If we know the *marginal propensity to consume,* it is possible to determine the *marginal propensity to save* by

   a. subtracting the marginal propensity to consume from 1.
   b. dividing 1 by the marginal propensity to consume.
   c. adding the marginal propensity to consume to 1.
   d. none of the above; one cannot be determined from the other.

7. In deciding whether to make an investment, what two factors is a businessperson likely to examine *most* closely?

   a. Tax rate and interest rate
   b. GDP and depreciation
   c. Unemployment and technological innovation
   d. Interest rate and expected rate of return

8. In an economy without exports, taxes, or government transfer payments, which of the following *best* describes the relationship between saving and personal consumption expenditure?

   a. They have no direct relationship.
   b. They are equivalent.
   c. The two together equal disposable income.
   d. The two together equal investment.

9. Suppose a business has regularly been investing $5 million a year on new facilities and expansion and then suddenly stops. Which of the following *best* describes the impact of this cut in investment?

   a. GDP decreases by $5 million.
   b. GDP increases by $5 million.
   c. The cut has no effect at all on GDP.
   d. GDP decreases by a multiplied amount well over $5 million.

10. Between 1929 and 1933, annual investment spending in the United States fell by about $216 billion (2003 dollars). Today's economists would most likely see this cut in spending as

    a. a result of the Depression, rather than a causal factor.
    b. a negligible factor on the Depression, with little real impact.
    c. a major cause of the Depression, given the multiplier process.
    d. one of the saving factors that kept the Depression from growing deeper.

True-False

____ 1. According to Keynesian economic theory, total private demand (demand for both consumption goods and investment goods) might be insufficient to sustain full employment.

____ 2. The creation of the Reconstruction Finance Corporation by the federal government in 1932 was a bold step that stopped the financial avalanche of the Depression and created new demand for goods and services.

_____ 3. During the early years of the Depression, the private demand for investment goods and consumption goods fell while government expenditures stayed about the same.

_____ 4. Keynes's ideas regarding aggregate demand and government intervention, published in *The General Theory of Employment, Interest and Money* in 1936, were instantly adopted by academic economists in the United States.

_____ 5. According to Keynes, when investment falls, consumption falls by a multiplied amount.

_____ 6. If GDP is above its equilibrium value, the total amount spent on goods and services exceeds the total amount produced. Inventories are reduced and firms increase their output rates, increasing GDP.

_____ 7. Consumption expenditures tend to vary from year to year by greater percentages than investment expenditures.

_____ 8. Franklin Roosevelt campaigned for the presidency in 1932 on the basis of a Keynesian program of public, deficit spending to repair the shattered economy.

_____ 9. Programs such as the NRA, CCC, and WPA did so much to relieve unemployment and increase revenues in the mid-1930s that Roosevelt was able to cut spending and achieve a balanced budget after the 1936 election, with no ill effects.

_____ 10. Keynes believed that investment demand plus consumers' demand might not be enough to reach the level of national income at which everyone is fully employed but that full employment could be achieved if government spending on goods and services was added to make up the difference.

Discussion Questions

1. Discuss the importance of nonincome factors on consumption expenditure. Include in your discussion facts concerning the postwar U.S. experience.

2. Describe the process that ensures that actual savings and actual investment are equal.

3. Many economists believe that, when consumers are pessimistic, they limit their borrowing, and when they are optimistic, they borrow. If this is true, what are the implications for the consumption function? For the saving function? How do changes in consumer confidence affect them?

4. Describe how the various rounds of spending result in the multiplier's assuming the value described in the text.

5. In a past issue, *Business Week* observed that inventories at the end of January were only slightly higher than they had been in the previous September, even though sales moved up substantially between September and January. "Order backlogs are (also) hefty. Going into February, manufacturers had $197.6 billion in unfilled orders on their books."

a. What does the existence of large unfilled orders suggest about the current relation between actual and equilibrium GDP? Why? Use a diagram with intended spending on the vertical axis to illustrate the situation.
b. Why specifically does *Business Week* conclude that inventory shortfalls and backlogs suggest that there will be a "substantial advance in production" this spring?

Problem Set

1. In the nation of Chaos on the Styx, there is the following relationship between consumption expenditure and disposable income (both in billions of dollars):

Consumption expenditure	Disposable income
120	100
200	200
270	300
330	400
380	500
420	600

a. Plot the consumption function for this nation in the graph:

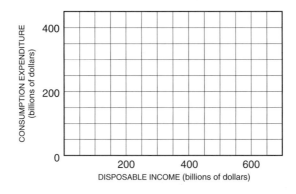

b. What is the marginal propensity to consume when disposable income is between $100 and $200 billion? When disposable income is between $300 and $400 billion? When disposable income is between $500 and $600 billion?

2. Suppose that the Bugsbane Music Box Company is considering investing in seven projects, identified as A to G. The expected rate of return from each project follows:

Project	Expected rate of return (percent)
A	12
B	8
C	7
D	15
E	25
F	11
G	9

a. If the firm can borrow money at 10 percent interest, which projects are clearly unprofitable
b. Suppose that the interest rate increases to 13 percent. Which projects are unprofitable now?

3. a. Country X's economists estimate the following very simple relationship between consumption expenditure C and gross domestic product Y:

$$C = 10 + 0.8Y,$$

where all figures are in billions of dollars. If gross domestic investment I is $100 billion and GDP = $C + I$, calculate GDP.
b. If investment increases by $10 billion dollars to $110 billion, what is GDP?
c. How much does GDP grow from one year to the next?
d. What is the multiplier in this economy?
e. What is the *MPS*? *MPC*?

4. Country X's consumption function is such that personal consumption expenditure equals $90 billion if disposable income equals $100 billion. The marginal propensity to save equals one-third.

a. Fill in the values of the personal consumption expenditure and the average propensity to consume corresponding to each of the following values of disposable income:

Disposable income (billions of dollars)	Personal consumption expenditure (billions of dollars)	Average propensity to consume
150	____	____
200	____	____
250	____	____
300	____	____

b. In 2004, Country X's economists believe that the consumption function just described is no longer valid. In that year, disposable income is $200 billion and personal consumption expenditure is $175 billion. Is there evidence of a shift in the consumption function?
c. Can we tell what the new marginal propensity to consume is? If so, how? If not, why not?

5. Suppose that a village contains three families. Let C_1 be the consumption expenditure of the first family and D_1 be its disposable income; let C_2 be the consumption expenditure of the second family and D_2 its disposable income; and let C_3 be the consumption expenditure of the third family and D_3 its disposable income. The consumption function for each family is as follows (the values of C and D are measured in thousands of dollars per year):

$$C_1 = 3,000 + 0.8D_1$$
$$C_2 = 2,000 + 0.8D_2$$
$$C_3 = 1,000 + 0.8D_3$$

a. For the village as a whole, what is the marginal propensity to consume?

b. If each family's disposable income is $10,000, what is the average propensity to consume in the village as a whole?
c. Derive an equation for the consumption function in the village as a whole.

LESSON REVIEW

If you had difficulty with the Self-Quiz or would like additional assistance, read the following lesson review. It should reinforce and help you understand the content presented in this lesson.

Equilibrium

The Concept of Equilibrium

In Lesson 4, we discussed the *equilibrium* of the national economy as the point at which the aggregate supply curve and aggregate demand curve intersect; in other words, the point at which supply equals demand. In this chapter, we consider equilibrium from a slightly different perspective—in terms of output, defined for our purposes here as gross domestic product, or GDP. *GDP is at its equilibrium value when income results in a level of spending just sufficient (neither too much nor too little) to take current production (goods and services) off the market.* In other words, equilibrium can be achieved at many different dollar values of GDP. If we plotted all these potential values together in a chart, they would produce a straight line at a 45-degree angle, with intended spending along the vertical axis, and GDP along the horizontal axis; equilibrium occurs only at that point where intended spending precisely equals GDP.

Three Simplifying Assumptions

To keep our discussion from becoming too complex for the time being, we focus on the private sector and make three simplifying assumptions:

1. In our current hypothetical U.S. economy, there are no government expenditures or net exports. Therefore, total spending, or GDP, equals *consumption* expenditure plus *investment*.

2. For now, we assume there are no taxes, transfer payments, undistributed corporate profits, or depreciation. Therefore, *disposable income* equals GDP. Remember, people can do two things with their income: spend it or save it. So, this is another way of saying that *consumption* plus *savings* = GDP (disposable income).

3. We also assume that the total amount firms and individuals intend to invest is independent of GDP level; this is a simplification, of course, since in real life, GDP is one factor that determines the tendency to invest.

Note: Taking assumptions 1 and 2 together, we get

$$\text{Consumption } C + \text{investment } I = \text{GDP}.$$
$$\text{Consumption } C + \text{saving } S = \text{GDP}.$$

So
$$C + I = C + S.$$

Hence in equilibrium, $S = I$ under these simplifying assumptions.

The Consumption Function

The *consumption function* can be defined as *the relationship between consumption spending and disposable income*. It is a way of verifying what logic tells us would be so: Families with higher incomes spend more on consumption than families with lower incomes. What this means to GDP is simply that the more disposable income available to the population, the more they are likely to spend and the more GDP grows. But, as income rises, the percentage of income spent falls. Higher-income individuals tend to save a greater fraction of their income.

Marginal Propensity to Consume

The fraction of each extra dollar of income that consumers are likely to spend is called the *marginal propensity to consume*. For example, if we determine that consumers probably spend 60 cents of each extra dollar, the marginal propensity to consume is 0.60. This represents the ratio of change in personal consumption spending to change in disposable income:

$$\frac{\text{Change in personal consumption spending}}{\text{Change in disposable income}} = \text{marginal propensity to consume}.$$

The Average Propensity to Consume

Simply put, the *average propensity to consume* differs from the marginal propensity in this way: The average propensity to consume is the proportion of total disposable income consumed, while the marginal propensity to consume is the proportion of extra disposable income consumed. The average propensity to consume is calculated by this formula:

$$\frac{\text{Personal consumption expenditure}}{\text{Disposable income}} = \text{average propensity to consume}.$$

So, if disposable income equals \$1,000 and personal consumption expenditure equals \$950, the average propensity to consume would be 950/1,000, or 0.95.

The Saving Function

We have two choices about what to do with disposable income: spend it or save it. If we know the levels of disposable income and the levels of personal consumption, we can easily calculate what people save at any given level of disposable income:

Disposable income – personal consumption = savings.

If disposable income equals $1,000, and personal consumption equals $920, the savings at that level is $80. By graphing the savings that occurs at many different levels of disposable income, we produce the *saving function*.

The Marginal Propensity to Save

Once we know the saving function, we can calculate the marginal propensity to save at any given disposable income level. The marginal propensity to save is the *proportion of any extra dollar of income saved*. The marginal propensity to save is calculated by this formula:

$$\frac{\text{Change in savings}}{\text{Change in disposable income}} = \text{marginal propensity to save.}$$

Suppose that disposable income rises from $1,000 to $1,050, a change of $50. At the $1,000 level, the savings equal $50. At the $1,050 level, savings equal $70. The change in savings equals $20. According to the formula, the marginal propensity to save equals 20/50, or 0.40.

Remember, regardless of the level of disposable income, *the marginal propensity to save plus the marginal propensity to consume must equal 100 percent of income, or 1.*

Determinants of Investment

What factors determine how much firms are willing to invest on new buildings and equipment, expansion, research, or inventory? While many factors play a part, including personal willingness to take a risk, the two most critical are

- The expected rate of return from capital invested.
- The current interest rate for borrowed capital.

Rate of Return. Investment costs money. Before businesses expand, they must ask whether the rate of expected return sufficiently outweighs the expenditures to allow a profit. Suppose the profit margin on a particular investment is calculated at 10 percent. That figure must then be compared with another (the current interest rate) to determine whether the profit is sufficient.

Interest Rate. The interest rate is the cost of borrowing money. At an annual interest rate of 10 percent, a borrower must pay 10 cents on the dollar per year for the privilege of borrowing money.

If the expected rate of return is greater than the cost of borrowing money to finance the project, a business is likely to decide in favor of the investment. If the reverse is true (the interest rate exceeds likely profits), the firm can seldom afford to invest. It will probably do better, if it has extra capital, to lend it. Thus, total economic growth depends heavily on the number of projects available for investment in which profit is likely to exceed the cost of financing. When interest rates run high, the number of such projects falls dramatically; this is one reason that high interest rates tend to hurt economic growth.

Income and Expenditure: Some Guiding Principles

Whenever GDP deviates from its equilibrium level, forces within the economy adjust production levels to push it back to equilibrium. Let us see how this works.

First, we must recognize the interrelationship between production and income. Output determines income. That is, as production of goods and services (GDP) goes up, the income consumers earn through producing these goods and services goes up too. Increased income, in turn, tends to push up spending. So long as spending is just sufficient to take the current output (GDP) off the market, the economy is in a state of equilibrium. But what happens if output and spending are *not* equal?

Case 1. Spending exceeds output. When spending exceeds GDP, firms' inventories are drained and must be replaced. Therefore, the answer is to increase production rates, pushing the economy to a higher level of equilibrium or output.

Case 2. Output exceeds spending. Here, inventories pile up and profits can be lost. To compensate, firms must lower their production rates, causing the value of output (GDP) to decrease, again pushing the economy toward equilibrium.

As we noted earlier, output (GDP) equals the sum of consumption and investment at the equilibrium level. But at what level of aggregate spending does equilibrium occur? We can find out by plotting the sum of consumption and investment ($C + I$) on the same graph with the 45-degree line that represents all points along which aggregate spending ($C + I$) and output, or GDP, are equal. The point at which these two lines intersect indicates the intended spending level at which equilibrium occurs.

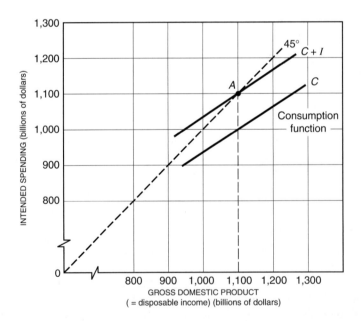

The Volatility of Investment

Investment expenditure tends to be relatively unstable, varying more year to year than consumption expenditure. Why? Here are three key reasons.

1. *Irregularity of innovation.* Innovations in technology do not occur at regular intervals; they tend to come in fits and starts, with peaks and slumps. Investment tends to increase during periods of high innovation.

2. *Durability of capital goods.* Firms may experience the need for new equipment or facilities long before doing anything about it. The tendency is to postpone expansion until it is clear what others plan to do, and most facilities and equipment are durable enough to withstand this delay. The general mood of the economy tends to influence investment heavily: When one major firm invests, others within that industry may follow.

3. *Capacity utilization.* Sales go up and down from one year to the next. When sales are brisk, and a firm is producing at or near capacity, the tendency to invest is far greater than during slack periods.

The Spending Chain and the Multiplier Process

An initial investment in the economy has both an immediate and a long-term effect on growth. For example, say a firm invests $1 billion dollars on equipment or inventory during a period when marginal propensity to consume is 0.60. In the first stage, that extra $1 billion is received by workers as extra income; this leads to the second stage, or consumer spending. How much will consumers spend? At the 0.60 rate, they spend 0.60 times $1 billion, or $0.6 billion. This extra income is once again received by firms and distributed again to workers, who once again spend 60 percent (0.60) of the $0.6 billion, or $0.36 billion, and so forth. The total increase in intended spending (autonomous plus induced) approaches $2.5 billion in this example. This is 2.5 times the initial increase in autonomous investment spending that set things in motion. This spending and respending process is called the *spending chain.*

At the same time, a decrease in investment has the opposite effect but with a reverse chain reaction. The notion that, once the demand for goods starts falling, it can continue to fall further, further, and still further is contrary to the reasoning of the classical economists, who felt the economy would always right itself eventually. But the lessons of the Great Depression and economist John Maynard Keynes convinced most students of economics that classical economics did not apply to that time period.

The Multiplier

We have seen how investment (or the withdrawal of investment) can trigger a chain reaction. The ultimate effect of this reaction can be calculated mathematically, using a ratio called the *multiplier.* The multiplier ratio is $1/MPS$, where MPS is the marginal propensity to save. In other words, suppose that MPS is 1/3 (which would make the marginal propensity to consume 2/3, since these figures always total 1). What is the increase in equilibrium GDP given a $1 billion investment?

The $1 billion investment increases equilibrium GDP by 1 divided by 1/3 billion dollars, or $3 billion dollars. Note that, since *MPS* is always less than 1 (marginal propensity to save and marginal propensity to consume must together equal 1), the *multiplier is always greater than 1*. This makes equilibrium GDP very sensitive to changes—up or down—in investment rates.

Shifts in the Consumption and Saving Functions

The consumption function, remember, is the relationship between consumption spending and disposable income. Generally, the more disposable income we have, the more we spend. This causes movement along the consumption function. Movement along one consumption function from point *A* to point *B* reflects consumers' propensity to spend their increased disposable income.

Consumers' spending decisions depend on more than their income level. Some non-income determinants of spending are wealth, credit availability, expectations, durable goods on hand, income distribution, and the size of the population. If people's wealth increases because of a booming stock market, the consumption function is likely to shift upward as consumers are willing to spend more at every level of income. A shift is quite different from a movement along a given consumption function. Keep in mind too that an upward shift in the consumption function is accompanied by a downward shift in the saving function. This is another way of saying that if people want to spend *more* out of a given level of income, it must follow that they wish to save *less*.

Keynes versus the Classical Economists: How Did They Differ?

Keynes and his followers took issue with the classical economists in two critical ways. First, the classical model held that equilibrium would spell prosperity: high employment, low inflation. Keynes thought otherwise. There was no assurance, said Keynes, that total intended spending would equal GDP at a level that would ensure high employment. In the classical view, people were pictured as either investing or saving. But the investors and the savers, Keynes pointed out, were often very different people with very different motivations. The savers tended to be families who were saving now to become consumers later. The investors, on the other hand, tended to be firms interested in increasing profits.

All this adds up to the fact that total intended spending might, in fact, equal GDP but not at a level of full employment.

The classical economists also held that wages and prices are flexible, a view Keynes considered totally unrealistic. The classical economists assumed that all businesses would compete on a relatively equal basis. Such, in our complex modern economy, is far from the case. Although significant price and wage changes have taken place in recent years, they are still not enough to automatically move the economy to a full-employment equilibrium.

And yet, in the year 2000, the United States experienced full-employment equilibrium amid the longest peacetime expansion in its history. And this followed the second longest peacetime business expansion. The two were separated only by a short and shallow six-month recession. The wonder of it is that, except for the classical-like reduction in marginal tax rates by the Reagan administration in the early 1980s and 1986, no government policies based on Keynesian theory have been carried out for over 20 years.

By the early part of 2001, however, the U.S. economy was hardly growing at all. The terrorist attacks on the World Trade Center and the Pentagon made matters worse, destroying what little optimism remained after the tech sector and stock market crash of the preceding year. Though describing it as a supply side tax cut, the new president, George W. Bush, asked for and Congress passed a Keynesian style tax cut meant to stimulate the economy. The recession was brief but the recovery, especially in employment, was slow. The recovery had started in 2002, but major improvements in employment did not begin until spring of 2004.

EXTENDED LEARNING

This section of the study guide is specifically designed for the two-semester student.

AUDIO

Before Listening

Read Exploring Further of Chapter 5, pages 137–139 in your text.

Next

Listen to the audiotape that accompanies Lesson 5.

After Listening

Answer the following questions:

1. How does the marginal propensity to consume differ from the average propensity to consume? Could the two ever be the same?
2. How is the saving function related to the consumption function?
3. What major factors affect the decision by firms to invest in plant and equipment?
4. What effect would each of the following events have on the amount firms invest in plant and equipment?
    a. A process is developed to convert coal into gasoline cheaply.
    b. There is a recession.
    c. One-fifth of California's capital stock is damaged by an earthquake.
    d. Interest rates fall by 2 percentage points.
    e. Costs in the construction industry suddenly rise rapidly.

5. A business periodical noted that "most businessmen . . . believe that an inflationary environment produces not more capital spending but less." What would explain that position?

ADDITIONAL READINGS

Collery, Arnold. *National Income and Employment Analysis,* 2d ed. New York: John Wiley, 1970.

> Chapters 1, 2, and 3 provide a clear development of the Keynesian concepts of unemployment equilibrium and the multiplier and highlight the difference between Keynesian theory and the previous analysis of unemployment. Simple mathematics and graphs.

Galbraith, J. K. *The Great Crash: 1929.* Boston: Houghton Mifflin Company, 1961.

> Chapters 6 and 10 provide a lively account of the events leading up to the stock market crash of 1929 and various possible causes, including the crash, of the 1930s Depression. No mathematics or graphs.

Gill, Richard T. *Evolution of Modern Economics.* Englewood Cliffs, NJ: Prentice-Hall, 1967.

> Chapter 6, "The Keynesian Revolution," details how Keynes departed from mainstream economic thought by focusing on economic aggregates, or macroeconomics, arguing that the economy would not quickly regain a full-employment equilibrium, urging temporary intervention by the state to promote full employment, and trying to unify monetary factors with economic activity in a new way. No mathematics or graphs.

Heilbroner, R. L. *The Making of Economic Society,* 7th ed. Englewood Cliffs, NJ: Prentice-Hall, 1985.

> Chapter 9, "The Evolution of Gilded Capitalism," provides a short description of the development of the idea of compensatory government spending against the background of the 1930s and World War II and how this concept became the basis for government policy in the 1960s. No mathematics or graphs.

Kimmel, Lewis H. *Federal Budget and Fiscal Policy: 1789–1958.* Washington, DC: Brookings Institution, 1959.

> Pages 213–228 detail the relationship between the economic theories of the 1930s and federal budget policy, and Chapter 6 discusses the extent to which Keynesian theory influenced the Truman and Eisenhower administrations. No mathematics or graphs.

ANSWER KEY

Video Questions

1. From our perspective today, Hoover's belief in a turnaround for the depression economy may seem very naive, but there is every reason to suppose that Hoover really believed his message of imminent prosperity, given that it was grounded in classical tradition. The classical economists had preached for years that the capitalistic economy—if left alone—would always right itself. The best course of action, from the classical view, was to leave the economy to its own course.

2. Today's economists often hail the RFC as a milestone—because it was such a revolutionary departure from the hands-off policies of the past. Most feel now that the RFC failed not because it was the wrong approach but because it simply provided too little help too late. Consumer demand cannot grow without income to support it. The RFC provided one tiny stimulus to a dying economy, hardly sufficient to generate the kind of income capable of boosting spending.

3. The rocking boat metaphor fits very nicely the classical idea of an economy battered by turbulence that is temporarily thrown off course but that always eventually rights itself and presses on toward calmer seas. As the Depression took hold, however, economists of that time increasingly doubted the validity of the rocking boat metaphor. The rocking was going on too long, and the boat was definitely sinking. Keynes's view of the economy, by contrast, is better reflected in the metaphor of an elevator capable of going up or down—or of stalling for a time and going nowhere at all unless someone steps in to rectify the problem.

4. Keynes's whole economic theory was revolutionary for its day. In particular, he surprised (and sometimes antagonized) economists with the notion that a decrease in investment would not automatically be offset by an increase in consumption; that, in fact, personal income would continue to plummet, thus weakening consumer demand and perpetuating low employment. But Keynes's conclusion really shook the economic world: Things would *not* get better without government intervention. While some young economists adopted his views with evangelistic zeal, others found them unthinkable. It took a long time, therefore, for Keynesian economics to gain a foothold.

5. Most economists now agree that Franklin Roosevelt's efforts to pump new life into the economy through the various New Deal programs was the right approach, but it was half-hearted at times and inconsistently applied. Roosevelt basically distrusted the idea that lowering taxes and increasing government spending would solve the problems of the Depression; he was what most economists today would call an economic conservative, even though politically he has always been regarded as a liberal. Largely because of Roosevelt's apprehension (and even though many of his economic advisers were admirers of Keynes), the government moved forward with spending, then alternately pulled back; and the economy reflected this to and fro footwork, so that slight improvements alternated with declines through the early 1940s. What really turned things around was the wartime economy as the country geared up to produce weapons for the

Allies. Ironically, Keynes himself worried over the stress this enormous sudden demand would place on the country. But Keynes's followers believed he underestimated the capacity of the country to produce. And apparently they were right, for through the war and beyond, the nation burst once again into prosperity.

Multiple Choice

1. d Text, 126–127.
2. a Text, 117–121.
3. b Text, 117–121.
4. b Text, 118–120.
5. c Text, 118–121.
6. a Text, 122.
7. d Text, 123–124.
8. c Text, 121.
9. d Text, 133–137.
10. c Text, 136.

True-False

1. True   Text, 134; Video.
2. False Video.
3. True   Video.
4. False Video.
5. True   Video.
6. False Text, 128.
7. False Text, 131.
8. False Video.
9. False Video.
10. True Video.

Discussion Questions

1. The consumption function is influenced by disposable income as well as factors such as wealth, the ease and cheapness with which consumers can borrow money, consumers' expectations, the amount of durable goods on hand, the distribution of income, the size of the population, and the expected inflation rate. After the war, the amount of durable goods on hand was low and this spurred consumption expenditure. In addition, the years after the war saw an unprecedented increase in the population, which also fueled consumption expenditure. Consumers, denied the opportunity to consume at their normal levels during the war, also had greater wealth from their enforced saving during the war.

2. In a closed economy with no government sector, savings necessarily equal investment. This is because consumption plus savings equals gross national income while consumption plus investment equals gross domestic product (see the identity on pages 79–80 of the text and page 94 here). Because consumption does not change, it must be true that investment is equal to savings.

3. When consumers become less confident, they cut back on their borrowing. This causes the consumption function to shift downward and the saving function to shift upward. When consumers feel more confident, they increase their level of consumption, and the result is a shift upward of the consumption function. When the consumption function shifts upward, the saving function must shift downward.

4. When autonomous consumption or investment changes, the result is a change in national income. If the change in autonomous consumption or investment is positive, then national income increases by the amount of the change. Subsequently, consumers receive this extra income and they spend a portion of it on goods and

services. Businesses receive this income and then distribute it again to workers, who take the extra income and spend a portion of that income. This cycle continues again and again until the change in income approaches zero. The portion of the extra income received by consumers that is spent in each cycle depends on the marginal propensity to consume. Thus, a change in autonomous consumption or investment induces consumer spending at a level far greater than its original amount due to the multiplier effect.

5. a. The existence of large unfilled orders suggests that intended spending is greater than the total output. This indicates that the economy currently produces at a level of output lower than the equilibrium level of output.
   b. *Business Week* anticipates that businesses will respond to the pressure exerted by this excess demand by producing a greater supply of goods. This will lead to a "substantial advance in production" during the spring.

Problem Set

1. a.

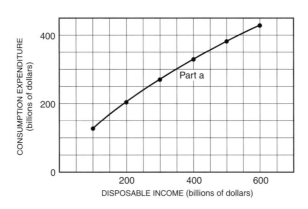

   b. 0.8. 0.6. 0.4.

2. a. Projects B, C, and G.
   b. Projects A, B, C, F, and G.

3. a. GDP $= C + I$
   $Y = 10 + 0.8Y + 100$
   $0.2Y = 110$
   $Y = 550.$
   GDP $= \$550$ billion.
   b. $Y = 10 + 0.8Y + 110$
   $0.2Y = 120$
   $Y = 600.$
   GDP $= \$600$ billion.
   c. $50 billion.
   d. 5.
   e. 0.2. 0.8.

4. a. 123.33   0.82
        156.67   0.78
        190   0.76
        223.33   0.74
    b. Yes.
    c. No, because we know only one point on the new consumption function.

5. a. 0.8.
    b. 1.00.
    c. $C = 6{,}000 + 0.8D$.

Audio/Text Questions

1. The marginal propensity to consume relates to the fraction of each incremental dollar used for consumption, whereas the average is the portion of *total* income spent on consumption. Since an individual is more likely to spend a higher fraction of her or his income for consumption when her or his income is low, the marginal propensity tends to be greater for low incomes than for high. Average and marginal propensities to consume are the same only if the individual saves (or consumes) a constant fraction of her or his income, regardless of the level of income and no consumption was autonomous of income.

2. If there are no taxes, savings equal income less consumption. It is the part of one's income left after money is spent on consumption. Therefore, if consumption is equal to 95 percent of income, savings are equal to the remaining 5 percent.

3. For an investment to be worthwhile, the expected net revenue (revenue minus operating costs) each year must yield a rate of return better than the interest rate the firm could get by placing the money in the bank. If a plant is cheap to build and holds out the promise of high net revenue for many years, then it is expected to yield a high rate of return. If, in addition, interest rates are low, the firm has a large incentive to borrow funds and invest in the project.

4. a. Tends to increase investment because the expected net revenue of such a project is high.
    b. Reduces investment because fear of low sales reduces expected net revenue.
    c. Increases investment to replace damaged productive capacity.
    d. Increases investment because projects that before promised a return slightly worse than the market interest rate now look like better investments.
    e. Reduces investment; increased costs of the initial investment in plant reduce the expected rate of return, even if the estimate of net revenue year to year remains unchanged.

5. Uncertainty about future economic conditions makes it difficult for investment planners to determine the expected rate of return on an investment. It is harder to forecast costs, revenues, and interest rates, and therefore businesses may shy away from committing as much to investment in plant and equipment as they would have in the absence of inflation.

LESSON 6. FISCAL POLICY: CAN WE CONTROL THE ECONOMY?

INTRODUCTION

For many years, the hands-off fiscal policies advocated by the classical economists held sway with U.S. government. When times were hard, the prevailing response was to tough it out, awaiting the "inevitable" turnaround. The lessons of the Great Depression and a booming wartime economy have since taught us, however, that government intervention is sometimes necessary and desirable—and that to an extent, we can take charge of our own economic lives.

Of course, government involvement does not solve everything. Sometimes, we are plagued by high unemployment rates and relatively high inflation rates. Unfortunately, the fiscal policies that government can use to combat inflation are often at odds with the policies called for to combat unemployment. When the two problems occur together, as they did starting in the late 1960s through the early 1980s, finding the appropriate fiscal policy can be a daunting task.

Under Franklin Roosevelt, the idea that the government could use its power to spend and tax to control national economics was just beginning to take root. Few could have predicted the many ramifications this change carried with it. At that time, government spending represented only about 10 percent of the total national output; now, that figure has increased to over 35 percent. This relatively high level of government spending gives us greater control, perhaps, over our economic destinies but also makes us more dependent on government.

What You Should Learn

By the end of Lesson 6, you should be prepared to

1. Identify major sources of tax revenue for federal, state, and local governments and identify major spending areas for tax money.

2. Describe the general relationship between fiscal policy and aggregate demand.

3. Identify three strategies government can use to combat high unemployment.

4. Identify three strategies government can use to combat inflation.

5. Explain the effects of government spending on GDP.

6. Use the *multiplier* to calculate the actual change in equilibrium GDP resulting from a change in government expenditure.

7. Explain the effects of a tax increase or tax cut on GDP.

8. Describe two *automatic stabilizers* that help keep the GDP near equilibrium.

KEY TERMS

equilibrium GDP
discretionary fiscal policy
Employment Act of 1946
Council of Economic Advisers
automatic stabilizers
government transfer payments

anti-unemployment
  fiscal policy
anti-inflationary fiscal
  policy
recessionary gap
inflationary gap

VIDEO

Watch

Economics U$A Program 6, "Fiscal Policy: Can We Control the Economy?"

Illustrative Events

Passage of Employment Act of 1946, which committed the government to using fiscal policy to maintain economic stability and gave birth to the Council of Economic Advisers with Leon Keyserling, former chair of the Council of Economic Advisers.

How automatic stabilizers worked to moderate the 1954 recession; featuring Herbert Stein, a member of President Eisenhower's Committee for Economic Development. Richard Gill shows with graphs how the stabilizers worked.

The "textbook" success of the Kennedy-Johnson tax cut of 1964; featuring economists Walter Heller and John Kenneth Galbraith, who opposed the tax cut.

After Viewing

Answer the following questions:

1. What were the origins of the Council of Economic Advisers and what responsibilities did the council have?

2. The Economic Employment Act of 1946 was passed in a form much different from what was originally intended by drafters of the bill. What was lost, and what was gained?

3. What impact did economic stabilizers have on the economy during the Eisenhower administration? Why did these stabilizing factors work so differently in 1954 than they had during the Great Depression?

4. When John Kennedy inherited a troubled economy in 1961, he received very different advice from two prominent economic advisers: Walter Heller and John Kenneth Galbraith. On what major point did their philosophies and recommendations disagree? Why?

Read

Read Chapter 6, "Fiscal Policy and National Output," pages 143–162 and 164–166 in your text. After completing your reading, try the Self-Quiz.

SELF-QUIZ

Multiple Choice

1. In the years since World War II, the idea that government should use its powers to spend and tax to control the national economy has

    a. pretty much gained acceptance throughout the world.
    b. gained some acceptance in the United States but not elsewhere.
    c. given way in most countries to a hands-off fiscal policy.
    d. never really been given a chance to prove itself.

2. If the government this year decides to purchase $50 billion worth of goods and services more than last year, this decision

    a. raises the level of total spending but has little effect on equilibrium GDP.
    b. raises both total spending and equilibrium GDP.
    c. raises equilibrium GDP but has no effect on total spending.
    d. has little effect on either total spending or equilibrium GDP.

3. The increase in government spending described in question 2 causes

    a. an upward shift in the $C + I + G$ line.
    b. a downward shift in the $C + I + G$ line.
    c. a movement to the right in the $C + I + G$ line.
    d. a movement to the left in the $C + I + G$ line.

4. Suppose the marginal propensity to consume is 0.6. A reduction in government spending of $1 billion

    a. has no effect on equilibrium GDP.
    b. decreases equilibrium GDP by $1.66 billion.
    c. increases equilibrium GDP by $1.66 billion.
    d. decreases equilibrium GDP by $2.5 billion.

5. As taxes go up, which of the following is *most likely* to occur?

   a. Equilibrium GDP rises.
   b. Inflation increases.
   c. Disposable income declines.
   d. Unemployment declines.

6. Suppose the economy is suffering from a high unemployment rate. Which of the following would probably *not* be a good strategy for dealing with this situation?

   a. Extend unemployment benefits.
   b. Cut back on expenditures for public works programs.
   c. Provide tax incentives to encourage business investment.
   d. Cut taxes.

7. Which of the following is probably the *most* accurate description of how fiscal policy is set?

   a. It is established by Congress, with direction and guidance from the U.S. public.
   b. It is established primarily by the president and his advisers and by Congress, within the guidelines of congressional laws.
   c. Since World War II, it has been established by the Council of Economic Advisers, under the direction of the Congress and the president.
   d. As yet, within our country, there really are no formal rules or guidelines for establishing fiscal policy.

8. Which of the following is the *best* definition of fiscal policy?

   a. A series of laws and regulations that determine how much and under what conditions people can be taxed.
   b. A method of gauging the relative prosperity of the country by analyzing figures for inflation and unemployment.
   c. The strategies a government uses to deal with unemployment and recession.
   d. Government's continual adjustment of taxes and spending for stabilization purposes.

9. Proportionately, how does government spending compare now to what it was in the days before the Great Depression?

   a. It is about triple what it was then.
   b. It is about twice what it was.
   c. It is about equal to what it was.
   d. It is about half what it was.

10. Which of the following is the single *largest* source of revenue for the federal government?

    a. Employment tax and Social Security tax
    b. Corporate income tax
    c. Personal income tax
    d. Excise tax

True-False

____ 1. Assuming the economy is below full capacity, an increase in government spending produces an even larger increase in GDP.

____ 2. In the simple Keynesian model, because not all of a tax cut is spent, an increase in government spending has more of an impact on GDP than a tax cut of the same size.

____ 3. Unemployment benefits, welfare payments, and the income tax act as automatic stabilizers during periods of recession and recovery.

____ 4. The rationale for using fiscal policy to maintain economic stability is based on classical economic theory.

____ 5. In the past 100 years, government spending has increased in absolute terms but decreased as a percentage of total output.

____ 6. The Employment Act of 1946 promoted maximum employment, production, and purchasing power rather than full employment.

____ 7. The nation's recovery from the recession of 1954 showed that the government could take advantage of the automatic stabilizers in the economy and use fiscal policy to minimize the effects of an economic downturn.

____ 8. The Kennedy administration attempted to counter the high unemployment that remained after the recession of 1960 by proposing an across-the-board tax cut.

____ 9. The tax cut of 1964 gave more disposable income to consumers, shifted the curve of private spending upward, and eliminated the gap between spending and full-employment GDP.

____ 10. A rise in transfer payments such as Social Security and welfare payments has the same impact on GDP as a tax cut.

Discussion Questions

1. If the economy is suffering from an undesirably high rate of unemployment, what measures can the government take to improve the situation? How quickly can these measures be adopted? If the economy is suffering from an undesirably high rate of inflation, what measures can the government take to improve the situation? How quickly can these measures be adopted?

2. In the primaries of the presidential election year in 2000, Governor George W. Bush of Texas proposed a substantial reduction in the federal income tax. He framed the cut as a stimulus that would help increase aggregate supply and keep the business expansion going and as a way to return part of the budget surplus to the taxpayers. Vice President Albert Gore, Bush's opponent in the November elections, and most newspaper editorials, except for the *Wall Street Journal,* opposed this cut as dangerous. For part of their argument against the tax cut, Vice President Gore and the editorialists used the analytical tools developed in this

chapter. Given that the economy was operating at full-employment output and using the same analytical tools, explain the argument against the tax cut.

3. "If defense spending were cut, we would have mass unemployment. Regardless of the worthiness of defense spending, it is required to prevent a massive, long-term depression." Comment and evaluate, using a production possibilities curve.

4. What are the automatic stabilizers for the U.S. economy? What are the major tools of discretionary fiscal policy? How do they differ? Why are both considered important?

Problem Set

1. Suppose that the consumption function in Debland is as follows (with all amounts in billions of dollars):

Disposable income	Consumption expenditure
900	750
1,000	800
1,100	850
1,200	900
1,300	950
1,400	1,000

a. Suppose that intended investment is $200 billion and government expenditure is $100 billion. Plot the $C + I + G$ curve and the 45-degree line in the following graph.

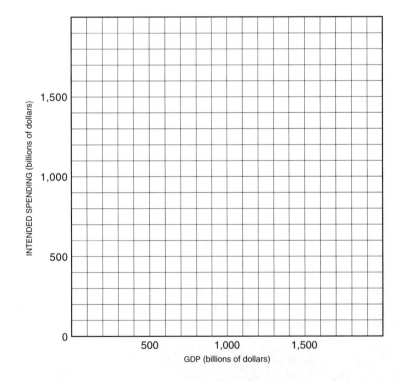

b. What is the equilibrium value of GDP?
c. Suppose that $1,400 billion is the full-employment GDP. Is there an inflationary gap? A recessionary gap?
d. What sorts of measures can be taken by the government to promote noninflationary full employment.

2. a. In the country of Badger, the consumption function (in millions of dollars) is as follows:

Disposable income	Consumption
900	700
1,000	750
1,100	800
1,200	850
1,300	900

Suppose intended investment is $100 million. What is the equilibrium level of GDP if government expenditures are $200 million (and taxes are zero)?

b. Suppose Badger increases its government expenditures by $10 million. What is the effect on its equilibrium GDP? Does GDP increase or decrease? By how much?

c. Suppose the government of Badger imposes a personal income tax that takes 16 2/3 percent (or one-sixth) of everyone's pretax income. What now is the relationship between GDP and consumption expenditure (in millions of dollars)? Specifically, fill in the blanks:

GDP	Consumption expenditure
_____	700
_____	750
_____	800
_____	850
_____	900

d. Given the consumption expenditure figures in part c, what is the equilibrium value of Badger's GDP if intended investment is $100 million and government expenditure is $350 million?

e. In the situation described in part d, if the economy is at the equilibrium level of GDP, is Badger's government running a surplus or a deficit, and how big is it?

3. The following set of equations defines a model of our basic economy with price level held constant:

(1) GDP $= Y = C_d + I_d + G$, where C_d and I_d are intended consumption and investment.

(2) $Y_d = Y -$ taxes, where Y_d is disposable (aftertax) income. (*Note:* Taxes in this problem are "lump sum" rather than "proportional" as in problem 2c.)

(3) $C_d = 200 + 0.8 Y_d$.

(4) $I_d = 160$.

(5) $G = 500$, where G is government spending on goods and services.

(6) Taxes = 500.

All figures are in billions of dollars.

a. Algebraically solve for equilibrium GDP by substituting the given information into equation (1).

b. What is the multiplier for this economy? Demonstrate your result by increasing government spending from $500 billion to $600 billion and finding the new equilibrium GDP. How much greater is the new equilibrium than the one found in part a? How many times greater is this change in GDP than the change in government spending that brought it about?

4. The following figures pertain to country Q's economy (in millions of dollars) at various levels of GDP:

Taxes	GDP	Disposable income	Intended consumption expenditure	Intended saving
25	1,000	975	898	77
30	1,100	1,070	983	87
38	1,200	1,162	1,066	96
50	1,300	1,250	1,145	105
67	1,400	1,333	1,220	113
90	1,500	1,410	1,289	121
120	1,600	1,480	1,352	128
158	1,700	1,542	1,408	134
205	1,800	1,595	1,456	139

Suppose that intended investment is $128 million and government expenditures on goods and services are $27 million. What is the equilibrium level of GDP? What is the status of the government's budget at this value of GDP?

5. Consider an economy in which:

$C_d = 500 + 0.9 Y_d$ $G = 225$

$I_d = 500$ $T = 250$,

where C_d equals intended consumption expenditure, Y_d equals disposable income, I_d equals intended investment, G equals government expenditure, and T equals taxes.

a. What is equilibrium GDP?
b. Full-employment GDP = $10,400 million. President Earnest is most interested in getting the economy to full employment, but she also feels a driving need to balance the government's budget. How would you change fiscal

policy (T and/or G) in an attempt to satisfy President Earnest's twin goals? Convince Earnest that your policy suggestions will work by using numerical values.

LESSON REVIEW

If you had difficulty with the Self-Quiz or would like additional assistance, read the following Lesson Review. It should reinforce and help you understand the content presented in this lesson.

Government Expenditure and GDP

In Lesson 5, we discussed how GDP was determined in a simplified economy with no government spending or taxation; these two elements are now included to make our hypothetical economy a little closer to the real thing. We talk about government spending first.

To begin with, we make the assumption that government spending does not affect the aggregate demand function; in other words, it does not reduce or increase intended investment by private industry or the amount individual consumers *want* to spend on things for themselves. It does increase the total intended spending level. In other words, *the total intended spending now equals the consumption expenditure plus the intended investment plus the intended government expenditure.* If we graph the result, we can see that adding government spending causes the aggregate spending function to shift upward (recall this discussion from Lesson 5), with a resulting increase in equilibrium GDP. By the same token, decreasing government spending creates a downward shift in the aggregate spending function, with a resulting decrease in equilibrium GDP.

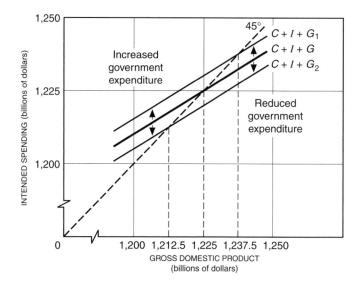

Note that, in this graph, a $5 billion increase in government spending raises equilibrium GDP (the point of intersection with the 45-degree line) from $1,225 billion to $1,237.5 billion. At the same time, a $5 billion decrease in government spending decreases equilibrium GDP from $1,225 billion to $1,212.5 billion. How are these figures calculated?

The Multiplier Effect

In Lesson 5, we saw that a $1 billion change in intended investment (which shifts the consumption function up or down) changes GDP by $1/MPS$ billions of dollars, where MPS is the marginal propensity to save. A change in government expenditure has precisely the same effect and is calculated the same way. So, for example, say the marginal propensity to consume is 0.6. What is the effect of an additional $1 billion in government expenditure? It's calculated this way:

$$MPS = 1 - \text{marginal propensity to consume}$$
$$MPS = 1 - 0.6$$
$$MPS = 0.4$$

Therefore, $1/MPS = 1/0.4 = 2.5$

An increase in government investment of $1 billion increases equilibrium GDP by $2.5 billion.

Taxation and GDP

We see the effect of government expenditures. What about taxes? For the sake of simplicity, this discussion assumes that all tax revenues come from personal taxes. For example, if consumers pay 10 percent of their income in taxes, their disposable income now equals 90 percent of GDP, whereas in the hypothetical economy without taxes, disposable income and GDP were the same. Clearly, people who pay taxes have less disposable income for consumption. Thus, the higher is the tax rate, the lower the equilibrium GDP; and the lower is the tax rate, the higher the equilibrium GDP.

The general impact of taxation on spending power seems pretty much a matter of common sense. But just how much do taxes really affect GDP? To get some idea, consider this graph, showing the differences in equilibrium GDP when the tax rate is $16^2/_3$ percent and $33^1/_3$ percent:

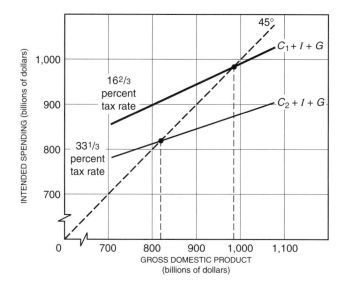

Had the tax rate been 0 percent, equilibrium GDP would be $1,225 billion. At a $16^{2}/_{3}$ percent tax rate, equilibrium GDP drops to $980 billion. And, at the $33^{1}/_{3}$ percent tax rate, equilibrium GDP falls clear to $816^{2}/_{3}$ billion; in other words, it drops by about a third.

The Nature and Objectives of Fiscal Policy

We see how government spending and taxation can shift the consumption function and cause equilibrium GDP to rise and fall. How does this affect government fiscal policy?

First, suppose we experiencing severe unemployment. What should the government do? We know from our previous discussions that employment is directly affected by production and that production in turn relies heavily on spending levels. The government can increase spending in one of several ways:

1. *Reduce taxes.*
   a. Personal taxes, giving people more disposable income to spend.
   b. Business taxes, encouraging more business investment.

2. *Increase government spending,* to shift the consumption function up.

3. *Encourage firms to invest more,* allowing tax credits for investment.

On the other hand, suppose high inflation is our problem. In this case, increased spending only drives prices higher still. What is needed is reduced spending or a downward shift in the aggregate spending function. To bring this about, the government can again do several things:

1. *Increase taxes.*
   a. Personal taxes, giving people less disposable income.
   b. Business taxes, discouraging investment.

2. *Cut government spending,* to reduce spending totals.

Most economists agree that these basic strategies are useful. Notice, however, that the strategies for dealing with unemployment and with inflation may be opposites. What happens then when, as in the 1970s and early 1980s, these situations occur together? This tricky problem will be the basis of future discussions.

Who Makes Fiscal Policy?

The most important player in this game is the president, who takes the lead in speaking for legislative reforms relating to taxation and spending.

Naturally, the president does not make decisions alone, but receives information and advice from numerous sources, including

- The House and Senate Budget Committees.
- The Congressional Budget Office.
- The Appropriations Committees.
- The House Ways and Means Committee.
- The Senate Finance Committee.
- The Office of Management and Budget (on expenditure policy).
- The Treasury Department (on taxation).
- The Council of Economic Advisers (established by the Employment Act of 1946).

All those who set fiscal policy for the nation must act within the context of tax and expenditure laws passed by Congress.

Automatic Stabilizers

If the classical economists were not entirely right that the economy would rectify its own problems given time, they were not entirely wrong either. Although some intervention is useful in setting directions, certain built-in stabilizers help boost the economy in down times and restrain spending in inflationary times. What are these stabilizers?

Tax Revenues. As productivity rises and more people are employed at better salaries, tax revenues also rise. In other words, the amount of income tax collected by the federal government goes up as GDP rises and down as it falls. This means that, when production goes down and unemployment mounts, tax collections fall because people have less income to be taxed. As a result, GDP falls more than disposable income. The decreased impact on disposable income means less of a fall in consumption; this, in turn, breaks the fall of GDP. On the other hand, when production is soaring, tax collections rise, restricting the increase in disposable income and restraining GDP by holding down spending.

Unemployment Compensation and Welfare. When GDP falls and unemployment rises, less money can be collected through taxes to fund unemployment benefits. At the same time, the amount paid out in benefits goes up because more persons are out of work. The benefits combined with decreased taxes boost consumer spending and curb the fall of GDP. When more people are working, benefit payments go down and taxes rise; this means less spending with a resulting restraint on inflation and GDP.

It is easy to overestimate the power of these stabilizers. They can help curb inflation and unemployment but cannot eliminate them. According to many (but not all) economists, discretionary spending and taxation are still necessary if we are to keep our economy growing and ward off recession. In addition, we must recognize that our economy has changed remarkably in the last century. There is no reason to suppose it will not continue changing. To deal with it effectively, therefore, some economists believe we need a well-defined set of rules and regulations; other economists advocate flexibility and skill in using the tools of discretionary fiscal policy.

Discretionary Fiscal Policy: What Can Government Do?

Suppose that the president and the Council of Economic Advisers determine that the economy is poised for decline. What steps can they take?

Here are the primary discretionary tools available.

1. *The government can vary its expenditure for public works and other programs.* This does not mean work for its own sake, but urban reconstruction programs, road projects, and other activities that work for the public good can boost production and improve our lifestyle at the same time. In times of inflation, on the other hand, such programs will likely be cut.

2. *The government can vary welfare payments and other types of transfer payments.* Benefits for Social Security, welfare, aid to dependent children, or veterans' programs can be increased, for example; or the government can decide to extend the length of time during which such benefits can be received. Either would give the economy a boost. Again, when inflation is high, such programs can be cut.

3. *The government can vary tax rates.* When unemployment is high, the government can cut taxes. A tax hike or surtax may help curb inflation.

Some Important Considerations for Discretionary Fiscal Policy

In deciding which discretionary tools to use, decision makers must weigh advantages and disadvantages carefully. Two factors are particularly critical: time and long-range implications.

Both public works programs and government-sponsored programs can take a long time to initiate. An urban reconstruction program, for instance, requires planning, purchase of land, acquisition of permits, contracting, materials purchase, budgeting, and a host of other steps so time consuming that when things finally get moving, the economic impetus for the whole project—unemployment—may now have given way to a whole new economic picture characterized by inflation and high production. In this scenario, the public works project may do more harm than good. Similarly, programs that require congressional support may get bogged down in political debate; further, politicians may be reluctant to support programs that raise taxes or decrease benefits, for fear they will not be reelected.

Increasingly, some economists believe that taxation should be the primary fiscal tool. Other programs, they argue, may have short-term benefits for stabilizing the economy but may have limited long-term desirability. The quality of the project itself, they say, and not just its immediate effects on the economy should be the basis for funding.

How Big Is Government?

Total government expenditures in 2001 totaled about $3.5 trillion. Since total national output was about $10.1 trillion, this means that government spending accounted for about one-third of our total output. This is a dramatic increase from 1929, when government spending was about 10 percent of the total. What are the primary reasons for this enormous growth?

1. *Government transfer payments have grown.* Demands have grown for welfare payments, unemployment, Social Security benefits, and so forth. The Social Security budget alone rose from $20 billion in 1965 to about $500 billion in 2004.

2. *Military spending.* Defense spending is our second largest single budget item at $390 billion in 2004.

3. *Demand for government services.* As incomes rise, people want better schools, more police and fire protection, more and better highways, park systems, and so forth.

Where the Money Comes from and Where It Goes

At the *federal* level, personal income tax is the biggest money raiser; it accounts for half the tax revenue raised by the federal government. Social Security, payroll, and employment taxes account for about a third. Other important taxes include corporate income and excise taxes, as well as death and gift taxes.

At the *state* level, sales and excise taxes are the most significant, followed by income and highway user taxes (including gasoline tax and license fees).

At the *local* level, the property tax is the most important revenue source by far, although some additional revenues are generated through local sales and income taxes.

Spending

About 20 percent of the *federal* expenditure goes for defense, veterans' benefits, and items connected with international relations, energy, space, and technology. About 60 percent goes for Social Security, welfare, health, and education programs. And around 10 percent goes to make interest payments on the national debt. The rest is used to support farm, transportation, and housing programs, as well as to run the Congress, the courts, and the executive branch of government.

State and *local* governments spend by far the greatest percentage of their revenues to support schools. In addition, they support hospitals, redevelopment programs, courts, and police and fire departments.

Relating Fiscal Policy to Aggregate Demand

As we see, discretionary fiscal policies tend to fall within one of two categories: anti-unemployment or anti-inflationary. As you should recall from the discussion in Lesson 4, the aggregate demand curve (sloping downward and to the right) intersects the short-run aggregate supply curve well within the horizontal range during periods of high unemployment.

During periods of inflation, the aggregate demand curve intersects the aggregate supply curve somewhere within the vertical range.

What does this imply for fiscal policy? It means that, generally, during periods of slow productivity, the government can employ expansionary strategies (lowering taxes, increasing government spending, encouraging investment) and move the aggregate demand curve to the right toward full-employment equilibrium (i.e., within the positively sloped range) *without* raising prices. It also means that, during periods of high inflation, when prices are up, the government can employ anti-inflationary strategies (raising taxes, decreasing government spending, and discouraging investment) and shift the aggregate demand curve to the left toward the noninflationary, full-employment equilibrium (within the positively sloped range) *without* hurting employment rates.

EXTENDED LEARNING

This section of the study guide is specifically designed for the two-semester student.

AUDIO

Before Listening

Read Exploring Further of Chapter 6, pages 162–164 in your text.

Next

Listen to the audiotape that accompanies Lesson 6.

After Listening

Answer the following questions:

1. Given the framework and assumptions used in this chapter, what would be the effect of each of the following on equilibrium GNP in the short run?

    a. An increase in the marginal propensity to save
    b. An increase in the income tax rate
    c. An increase in transfer payments
    d. A decrease in the amount of plant and equipment needed to generate the existing level of output

2. "The whole purpose of automatic stabilizers is to reduce the value of the multiplier." Discuss.

3. Which of the following are automatic stabilizers and why?

    A progressive income tax
    A proportional income tax
    Consumption according to the permanent income hypothesis
    Durability of capital goods
    Corporate dividends
    Property tax
    Unemployment compensation

4. What does the size of the government today, as compared to 1929, imply as far as the likelihood that a depression like the 1930s will occur again?

5. A tax is defined as being progressive if the rich pay a higher percentage of their incomes than the poor.

    a. Is the federal income tax progressive?
    b. Are property taxes progressive?
    c. Is a tax in which the marginal tax rate decreases as the income increases progressive?

ADDITIONAL READINGS

Blough, Roy. "Economic Problems and Economic Advice: A Half Century of Evolution." In *Economic Advice and Executive Policy*, edited by Werner Sichel. New York: Praeger, 1978.

> The author shows how the economic policies the government should follow have evolved from 1926 to 1976 because of changes in the economy and increased knowledge and tools for affecting the economy. No mathematics or graphs.

Council of Economic Advisers. "The Employment Act: Twenty Years of Policy Experience." *Economic Report of the President*. Washington, DC: Government Printing Office, 1966.

> Chapter 7 of the *Economic Report* discusses the period from 1946 to 1966 from a narrow Keynesian viewpoint, which stresses the importance of fiscal policy. No mathematics or graphs.

Eckstein, Otto. "The Economics of the 1960s—A Backward Look." *Public Interest*, 19 (Spring 1970): 86–97.

> Details the way economic policy was made and the repercussions of those policies. Argues that, because fiscal and monetary policies swung to extremes, the economy did not perform as well as it could have in the 1950 to 1970 period. No mathematics or graphs.

Gordon, Robert A. *Economic Instability and Growth: The American Record*. New York: Harper & Row, 1974.

> Chapters 4, 5, and 6 detail the macroeconomic policy responses to the events of the 1946 to 1973 period, showing the development of Keynesian policies and the mismanagement of the economy in the late 1960s. No mathematics or graphs.

Stein, Herbert. *Presidential Economics*. New York: Simon & Schuster, 1984.

> Chapters 3 and 4 discuss the consolidation of Keynesian theory in the 1950s and 1960s in economic policy, but the author stresses the weaknesses of a simple Keynesian approach and how those weaknesses became evident in later years. No mathematics or graphs.

ANSWER KEY

Video Questions

1. Following the Great Depression and the booming economy of the war years, many were ready to accept the pro-government-intervention theories of John Maynard Keynes. To help bridge the gap between theory and political reality, the Employment Act of 1946 required the president to form a group called the *Council of Economic Advisers*. The job of this group was to assist the president (and others) in accurately assessing the current economic climate, forecasting the future, and making difficult decisions on fiscal policy. In particular, the council was charged with helping the president fulfill the intent of the Employment Act of 1946: "to promote maximum employment, production and purchasing power."

2. Talk of public policies promoting full employment was one thing, but many persons felt apprehensive about how much power such an approach might give the government. The bill that ultimately became the Employment Act of 1946 was

first introduced in the U.S. Senate in 1945. But through a year of compromise and debate, its straightforward, strong language guaranteeing "full employment" for all citizens was replaced by the less direct phrase: "to promote maximum employment, production and purchasing power." What was lost was the citizen's right to a job, protected and ensured by government. On the other hand, the bill did ensure government commitment—both philosophical and political—to promoting employment through fiscal policy. Many government programs, called *hollow season* programs, had been initiated to deal with employment problems. But these various programs lacked coordination and order; among the benefits of the Employment Act of 1946 was the evaluation of these programs as part of a coordinated, centralized effort.

3. As the U.S. involvement in the Korean War ended, the economy stalled, with no subsequent rise in consumer demand. With unemployment at its highest levels since the Depression, Eisenhower found himself besieged with diverse, strongly voiced recommendations. Traditionalists favored a tax increase. But the Committee for Economic Development urged a "stabilizing budget policy," meaning a reliance on the economy's built-in automatic stabilizers. The theory was that, if the tax rate were kept stable for a sufficient period, as GNP began to fall, tax revenues would also fall because people would have less income to be taxed. This, in turn, would put more money in the hands of consumers so that spending would not decline as much as one might expect, and instead of a declining spiral into ever deeper recession, the economy would be cushioned by the relatively high levels of consumer spending and gradually inch its way toward prosperity again. That is precisely what happened during the Eisenhower administration. And, by the summer of 1954, the recession that had appeared so ominous only months before was just a memory. Why had these stabilizers worked so well in 1954 and virtually not at all during the Great Depression? The answer was simply that government spending was already playing a much bigger role in the economy than it had during the 1930s; and precisely this high level of government involvement was what John Maynard Keynes and his followers had been advocating.

4. When President Kennedy took office in 1961, economists agreed that the country was beginning to recover from the 1960 recession, yet unemployment rates remained distressingly high. There were two obvious options: increase government spending on social programs, or cut taxes. John Kenneth Galbraith strongly favored the government spending approach. Kennedy's new economic advisor, Walter Heller, thought differently, however. A pragmatist, he saw that Kennedy was making little progress in Congress with proposed spending packages. If the tax cut alone stood the best chance in Congress, then he would support that approach, and he did. Although Kennedy resisted at first, in part because of heavy lobbying from Galbraith, a new slump in 1962 made Heller's argument increasingly convincing. By the middle of 1962, an across-the-board tax cut was under consideration. What made Heller and Galbraith differ so strongly in their approaches? Heller was concerned predominantly with ensuring that the economy did not slip again into recession. Galbraith, by contrast, was more concerned with the long-range implications of fiscal policy. He felt that the tax cut approach

might open the doors to future tax cuts, with questionable results. In addition, he felt an obligation to promote programs that would serve a social purpose.

Multiple Choice

1. a   Text, 143.
2. b   Text, 145.
3. a   Text, 145.
4. d   Text, 146.
5. c   Text, 146–148.
6. b   Text, 151–157.
7. b   Text, 152.
8. d   Text, 143, 149–152.
9. a   Study Guide, 105.
10. c   Text, 161.

True-False

1. True   Text, 143–146.
2. True   Text, 146–148.
3. True   Text, 154–155.
4. False   Video.
5. False   Text, 159.
6. True   Video; Text, 154.
7. True   Video; Text, 156.
8. True   Video; Text, 158.
9. True   Video; Text, 158.
10. True   Text, 155–157.

Discussion Questions

1. In the case of unemployment, the government can reduce taxes, increase government spending, or encourage firms to invest more by legislating tax credits. Unfortunately, all three of these possible stimuli to the economy are relatively difficult for the government to implement. Each stimulus is subject to implementation delays; taxation policies typically are quickest to implement. In the case of inflation, the government can increase taxes or cut government spending. Both these anti-inflationary responses are potentially difficult to implement due to the adverse consumer response to tax increases and cuts in government programs.

2. Although Governor Bush claimed that his tax cut would help increase aggregate supply, his critics focused on its impact on aggregate demand. A substantial tax cut, magnified by the multiplier, would significantly increase aggregate demand. If the economy was at a full-employment equilibrium, this shift of the aggregate demand curve to the right would throw the economy out of equilibrium and cause an inflationary gap. This is something that his opponents argued should be avoided.

3. If one assumes that the economy is faced with the choice of producing either consumer goods or military goods and the economy is currently producing a combination of these two goods such that it is on the production possibilities curve, it does not follow that a reduction in the production of military goods must necessarily result in mass unemployment. One can choose from an infinite number of efficient points on the production possibilities curve, where each point represents an efficient combination of military and consumer goods. Only if military production is decreased and consumer goods production remains unchanged or decreases does the economy end up at a point of inefficiency, where there is unemployment. This type of point would be represented by a point interior to the production possibilities curve.

4. The automatic stabilizers for the U.S. economy are tax revenues, unemployment compensation and welfare, corporate dividends, family saving, and farm

programs. The major tools of discretionary policy are the level of government expenditure on public works and other programs, the level of government expenditure on welfare programs and other types of transfer payments, and the tax rates the government imposes. Automatic stabilizers automatically help the economy move toward equilibrium: These stabilizers help boost the economy during recessionary periods and slow down the economy during inflationary periods. In contrast, discretionary spending and taxation policies must be actively implemented by the government in times of recession or inflation. Stabilizers can help curb inflation and recession, but they are not necessarily strong enough to eliminate these problems. Some economists feel that discretionary spending and taxation policies are necessary if the economy is to be kept growing at the appropriate rate (a rate that results in neither recession nor inflation).

Problem Set

1. a.

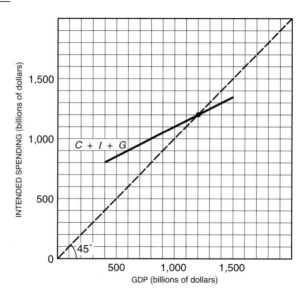

  b. $1,200 billion.
  c. There is a recessionary gap.
  d. The government can increase its expenditures by $100 billion or it can encourage private investment or cut taxes.

2. a. $1,100 million.
  b. Equilibrium GDP increases by $20 million.
  c. *Hint:* If consumption expenditures are $700 million, then disposable income is $900 million. Disposable income is five-sixths of GDP.

GDP (millions of dollars)
1,080
1,200
1,320
1,440
1,560

    d. $1,200 million.
    e. Government expenditure is $350 million, and taxes are $200 million, so the government is running a deficit of $150 million.

3. a. $Y = 200 + 0.8(Y - 500) + 160 + 500$,
        $0.2Y = 460$,
        $Y = 2,300$.
        GDP = $2,300 billion.
   b. The multiplier is 5.
     $Y = $2,800 billion = GDP.
     Greater by $500 billion.
     5 times greater.

4. Intended consumption expenditures plus intended investment plus government spending must equal GDP to be in equilibrium. This happens when GDP = $1,300 million ($1,145 million + $128 million + $27 million). So, equilibrium GDP is $1,300 million. The government is running a surplus of $23 million.

5. a. GDP = $500 + 0.9(\text{GDP} - 250) + 500 + 225$ (all figures in millions of dollars). Thus, $0.1\text{GDP} = 500 - 225 + 500 + 225 = 1,000$, so the equilibrium value of GDP is $10,000 million.
   b. Earnest wants GDP = $10,400 million and $T = G$. Therefore, GDP = $500 + 0.9(\text{GDP} - G) + 500 + G = 10,400$, which means that $0.1G = 10,400 - 500 - 500 - 9,360 = 40$ (all figures in millions of dollars). Hence, both G and T should be set equal to $400 million.

Audio/Text Questions

1. The increase in the marginal propensity to save, the decrease in the amount of plant and equipment necessary to generate the existing level of output, and the tax rate increase would all cause GNP to fall in the short run. All three reduce the aggregate demand. The transfer payment increase, unless totally offset by higher taxes, would be expansionary.

2. Automatic stabilizers reduce income when the economy is growing and increase it when it is contracting, so they effectively reduce the multiplier.

3. Income taxes are stabilizers, regardless of whether they are progressive or proportional. Consumption, corporate dividends, and unemployment compensation all tend to increase as a percentage of national income when national income falls, so they too tend to stabilize the economy.

The durability of capital goods is a destabilizing influence since firms can cut back drastically on investment spending and still produce. The property tax, because it remains constant as income falls, is also a destabilizer.

4. Government spending tends to be very stable over the business cycle, and since total government spending is now approximately 35 percent of GNP, compared to less than 15 percent in 1929, the very size of the government tends to preclude the recurrence of the Depression.

5. a. Federal income tax structure is progressive as far as the tax brackets are concerned, but various legal exemptions reduce the degree of progressivity.
   b. Property taxes tend to be regressive.
   c. Any income tax in which the marginal rate falls as income increases is regressive.

LESSON 7. INFLATION: HOW DID THE SPIRAL BEGIN?

INTRODUCTION

Think of the shoes you wear, the groceries you purchased within the last few days, the car you drive, or the home you live in. How much would these same items have cost 10 years ago? Twenty? Fifty? For almost any item or service you can think of, prices have gone up. For many items, prices have increased by 32 percent within the past 10 years alone.

All of us are victims of inflation, the general upward movement of prices that eats away at our spending capability. Economists have long known that inflation and unemployment were the two major economic evils; what we are now discovering is just how complex the relationship between these two can be. In the simplest Keynesian models, inflation and unemployment tended to occur alternately, resulting from different circumstances and requiring opposite remedies. Since the mid-1960s, however, things have not been so simple. Inflation and unemployment, we find, can occur together, making the old solutions less effective. What can we do to help ourselves? The first step lies in gaining a better understanding of the problem: What is inflation? How did it become what some economists consider the most serious economic problem of our time? Answering those questions is what Lesson 7 is all about.

What You Should Learn

By the end of Lesson 7, you should be prepared to

1. Define *inflation,* and distinguish between creeping inflation and runaway inflation.

2. Describe the effects of runaway inflation on the German economy following World War I.

3. Describe the general pattern of inflation that has characterized the U.S. economy for the past 50 years.

4. Define the *consumer price index* and explain how this measure is used by economists.

5. Explain what is meant by the *redistributive effects* of inflation.

6. Distinguish between *money income* and *real income*.

7. Describe the general effects of inflation on *lenders* and *savers*. Who benefits?

8. Describe the relationship between aggregate demand and inflation.

9. Define *demand-side inflation*.

10. Define *supply-side inflation*.

11. Define the *inflationary gap*.

12. Explain how economists use the *Phillips curve* to show the relationship between the rate of increase of wages and the level of unemployment.

13. Describe the ways in which demand-side inflation affected our economy under the Johnson administration.

14. Identify several ways that Presidents Johnson and Nixon tried to deal with inflation during their administrations.

KEY TERMS

inflation
runaway inflation
creeping inflation
consumer price index
redistributive effects of inflation
money income
real income

"arbitrary tax"
inflationary gap
demand-side inflation
Phillips curve
supply-side inflation
anticipated inflation
unanticipated inflation

VIDEO

Watch

Economics U$A Program 7, "Inflation: How Did the Spiral Begin?"

Illustrative Events

The inflationary spiral set off by the Vietnam War and President Lyndon Johnson's Great Society; featuring economist Walter Heller, chair of the Council of Economic Advisers under LBJ, and *Washington Post* reporter Myra MacPherson. Richard Gill introduces demand-pull inflation.

The inflation of the late 1960s and early 1970s—who it helped and who it hurt, with William Hutton, director of the National Council of Senior Citizens; Michael Harrington, author of *The Other America*; and Victor Gottbaum, New York City labor leader.

The failure of wage and price controls to stop inflation when they were applied by President Richard Nixon as a last resort; featuring economists Paul McCracken, chair of the Council of Economic Advisers under Nixon, and Herbert Stein, a member of the council at that time. Host David Schoumacher discusses a new economic problem, stagflation.

After Viewing

Answer the following questions:

1. Walter Heller, former chair of the Council of Economic Advisers, makes the statement that "Kennedy was our first Keynesian president." Given that other presidents also found merit in Keynesian economics, what causes Heller to make this statement?

2. What major factors contributed to the severe inflation problems that began during the Vietnam War era?

3. According to Keynesian economics, a tax increase might have helped curb inflation during President Johnson's administration. Why did Johnson oppose such an increase?

4. What prompted the 10 percent surtax of 1968, and how effective was it?

5. What strategies were tried during the Nixon administration to curb inflation? How effective were they?

6. What is the primary limitation of Keynesian economics in dealing with today's economic problems?

Read

Read Chapter 7, "Inflation," pages 167–181 in your text. After completing your reading, try the Self-Quiz.

SELF-QUIZ

Multiple Choice

1. Suppose wheat costing $10 a bushel suddenly rose to $30 a bushel. To an economist, this change in cost would *probably* indicate

   a. runaway inflation.
   b. creeping inflation.
   c. a change in the consumer price index.
   d. a change in the price for one commodity only.

2. Which of the following is the *best* definition of inflation?

    a. A reflection of the current value of money
    b. The ratio between the value of money now and the value during some base year of comparison
    c. A measurable upward shift in the price of any given commodity
    d. A general upward movement in the average prices of most goods and services

3. Which of the following probably *best* characterizes our own U.S. economy during the past 50 years?

    a. We have experienced creeping inflation except during the 1970s.
    b. We have experienced alternately creeping inflation and runaway inflation.
    c. We experienced very little inflation prior to 1965, then a period of runaway inflation that plagued us into the early 1980s.
    d. We have experienced primarily runaway inflation that has only been checked in recent years.

4. Which of the following groups is likely to be hurt *most* by inflation?

    a. Government workers on salary
    b. Retired persons on fixed pensions
    c. Families borrowing money for new homes
    d. Persons investing in stocks and commodities

5. During periods of runaway inflation, which of the following are consumers *most* likely to do with their money?

    a. Spend it as fast as possible.
    b. Save as much as they can.
    c. Invest in the hopes of getting some money back later.
    d. None of the above, since all their money is consumed by taxes.

6. Suppose that goods and services that cost $100 in 1967 now cost $400. Using 1967 as the base year, what is the current consumer price index?

    a. 300
    b. 100
    c. 400
    d. 500

7. Generally, how would economists today probably characterize the seriousness of inflation as a national economic problem?

    a. Important enough to merit continued attention but nowhere near as serious as in John Maynard Keynes's day
    b. More serious than in the 1950s, but dwarfed by the more devastating problems of unemployment
    c. Along with unemployment, the most serious economic problem of our time
    d. Thanks to the new fiscal policies of the 1980s, no longer a serious threat to our economy

8. Last year the Smiths earned $40,000. This year, their income is $42,000. In an economy with an inflation rate of 8 percent, which of the following would be true?

   a. The Smiths' money income and real income have both gone up.
   b. The Smiths' money income and real income have both fallen.
   c. The Smiths' money income has fallen, though their real income has increased.
   d. The Smiths' real income has fallen, though their money income has increased.

9. As real GDP approaches potential GDP, which of the following is *most* likely to occur?

   a. Shortages become severe.
   b. Unemployment rates rise.
   c. Production capacity rises.
   d. Government spending declines.

10. Both the unemployment rate and inflation rate are largely determined by

    a. the total level of spending.
    b. equilibrium GDP.
    c. the maximum national output.
    d. government spending.

True-False

_____ 1. The consumer price index, published monthly by the Bureau of Labor Statistics, is the key measure of the rate of inflation.

_____ 2. High rates of inflation tend to stabilize the distribution of income and wealth.

_____ 3. Savers and people with relatively fixed incomes tend to fare best in an inflationary period.

_____ 4. Businesses are relatively unaffected by periods of inflation.

_____ 5. Demand-induced, or demand-side, inflation occurs when the level of equilibrium GDP is lower than the full-employment output.

_____ 6. If the Phillips curve remains fixed and unemployment is reduced, inflation increases.

_____ 7. Many economists trace this country's inflationary problems in the 1960s and 1970s to the Great Society legislation of the Johnson administration and expenditures related to the Vietnam War.

_____ 8. In the period during and following the Vietnam War, inflation became a problem not only because of a stimulative fiscal policy but also because of supply-side oil shocks.

____ 9. When an economy is *not* in a depression or recession, monetary influences on both GDP and prices become more important, a factor given little attention by most of Keynes's followers.

____ 10. In the long term, wage and price controls initiated by the Nixon administration were extremely effective in putting the brakes on the inflationary spiral.

Discussion Questions

1. In his 1979 *Economic Report,* President Carter said, "A large part of the worsening of inflation last year . . . stemmed from poor productivity." By *poor productivity,* he meant that output per hour of labor did not increase as fast as in previous years. Why would this affect the rate of inflation?

2. Suppose that the unemployed refuse to work unless they receive unrealistically high wages. For example, a high school dropout worth no more than $3 per hour may insist on receiving $6 per hour. If so, isn't it inflationary and foolish to try to achieve full employment?

3. "Unless some people benefited from inflation, the nation would not tolerate it." Do you agree? Why or why not?

4. In his 1982 *Economic Report,* President Reagan said, "We simply *cannot* blame crop failures and oil price increases for our basic inflation problem. The continuous, underlying cause was poor government policy." How can poor government policies cause inflation? What sorts of policies was President Reagan referring to? Do you agree that these policies were poor?

5. In Israel, the annual inflation rate was about 50 percent in 1978, and nearly 100 percent during the summer of 1979, according to William C. Freund of the New York Stock Exchange. In the *New York Times* on June 24, 1979, Freund concludes that: "The solution lies in marshalling the necessary political courage and consensus. . . . It is political fortitude, above all else, which is needed now— to cut back on excess claims against resources, to promote production and productivity, and to relieve intense demand pressures." Indicate how this advice is related to the discussion presented in this chapter. What specific measures would you suggest to accomplish these results?

Problem Set

1. Suppose that James Johnson's balance sheet is as follows as of January 1, 2003:

	Assets	Liabilities and net worth
Cash and bank accounts	$20,000	Mortgage $35,000
House	$50,000	Net worth $35,000

Suppose that the price level rises by 50 percent and Johnson's house goes up in value at the same rate as the price level.

a. In terms of current dollars, what is Mr. Johnson's net worth after this increase in the price level?
b. In terms of 2003 dollars, what is Mr. Johnson's net worth after this increase in the price level?
c. Has Mr. Johnson benefited from or been hurt by this inflation? Can you tell?

2. Suppose there are only three commodities, X, Y, and Z. The price per pound of each commodity in 2003 follows, together with the number of pounds of each commodity consumed in 2003:

	2003	
Commodity	Price per pound (dollars)	Number of pounds consumed (millions)
X	1	5
Y	2	8
Z	3	12

a. What is the total amount spent on these commodities in 2003?
b. The price per pound of each commodity in 2004 follows, together with the number of pounds of each commodity consumed in 2004:

	2004	
Commodity	Price per pound (dollars)	Number of pounds consumed (millions)
X	1.08	6
Y	2.15	8
Z	3.30	13

What is the total amount spent on these commodities in 2004?

c. If we divide the answer to part b by the answer to part a, do we get a proper price index? Why or why not?
d. If we average the 2004 prices of the three commodities, we get

$$\frac{\$1.08 + \$2.15 + \$3.30}{3} = \frac{\$6.53}{3} = \$2.177.$$

If we average the 2003 prices of the three commodities, we get

$$\frac{\$1 + \$2 + \$3}{3} = \frac{\$6}{3} = \$2.$$

One way to obtain a price index is to divide $2.177 by $2.00 and multiply the result by 100. If we do this, we get 108.8. Why do statisticians regard an index number of this sort as being too crude for most purposes?

e. Another way to calculate a price index is by calculating how much the amounts of these commodities consumed in 2003 would have cost in 2004 and dividing this cost by how much they actually cost in 2003. (The result should be multiplied by 100.) Compute this price index, using the data on the given previously. What advantages do you think this price index has over the one computed in part d?

3. Suppose that the Phillips curve in France in 1997 is shown on the following graph. What rate of increase of prices would be associated with a 5 percent unemployment rate? What unemployment would be associated with a 6 percent rate of increase of prices?

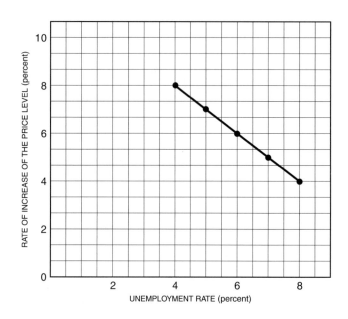

4. The Phillips curve in question 3 pertained to 1997. Suppose that the Phillips curve in France in 2000 is as follows (amounts in percent):

Unemployment rate	Rate of increase of price level
2	6
4	5
6	4
8	3

Plot the 2000 Phillips curve in the following graph:

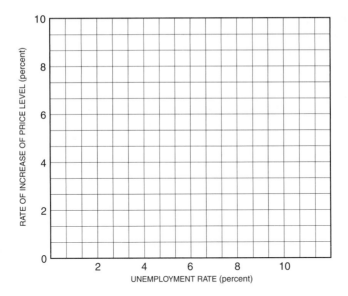

LESSON REVIEW

If you had difficulty with the Self-Quiz or would like additional assistance, read the following Lesson Review. It should reinforce and help you understand the content presented in this lesson.

Inflation: What Is It?

Simply put, inflation is a general upward movement in the prices of most goods and services. In practical terms, in the 1970s, it meant that a house bought for $20,000 in 1968 might sell for $80,000 in 1980.

In talking about inflation, we must distinguish between fluctuations in the prices of individual commodities and the movement of the general price level. If the price of wheat doubles tomorrow, that may not be a sign of inflation, since other goods may not be changing, keeping the average level of prices about the same. Inflation occurs when the prices for most goods and services within a society move upward so that the average price level increases.

Runaway Inflation versus Creeping Inflation

Inflation diminishes the value of money. Runaway inflation does so thoroughly and rapidly, while creeping inflation erodes the value over a long period of time.

- *Runaway inflation in Germany's postwar economy*. In the years following World War I, Germany was required to pay large reparations to the Allies. Rather than tax its people, the German government simply printed more money. The new money increased spending; this, in turn drove up prices because Germany's war-ravaged economy could not produce enough to meet demands. By 1923, it took a trillion marks to buy what a single mark would have purchased in prewar days.

- *Creeping inflation in the U.S. economy.* Our economy has been characterized by creeping inflation over the past 50 years. Between 1969 and 1980 that rate accelerated dramatically, causing many economists and consumers alike to view inflation as the most important economic problem during that period of time. Although creeping inflation is less damaging overall to an economy than runaway inflation, it carries serious consequences nevertheless, as we shall see.

Consumer Price Index: Measuring Inflation

The consumer price index, calculated monthly by the Bureau of Labor Statistics, is the most common measure of inflation for our society. The first step in calculating the index is to find out how much it costs in a particular month to purchase a "market basket" of goods and services typical of what U.S. consumers really buy. The contents of the market basket (clothing, food, drug items and doctors' fees, homes, furniture, repairs, transportation costs, recreational goods, automobiles, fuel, and so forth) are selected through a careful survey of U.S. consumers' buying habits.

The next step is to calculate the current cost of the market basket and compare it to the base-year cost in the form of a ratio. Presently, 1982–84 is used as the base year. So, for example, if the market basket now costs $600, and in 1982–84 it cost $200, then the ratio is 600/200, or 3. To obtain the consumer price index, we then multiply by 100: $3 \times 100 = 300$. In fact, the consumer price index for December 1990 was 133.8, which is another way of saying that with a 1982–84 base of 100, it cost 33.8 percent more to buy typical goods and services than in 1982–84.

Sales taxes, excise taxes, and real estate taxes are included in the index. Income taxes and personal property taxes are not. In addition, the consumer price index does not include prices of industrial machinery or raw materials.

In addition to the overall index, separate price indexes are computed for various goods and services, such as food, rent, medical fees, and so on. Economists can then determine not only whether prices as a whole are going up but whether, for instance, medical, housing, and transportation costs are rising disproportionately to other costs. Labor union representatives may use the index to substantiate requests for higher wages. Similarly, welfare, Social Security, pension, and other payments or benefits may be linked to the index.

Redistributive Effects of Inflation

Although inflation affects everyone to an extent, it hits some people harder than others. To see why, we need to distinguish between money income and real income. *Money income* is measured in current dollars; *real income* is adjusted for changes in price level.

For example, suppose you earned $20,000 last year. This year, you earn $22,000. Has your income really gone up? Assuming no inflation, yes. But suppose we have an inflation rate of 10 percent. Now we see that the increase in your income just matches the rate of inflation; in effect, your money income has gone up $2,000, but your real income is just the same. This situation may be frustrating for those who cannot keep ahead of inflation, but what about those living on a fixed income?

- *Fixed income consumers.* People who live on fixed incomes cannot increase their incomes regardless of inflation rates. For these groups, the impact of inflation can be devastating.

- *Lenders and savers.* Inflation hurts lenders and benefits borrowers. Why? Because, as inflation goes up, dollars are worth less and less. If you borrow $100 today and pay it back a year from now when it is worth much less, you benefit. The only way the lender can benefit is to charge a rate of interest that more than makes up for inflation, but since inflation is hard to predict, this is difficult to do.

- *The "arbitrary tax."* Why is inflation sometimes called the *arbitrary tax*? Because the rewards and penalties imposed by inflation have no relation to a society's values or goals. Generally, the elderly and the poor suffer most from inflation. Those who fare best are often the sophisticated investors who can afford to speculate on land, gold, or other commodities, and who (because they can afford enormous risk) may make substantial profits. In other words, those who need to benefit least, because they already have substantial income or savings, are usually those who benefit most. The average consumer who is simply "saving for a rainy day" stands little chance of even keeping pace with inflation.

Effects of Inflation on Output

Runaway inflation, as we see, can utterly disrupt production capabilities. Creeping inflation, by contrast, does not seem to reduce national output, and may even—in the short run—increase it.

As inflation continues and the rate grows, however, the effects on production become negative. Inflation encourages speculation, rather than productive investment. If everyone is buying gold and art works, this may spell huge profits for the speculators but benefit the economy very little. Business investment may suffer, and businesses themselves may put off improvements or expansions, feeling leery of long-range projects while future inflation rates remain uncertain.

Pushed to the extreme, inflation can actually destroy a country's monetary system. Eventually consumers insist on trading goods and services directly for other goods and services. The result is inefficiency and an enormous drop in national production.

Aggregate Demand and Inflation

One way that inflation gets started is when demand exceeds the ability of the economy to produce. There is a trade-off; both inflation and unemployment rates are determined by total spending.

When expenditures are low, national output is far below the maximum (in other words, actual GDP is far below potential GDP). Without sales, firms do not hire all the workers who want jobs. According to the Keynesian model, demand is low enough to keep prices down, so inflation is low too.

As spending goes up, jobs open up and more people go to work. At first prices remain stable. But, if the demand continues, shortages develop in one segment of the economy and then another, gradually driving prices up. Eventually, output hits maximum capacity everywhere. Employment can no longer rise because businesses are already producing at capacity; hiring more workers will not raise production. But prices soar because consumer demand continues to apply upward pressure.

Demand-Side Inflation

Demand-induced inflation is sometimes called *demand-side inflation*. This was the kind of inflation we began to experience during the Vietnam War.

With demand-side inflation, the economy may be already operating within the vertical range of its short-run aggregate supply curve *before* the increase in aggregate demand.

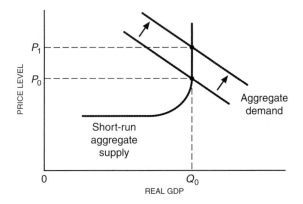

Note that, once the aggregate demand curve is within the vertical range, any further pressure caused by consumer demand, in effect, pushes that curve up rather than to the right. Output is already at its peak and thus operating at a fixed level: It cannot increase. Therefore, *the rise in the price level (up the vertical range) must be proportional to the increase in total spending.*

Supply-Side Inflation

Supply-side inflation is sometimes called *cost-push inflation*. This was the kind of inflation we experienced during the 1970s, when the oil-producing countries increased the price of crude oil by very large percentages.

With supply-side inflation, the short-run aggregate supply curve shifts to the left. Why? Because firms will supply a particular amount of output only if they receive higher prices. As indicated in the following graph, the result is an increase in the price level, from P_0 to P_2.

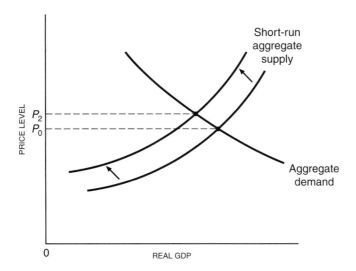

Phillips Curve

The Phillips curve (named after British economist A. W. Phillips) shows the relationship between the rate of increase of the price level and the *level of unemployment*.

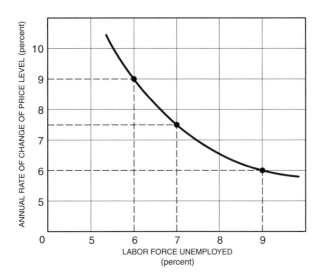

As the figure indicates, the relationship is inverse: As unemployment goes up, the rate of increase for the price level goes down, and vice versa. Hypothetically, when unemployment (in this chart) is running about 6 percent, prices rise at an annual rate of 9 percent. When unemployment rises to 9 percent, prices rise at an annual rate of 6 percent.

To make matters even more complicated, the simple trade-off between employment and inflation has been replaced by a phenomenon economists call *stagflation,* in which high unemployment and high inflation occur simultaneously. Recall from our discussion in Lesson 6 that the strategies government has at its command to deal with these two phenomena are essentially opposed. What happens then when inflation and unemployment occur together? We deal more with this issue in Lesson 10.

EXTENDED LEARNING

This section of the study guide is specifically designed for the two-semester student.

AUDIO

Listen

Listen to the audiotape that accompanies Lesson 7. There is no specific reading assignment.

After Listening

Answer the following questions:

1. If everybody's income could be indexed to inflation, would anybody be hurt?
2. How does a low or negative growth rate in productivity affect inflation?
3. How valid is the statement, "Every society must choose where it wants to be on the Phillips curve"?
4. For four years in the late 1960s, the nation's unemployment rate was below 4 percent. Does this mean there was an inflationary gap at the time?
5. Why is inflation sometimes called an *arbitrary tax*?

ADDITIONAL READINGS

Bach, G. L. "Inflation: Who Gains and Who Loses?" *Challenge* 17 (July–August 1974): 48–55.

> Discusses how unanticipated inflation shifts real wealth from lenders to borrowers and how the various sectors of the economy (households, business, and government) fared in the 1950 to 1973 period. No mathematics or graphs.

Feige, Edgar L., and Douglas K. Pearce. "The Wage and Price Control Experiment—Did It Work?" *Challenge* 16 (July–August 1973).

> Argues that the wage-price controls of the Nixon administration did not significantly reduce inflation and unemployment below what would have prevailed in the absence of controls. No mathematics or graphs.

Galbraith, J. K. *Money: Whence It Came, Where It Went.* Boston: Houghton Mifflin Company, 1975.

> Chapter 19, "New Economics at High Noon," discusses what Galbraith considers to be the three main problems with the use of Keynesian policy in the postwar period: excessive market power of unions and firms, political resistance to reducing federal expenditures when necessary, and excessive reliance on monetary policy.

Gordon, R. J. "Alternative Responses of Policy to External Supply Shocks." *Brookings Papers on Economic Activity.* Washington, DC: Brookings Institution, 1975.

> Develops a model of price behavior that includes the "indexing" of wages and analyzes the effectiveness of possible macroeconomic policy responses. Some difficult mathematics, but the paper can be understood without following the mathematics.

ANSWER KEY

Video Questions

1. In a sense it might have appeared that Roosevelt was following Keynesian economic theories when he launched his New Deal spending programs, but remember that Roosevelt's approach was very cautious and, at times, even sporadic. He remained suspicious of the spending approach to achieving prosperity, and so was alternately liberal and conservative about government spending, with the result that his programs were never as stimulating to the economy as they might have been. Kennedy, by contrast, was cautious at first, then very much committed to a more-liberal economic approach. According to Heller's perception, Kennedy used Keynesian economics in "an avowed and perceptive way," characterized by the massive tax cut proposed in 1962.

2. The 1962 tax cut boosted consumer spending enormously. Business activity skyrocketed. New factories opened. Unemployment neared an all-time low. Unfortunately, this high demand continued unchecked as other factors began to exert inflationary pressure. Among these were President Johnson's War on Poverty programs, which augmented government spending. In addition, the costs of the Vietnam War boosted total spending further yet. By 1965, aggregate demand was rising at a rate of 8 percent per year and continuing to grow. Production could not begin to keep pace. Shortages and inflation were inevitable, unless some measures were used to check spending. President Johnson opposed any tax

increase, however; nor would he consider suspending the War on Poverty programs that were part of his Great Society vision. Therefore, spending continued to race along at an accelerating rate.

3. Johnson felt such an increase would be unpopular, both in Congress and with the U.S. people. He believed, probably correctly, that such an increase would be viewed by the U.S. public strictly as government's way to fund an unpopular war that was costing the country from $2 to $3 billion monthly. Further, Johnson felt highly protective of his War on Poverty programs; if anything, he wanted to enhance spending, not cut it. In addition, inflation had been relatively low during the early 1960s; despite the warnings of economists, few people as yet had begun to take the threat of inflation with great seriousness.

4. By 1967, inflation had become severe enough that it was being felt everywhere. Shortages were occurring. Clearly, something had to be done. Johnson had held off as long as he reasonably could, and still he did not favor a large tax increase. He compromised with a one-year surtax signed into law in 1968. It was the right idea, but it was much too slight a measure to effectively anchor the full-sail economy of the late 1960s. Government spending splurged ahead, along with consumer demand, and the path was cleared for demand-pull inflation that would run unchecked for years.

5. Nixon, like Johnson, felt reluctant to impose a tax increase. He feared an economic slowdown and was basically a conservative who opposed increasing the size and role of government through taxation. He did, however, attempt two other measures. First, he approved a restriction of the money supply, the amount of money printed. At first, this seemed to have little effect, but as it took hold, unemployment went up and public protest went up with it. Some economists called for a measure that had been used successfully in wartime to curb inflation but never before in peacetime, that was to freeze wages and prices. Nixon responded with a 90-day price and wage freeze. It did not work. People simply did not alter their expectations about inflation; they just suspended them for a bit. Businesses continued to plan for price increases, and workers continued to seek wage hikes in anticipation of the inflation-as-usual economics they expected to resume after the freeze.

6. Keynesian economics assumes an economy in which production can grow to meet demand. During Johnson's administration and since, demand grows when production is already at capacity—already within the vertical range of the supply curve. As demand goes up, shortages occur because there is no increase in output. Prices rise, inflation mounts, and unemployment remains a problem because there are no more jobs despite the increased demand. In the world of Keynesian economics, there are logical strategies for combating inflation or unemployment, and somewhere it is expected that there will be a balance, a point of equilibrium GNP where both inflation and unemployment exist, if not at zero, at tolerable levels. We are learning that it simply does not work like that. Often we must live with a trade-off in which we cannot fight one economic problem without making the other worse. Further, we are also learning that unemployment and inflation can rise together, giving us stagflation, or even fall together.

Multiple Choice

1. d   Text, 167–168.
2. d   Text, 167.
3. a   Text, 168–169.
4. b   Text, 171.
5. a   Text, 168.
6. c   Text, 169.
7. c   Text, 167.
8. d   Text, 171.
9. a   Text, 174–179.
10. a   Text, 174–179.

True-False

1. True   Text, 169.
2. False   Text, 171–174.
3. False   Text, 171.
4. False   Video; Text, 174.
5. False   Text, 174–175.
6. True   Text, 175–179.
7. True   Video; Text, 176.
8. True   Text, 175.
9. True   Video.
10. False   Video.

Discussion Questions

1. President Carter's focus on productivity suggests that he felt inflation would have been diminished had productivity increased and the aggregate supply curve shifted out to the right. With poor productivity in the economy, this shift did not occur. By itself, this would not have resulted in increasing the level of inflation: If inflation increased during the year, either demand pressures must have caused the aggregate demand curve to shift to the right or supply pressures caused the aggregate supply curve to shift to the left. Without increases in productivity, either of these changes would have resulted in worsening inflation.

2. Full employment does not imply that every individual can work at whatever wage rate he or she deems acceptable. If the wage rate demanded by an individual or a group of individuals is greater than the market-determined wage rate, then that group of individuals do not find employment. Wage pressures are inflationary only if the level of output in the economy is at full employment and the aggregate demand curve shifts to the right.

3. This quote deserves two comments. First, there are people who do benefit from inflation: speculators, who are lucky in their speculations, and borrowers both benefit from inflation. Second, the quote overlooks the fact that inflation may be extremely difficult to control in an economy. If this were not the case, then it would be a simple matter to have the economy stay at full employment with no change in the price level.

4. President Reagan believed that focusing on the impact fiscal policy had on aggregate demand was inflationary. He thought some of these policies also had a negative impact on aggregate supply that aggravated the inflationary problem. He wanted to turn attention away from aggregate demand and focus on aggregate supply. That is why his tax cut and deregulation policies focused on the impact they would have on encouraging output. His policies were called *supply-side economics.*

5. Freund suggests policies that aim to curb both aggregate demand (i.e., shift aggregate demand back toward the left) and stimulate aggregate supply (i.e., shift aggregate supply to the right). His suggestions with regard to resources,

productivity, and production are directed toward the aggregate supply curve side of the model, whereas his reference to intense demand pressures is directed toward the demand side of the model. Increased taxes and reductions in government spending could be implemented to slow down the inflation in Israel. In addition, attention should be paid to the money supply and its growth rate because the experience in Germany after World War I provides evidence that excessive money supply growth can result in runaway inflation.

Problem Set

1. a. His assets are now worth $95,000, so his net worth is $60,000.
   b. $40,000.
   c. He has benefited.

2. a. $57 million.
   b. $66.58 million.
   c. No, because the amount consumed of each commodity is not held constant.
   d. Because the price of each commodity is not weighted by the amount of the commodity consumed. Also, the result depends on the units to which the prices pertain. For example, if the price of commodity Y pertains to an ounce, not a pound, the result differs.
   e. ($62.20 million/$57 million) × 100 = 109.1. This index does not have the limitations cited in part d.

3. 7 percent. 6 percent.

4.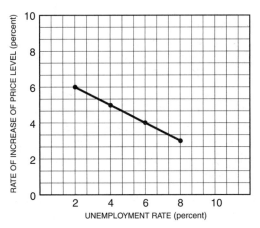

Audio/Text Questions

1. Inflation tends to reduce the level of output (and therefore the level of consumption) of the entire economy because

   a. It encourages speculation and discourages investment in plant and equipment that is useful for society in the long run.

b. It discourages savings.
   c. As inflation worsens, the risk of a massive disruption of production grows.

2. If workers get a 5 percent wage increase and their output per hour increases 5 percent, there is no need for the firm to raise prices, since the unit labor cost has not changed. But, if productivity rises only 1 percent when workers get a 5 percent raise, the firm would have to increase prices to try to cover the greater costs.

3. During the late 1950s and 1960s there was a close relationship between the rate of inflation and the rate of unemployment. This relationship traced out a curve called the *modified Phillips curve*. If a society wanted to reduce the unemployment rate from 6 to 4 percent, for example, it could do so by stimulative monetary and fiscal policies, but it would have to realize that inflation would rise about 2 percentage points as a result. This relationship no longer seems to hold, but at the time, it was thought that every society could manage its policies in a way to choose the combination of unemployment and inflation it could live with.

4. In retrospect, it is obvious that fiscal and monetary policies stimulated the economy so much that the unemployment rate fell below the full-employment unemployment rate. There was an inflationary gap (intended spending at stable prices was greater than the value of goods and services that could be produced), and those years of low unemployment saw inflation become a severe problem in the United States.

5. Inflation reduces the real purchasing power of peoples' incomes just as a tax does, but it does so in a way that is not controlled by legislatures. Some people suffer more by inflation than others, and therefore have a higher "tax" burden than others. The costs of inflation are not distributed according to society's goals but in a haphazard way.

LESSON 8. THE BANKING SYSTEM: WHY MUST IT BE PROTECTED?

INTRODUCTION

When you think of banking, what do you picture? Executives in gray flannel suits sitting behind mahogany desks totaling up assets and making decisions about loans?

Think of the money you may have right now in your pocket or wallet. Where did it come from? How is its value determined? In what other forms does money exist?

In answering these and a host of other questions, we discover that banking is really a dynamic process of creating, defining, and manipulating money, a process that helps keep our economy thriving. We also see how the banking system has changed dramatically over the past hundred years: How it has become very much a business in its own right and how its sophisticated efficiency in keeping money flowing means both convenience and increased security for U.S. consumers.

What You Should Learn

By the end of this lesson, you should be prepared to perform the following tasks related to banking:

1. Define *money* in terms of the three primary purposes it serves.
2. Distinguish between the *money supply, narrowly defined (M1), and the money supply, broadly defined (M2)*.
3. Describe at least three forms in which money exists in our society.
4. Explain what is meant by *demand deposits* and *checkable accounts*.
5. Identify the two primary functions of commercial banks.
6. Identify and explain three guiding principles that govern the way banks today operate.
7. Define *fractional-reserve banking* and explain how it evolved in this country.
8. List the primary functions of the Federal Reserve System.

9. Define *legal reserve requirements* and explain why they exist.

10. Explain how and why the role of government in monitoring the banking system has been changing during the past hundred years.

11. Explain the process by which banks create money.

KEY TERMS

money
currency
fiat money
demand deposits
checkable accounts
NOW accounts
money supply, narrowly defined (M1)
money supply, broadly defined (M2)
medium of exchange
barter
standard of value
store of value
secondary reserves
Federal Reserve System
balance sheet

assets
liabilities
net worth
fractional-reserve banking
legal reserve requirements
excess reserves
FDIC
savings
time deposits
commercial banks
savings and loan associations

VIDEO

Watch

Economics U$A Program 8, "The Banking System; Why Must It Be Protected?"

Illustrative Events

The failure of New York City's Knickerbocker Bank and the ensuing panic of 1907, with economic historian Robert Sobel. Richard Gill explains fractional reserve banking.

The banking panic of 1930 to 1933 and how it led to Franklin Roosevelt's bank holiday, featuring economist Merritt Sherman, secretary of the Board of Governors of the Federal Reserve in the 1930s.

After Viewing

Answer the following questions:

1. What was the *main* reason behind the failure of the Knickerbocker Trust in 1907?

2. What important decisions relating to the future of U.S. banking resulted from the panic of 1907?

3. How did multiple credit contraction contribute to economic slowdown during the 1930s?

4. What was the purpose of the national banking holiday declared by President Franklin Roosevelt, and what was the impact of this decision?

Read

Read Chapter 8, "Money and the Banking System," pages 187–207 and 208–210 in your text. After completing your reading, try the Self-Quiz.

SELF-QUIZ

Multiple Choice

1. Which of the following is probably the *best* definition of money? Money is

    a. any form of coin or currency that is backed by gold or some other valuable commodity.
    b. anything a person will trade for goods or services on the open market.
    c. anything that can be turned readily into cash.
    d. any medium of exchange that acts as a standard of value and a store of value.

2. Which of the following *best* describes the difference between M1 and M2?

    a. There is no real difference; they are interchangeable.
    b. M1 can be more readily spent on the open market.
    c. M2 exists primarily in the form of cash.
    d. M1 includes real estate, stocks, and other long-term holdings.

3. More than any other factor, what really gives money its value is the fact that it

    a. is backed by gold reserves.
    b. will buy things.
    c. is sanctioned by the Federal Reserve Board.
    d. can be readily converted to silver.

4. Demand deposits are those deposits that

    a. are subject to payment on demand.

b. draw interest from the bank.
   c. are considered a bank's assets.
   d. are not accessible by check.

5. Which of the following is *not* part of the money supply narrowly defined (M1)?

   a. Coins and currency
   b. Checking accounts
   c. Traveler's checks
   d. Credit and balances

6. It is sometimes hard to draw the line between money and nonmoney. The *main* reason for this is that

   a. no one has ever really defined what money is.
   b. money takes different forms in different societies.
   c. many valuable assets have some of the functional characteristics of money.
   d. what serves as money one day may well have little value the next.

7. Which of the following *best* describes the current banking system in the United States?

   a. We have basically one bank with many branches controlled by the Federal Reserve.
   b. We have thousands of banks that operate within federal guidelines but set their own policies.
   c. We have several hundred different banks, most of which have a number of branches.
   d. Banks generally tend to start up and fail at such a rapid rate that no one really knows how many there are.

8. In general, how much cash do most banks keep on hand?

   a. Only a small fraction of the amount needed to match liabilities
   b. About half the amount needed to match liabilities
   c. An amount about equal to their liabilities
   d. An amount well in excess of their liabilities

9. Fractional-reserve banking works effectively *mainly* because

   a. it is highly profitable.
   b. it is endorsed by the Federal Reserve.
   c. not all depositors withdraw their money at once.
   d. it is the only system that does not depend on creation of "new" money.

10. Banks can create money by

    a. calling in overdue loans.
    b. increasing their net worth.
    c. charging more for their services.
    d. loaning a portion of their excess reserves.

True-False

____ 1. The money supply, narrowly defined, is composed of coins, currency, demand deposits, and other checkable deposits.

____ 2. Most of our money supply is in coin and paper currency.

____ 3. Early banks held reserves equal to their deposits, but modern banks need only a small fraction of their deposits in cash to handle withdrawals.

____ 4. To control the money supply, the Federal Reserve System requires every commercial bank and every thrift institution with checkable deposits to hold a certain percentage of their deposits as reserves.

____ 5. A balance sheet tallies a bank's assets (primarily deposits) and liabilities (primarily cash and loans).

____ 6. The banking system itself has the authority, without limitation, to expand the amount of money in circulation at any given time by making loans.

____ 7. To reduce the risk of bank failure and consumer risk, the Federal Deposit Insurance Corporation (FDIC) insures the deposits of all banks.

____ 8. The Federal Reserve acts as a lender of last resort, loaning money to banks that are basically sound but temporarily in need of shoring up.

____ 9. Banks earn money by making loans and investments.

____ 10. The safeguards initiated by various government agencies since the Great Depression make it impossible for a bank to fail.

Discussion Questions

1. "Deposits at the Main Line Savings and Loan are just as much money as deposits at the Philadelphia National Bank, and short-term obligations of the U.S. Treasury are just as much money as either of the others." Do you agree?

2. Why does the Federal Reserve impose legal reserve requirements? Are the banks safer than they were a hundred years ago? Why or why not?

3. In reality the reserve requirement on time deposits is lower than the reserve requirement on demand deposits. What, then, would be the impact on the money supply if $1,000 were transferred from a savings account to a checking account? From a checking account to a savings account?

4. Suppose that someone receives $10,000 in newly printed currency and deposits it in a bank.
    a. Can this bank create $50,000 of additional new money if the legal reserve requirement is 16.67 percent?
    b. Can this bank create $8,333 in new money? If so, how?
    c. Can the banking system as a whole create $50,000 of additional new money?

5. a. Suppose that the legally required ratio of reserves to deposits is 20 percent. If there are no excess reserves and the total reserves of the banking system are reduced by $5 billion, what is the effect on demand deposits?
   b. If the legal reserve requirement is 20 percent, what effect would currency withdrawals on excess reserves have on the amount of demand deposits the banks can support?

Problem Set

1. The following data come from the 2004 *Economic Report of the President* (amounts in billions of dollars):

Year	M1	M2	Nominal GDP
1969	203.9	587.9	984.6
1974	274.0	901.9	1500.0
1979	381.4	1473.3	2563.3
1984	551.2	2309.6	3933.2
1989	792.1	3157.4	5484.4
1994	1149.9	3496.2	7072.2
1999	1121.5	4650.2	9268.4
2004	1263.0	6010.9	10987.9

   When M2 is used rather than M1, is the ratio of nominal GDP to the money supply more stable over time?

2. Suppose that the balance sheet of Crooked Arrow National Bank (in millions of dollars) is currently as follows:

Assets		Liabilities and net worth	
Reserves	0.5	Demand deposits	2.5
Loans and securities	3.0	Net worth	1.0

   a. Suppose that the Federal Reserve reduces the reserve requirement from 20 to 15 percent while the bank's balance sheet is as shown. After the reduction, will the bank have excess reserves? If so, how much?
   b. Suppose that the Federal Reserve increases the reserve requirement from 20 to 25 percent while the bank's balance sheet is as shown. After the increase, will the bank be short of the legally required reserves? If so, by how much?

3. Bank C lends $5,000 to a depositor, Mary Monroe, by crediting her checking account balance with a $5,000 deposit.

   a. What is the effect of this transaction on the bank's assets?
   b. What is the effect of this transaction on the nation's money supply (defined as M1)? What is its effect on M2?
   c. If Monroe transfers the $5,000 from her checking account to her savings account at the bank, what is the effect on M1? What is the effect on M2?

4. What is the effect on M1 of each of the following transactions (taken alone)?

   a. Mary Malone deposits $2,000 in currency in First Federal Savings and Loan.
   b. The Chase Manhattan Bank sells a $5,000 U.S. government bond to Merrill Lynch, a large stock brokerage firm, which pays Chase with a check.
   c. The Chase Manhattan Bank sells a $5,000 U.S. government bond to Mary Malone, who pays for the bond in currency, which Chase adds to the cash it holds.

5. Bank E has the following balance sheet (in millions of dollars):

Assets		Liabilities and net worth	
Cash	1	Demand deposits	29
Reserves at Fed	5	Net worth	1
Loans	10		
Securities	14		

All cash is held in the bank's vault and is part of its legal reserves. The item "Reserves at Fed" is the bank's legal reserve deposit at the Federal Reserve. Indicate the effect on reserves at the Fed for this bank for each of the following transactions (taken alone):

   a. Bank E increases its vault cash by $1,000 by obtaining this amount from the Fed. Then it uses this $1,000 to cash 10 $100 checks of depositors.
   b. A depositor at Bank E writes a check for $10,000 on Bank E, which is deposited in Bank F and clears.
   c. A depositor at Bank F writes a check for $10,000 on Bank F, which is deposited in Bank E and clears.

LESSON REVIEW

If you had difficulty with the Self-Quiz or would like additional assistance, read the following lesson review. It should reinforce and help you understand the content presented in this lesson.

What Is Money?

This question seems obvious. Isn't money dollar bills, the change in our pockets, traveler's checks, or bank checks? Yes, it can take all these forms in our society, and many others as well. We cannot realistically define money by its form at all. Anything generally acceptable as money can serve as money. For example, in other societies, precious rocks and metals, tea, salt, cattle, whales' teeth, and hundreds of other commodities of recognized value have served as money.

It makes more sense to define money by its function, and it serves three main functions:

1. *Money is a medium of exchange.* Money facilitates exchange. Say you are a painter. How troublesome and awkward it would be if, for instance, you wanted to buy a pair of shoes and had to find a shoe manufacturer who would trade its product for a few hours of your painting time. Not only would this be inefficient and inconvenient for you personally, it would also slow the entire economy to a crawl. Consider how many goods and services we purchase that do not originate in our home towns or states or even within this country. Without some recognized medium of exchange, much of what we purchase would never be accessible to us at all, and many producers would not have a sufficient market to keep a business alive.

2. *Money is a standard of value.* Money is a way of measuring how much various goods and services are worth. In a world without money, how would you decide how much of your painting time was equal in value to the shoes you wanted? Things are greatly simplified if you can determine that your time as a painter is worth $25 an hour and if the shoe manufacturer determines that it must have $50 for a pair of shoes to realize a profit. Now you have a solid basis for negotiation, and anyone who wants painting services or shoes knows the present market value of those things.

3. *Money is a store of value.* Money allows us the convenience of deferring purchases until we are ready. You need not lay down your paint brush and rush out to buy shoes. You can put the money in the bank if you want and save it for a month, or a year, or 50 years. This is a way of holding onto the established market value of whatever goods or services you sell for an indefinite period, until you are ready to make an exchange.

In summary, anything that is a medium of exchange, a standard of value, and a store of value is, regardless of its form or characteristics, defined as money.

The Money Supply, Narrowly Defined (M1)

The money supply, narrowly defined, includes those forms of money readily accessible and spendable: coins, currency, and checking accounts (also called *demand deposits*). A savings bond, for example, would not fall in this category because, even though it certainly has monetary value, you could not take it to the grocery store and spend it. You would have to first exchange it for some spendable form of money.

- *Coins.* Coins are a very small proportion (less than 5 percent) of the total money supply in the United States. It is easy to understand why, if you think of it for a moment, coins come in very small denominations. If you paid for everything in coins, you would actually have to haul them around in a wheelbarrow to have enough to buy what the average American consumes.

- *Currency.* Currency, or paper money, makes up a much larger percentage (about 45 percent) of our total money supply. Together, outstanding currency and coins total about $669.5 billion, on the basis of 2004 figures. The Federal Reserve System issues practically all our currency in the form of Federal Reserve notes. Before 1933, you could have exchanged this currency for a stipulated amount of gold. Such is no longer the case. All U.S. currency and coin is now *fiat* money, which means simply that it is money because the government and the people say so. Many people are troubled by the fact that our money is not backed by gold any longer. However, gold backing does not give money its value but *the willingness of people to accept it as a medium of exchange*. To ensure this acceptability, the government must limit the quantity of money; and this, as we shall see, is one important role of the Federal Reserve System.

- *Demand deposits and other checkable deposits*. Demand deposits are bank deposits subject to payment on demand, in other words, checking accounts. Demand deposits constitute a much larger portion of the total money supply (about 55 percent) than either coins or currency. You may not be accustomed to thinking of your checking account—if you have one—as money. But, if you think about it, you can pay for most things with a check just as easily as with cash. And in fact, Americans buy much more with checks than they do with cash; consider, for instance, how many bills are paid through the mail in this way. About 90 percent of the transactions in this country are carried out through checkable deposits. Other checkable deposits (that is, those accessible by check) include NOW accounts: negotiable order of withdrawal accounts, or interest-bearing checking accounts. Such accounts were approved for federally chartered thrift institutions by Congress in 1980. Numerous savings and loan associations, mutual savings banks, and credit unions now provide interest-bearing accounts against which checks can be drawn. Therefore, the distinction between so-called checking accounts and savings accounts is a bit fuzzy.

- *The growth of the money supply (M1)*. The money supply is far from constant. The narrowly defined money supply (coins, currency, and checkable deposits) has grown from about $100 billion in 1960 to about $1,250 billion in 2004, but the year-to-year rate of growth has fluctuated.

The Money Supply, Broadly Defined (M2)

The money supply, broadly defined, includes savings, small time deposits (under $100,000), money market mutual fund balances, and money market deposit accounts, as well as coins, currency, demand deposits, and other checkable deposits. The money supply narrowly defined is sometimes termed M1, while the money supply broadly defined is often termed M2.

Why are savings accounts excluded from M1 but not M2? Certainly, if you had a savings account, you could go down to the bank and withdraw some money to spend on a new dishwasher or lawnmower. But you could not transform your savings into cash quite as readily as if you were drawing on your checking account. The ease and speed with which you can transfer an asset into readily spendable cash is the key criterion in determining whether a resource is rightly categorized as narrowly or broadly defined money.

All economists do not agree about what is or is not money under the broad definition because so many assets have some of the characteristics of money. It is not necessary for our purposes to resolve this argument but only to realize that the line between money and nonmoney is not one easily drawn.

Commercial Banks in the United States

Over 10,000 commercial banks exist in the United States. This situation is in direct contrast with that in England and many other countries, where there are only a handful of banks with many branches. Americans traditionally have been suspicious of big, powerful bankers; independence and competition within the banking network keep the power divided.

Generally, banks (together with other financial institutions like savings and loan associations) serve as intermediaries between savers and borrowers. They supply investors with money received from savers, and this process of converting savings into consumption, investment, and public spending—a process that in most cases would never occur without the intervention of the banks—is critical in determining GDP.

Commercial banks serve two important functions:

1. They hold demand deposits and allow checks to be drawn on these deposits.
2. They lend money to government industrialists, merchants, homeowners, and other individuals and firms.

How Banks Operate

Because of the way our banking system evolved, banks operate relatively autonomously (although often cooperatively), so regulations and procedures differ greatly from one to the other. Nevertheless, the following three principles serve as general guidelines of operation:

1. *Banks generally make loans to both firms and individuals and invest in securities, particularly government bonds (in effect IOUs of federal, state, and local governments).* Banks and businesses often have a long-term, close relationship. The bank receives deposits from the business over a long period of time and, in return, provides the business with loans from time to time to support repair or expansion projects. The relationship between a bank and an individual consumer tends to be more casual. In addition to dealing with businesses and individuals, banks buy large quantities of federal, state, and local government bonds.

2. *Banks operate to make a profit.* Although banks charge for some services, this is not the way they make profits. They earn a profit by making loans and investments that yield a higher rate of interest than they must pay their depositors. Commercial banks pay interest on some deposits, not all.

3. *Banks must constantly balance their wish for high returns on loans and investments against the requirement that such loans and investments be safe and liquid.* High profits are highly desirable, of course. But a bank that consistently invests in risky ventures will not remain solvent long because too many loans go unpaid.

Confidence in the Banks

Until about 70 years ago, bank failure was common. Even during the 1920s, banks failed at a rate of more than one a day. From 1929 to 1933, one-third of all banks failed. Since then, however, public confidence has grown considerably, although lots of problems remain. In the 1980s, huge numbers of savings and loan associations and even a few banks failed, but there was no banking run or panic. This is largely attributable to the fact that the federal government insures most deposits up to $100,000.

The Balance Sheet of an Individual Bank

The following table shows the balance sheet of one of the nation's largest commercial banks, the Bank of America, as of 2003:

Assets		Liabilities and net worth	
Cash	27.0	Deposits	414.1
Securities	241.8	Other liabilities	274.4
Loans	365.3	Net worth	47.9
Other assets	102.3		
Total	736.4	Total	736.4

(*Source:* Bank of America, Annual Report. 2003, in millions.)

On the left-hand side of the balance sheet are the assets:

- Cash
- Securities
- Loans
- Other assets

Note that these assets total $736.4 billion.

On the right-hand side of the balance sheet are the liabilities:

- Deposits
- Other liabilities

Note that these liabilities total $688.5 billion.

The difference between assets and liabilities ($736.4 billion minus $688.5 billion) is the *net worth* of the bank: $47.9 billion. *Net worth* is also defined as the value of the claims the firm's owners have against the firm's assets.

Note that deposits are listed as liabilities. Why? Because the bank owes its depositors the amount of money in their deposits and must be prepared at any time to pay this money out if it is requested. Fortunately for the bank, the odds that all the deposit money is requested at the same time are very slight indeed, and recognition of this low probability led to a revolutionary approach to banking in this country, as we shall see shortly.

Cash

Note that the cash amount held by the bank ($27.0 billion) is far less than the value of the deposits ($414.1 billion). In other words, the cash reserves represent just a fraction of the value of deposits. This is a workable system because, on any given day, certain customers deposit money while others withdraw and most do neither. Therefore, banks have learned from experience that they need not keep enough cash on hand to cover all deposits at all times. This realization provided the basis for the fractional-reserve banking system we know today.

Fractional-Reserve Banking

Fractional-reserve banking refers to the practice of keeping on hand only a fraction of the cash reserves required to meet liabilities; in other words, a fraction of the amount owed depositors. How did this practice come about?

Perhaps early bankers kept reserves equal to the amounts they owed depositors; in effect, they were storehouses for gold. Gradually, though, it became clear that this approach was unnecessary. Not everyone was making withdrawals every day. Surely there would be a better way to use the money, say, for loans or investments. And, in fact, banks that tried this approach found it worked very well, and they could justify it with the following arguments:

1. None of the depositors lost money, for withdrawals could still be made at any time by those depositors who needed cash.

2. The interest earned by the bank on loans made it possible to charge depositors less for storing their gold/money—and eventually would make it possible to pay them a rate of interest.

3. Putting the money to work instead of merely storing it benefited the economy as a whole.

Legal Reserve Requirements

History has shown us that the fractional-reserve banking approach is sound and workable and that the three arguments advanced in the preceding paragraph hold up. However, it might be dangerous to allow banks to set their own "fractions," that is, to determine what percentage of reserves they should be required to hold.

The Federal Reserve System (commonly called the *Fed*) requires every commercial bank (whether or not it is a member of the system) to hold a certain percentage of its deposits as reserves. In extraordinary circumstances, the Fed can set the percentage at any level it deems necessary for a period of 180 days.

Suppose that the Fed has determined that the average bank should hold about $1 in reserves for every $6 of demand deposits (about 16.67 percent). Not all the reserves are held as cash right on the bank's premises. Most are held in the form of deposits by banks at the Federal Reserve. Either way, the cash reserves are equal to the amount entered under "Cash" on the bank's balance sheet.

What Is the Federal Reserve System?

It is our nation's central bank. Its most important functions are as follows:

> Control the quantity of money.
>
> Serve as a lender of last resort.
>
> Serve as fiscal agent for the United States and many foreign governments.
>
> Provide facilities for the collection of checks.
>
> Supply the public with currency.
>
> Supervise the operation of commercial banks.

Why does the Fed impose legal reserve requirements? It might seem that its main reason would be to keep banks safe. This is part of the reason but not the most important one. *The most important reason for legal reserve requirements is to control the money supply.*

Bank Safety

Although legal reserve requirements are imposed primarily to control the money supply, they *do,* particularly from the depositor's standpoint, contribute to the perception of bank safety. These regulations are not sufficient in themselves, however. What other factors are important?

- *Bank Management.* Banks should be circumspect about making loans and investments. Also, a bank must be prepared to meet a temporary upswing in withdrawals. Even though it is unlikely that all depositors want their money at once, there is always a chance that a sizable proportion do. How does the bank prepare for this? One way is by investing in securities that are readily turned into cash—short-term government securities, for instance, that vary only slightly in price day to day. Such securities may be termed *secondary reserves.*

- *The Role of Government.* The most important reason why banks are safer today than 80 years ago is that the banking system is supported by the power of government. What this means is that the government—including the Federal Deposit Insurance Corporation (FDIC), the Federal Reserve, and other public agencies—virtually guarantees the U.S. public that its deposits will be safe and insured. The FDIC insures accounts of depositors in nearly all banks up to $100,000. In addition, the government sends bank examiners to review balance sheets and banking practices and ensure that operating banks are solvent. Although banks are generally considered safe, the incidences of bank failure in the 1980s raised new questions. In the early 1990s, there were persistent rumors that many huge New York banks, as well as a host of smaller banks elsewhere, were in serious financial trouble.

How Banks Create Money

The notion of banks creating money may sound mysterious, but in fact, it is a simple and logical process that depends on two principles:

1. Money kept in circulation benefits the economy more than money simply stored.
2. Not all consumers use money in the same way at the same time; in other words, some spend, while others save or invest.

Consider a specific example. Bank A receives a deposit of $10,000 from R. Black. Suppose the legal reserve ratio is 20 percent. In other words, $1 of every $5 must be held in cash reserves to meet the legal requirement. This means that bank A must hold onto 20 percent of the $10,000, or $2,000, as legal reserves. But what about the other $8,000? This extra $8,000 (above the amount required for legal reserves) is known as *excess reserves*. Bank A could hold onto that too, but if it is going to make a profit, it would be better off to invest or loan that money.

Suppose that bank A decides to loan the $8,000 to J. Smith. Smith puts the money in a checking account at bank A, writes a check for the whole amount, and delivers the check to P. Brown in exchange for a new automobile. Brown, in turn, deposits the whole $8,000 in bank B.

What has happened up to this point? Bank A's deposits have gone up by $10,000 and Bank B's deposits by $8,000. (Note that bank A's deposits at one point were increased by $18,000 but that the immediate withdrawal of the $8,000 by check diminished this amount.) Black still has her deposit of $10,000; it says so right in her passbook savings ledger. But Brown also has $8,000 on account at bank B. In other words, bank A "created" $8,000 in new money.

Now what? Bank B, like bank A, could hold on to the money or could use a portion of it to support loans or investments. Again, the required reserve ratio is 20 percent, or 1 to 5. Therefore, bank B must hold onto $1,600 of the $8,000 deposit but can use $6,400 for loans and investments. Bank B subsequently approves a loan of $6,400 to Q. Jones, who uses the money to finance a course on Innovative Banking at High Rollers College. High Rollers, in turn, deposits the $6,400 in bank C, . . . , and so it goes.

What Is the Ultimate Impact on the Economy?

How long can this process of creating money continue, and how big an increase in the money supply can we expect as a consequence of the original $8,000 in excess reserves (from the $10,000 deposited by Black). Clearly the process can be a good deal more complex than our simple scenario indicates, and it could prove difficult indeed to track every transaction with every investor at every bank. Fortunately, we do not need to do that. We can compute the total increase in the money supply using a simple formula:

$$\frac{\text{Excess reserves}}{\text{required ratio of reserves to deposits}} = \text{total increase in the money supply.}$$

In our example, the excess reserves from the original $10,000 deposit totaled $8,000. If we divide this figure by the required ratio of reserves to deposits (1/5), the result is

$$\frac{\$8,000}{1/5} = \$8,000 \times 5 \text{ (the reciprocal of the ratio 1/5)}$$

$$= \$40,000, \text{ the total increase in the money supply.}$$

In other words, given the required ratio of 20 percent, or 1 to 5, the original $10,000 deposit can ultimately increase the money supply by $40,000. (When we calculate the total increase in the money supply, we assume all transactions are carried out within the banking system.)

What about a Decrease?

Reserves can be decreased in essentially the same way. The rule is this:

Given a deficiency in reserves of a certain amount, the banking system as a whole reduces demand deposits by an amount equal to the deficiency in reserves multiplied by the reciprocal of the required ratio of reserves to deposits.

So, say that our banking system has a deficiency of $8,000, instead of excess reserves in that amount. We use the same formula to determine the amount by which the money supply decreases:

$$\frac{\$8,000}{1/5} = \$8,000 \times 5$$

$$= \$40,000\text{, the total decrease in the money supply.}$$

EXTENDED LEARNING

This section of the study guide is specifically designed for the two-semester student.

AUDIO

Before Listening

Read Exploring Further of Chapter 8, pages 207–208 in your text.

Next

Listen to the audiotape that accompanies Lesson 8.

After Listening

Answer the following questions:

1. Why is it so difficult to determine exactly what to count when calculating the nation's money supply?

2. Why are deposits in a bank called a *liability* and loans called an *asset*?
3. How is the net worth of a bank determined and what might cause the net worth to change from one year to the next?
4. How do commercial banks make a profit? Do they make a profit by "creating" money?
5. What makes banks so vulnerable to runs? Why is a lender of last resort or insurance necessary?

ADDITIONAL READINGS

Chandler, Lester V. *The Economics of Money and Banking,* 6th ed. New York: Harper & Row, 1973.

> Chapter 7, "Bank Expansion and Contraction," details how the loan activity of the banking system can cause the money supply to expand or contract independent of Federal Reserve policies. Moderately difficult mathematics, no graphs.

Dince, Robert R. "Penn Square, Upstream Lending, and the Bank Examination Dilemma." *Bankers Magazine* 165 (November–December 1982). In *Commercial Banking*, edited by John R. Brick, 121–128. Haslett, MI: Systems Publications, 1984.

> The failure of the Penn Square Bank is used as an example of how difficult it is for regulators to rate the solvency of a bank given new banking practices. No mathematics or graphs.

Federal Reserve Bank of Chicago. "The Depository Institutions Deregulation and Monetary Control Act of 1980." In *Commercial Banking*, edited by John R. Brick, 17–38. Haslett, MI: Systems Publications, 1984.

> This article explains the reasons for the legislation that reduces the level of regulation of U.S. financial institutions, and what the various provisions of the act imply for interest rates, monetary control, and institutional behavior. No mathematics or graphs.

Haslem, John A., and George H. Hempel. "Commercial Banking as a Business." In *Financial Institutions and Markets,* 2d ed., edited by Murray E. Polakoff et al., 63–80. Boston: Houghton Mifflin Company, 1981.

> Describes the functions of a commercial bank, how a bank makes its profits, and the risk-reward trade-off of banking. No mathematics or graphs.

Nadler, Paul S. *Commercial Banking in the Economy,* 4th ed. New York: Random House, 1986.

> Chapter 2 covers the functions of commercial banks, their balance sheets, how they are affected by regulations, and the money creation process. Chapter 3 details the sources and uses of bank funds, and discusses how banks have

managed to increase their capitalization without reducing the rate of return to stockholders. Simple mathematics, no graphs.

ANSWER KEY

Video Questions

1. Several factors contributed to the collapse of the Knickerbocker. First, the Knickerbocker's president, Charles Barney, may have been guilty of bad management. Second, it could be plausibly argued that, since J. P. Morgan ultimately saved the bank anyway, earlier interference on his part might have prevented the general run on funds that eventually turned into the panic of 1907. But more than anything else, what really contributed to the downfall of the Knickerbocker was lack of faith among depositors. As soon as they feared they would not see their money again, they panicked. The inherent weakness in the fractional-reserve banking approach is that it cannot support the withdrawal of funds by all depositors at once. So long as people retain their faith in the banking system, and this mass withdrawal does not occur, the system not only remains solvent but actually functions to depositors' benefit. Therefore, it is in their best interests *not* to panic. But it would have been difficult indeed to persuade Knickerbocker depositors with such reasoning.

2. Bankers faced two important decisions: First, did they want the fractional-reserve system to continue? Second, did they want the power to save banks to remain in the hands of individual investors like J. P. Morgan? The answers to these two questions would be different.

    Despite its inherent problems, bankers certainly did want the fractional-reserve system to survive. Without such a system, banks could not realize a profit unless they charged depositors exorbitant sums for holding their money and providing other services. Clearly, this would be to no one's benefit, including that of the economy as a whole. So long as the panics and rushes on withdrawals could be prevented, the fractional-reserve system could work very well indeed.

    Bankers and business executives alike agreed, however, that they did not want the power to save failing banks to rest on the whims of investors like J. P. Morgan who might act to protect their own interests (as Morgan partly did). They accepted the need for a central bank—what was to become the Federal Reserve—to offer assistance to banks that were generally solvent but experiencing temporary problems and monitor the system as a whole.

3. During the prosperous 1920s, the banks generally had become too liberal in their loan policies, funding projects that in less prosperous times would likely not have received support. When the stock market crashed, the banks recognized their perilous position and changed policy drastically. Loans were no longer granted to new customers. Businesses were unable to pay back the loans they

already received, and many failed. As fewer loans were repaid, banks pulled back even further, struggling to build or maintain reserves. Recall that, as banks build reserves and decline to loan money, they can contract the money supply in much the same way that they create money in good times. In fact, the total money supply, including checking accounts, shrank drastically between 1929 and 1933.

4. Franklin Roosevelt was convinced that the banking system could succeed through proper management, and he wanted to create a period in which the whole system, bank by bank, would be reviewed by experts. The idea was that those banks operating with appropriate procedures would be granted a license to reopen. This policy, Roosevelt rightly reasoned, would give the U.S. people faith that their banks were being run correctly. He further promised to continue this monitoring procedure with tougher regulatory standards imposed by the federal government, ensuring that banks allowed to reopen would be able to remain open. In addition, he initiated legislation that created the Federal Deposit Insurance Corporation to guarantee each customer's account up to $10,000, an amount that has since been expanded considerably. Roosevelt's action was a huge success. He did indeed—as he hoped—increase the people's faith in the banking system. And further, he set a precedent for ensuring better bank management and providing federal support for the banking system as a whole.

Multiple Choice

1. d   Text, 187–189.
2. b   Text, 189–192.
3. b   Text, 187–188.
4. a   Text, 190.
5. d   Text, 189–191.
6. c   Text, 192.
7. b   Text, 192.
8. a   Text, 196.
9. c   Text, 196.
10. d Text, 202.

True-False

1. True   Text, 189–191.
2. False   Text, 189–190.
3. True   Text, 197.
4. True   Text, 198.
5. False   Text, 194–196.
6. False   Video; Text, 198–199.
7. False   Text, 201.
8. True   Video.
9. True   Text, 193.
10. False Text, 199.

Discussion Questions

1. No. The deposits at the Main Line Savings and Loan and the deposits at the Philadelphia National Bank, provided they are checkable deposits, are money in the narrowly defined, M1, sense. The short-term obligations of the U.S. Treasury would not be included in M1 or in M2 because they could not easily be used to make purchases of goods and services.

2. The Federal Reserve imposes legal reserve requirements for two reasons: (1) to control the money supply and (2) to promote financial soundness in the banking system. The existence of both the Federal Reserve System and federally insured deposits has led to greater bank safety. However, it is worthwhile to note that the catastrophic bank panic of the 1930s occurred even though the Federal Reserve System was created to deal with precisely this type of problem.

3. When funds are transferred from a savings account to a checking account, the money supply, as measured by M2, is lowered because the reserve requirement is greater for the checking account than the savings account. Conversely, when funds are transferred from a checking account to a savings account, the money supply, as measured by M2, increases because of the relatively smaller required reserve on the savings account.

4. a. If this bank is one of many in the banking system, then it can create money only equal to the excess reserves that result from the deposit of the $10,000 of newly printed money (i.e., $8,333). However, if the bank is the only bank in the banking system and all transactions remain in the bank, then this bank can create $50,000 of additional money.
   b. Yes. When it receives the $10,000 in newly printed money, it can place 16.67 percent of it in its required reserve account then loan out the remaining excess reserves. The required reserve account would have $1,667 in it, whereas the excess reserves to be loaned out would equal $8,333.
   c. Yes. If more than one bank is in the banking system, the first bank can loan out $8,333 to a customer who then deposits it in a second bank. This second bank puts 16.67 percent of this money into its required reserve account and loans out the rest of the money. This second loan is then deposited in a third financial institution, which places 16.67 percent of this deposit in its required reserve account and loans out the remainder. This process continues until $50,000 of additional new money is created.

5. a. The effect is a decrease in demand deposits of $25 billion.
   b. This reduces the amount of demand deposits that the bank can support because it reduces the amount of excess reserves the bank can loan out. This currency drain effectively reduces the money multiplier effect.

Problem Set

1. The ratio of nominal GDP to M1 and M2 is as follows:

Year	Based on M1	Based on M2
1969	4.83	1.68
1974	5.48	1.67
1979	6.73	1.74
1984	7.14	1.71
1989	6.93	1.74
1994	6.16	2.03
1999	8.27	2.00
2004	8.70	1.83

   The ratio is more stable when M2 is used than when M1 is used.

2. a. Yes. $125,000.
   b. Yes. $125,000.

3. a. They increase by $5,000.

b. Both M1 and M2 rise by $5,000.
   c. M1 decreases by $5,000, but there is no effect on M2.

4. a. No effect.
   b. M1 decreases by $5,000.
   c. M1 decreases by $5,000.

5. a. Reserves at Fed decrease by $1,000.
   b. Reserves at Fed decrease by $10,000.
   c. Reserves at Fed increase by $10,000.

Audio/Text Questions

1. Normally, one would count as money any asset that can be readily used in an economic transaction, such as coins, currency, and checking account deposits. But other assets might be used for transactions, such as other checkable deposits (NOW and ATS accounts), savings accounts, and small time deposits. The latter two categories are included in a broad definition of the money supply (M2) and not in the narrow definition (M1).

2. If an individual deposits her money in a bank, the bank essentially borrows from that individual, it owes him or her an amount equal to the deposit. Similarly, a loan is money owed to the bank, an asset the bank can draw on (i.e., call in) if it needs cash.

3. The net worth is equal to assets (cash, securities, loans, etc.) less liabilities (deposits and other debts of the bank). Part of the profits a bank earns can be retained by the bank every year, thereby increasing its net worth. If the bank fails to make a profit or loses money (most commonly because it has made some loans that default or made loans at interest rates that turn out to be too low), its net worth falls.

4. The two main categories of bank revenue are fees for services (such as arranging a loan or managing a trust) and interest or on the difference between the interest rate it pays out to depositors and the interest it charges its borrowers. Money is "created" by the banking system as a whole, and no bank profits in the process of money creation.

5. Banks have on hand only a small fraction of the money deposited with them. A large percentage of this money is loaned out to individuals and firms, so if many depositors suddenly demand their money back, the banks may not have it. The bank will try to call in its loans, but if many of its borrowers cannot raise cash quickly, the bank may have to close (at least temporarily). Insurance calms fears of losing money and prevents runs. A lender of last resort can provide the ready cash to temporarily tide over a bank in trouble.

LESSON 9. THE FEDERAL RESERVE: DOES MONEY MATTER?

INTRODUCTION

A May 21, 2004, headline in the *Wall Street Journal* stated, "Fed Shifts Focus from Job Growth to Rising Prices." The article began this way:

> *An unexpected quickening in the pace of price increases is challenging the Federal Reserve's plan to raise short-term interest rates only slowly from today's 46-year lows.*
>
> *Prices have risen faster in the past two months than Fed officials expected. That is at odds with their forecast that the combination of unemployment, unused industrial capacity and rapid growth in productivity would keep inflation very low for another year or two.*
>
> *That forecast has underpinned the Fed's expectation that when it starts to raise rates, probably in June, it will do so slowly.*
>
> *Fed officials, though not ready to abandon the forecast, acknowledge that their primary concern has shifted in the past few months from sluggish job growth to rising prices. If inflation moves higher in the coming months, they are likely to re-examine their public assessment, made earlier this month, that rates will rise "at a pace that is likely to be measured."*

A news story like this one should lead to these questions: How are decisions about interest rates made? Who makes these decisions? What do rising interest rates really mean for us as consumers?

When the monetary authorities "tighten" the money supply, it becomes harder to finance a new house, a car, or a college education. As fewer consumers borrow money and spend it to finance these and other items, GDP slows and perhaps even falls. In effect, the corresponding decrease in the money supply and the rising interest rates provide an important means for combating inflation.

As you may have concluded already, monetary policy and fiscal policy have similar goals: Both are aimed at promoting full employment without inflation. But they use different approaches. Whereas fiscal policy uses the power of government to spend and tax, monetary policy relies on the government's power over the money supply.

When recession seems imminent, the monetary authorities are likely to increase the supply of money; when the economy is speeding toward inflation, they are likely to reduce the money supply. How do they do it? To a considerable extent, the money supply is influenced by control of bank reserves. As we saw in earlier lessons, the banks can increase or contract the total money supply through lending (or holding onto) their excess reserves. Those reserves, in turn, are manipulated in large part by the Federal Reserve, a system of federally operated banks that function under the auspices of the Federal Reserve Board.

In this lesson, we learn how that board functions, what powers the Federal Reserve has over the money supply, and what strategies it uses to expand or contract that supply. We also examine the effects of monetary policy on our personal and national economic lives.

What You Should Learn

By the end of Lesson 9, you should be prepared to

1. Describe the effects of monetary policy on our national output and price level during low, moderate, and high levels of employment.
2. Describe the composition and the powers of the Federal Reserve System.
3. Name three strategies the Federal Reserve System uses to control the money supply, and identify the most important of these.
4. Define *open market operations*.
5. Describe the impact on the money supply resulting from the Federal Reserve buying or selling securities.
6. Explain the functions of the Federal Open Market Committee.
7. Describe the impact of an increase or decrease in *legal reserve requirements*.
8. Describe the impact of an increase or decrease in the discount rate.
9. Describe the relationship between monetary policy and the aggregate demand curve.

KEY TERMS

monetary policy
easing money/credit
tightening money/credit
Federal Reserve
Federal Reserve System
Federal Reserve Board
Federal Open Market Committee
fiscal policy
central banks

gold certificates
open market operations
discount rate
securities
U.S. government bonds
U.S. government notes
U.S. government bills
Federal Reserve Notes

VIDEO

Watch

Economics U$A Program 9, "The Federal Reserve: Does Money Matter?"

Illustrative Events

The establishment of the Federal Reserve, and its ill-fated attempt to stem the gold crisis of 1931 by raising the discount rate; featuring former members of the Federal Reserve Board, Merritt Sherman and Andrew Brimmer.

The Accord of 1951, resulting in the Federal Reserve's independence from the Treasury, with Andrew Brimmer.

The Fed's attempt to curtail inflation during the Johnson administration, which led to a severe credit crunch; with Brimmer and James Duesenberry, former member of the Council of Economic Advisers.

After Viewing

Answer the following questions:

1. How did the Federal Reserve Act come into being, and what was its primary function?

2. What action did the Fed take to protect member banks in 1931, and what was the overall effect of that action?

3. What did the Fed and the Treasury agree on in the Accord of 1951?

4. When the Fed decided to tighten the money supply in the mid-1960s, what were the immediate and long-term effects?

Read

Read Chapter 9, "The Federal Reserve and Monetary Policy," pages 211–224, and 228–229 in your text. After completing your reading, try the Self-Quiz.

SELF-QUIZ

Multiple Choice

1. Monetary policy is *best* defined as
    a. the government's use of its powers to spend and tax to control GDP.
    b. exercise of the central bank's control over the quantity of money.
    c. the power of the Fed to set ceilings on discount and interest rates.
    d. the tendency of the Fed to purchase or sell securities on the open market.

2. Most economists today would probably agree that monetary policy has

    a. a major impact on the economy.
    b. less impact generally than fiscal policy.
    c. a substantial impact on inflation, but little effect on unemployment.
    d. only a minor impact unless it is backed by support from Congress.

3. When the monetary authorities tighten credit, which of the following is *most likely* to occur?

    a. Inflation soars.
    b. Employment rises.
    c. The economy overheats.
    d. GDP falls.

4. The Fed has power to do all of the following *except*

    a. enact new legislation affecting fiscal policy.
    b. control the amount of reserves available to its member banks.
    c. buy or sell U.S. government bonds.
    d. increase or decrease the total money supply at will.

5. The *leading* role in establishing monetary policy is played by the Federal Reserve Board and the

    a. Congress.
    b. president.
    c. Federal Open Market Committee.
    d. 12 member banks.

6. It is the job of the Federal Open Market Committee to establish policy concerning the

    a. purchase and sale of government securities.
    b. discount rate.
    c. legal reserve limit.
    d. congressional control over the Fed.

7. All of the following entries would be assets *except* for

    a. gold certificates.
    b. reserves of member banks.
    c. securities (U.S. government bonds, notes, and bills).
    d. loans to commercial banks.

8. The *single most important* means by which the Fed can control bank reserves is through

    a. manipulation of the discount rate.
    b. influence over fiscal policy.
    c. purchase and sale of securities.
    d. influence over the legally required reserve rate.

9. Within broad limits, the Fed has the power to change legal reserve requirements whenever

   a. it wants to.
   b. the 12 member banks approve such a measure.
   c. Congress agrees to this step.
   d. the Federal Open Market Committee initiates such action.

10. The interest rate that the Fed charges member banks for loans is called the

    a. percentage rate.
    b. reserve rate.
    c. short-term market interest rate.
    d. discount rate.

True-False

_____ 1. Although the Federal Reserve System is responsible for regulating and controlling the money supply, it does not concern itself with inflation or the level of interest rates.

_____ 2. The Federal Reserve System coordinates all banking operations in the United States from a large central bank in Washington, DC.

_____ 3. Monetary policy and fiscal policy are aimed at many of the same goals but use different methods to promote them.

_____ 4. Although monetary policy is influenced by the Federal Reserve Board and the Federal Open Market Committee, the chief responsibility for the formulation of monetary policy lies with Congress and the Treasury.

_____ 5. One advantage of fiscal policy over monetary policy is the relatively short lag time between decision and enactment.

_____ 6. One of the most important tools of monetary policy is buying and selling government securities in the open market by the Federal Reserve.

_____ 7. When the Fed buys government securities, bank reserves are decreased.

_____ 8. The Fed can tighten or ease money by raising or lowering the discount rate or increasing or decreasing legal reserve requirements.

_____ 9. If the rate of growth of the money supply is slowed, interest rates initially rise and both economic activity and inflation tend to slow down.

_____ 10. The Federal Reserve is much less active today than it was in the early 1930s.

Discussion Questions

1. What is the effect of increases in the legal reserve requirements on the amount of demand deposits? Use a numerical example in your response.

2. What is the effect of changes in the discount rate? What variables has the Fed looked at to determine whether to change the discount rate?

3. Suppose the Fed buys $1 million of government securities from U.S. Steel. What is the effect on the quantity of bank reserves? Suppose it sells $1 million of government securities to U.S. Steel. What is the effect on the quantity of bank reserves?

4. Explain how the citizens of the United States can affect the money supply through their willingness to go into debt. What does this say about the ability of the Federal Reserve System to keep very close control of the exact amount of money in circulation? Could the willingness of borrowers to borrow or the willingness of bankers to lend be reflected in the amount of excess reserves in the whole banking system? How?

5. In the early 1980s, a business publication reported that, "The decline in the money growth rate has the financial markets breathing a sigh of relief. Interest rates generally declined in the past week." Explain why the decline in the rate of growth of the money supply was interpreted as having this effect.

Problem Set

1. Suppose that the Crooked Arrow National Bank has the following balance sheet (in millions of dollars):

Assets		Liabilities and net worth	
Reserves	0.5	Demand deposits	2.5
Loans and securities	3.0	Net worth	1.0

   a. If the legal reserve requirement is 20 percent, does the bank have any excess reserves? If so, how much?
   b. Suppose that the Fed lowers the reserve requirement, with the result that the bank has excess reserves of $25,000. What is the new legal reserve requirement?
   c. Suppose that the Fed lowers the reserve requirement, with the result that the bank has excess reserves of $100,000. What is the new legal reserve requirement?

2. From the following figures, construct the consolidated balance sheet of the 12 Federal Reserve banks. (All figures are in billions of dollars.)

Gold certificates	10	Reserves of member banks	30
Other liabilities and net worth	5	Other assets	10
Securities	100	Treasury deposits	5
Outstanding Federal Reserve notes	90	Loans to commercial bank	10

3. The public wants to hold $1 in currency for every $3 in demand deposits. It holds $30 billion in currency and $90 billion in demand deposits. The legal reserve requirement is 20 percent, and commercial banks hold no excess reserves. The banks hold $18 billion in reserves. There are no checkable deposits other than demand deposits.

a. If the Federal Reserve wants to reduce the quantity of money by $2 billion, how much of a decrease must occur in demand deposits?
b. To obtain this decrease in demand deposits, by how much must bank reserves decline? What are the banks reserves now?
c. To reduce bank reserves by this amount, how many billions of dollars worth of government securities should the Federal Reserve sell? (Be careful, note that, because of the $2 billion decrease in the quantity of money, the public wants to hold $0.5 billion less in currency.)

4. Suppose that the Federal Reserve purchases $100 million of U.S. government securities from *commercial banks*.

    a. What is the effect on the balance sheet of the Federal Reserve banks?
    b. What is the effect on the balance sheet of the commercial banks?
    c. What is the effect on the potential money supply if the legal reserve requirement is 20 percent?

5. Suppose that on May 1, 2002, the Federal Reserve sells $100 million of U.S. government securities to the public, which pays for them by check.

    Show the effect of this sale on the balance sheets of the Federal Reserve and the commercial banks:

Federal Reserve

Assets		Liabilities	
Government securities	____	Member bank reserves	____

Commercial banks (balance sheet for all banks combined)

Assets		Liabilities	
Reserves	____	Demand deposits	____

LESSON REVIEW

If you had difficulty with the Self-Quiz or would like additional assistance, read the following lesson review. It should reinforce and help you understand the content presented in this lesson.

The Aims of Monetary Policy

Monetary policy is the exercise of the central bank's control over the quantity of money and interest rates to promote the objectives of national economic policy. The central bank in this country is the Federal Reserve System, consisting of the Federal Reserve Board of Governors (which has seven members) located in Washington, DC, and 12 Federal Reserve Banks located regionally.

In formulating its monetary policy, the Fed seeks reasonably full employment without excessive inflation. So, when a recession appears imminent, the monetary authorities generally increase the money supply and push down interest rates. This is commonly described as "easing money" or "easing credit." Expanding the money supply increases aggregate demand.

On the other hand, when the economy is steaming ahead and inflation is a threat, the Fed tightens credit or tightens money. Decreasing the money supply reduces aggregate demand.

Fiscal policy and monetary policy seek to achieve the same goals: Full employment without inflation. But they use very different methods. Fiscal policy relies on the government's powers to spend and tax, while monetary policy relies on a tightening or loosening of the money supply. This difference in strategies is significant with respect to timelines for implementation and effect. Getting new tax legislation approved can take months, even years. And often, precisely because of this time lag and the amount of discussion and debate that can occur, final legislation bears little resemblance indeed to what was originally intended. But once it is implemented, its impact is immediate. Monetary policy can be implemented relatively quickly. But it may be a year or so from the time the Fed takes action until significant indicators reflect the start of a turnaround in the economy.

The Central Role of Bank Reserves

The chief way in which the Federal Reserve controls the money supply is by controlling the reserves of the banking system. As we have already seen (Lesson 8), if the legal reserve requirements are that $1 in reserves must be kept for every $6 in deposits, the banking system can increase the money supply by $6 for every $1 of excess reserves. When inflation threatens, the Federal Reserve finds a way to cut reserves and the growth of the money supply. If the Fed increases the legal reserve ratio, raises the discount rate, or sells government securities, it decreases or eliminates excess reserves; this can decrease the money supply.

On the other hand, in times of recession and low employment, the Federal Reserve finds a way to expand reserves and the growth of the money supply. If the Fed decreases the legal reserve ratio, lowers the discount rate, or buys government securities, it increases excess reserves; this can increase the money supply.

Who Are the Makers of Monetary Policy?

Who decides whether our current economy warrants expansion or cutback? This is a complex question indeed because, as with fiscal policy, there are many actors. Certainly the primary source of power rests with the Federal Reserve System, which consists of a seven-member Federal Reserve Board of Governors and 12 Federal Reserve Banks, located in New York, Chicago, Philadelphia, San Francisco, Boston, Cleveland, St. Louis, Kansas City, Atlanta, Richmond, Minneapolis, and Dallas. These Federal Reserve Banks are "bankers' banks"; that is, they perform much the same functions for banks that your bank performs for you. They hold deposits for member banks and make loans to them. In addition, they perform a function no commercial bank can perform: They issue Federal Reserve notes—paper money.

The components (other than the banks) of the Federal Reserve System include

- *The Board of Governors.* The Board of Governors consists of seven members appointed for 14-year terms by the president. One term expires every two years. Since many governors do not serve full terms, a president who is reelected may have an opportunity eventually to appoint a majority of board members. The length of the terms, however, is intended precisely to prevent the president—or anyone—from having too much political influence over the board's composition.

- *The Federal Open Market Committee.* The Federal Open Market Committee consists of the board plus the presidents of five Federal Reserve banks, who serve on a rotating basis. The function of this committee is to make policy concerning the purchase or sale of government securities, which is the primary means available to the Fed for controlling the money supply.

- *The Federal Advisory Council.* This group of 12 commercial bankers advises the board on banking policy.

Independence of the Federal Reserve System

The Federal Reserve System was established by Congress in 1913, largely as a result of public pressure to strengthen the banking system. The Fed is responsible to Congress technically, but since no formal guidelines have been established for governing its behavior, in practice, it has a good deal of independence and wide discretionary powers over monetary policy.

Who has influence over the Fed? In addition to the president, who appoints the Federal Reserve Board of Governors, and advisory groups like the Federal Advisory Council, the business community and the board's professional staff of senior economists wield considerable influence. Staff economists often remain from one administration to the next, and their continuous exposure to a wide range of economic policies and issues gives them an unmatched perspective.

Functions of the Federal Reserve

What are the key functions and responsibilities of the Federal Reserve? As noted already, their most important job, like that of any central bank, is to control the quantity of money. But they have other functions as well:

1. *Holding deposits.* The Federal Reserve banks hold the deposits or reserves of member banks.

2. *Collecting checks.* Federal Reserve banks provide a facility for check collection so that banks can collect funds for checks drawn on other banks.

3. *Issuing currency.* Federal Reserve banks supply us with paper currency, called Federal Reserve notes.

4. *Acting as fiscal agents.* These banks act as fiscal agents for the federal government. They hold some checking accounts of the U.S. Treasury and engage in the purchase and sale of government securities.

5. *Supervising banks.* Finally, the Federal Reserve banks supervise the operations of commercial banks and thrift institutions to make sure they meet the legal reserve requirements.

6. *Lending money to banks.* The Federal Reserve Board acts as a lender of last resort and provides reserves to banks as necessary.

Consolidated Balance Sheet

If we were to examine the consolidated balance sheet for the 12 regional Federal Reserve banks, what would we find? First, on the left-hand side, we find these assets:

1. *Gold certificates.* Warehouse certificates issued by the Treasury for gold bullion.
2. *Securities.* U.S. government bonds, notes, and bills, which are, respectively, long-term, medium-term, and short-term IOUs.
3. *Loans.* Loans made to commercial banks whether or not they are members of the Federal Reserve System.

On the right-hand side, we find the following liabilities:

1. *Outstanding Federal Reserve notes.* In other words, the paper currency we currently use.
2. *Treasury deposits.* Deposits the U.S. Treasury maintains and on which it can draw checks.
3. *Reserves of banks.* The deposits banks make, which are assets from the viewpoint of the commercial banks but liabilities from the viewpoint of the Fed, which must return them on demand.

Open Market Operations

Now that we see what the basic balance sheet contains, we can talk about the effects on that balance sheet of buying and selling securities, that is, participating in open market operations. Buying and selling securities is the single most important means the Federal Reserve has to control the quantity of banks reserves.

Buying Securities

Suppose the Federal Reserve buys $1 million worth of government securities on the open market. What is the effect on the balance sheet? There is an increase of $1 million in assets but also an increase of $1 million in liabilities in the form of reserves. This means that the reserves of member banks also increase. In other words, member banks can obtain more money from the Federal Reserve with which to make loans.

Suppose the Federal Reserve purchases its securities from General Motors with a check for $1 million and GM deposits this check in the Chase Manhattan Bank. The balance sheet for Chase Manhattan will show a $1 million increase in demand deposits and a $1 million increase in reserves; in other words, it too has more money available with which to make loans, increasing the money supply.

Effect on Fed's balance sheet:

Assets		Liabilities and net worth	
Government securities	+1	Member bank reserves	+1

Effect on balance sheet of the Chase Manhattan Bank:

Assets		Liabilities and net worth	
Reserves	+1	Demand deposits	+1

Selling Securities

Suppose, on the other hand, that the Fed determines to sell $1 million worth of securities as a means of tightening the money supply and holding down inflation. What happens? Essentially the same steps in reverse. For example, Merrill Lynch, a large brokerage firm, buys $1 million worth of securities from the Fed, and the Fed in turn presents a check for $1 million to the Chase Manhattan for payment. The Chase Manhattan, after making payment on this check, loses $1 million in demand deposits and $1 million in reserves; its lending power is diminished by $1 million. Similarly, the Fed's member bank reserves decline by $1 million, along with its assets in the form of government securities. In effect, the Fed has reduced member banks' reserves by $1 million, decreasing their power to make loans and tightening the total money supply.

The Federal Open Market Committee

The responsibility for open market operations rests largely with the Federal Open Market Committee, which meets monthly to review current economic trends. This committee in turn gives instructions on buying or selling to the manager of the Open Market Account at the Federal Reserve Bank of New York, who handles the actual transactions for the Fed.

Other Means for Controlling the Money Supply

In addition to buying or selling securities on the open market, the Federal Reserve has two other means for controlling the money supply:

1. Changing the legal reserve requirements.
2. Changing the discount rate.

While none of these has the immediate, dramatic effect of the open market exchanges, each merits consideration.

Changing the Legal Reserve Requirements

The Federal Reserve has the power to change the amount of reserves banks must hold for every dollar of demand deposits. According to the 1980 Financial Reform Act, the

Fed can establish this limit between 8 and 14 percent for checkable deposits. And, on the affirmative action of five out of its seven member governors, it can impose an additional reserve requirement of up to 4 percent. In extraordinary economic circumstances, the Fed can set the percentage at any level it deems appropriate.

What is the effect of increasing reserve requirements? If a bank has sufficient reserves to more than meet current requirements, then an increase still allows the bank some funds to use in making loans. On the other hand, if a bank is just barely meeting legal reserve requirements, an increase forces the bank to sell securities, refuse to renew loans, and reduce demand deposits to meet new reserve requirements.

What happens to the banking system as a whole when legal reserve requirements increase? This increase in required reserves overall means less in excess reserves, hence less money available for loans and a general shrinking of the money supply.

What is the effect of a *decrease* in legal reserve requirements? Suppose a bank has been just meeting the legal reserve limits. Suddenly, those limits are lowered. Now the bank has more excess reserves and is in a position to lend and invest more, thus increasing the money supply.

Changes in the legal reserve requirements are considered by economists to be a fairly drastic measure. The impact is immediate and rapid, and in cases of an increase, can spell financial difficulty for banks that have been living on the edge, barely meeting requirements. Such changes, therefore, tend to be fairly infrequent and relatively moderate.

Changing the Discount Rate

The discount rate is the rate of interest that the Fed charges banks for loans. The Fed can alter this rate whenever it chooses, thus either encouraging or discouraging borrowing. The discount rate increased gradually (with occasional alternating decreases) from 3.53 in 1960 to 7.46 in 1978, then took a big leap forward to 10.28 in 1979. It peaked at 13.41 in 1981, and decreased to 5.5 percent in 1987, and dropped all the way down to 3 percent in 1993. It was back up to 6 percent in May 2000 but had dropped to a post–World War II low of 0.75 percent in November 2002.

When the Fed increases the discount rate (relative to other interest rates), it makes it more expensive for banks to increase their reserves. Similarly, when it decreases the discount rate, the Fed encourages borrowing. Member banks are expected to borrow money to see them through difficult times; they are *not* expected to make a practice of borrowing from the Fed then loaning that money for profit. To discourage excessive borrowing, the Fed keeps the discount rate relatively close to short-term market interest rates.

Overall, most economists agree that the impact of changes in the discount rate is minor in comparison to that of open market operations. However, these changes do affect the public attitude and thus may encourage or discourage borrowing and investment. When the Fed decreases the discount rate, the public may view this as a sign of easier money and be more likely to invest and borrow.

EXTENDED LEARNING

This section of the study guide is specifically designed for the two-semester student.

AUDIO

Before Listening

Read Exploring Further of Chapter 9, pages 224–228 in your text.

Next

Listen to the audiotape that accompanies Lesson 9.

After Listening

Answer the following questions:

1. What are *open market operations*, and what is the immediate effect of open market operations on the money supply and the overall wealth of the economy?
2. Why did the public's response to the bank failures in the early 1930s cause a sharp reduction in the money supply?
3. How does an expansionary monetary policy resemble "pushing on string"?
4. What is the *reserve requirement,* and how can changing the reserve requirement change the money supply?
5. What is the *discount rate?* If the Federal Reserve lowers the discount rate, what is likely to happen to the money supply?

ADDITIONAL READINGS

Chandler, Lester V. *The Economics of Money and Banking,* 6th ed. New York: Harper & Row, 1973.

> Chapter 11, "Instruments of Monetary Management," provides a clear explanation of the three basic tools of monetary policy and examples of how they were used in the 1950 to 1970 period. The need to coordinate the use of these tools and other, lesser-known monetary policy instruments is also discussed. Moderately difficult, no mathematics or graphs.

Chandler, Lester V. *The Economics of Money and Banking,* 6th ed. New York, New York: Harper & Row, 1973.

> Chapters 22 to 26 detail U.S. monetary policies from 1914 to 1971. Of most interest are Chapter 23, which covers the 1930 to 1941 period, and Chapter 26, which covers the 1960 to 1971 period. No mathematics or graphs.

Cook, Timothy Q., and Bruce J. Summers. *Instruments of the Money Market,* 5th ed. Richmond, VA: Federal Reserve Bank of Richmond, 1981.

> Chapters on "The Money Market," "Treasury Bills," and "Federal Funds" detail the mechanics of money market transactions. Other chapters cover repurchase agreements, commercial paper, euro-dollars, and so on. No mathematics or graphs.

Durkin, Thomas A., and Robert O. Edmister. "The Supply of Money and Bank Credit." In *Financial Institutions and Markets,* 2d ed., edited by Murray E. Polakoff et al., 81–104. Boston: Houghton Mifflin Company, 1981.

> Details how elastic the creation of money is and how money creation depends on the behavior of financial institutions and borrowers. Notes how this complicates monetary policy formulation. Simple mathematics, no graphs.

Galbraith, J. K. *Money, Whence It Came, Where It Went.* Boston: Houghton Mifflin Company, 1975.

> Chapters 9 and 10 provide a lively discussion of the political rivalries that affected the creation of the Federal Reserve System. No mathematics or graphs.

ANSWER KEY

Video Questions

1. Before the Fed existed, early in the twentieth century, the U.S. economy was expanding at a rapid clip with growth of industries, highway systems, railroads, and the banking business. However, without any means of central control, there was no way to shift monetary reserves to banks with temporary problems. As a result, a series of financial panics prior to 1910 spelled the demise of numerous banks, and a threat to other segments of the economy. At this time, J. P. Morgan, the wealthy business magnate and financier, stepped in to bail out the economy. His actions precipitated serious discussion about the vulnerability of an economy dependent on an individual banker or business executive, and as a result of that discussion, the president and Congress agreed that formation of a central bank would be a boon to the country and the economy. Just before Christmas 1913, President Wilson signed the Federal Reserve Act into law. The function of the Federal Reserve was to act as a central bank. It would keep member banks solvent (the Federal Reserve saw this as its primary function), providing loans in time of financial difficulty, and also regulate member banks, ensuring, among

other things, that all members held a minimum amount of reserves to back financial transactions.

2. In keeping with traditional banking policies, the Fed loaned money to member banks but raised the discount rate. The theory was that a higher discount rate would discourage borrowing (although banks that needed money to stay afloat would still borrow) and discourage foreign investors from cashing in their assets (because the rate of return would now be lower). Unfortunately, this tight money policy occurred at a time when the economy was badly in need of stimulation. Member banks were kept alive, but more than 1,000 nonmember banks went under. Business investment also died a slow death, and the economy in general stagnated. Clearly, the Fed had kept its members solvent at a staggering cost to the economy in general.

3. Prior to the Accord of 1951, the Fed had been pushing hard for greater autonomy. As an example, the Fed's Open Market Committee had demonstrated its independence by increasing short-term rates without the direct approval of the Treasury. It was expected that the Fed would help finance the Korean War effort through the purchase of bonds, but the Fed balked at this, wanting to be something more than a political arm of the Treasury. When President Truman ordered a special committee to help settle the dispute, the Fed and the Treasury determined that they would work out the differences, rather than let a third party become involved. The result was the Accord of 1951. In that accord, the Fed agreed to support—temporarily—long-term government securities in exchange for the freedom to follow a more flexible policy in the future. The Fed would communicate openly with the Treasury in hopes of maintaining a spirit of collegial support for financial policy, but the Fed would retain autonomy to act in its own (perceived) best interests with or without direct Treasury approval.

4. The most notable immediate effect of the Fed's action was that interest rates soared during the summer of 1966. Businesses dependent on borrowing, particularly the housing industry, suffered as a result. Mortgage money was scarce. Eventually, the entire economy was slowed, but the total impact was not felt for over a year. This was due to the lag time between any action taken by the Fed and the ultimate impact of shock waves on the economy as a whole. By the time the Fed reacted to its overcorrecting policies and tried to stimulate the economy by loosening the money supply, the United States was heavily involved in the Vietnam War. The total effect was severe inflation—more than two and one half times greater than it had been in the early 1960s.

Multiple Choice

1. b   Text, 211.
2. a   Text, 211.
3. d   Text, 211.
4. a   Text, 215–224.
5. c   Text, 215.
6. a   Text, 215.

True-False

1. False   Text, 211–212.
2. False   Text, 214.
3. True   Text, 211–212.
4. False   Text, 213.
5. False   Video.
6. True   Text, 217.

7.	b.	Text, 216.	7. False	Text, 217–218.
8.	c	Text, 217.	8. True	Text, 220–224.
9.	a	Text, 220.	9. True	Video; Text, 212.
10.	d	Text, 223.	10. False	Video.

Discussion Questions

1. An increase in the legal reserve requirement can reduce demand deposits if a bank does not have excess reserves at the time the legal reserve requirement is increased. The bank also has the option of selling securities or refusing to renew loans to meet the new reserve requirement. If a bank currently has $1 million in demand deposits and the reserve requirement is 20 percent, then it must have $0.2 million in legal reserves. If the required reserve is increased to 25 percent and the bank meets this requirement by reducing its demand deposits, the bank must reduce its demand deposits by $0.2 million.

2. The discount rate measures the cost of borrowing from the Fed. When the discount rate increases, banks find that the cost of borrowing from the Fed increases. With higher discount rates, banks borrow less and the money supply does not expand as rapidly as it would with a lower discount rate. Conversely, when the discount rate decreases, the cost of borrowing falls and this encourages greater borrowing by banks from the Fed. In setting the discount rate, the Fed looks primarily at short-term market interest rates.

3. The purchase of these securities by the Fed increases the level of bank reserves. The selling of securities by the Fed decreases the level of bank reserves.

4. In thinking about the desire to increase or decrease debt in the aggregate economy, it seems likely that if one group decides to increase its debt level that some other group, in all likelihood, decides to decrease its debt level. One would think that, generally speaking, the two counterforces would tend to balance each other. However, if the desire for debt in the aggregate either increases or decreases, there is an impact on the money supply. A diminished desire for debt is reflected in increased excess reserves in the banking system, while an increased desire for debt is reflected in decreased excess reserves in the banking system.

5. The most likely explanation for this effect is that people interpreted the decline in the money growth rate as a signal that inflationary pressures were being dampened. As expected inflation falls, one anticipates that interest rates will decline, since lenders need not charge as high a nominal rate to receive the same real rate.

Problem Set

1. a. No. Its reserves are just equal to the legally required amount.
   b. 19 percent.
   c. 16 percent.

2.

Assets		Liabilities and net worth	
Gold certificates	10	Outstanding Federal Reserve notes	90
Securities	100	Reserves of member banks	30
Loans to commercial banks	10	Treasury deposits	5
Other assets	10	Other liabilities and net worth	5
	130		130

3. a. $1.5 billion.
   b. $0.3 billion. $17.7 billion.
   c. $0.8 billion of securities need to be sold, $0.3 billion to reduce the bank's reserves to $17.7 billion and $0.5 billion to soak up the currency people do not want to hold anymore.

   To meet its target the Fed needs to reduce bank reserves to $17.7 billion. As the Fed sells securities, thus reducing reserves and the demand deposits the reserves support, people want to hold less currency (at least according to this problem). the only rational way the people can reduce their currency holdings is to deposit unwanted currency in their checking accounts. This will increase bank reserves above the Fed's target of $17.7 billion, so the Fed will have to keep reducing the reserves by buying securities in order to hit its target.

4. a. Government securities + $100 million; member bank reserves + $100 million.
   b. Securities – $100 million; commercial bank reserves + $100 million
   c. It increases by $500 million.

5.

Federal Reserve

Assets		Liabilities	
Government securities	–100	Member bank reserves	–100

Commercial banks (balance sheet for all banks combined)

Assets		Liabilities	
Reserves	–100	Demand deposits	–100

Audio/Text Questions

1. The Federal Reserve's open market operations are buying or selling government securities from or to the public. When the Fed buys a government bond, it pays for it by writing a check on itself, which the seller deposits in his or her bank. The bank then has more deposits than before, increasing the money supply, and it can make more loans that increase the money supply even more. The overall

or aggregate wealth of the economy is not affected by open market operations. The way in which wealth is held is changed somewhat, however, in that a larger percentage of the nation's wealth is held in a more liquid form (that is, as a checking account deposit rather than as a government bond).

2. Depositors withdrew their money to hold it as currency for fear of bank failures. The reduction in deposits caused banks to have fewer reserves, so they tended to call in loans and refuse to extend more loans to build up their reserve position. This reduction in loan activity reduced the money supply.

3. If expectations about the future of the economy are so low that people are unwilling to borrow money for investment or consumption or if banks are so worried about failure that they hold massive amounts of excess reserves, then increasing the money supply may have very little effect on the economy. Although restrictive policies are effective, expansionary monetary policy depends for its success on the responsiveness of firms, individuals, and banks.

4. The reserve requirement is the percentage of a bank's deposits that the bank is required to hold in the form of cash. If the reserve requirement is lowered, banks can loan out a greater percentage of their deposits, thereby enhancing the money creation process of the banking system. The banking system's ability to create a money supply that is a multiple of the Federal Reserve's monetary base depends on the reserve requirement.

5. The discount rate is the interest rate that the Federal Reserve charges member banks. The higher is the rate relative to the prevailing short-term market interest rates, the less the banks lend their customers. If the discount rate is lowered, the money supply tends to increase because banks feel easier about extending loans, which increases the money supply.

LESSON 10. STAGFLATION: WHY COULDN'T KEYNESIAN POLICIES BEAT IT?

INTRODUCTION

The solutions to economic ills, according to Keynesian economics, are relatively straightforward and obvious: tax less and spend more during periods of sluggish productivity and unemployment, tax more and spend less during periods of inflation. What Keynesian economics did not take into account, however, was the situation in which serious inflation and unemployment occur together—a situation we call *stagflation.* Under these circumstances, it may appear that the traditional Keynesian solutions do not seem to work well, since we cannot alleviate one problem without aggravating the other.

To make matters worse, stagflation worsened during the 1970s and early 1980s, yet economists remained largely baffled concerning viable solutions. This is not to say that the economic lessons of the past 70 years have been wasted, but a couple of anti-inflationary measures were tried in the 1960s and 1970s that went well beyond the prescriptions of Keynesian economics. In the 1960s, an incomes policy was tried by the Kennedy administration, and in the 1970s, wage and price controls were tried by the Nixon administration. While each might have had some success in the short run (this is debatable), in the long run both failed. In this chapter we examine the benefits and potential pitfalls inherent in these economic policies.

What You Should Learn

By the end of Lesson 10, you should be prepared to

1. Define *supply-side* (i.e., *cost-push*) *inflation* and contrast it with *demand-side* (i.e., *demand-pull*) *inflation*.

2. Describe the economic impact of a shift upward and to the left of the short-run aggregate supply curve.

3. Discuss the role of the oil price hikes on the U.S. economy of the 1970s.

4. Define and explain the applications of the short-run and long-run Phillips curves.

5. Explain what is meant by the *natural rate of unemployment,* and the ways it is influenced by structural unemployment.

6. Describe the consequences when the government attempts to lower the unemployment rate below the natural unemployment level.

7. Describe the purposes, advantages, and disadvantages of wage and price controls.

8. Define and explain the applications of an *incomes policy*.

9. Explain how the Fed can "accommodate" supply-side inflation.

KEY TERMS

supply-side inflation
demand-side inflation
long-run Phillips curve
natural rate of unemployment
wage and price guidelines
wage-price spiral

short-run Phillips curve
stagflation
wage and price controls
incomes policies
inefficiency
expectations

VIDEO

Watch

Economics U$A Program 10, "Stagflation: Why Couldn't We Beat It?"

Illustrative Events

The food and petroleum supply shocks of 1972–73, leading to supply-side inflation, with Princeton economist Alan Blinder.

The 1974 cost of living adjustment (COLA) agreement between the UAW and the Big Three auto companies, and its inflationary results; with Leonard Woodcock, president of the UAW; Richard Lesher, president of the U.S. Chamber of Commerce; and Selmon Knudsen, former president of the Ford Motor Company.

The failure of government efforts to fight the damaging stagflation of the 1970s, featuring Arthur Burns, former chair of the Federal Reserve; and Stanley Fischer, professor of economics at MIT.

After Viewing

Answer the following questions:

1. During the 1950s and 1960s, the U.S. government gained great skill in manipulating monetary and fiscal policies to regulate the economy. Why were these strategies less successful in combating the recession of the 1970s?

2. How did the inflationary picture of the 1970s differ from that witnessed in earlier years?

3. Almost immediately on taking office, President Gerald Ford called an economic summit conference. What was the impact of that conference on U.S. economic policy?

4. In the 1990s, the U.S. economy experienced the exact opposite of what it experienced in the 1970s. Explain these differences using only the concept of aggregate supply. What events had an impact on the aggregate supply in the 1970s? In the 1990s?

Read

Read Chapter 10, "Supply Shocks and Inflation," pages 230–244 and 245–246 in your text. After completing your reading, try the Self-Quiz.

SELF-QUIZ

Multiple Choice

1. Supply-side inflation tends to be triggered by
    a. fluctuations in GDP.
    b. wage increases exceeding productivity increases.
    c. shifts in the aggregate demand curve.
    d. new technology.

2. Joe's union is seeking a cost of living wage increase. "Everything is getting more expensive these days," says Joe. "If we're going to have to pay more for everything, they're going to have to give us more to begin with." Joe's boss is concerned about the wage increase, although he feels confident a fair agreement can be reached. "It isn't that we don't want to increase wages," he claims, "but it's going to mean higher price tags on everything we produce." This scenario is an example of
    a. demand-side inflation.
    b. price indexing.
    c. the wage-price spiral.
    d. the Phillips curve.

3. According to many economists, the inflation of the 1970s was due in large part to
    a. a leftward shift in the short-run aggregate supply curve.
    b. a rightward shift in the aggregate demand curve.
    c. a rightward shift in the short-run aggregate supply curve.
    d. a leftward shift in the aggregate demand curve.

4. When the oil-producing countries increased the price of crude oil in 1974, the impact on the U.S. economy was
    a. negligible because that increase was offset by drops in other prices.

b. slight and relatively short lived, thanks to alternative product sources.
   c. moderate, largely because the increase was not predicted.
   d. substantial because the cost of oil affected the cost of many other products.

5. The relationship between inflation and unemployment during the 1960s seemed to illustrate that the Phillips curve

   a. really did not exist at all.
   b. existed only as a straight line.
   c. was accurate for short periods.
   d. reflected a stable, predictable relationship.

6. Economist Sara R. believes that the government should devote less attention to problems of unemployment and worry more over inflation. "Government spending to curb unemployment brings only temporary relief of our symptoms," Sara claims, "and intolerable increases in inflation over the long run. What good is it getting a few more people to work when the wages they earn won't support them?" On the basis of the viewpoint she expresses here, Sara could *best* be classified as

   a. a supporter of Milton Friedman and Edmund Phelps.
   b. a Keynesian.
   c. a classicist.
   d. a supporter of Karl Marx.

7. Judging by her apparent philosophy (question 6), Sara probably believes that the relationship between unemployment and inflation, in the long run, is represented by

   a. the traditional Phillips curve.
   b. an upward right shift of the Phillips curve.
   c. a line sloping downward and to the right.
   d. a vertical line.

8. According to Friedman, the so-called natural unemployment rate is

   a. zero when inflation is under control.
   b. somewhere between 2 and 4 percent.
   c. generally well over 5 percent.
   d. dependent on how long workers search before taking a job.

9. Even with the looming threat of recession, President Ford requested a tax surcharge in 1974. The *main* reason for this was probably that

   a. Ford, like many members of Congress, viewed inflation as the number one economic problem of the times.
   b. like many economists, Ford hoped that the surcharge would stimulate the economy.
   c. this was virtually the only economic strategy that the Congress would sanction.
   d. unemployment had finally fallen to such low levels that almost no one was concerned about it any longer.

10. The *main* difference between wage and price controls and incomes policies is that incomes policies

   a. tend to be administered during wartime rather than peacetime.
   b. carry a tax liability for noncompliance.
   c. are voluntary rather than mandated.
   d. are the result of legislative action rather than presidential directive.

True-False

_____ 1. During the 1950s and 1960s, various administrations were able to maintain the classic balance between unemployment and inflation. When unemployment increased, inflation correspondingly fell.

_____ 2. Typically, the major cause of inflation is the excessively rapid growth of aggregate demand, a demand for goods and services that outstrips the rate at which the economy's productive capacity is increasing.

_____ 3. The use of wage and price controls to reduce the inflation rate is difficult to administer and tends to distort the allocation of resources.

_____ 4. Rising inflation and rising unemployment can occur simultaneously when there is a supply shock, such as an oil embargo or crop failure, and the supply grows very slowly or, in some cases, contracts.

_____ 5. During periods of stagflation, there is an increase in GDP, an increase in unemployment, and an increase in inflation.

_____ 6. During the 1970s and 1980s, U.S. auto workers were shielded from any of the effects of inflation because of the cost-of-living adjustments included in their contracts with automobile manufacturers.

_____ 7. Cost-of-living adjustment clauses build inflationary expectations into the economic structure and can actually contribute to the inflationary spiral.

_____ 8. In the early stages of demand-side inflation, demand management policies may be able to reduce inflation without causing unemployment to rise to high levels; but to fight *demand-side* inflation that is entrenched or inflation caused by supply shocks, the government would have to reduce aggregate demand significantly causing a high level of unemployment.

_____ 9. In Milton Friedman's view, if the government, through its expansionary policies, attempts to reduce unemployment below its natural level, higher and higher rates of inflation result.

_____ 10. Economists agree that efforts to solve the stagflation problems of the 1970s were successful primarily because of the consistency of monetary and fiscal policies during that period.

Discussion Questions

1. During the late 1970s, the United States experienced unusually high rates of inflation and unemployment. Briefly try to explain why you feel we suffered from these ills. Pretend you must give your presentation to two separate groups: a meeting of economists and a local civic organization interested in contemporary problems.

2. What is the nature of supply-side inflation? What factors can cause shifts in the Phillips curve? What does the Phillips curve look like in the long run?

3. During the 1970s and early 1980s, some economists came to the conclusion that there no longer was a trade-off between inflation and unemployment. Do you agree with them? Why or why not?

4. What are the disadvantages of adopting price and wage controls? What are the three elements of an incomes policy? Can guidelines save the day if monetary and fiscal policies generate strong inflationary pressures?

Problem Set

1. Labor productivity is increasing at an annual rate of 2 percent in economy C.

    a. If the wage level is increasing at an annual rate of 3 percent, are unit labor costs increasing or decreasing, and at what rate are they increasing or decreasing?
    b. Suppose that the wage level in the economy increases at a rate such that unit labor costs remain stable. At what rate is the wage level increasing?
    c. If the wage level in economy C's steel industry increases at the rate indicated in part b, at what rate do unit labor costs rise in the steel industry if labor productivity in steel is increasing at 1 percent per year?
    d. If the steel industry's price level increases at the same rate as its unit labor costs, at what rate does it rise under the circumstances in part c?
    e. Wage and price guidelines are established in economy C. Wages are allowed to increase at a rate equal to the rate of increase of labor productivity in the economy as a whole. Prices are allowed to increase at a rate equal to the rate of increase of unit labor costs. Do prices increase in all industries? If not, in which industries do prices not increase?

2. The following table applies to a firm in economy D, which has an incomes policy stating that wage rates should rise by 8 percent per year. Assume that the firm and the union adhere to this policy.

Year	Wage rate per hour	Hours of labor	Wage bill	Total output	Price of product	Profits and nonwage costs
1989	$8.00	200	___	1,500	$2	___
1990	___	___	$1,728	1,650	$2	___
1991	___	200	___	1,800	$2	___

   a. Fill in the blanks in the table.

b. What is the rate of increase of labor productivity between 1989 and 1990? Between 1990 and 1991?
c. What is the rate of increase of unit wage costs between 1989 and 1990? Between 1990 and 1991?
d. What is the rate of increase of unit profits and nonwage costs between 1989 and 1990? Between 1990 and 1991?
e. What changes occur in the proportion of total revenue going to labor?

3. The Phillips curve in economy D shifts upward and to the right.

   a. Economy D's leading liberal legislator says that this shift means an increase in unemployment. Is he right? Why or why not?
   b. Economy D's leading conservative legislator says that this shift means an increase in inflation. Is she right? Why or why not?
   c. Economy D's prime minister says that, despite this shift, his administration will reduce both unemployment and inflation. Is he right? Why or why not?

LESSON REVIEW

If you had difficulty with the Self-Quiz or would like additional assistance, read the following lesson review. It should reinforce and help you understand the content presented in this lesson.

Supply-Side Inflation

Even while GDP is below its potential, costs sometimes rise, perhaps because union workers seek higher wages. The firms that pay those wages protect their profit margins by increasing prices; in other words, they pass the costs along to consumers. As the cost of living rises, however, labor seeks further increases in wages. This continuing upward cycle of wages and prices, the *wage-price spiral*, is at the heart of supply-side inflation.

In certain cases, increases in the prices of materials may trigger supply-side inflation too. For example, when the price of crude oil shot up in the 1970s, the impact on the economy was severe because many products are directly or indirectly made from petroleum. When these price increases were not offset by price decreases for other products, the overall effect was a shift upward and to the left in the aggregate supply curve, resulting in decreased output and higher prices.

Instability of the Phillips Curve

Recall that the Phillips curve illustrates the relationship between the inflation rate and the unemployment rate. The inverse relationship between these two variables is reflected by the fact that the Phillips curve slopes downward to the right—or at least, this is the way economists generally pictured it through the 1960s, when the relationship between unemployment and inflation seemed highly predictable.

During the 1970s and 1980s, however, the relationship turned out to be rather unpredictable as both inflation and unemployment rose or fell at the same time.

The economic conditions of the 1970s resulted, at least in part, from the following:

1. A shift to the left in the aggregate supply curve, resulting from price hikes in oil and other commodities.
2. Higher inflation and unemployment resulting from this shift.
3. Reduced consumer spending because of higher prices.
4. Increased taxation as inflation pushed consumers into higher tax brackets.
5. Higher taxes to firms because of increased paper profits.
6. Decline in the stock market.

Long-Run versus Short-Run Phillips Curve

Many economists, on viewing the inflationary trends of the 1970s, ceased to believe that the Phillips curve, as originally presented, existed except as a short-run phenomenon. The long-term relationship, they argued, would exist as a straight vertical line, which would induce prices to rise with no reduction in unemployment whatever.

Expansionary fiscal policies of the government, these economists felt, would reduce unemployment only temporarily, and then as inflation increased, unemployment would rise again. Trying to reduce unemployment again and again would only accelerate the inflation rate.

Stagflation

This term was coined to describe the combination of high unemployment and high inflation that characterized the 1970s and early 1980s. According to many economists, stagflation results from a shift upward and to the left in the aggregate supply curve. What caused such a shift during the 1970s? Generally, the following three reasons are the most-frequently cited:

1. Dramatic increases in food prices because of crop failures and shortages worldwide.
2. Other price increases triggered by worldwide materials shortages.
3. Increases in crude oil prices.

Although the economic problems of the 1970s may not seem severe in comparison to the Great Depression of the 1930s, the seriousness may seem more consequential when we realize that, despite a relatively sophisticated knowledge of economics, the problems persisted without resolution for a variety of reasons, at least some of which were political as well as economic.

The "Natural" Rate of Unemployment

As noted earlier, most economists do not expect, realistically, that the unemployment rate will ever hit zero. New job seekers are always entering the market, persons are between jobs for one reason or another, and people whose present training does not qualify them for jobs demand new technical knowledge or skills. Thus, some economists claim, there is a certain "natural" or full-employment rate of unemployment below which we cannot realistically hope to go. This rate is determined partly by the length of time workers are willing to search before taking a new job and the rate at which technological changes demand new job skills.

Suppose that the government uses expansionary fiscal policy to increase demand when the unemployment rate is already at the natural (full-employment) level. What happens?

1. At first, expanded output and higher employment (in accord with the Phillips curve).
2. Higher inflation.
3. Changes in consumers' expectations, as they experience higher inflation rates.
4. Wage hikes to match expected inflation.
5. More price increases and inflation.
6. Renewed increases in unemployment, this time with accelerated inflation.

What if the government continues to use its fiscal powers to generate demand in the hope of alleviating this situation? *Inflation will continue to rise, and unemployment will be reduced only in brief, temporary cycles, after which it will resume.*

Wage and Price Controls

One way that the government can try to reduce inflation and unemployment is through wage and price controls, measures designed to ensure that wages and prices do not increase more than a fixed amount. Such controls usually have been imposed during wartime emergencies and to varying degrees during other periods. Many economists oppose governmental wage-price controls on the following grounds:

1. Wage and price controls encourage inefficiency and wasted resources (because the natural capacity of the price system to determine allocation and use of resources is distorted).
2. Wage and price controls are difficult, cumbersome, expensive, and many economists believe, ineffective in their application.
3. Wage and price controls, according to some, jeopardize economic freedom.

Incomes Policies (Guidelines)

Higher inflation during the 1970s and early 1980s increased interest here and abroad in the use of incomes policies to curb inflation without cutting back on aggregate demand. An incomes policy is characterized by these three elements:

1. Overall targets for economic achievement, for example, "Over the coming year, wages will not be allowed to increase by more than 5 percent."

2. Detailed guides to assist individual industries and firms in making decisions on wages and prices.
3. Some means for ensuring firms' compliance (although ultimately, compliance is voluntary).

Exceptions. The Council of Economic Advisers may specify particular situations under which the guidelines would be modified, for example, when there is a labor shortage, when one industry has lower wages than another comparable industry, when there are insufficient profits to attract needed investment capital, or when there is an increase in an industry's nonwage costs.

Some Criticisms. Guidelines do not escape criticism. Economists charged that they would result in

1. *Inefficiency*, as a hampered price system allows shortages and surpluses to build.
2. *Loss of economic freedom*, especially if firms did not respond to government pressures. How far would government eventually go to ensure enforcement?
3. *Infeasibility*, because for some industries it would be hard to obtain accurate data on productivity and rules regulating exceptions are vague and hard to apply.
4. *Faulty perspective*, focusing attention on the symptoms of inflation, rather than on the causes, which many economists felt could be traced directly to faulty government monetary policy.

Overall Impact

The guidelines initiated by Kennedy-Johnson seemed to work well during the early 1960s, but critics would later argue that this was because of firms' general willingness to comply. As the economy heated up to finance the Vietnam War, compliance grew costlier, and firms grew increasingly willing to ignore the guidelines. By 1968, no one was paying the slightest attention to them.

Economists still argue about the relative impact of the guidelines overall. Some feel they were very effective in reducing supply-side inflation in the early 1960s, while others feel their impact is highly questionable. The question has yet to be resolved.

Perhaps most important, though, is the realization that no guidelines or "cures" make up for faulty monetary and fiscal policies. Treating symptoms does not make inflation go away, and it may even be economically dangerous if it lulls us into believing that we accomplished more than we really have.

The Fed and Accommodation

The Fed can "accommodate" supply-side inflation by increasing the money supply. Here is how. Under supply-side inflation, the short-run aggregate supply curve shifts upward and to the left. As the point of intersection between aggregate demand and supply changes, real output falls, and unemployment rises. By increasing the money supply, the Fed pushes the aggregate demand curve to the right. If it pushes it far enough, it can raise GDP to its former level. Prices are still high but without the resulting additional unemployment. The result is known as *accommodation*.

EXTENDED LEARNING

This section of the study guide is specifically designed for the two-semester student.

AUDIO

Before Listening

Read Exploring Further of Chapter 10, pages 244–245, in your text.

Next

Listen to the audiotape that accompanies Lesson 10.

After Listening

Answer the following questions:

1. Did Federal Reserve chair Arthur Burns follow the correct monetary policy in 1972 when President Nixon was trying to slow inflation with wage and price controls?

2. What is the primary reason most economists oppose wage and price controls?

3. Why have "jawboning" techniques to keep prices and wages from increasing been ignored in recent years?

4. What is a tax-based incomes policy (TIP), and why might it be better than ordinary wage-price controls?

5. Did President Nixon's wage and price controls work? Did special problems keep them from working?

ADDITIONAL READINGS

Blinder, Alan S. *The Great Stagflation*. New York: Academic Press, 1979.

>A thorough analysis of the economic events of the 1971 to 1976 period, including the food and petroleum supply shocks, price controls, and the fiscal and monetary policy response to the supply shock. Moderately difficult graphics.

Cagan, Philip. *Persistent Inflation: Historical and Policy Essays*. New York: Columbia University Press, 1979.

> Details the historical evolution of inflation from the Vietnam War era to 1975, and discusses the various theoretical explanations of the causes of inflation. No mathematics or graphs.

Feldstein, Martin. "Inflation and the American Economy." *Public Interest* 67 (Spring 1982).

> Feldstein analyzes the inflation of the 1970 to 1981 period and stresses how policy has been misled by the failure to understand how the nature of unemployment has changed, how the Phillips curve was deceptive, how tax rules must be taken into account when formulating monetary policy, and how costly inflation truly is. No mathematics or graphs.

Fellner, William. "On the Merits of Gradualism and on a Fall-back Position If It Should Nevertheless Fail." In *Contemporary Economic Problems,* 3–18. Washington, DC: American Enterprise Institute, 1981.

> Advocates a slow reduction in inflation because the "credibility effect" would cause high unemployment if policies tried to reduce inflation quickly. Also discusses the possibility of returning to a gold-based money to stop inflation. No mathematics or graphs.

Stevens, Robert Warren. *Vain Hopes, Grim Realities: The Economic Consequences of the Vietnam War*. New York: New Viewpoint, 1976.

> Chapter 6, "Escalating the War in Vietnam: How Not to Finance a War," provides a brief description of the political roadblocks to implementing a proper fiscal policy in the late 1960s. No mathematics or graphs.

ANSWER KEY

Video Questions

1. For years, unemployment and inflation had seemed to exist in a kind of trade-off situation. When one went up, the other went down. Under these circumstances, the government could take one of two fairly direct actions: To combat unemployment, it could stimulate consumer demand, lower taxes, make more money available, or encourage spending. To fight inflation, the government could reduce consumer demand, decrease public spending, tighten the money supply, or impose heavier taxes. Suddenly, however, unemployment and inflation were hitting at the same time. Each seemed to exacerbate the problems of the other, and since government could not employ contradictory policies at the same time, it was virtually helpless to fight what came to be known as *stagflation*.

2. In previous years, economists had become used to witnessing demand-side inflation, stimulated by growing consumer demand. During the 1970s, although many persons did not recognize it at the time, we experienced supply-side inflation, triggered by shortages rather than increases in demand. The supply-side inflation of this period was triggered by, among other things, food shortages worldwide, the result of drought, storms, and numerous crop failures. To make things worse, in 1973 we were faced with the beginning of a severe oil shortage. Oil and all oil products became scarce and very expensive, and prices in general skyrocketed. Consumers reacted by spending less and less. Therefore, whereas we had previously experienced inflation mainly in periods of high consumer demand and an expanding economy, we now experienced inflation in a period of very low consumer demand and a shrinking economy, one with high unemployment.

3. The theme of the economic summit conference was defining "a battle plan against inflation." Of those nongovernment economists who attended, however, the overwhelming majority were more concerned with problems of recession than inflation. They urged an easing of the money supply and stimulation of the economy. Their voices went largely unheard for some time to come. The president, Congress, and the U.S. people were in virtual agreement that the most serious economic problem of the times was inflation and this should be the number one priority. It was to remain the chief priority for the next several years. Shortly following the economic conference, President Ford asked for a stringent ceiling on federal spending and a tax surcharge. The Fed, in turn, held the money supply tightly in check. Meanwhile, both inflation and unemployment continued to mount.

4. The early 1970s experienced a couple of supply-side shocks to the economy. First, there were several years of bad crops worldwide. This pushed the price of food products and agricultural raw materials higher. Second was the Arab oil embargo, which tripled oil prices. Both events raised the costs of producing goods and services and, hence, shifted the aggregate supply to the left. A less obvious problem at the time was declining output, stagflation in short. In the 1990s, on the other hand, circumstances worked in the opposite direction. First, information technology came of age and dramatically increased productivity and lowered costs. Second, with western Europe and Japan mired in no-growth recessions and South Asia imploding financially, raw material prices were very low. This caused the aggregate supply curve to shift to the right, resulting in a falling inflation rate and greater output.

Multiple Choice

1. b   Text, 230–231.
2. c   Text, 231.
3. a   Text, 231.
4. d   Text, 231.
5. d   Text, 232.

True-False

1. True   Video.
2. True   Video.
3. True   Text, 239.
4. True   Video; Text, 230–231.
5. False   Video; Text, 234.

6.	a	Text, 235.	6.	False	Video.
7.	d	Text, 235.	7.	True	Video.
8.	d	Text, 235.	8.	True	Video.
9.	a	Video.	9.	True	Text, 235.
10.	c	Text, 239–244.	10.	False	Video.

Discussion Questions

1. a. The major cause of stagflation in the late 1970s was a shift upward and to the left in the aggregate supply curve.
    b. The major causes of stagflation in the late 1970s were dramatic increases in food prices due to worldwide crop failures and shortages, other price increases due to worldwide shortages, and crude oil price increases. All three increases led to a leftward and upward shift in the aggregate supply curve with higher inflation and unemployment resulting.

2. Supply-side inflation is the result of increases in wages paid to labor or the prices of other materials used to produce goods and services. When these price increases occur, the aggregate supply curve shifts upward and to the left. The Phillips curve in the long run is thought to be a vertical line stating that unemployment in the long run will be at the natural unemployment level regardless of the rate of inflation.

3. In the long run, there is no trade-off between inflation and unemployment. In the long run, the natural rate of unemployment is the equilibrium rate and the accompanying inflation rate depends on government monetary policy. Efforts to reduce unemployment below this natural level result in only increased inflation.

4. The disadvantages of adopting price and wage controls are (1) the encouragement of inefficiency and wasted resources, (2) the difficulty and expense of implementing these controls and their relative ineffectiveness, and 3) the loss of economic freedom due to the imposition of these controls.

   An incomes policy must set overall targets for achievement; provide detailed guidelines to industries and firms on how to make wage and price decisions; and provide a means of ensuring compliance with the policy. During periods of strong inflationary pressure, guidelines typically are not effective: Compliance with the guidelines becomes increasingly costly for firms, and the result is that fewer and fewer firms are willing to comply with the guidelines.

Problem Set

1. a. They are increasing at the rate of 1 percent per year.
    b. 2 percent per year.
    c. 1 percent per year.
    d. 1 percent per year.
    e. No. They will not increase in industries where the rate of increase of labor productivity is higher than in the economy as a whole.

2. a.

1989	$8.00	200	$1,600	1,500	$2	$1,400	
1990	$8.64	200	$1,728	1,650	$2	$1,572	
1991	$9.33	200	$1,866	1,800	$2	$1,734	

b. 10 percent. 9 percent.
c. 2 percent decline. 1 percent decline.
d. 2 percent increase. 1 percent increase.
e. It is 53 percent in 1989, 52 percent in 1990, and somewhat less than 52 percent in 1991.

3. a. Not necessarily. If the country is willing to tolerate more inflation, it may be able to avoid an increase in unemployment.
   b. Not necessarily. If the country is willing to tolerate more unemployment, it may be able to avoid an increase in inflation.
   c. No, not unless the curve can be shifted downward and to the left.

Audio/Text Questions

1. Some say no, because Burns let the money supply grow quite rapidly. This stimulated economic activity and created inflationary pressure, undermining the effectiveness of the wage and price controls.

2. Prices act as signals to producers and consumers; they tell producers what and how much to produce and they guide consumers' buying patterns. When those signals are distorted, artificial shortages develop and the economy does not use its scarce resources to its best advantage.

3. When inflation seemed to originate in excessive wage and price increases of large, union-dominated oligopolies, jawboning seemed like a policy that might have some moderate success. Since the late 1960s, however, the degree to which inflation has appeared embedded in the economy has made jawboning an unworkable policy.

4. A TIP rewards (or punishes) firms for keeping their price increases down (or for raising prices too quickly) by changing the amount of taxes they have to pay. A TIP is more flexible than a strict wage-price controls policy. Firms can raise prices in response to increased demand, avoiding some of the problems of controls such as stultifying supply.

5. Most analysts have concluded that the wage-price controls kept general inflation down somewhat while they were in effect, but prices rose very quickly after they were relaxed; this largely offset any gain. During the period of controls, both fiscal and monetary policy were inflationary, and also there were some extraordinary commodities shortages (grains, soybeans, petroleum).

LESSON 11. PRODUCTIVITY: CAN WE GET MORE FOR LESS?

INTRODUCTION

The United States has enjoyed a spirited rate of growth during the past 165 years. That growth has not been steady, however. For example, output per person-hour was much higher after World War I than before and again after World War II than before. And growth during some decades, like the 1920s, was relatively fast, while during other decades, like the 1930s, it was extremely slow. But overall, despite these variations in rates, growth generally tended upward at a fairly healthy rate. Many factors contributed to this growth, including growth in technology, great attention to education, investment in capital, and a value system that supports hard work and the acquisition of material goods as one indicator of success.

During the 1970s and 1980s, however, the United States experienced a marked slowdown in its rate of per-capita output. Many observers attributed this slowdown to a declining rate of innovation, and although the evidence to support this assertion is somewhat limited, there is enough support to justify our close examination of this potential cause. Other factors often cited as causes for slowdown include changes in the composition of the labor force, reduction in the rate of growth of the capital-labor ratio, increased government regulation, and declines in research and development. By the late 1990s and early 2000s, another period of more rapid productivity growth had commenced.

What You Should Learn

By the end of Lesson 11, you should be prepared to

1. Compare per-capita output in the United States with that of other major industrial nations.

2. Describe the effects of the following factors in per-capita growth:

   - Population
   - Education
   - Technological change

- Capital formation
- Natural resources
- Social and entrepreneurial environment

3. Describe the productivity slowdown in the 1970s and 1980s and its impact on the U.S. economy.
4. Cite five factors generally held to be responsible for this slowdown.
5. Describe the evidence, if any, indicating that (1) the rate of innovation declined in the United States and (2) the United States lost much of its technological lead in the world.
6. Discuss the relationship between R & D and productivity slowdown.
7. Explain why the federal government is more likely to support research and development in one field than in another.

KEY TERMS

productivity
technological change
research and development
innovation
domestic policy review on industrial
   innovation
rate of economic growth

technological lead
per-capita output
advance of knowledge
capital formation
R & D tax credits
supply-side economics
Laffer curve

VIDEO

Watch

Economics U$A Program 11, "Productivity: Can We Get More for Less?"

Illustrative Events

The serious slowdown in U.S. productivity during the 1970s; featuring economist Edward Denison, Brookings Institution, and Walter Williams, president of Bethlehem Steel.

President Jimmy Carter's attempt to increase productivity through government investment in research and development, featuring Edwin Mansfield, professor of economics, University of Pennsylvania, and Jordan Baruch, former Commerce Department Official.

The 1981 Reagan tax cut, and the strong disagreements on its effects, featuring economist Arthur Laffer; Norman Ture, former undersecretary of the Treasury; Nariman Behravesh, former Congressional Budget Office economist and now chief international economist at Standard & Poor's; and former U.S. Representative Barber Conable.

After Viewing

Answer the following questions:

1. According to the video presentation, what factors were probably most significant in accounting for the productivity slowdown of the 1970s?

2. Why do economists place such great importance on a 1 or 2 percent change in productivity growth?

3. How significant is new technology to productivity?

4. In what ways can government involvement affect productivity both positively and negatively?

5. What is the basic economic philosophy of the supply-siders, and how has it been realized in recent years?

Read

Read Chapter 11, "Productivity, Growth, and Technology Policy," pages 247–261 and 262–264 in your text. After completing your reading, try the Self-Quiz.

SELF-QUIZ

Multiple Choice

1. Which of the following statements about U.S. productivity is probably *most* accurate?

    a. It has generally increased over the past hundred years, although the growth has been far from steady.
    b. It grew steadily till the 1950s, then began a gradual decline.
    c. It rose and fell alternately until the middle of the twentieth century, then began a sharp turn upward.
    d. It has gone steadily upward every year since 1840.

2. How does the U.S. growth rate generally compare to that of other countries?

    a. Throughout its history, the United States has held the number one position in per-capita rate of growth.
    b. Despite our early lead, many industrialized countries have shown growth rates equal to or greater than ours over the last 70 years.

c. For the past 50 years, the United States has vied for the number one position with its chief rival, Japan.
d. We were number one in rate of growth till the early 1980s, when both Japan and Germany surpassed us.

3. According to estimates by Stephen Oliner and Daniel Sichel, which of the following contributed *most* to the growth of real national income in the United States between 1974 and 1999?

   a. Increase in the quantity of capital
   b. Improved education and training
   c. Increase in labor hours
   d. Total factor productivity

4. It is somewhat difficult to determine just how significant a contribution education has made to our economic growth *mainly* because

   a. the percentage of persons who complete high school is still fairly small.
   b. large numbers of persons with excellent education are underemployed.
   c. not everyone who goes to school chooses to work.
   d. the effects of education are difficult to sort out from those of technology or investment.

5. At present, the federal government provides about what percentage of the total research and development funds?

   a. Less than 5 percent
   b. Between 25 and 30 percent
   c. Between 30 and 35 percent
   d. Well over 50 percent

6. Which of the following contributed *most* to the productivity slowdown in the United States between 1973 and 1995?

   a. Low rates of investment
   b. Poor enforcement of government regulations
   c. Too much expenditure of resources on research and development
   d. Shift from production of services to production of goods

7. Given the current available evidence, the *most logical* conclusion we can reach about the innovation rate in the United States is that it is

   a. probably rising.
   b. unquestionably rising.
   c. probably declining.
   d. unquestionably declining.

8. Which of the following statements is *most* accurate? Implementation of an R & D tax credit has

   a. had only a modest effect on industrial R & D expenditures.
   b. decreased industrial R & D expenditures.
   c. had no effect on industrial R & D expenditures.
   d. greatly increased industrial R & D expenditures.

9. In periods of high unemployment or high inflation, an economy's rate of innovation generally

   a. decreases.
   b. increases.
   c. remains the same.
   d. cannot be determined.

10. Computer sales representative Marvin K. feels that some concern over the declining rate of innovation may be unwarranted. "Things are changing so fast in our industry we can barely keep up," Marvin maintains. "Even with heavy competition from the Japanese companies, we're still holding our own." Marvin is able to draw this conclusion *mainly* because

    a. it is becoming increasingly clear with new evidence that the slowdown in innovation is largely a myth.
    b. while the slowdown is apparent to researchers, virtually no one else is likely to be aware of it.
    c. he is confusing rate of sales with innovations in new technology.
    d. in certain industries like microelectronics, innovation really is on the rise.

True-False

_____ 1. At its simplest, demand is the appetite to consume, and supply is the ability to produce.

_____ 2. Labor productivity is defined as output per hour of employed labor.

_____ 3. The supply-side factors that determine productivity are education and training. Research has shown that technological innovation and the amount of capital per worker invested in machinery and factories are not relevant and therefore not included.

_____ 4. Throughout most of the twentieth century, the United States enjoyed the highest rate of productivity growth in the industrial world, but by the end of the 1970s, the country was not even included among the top 10.

_____ 5. The decline of U.S. productivity in the 1970s was blamed in part on the relative inexperience of the baby-boom generation and the uncertainty caused by inflation and the vagueness of economic policy.

_____ 6. Pay raises that are expected and granted without an increase in productivity contribute to inflation.

_____ 7. During the period of productivity decline in the 1970s, the United States was increasing its investment in research and development.

_____ 8. Seventy-five percent of the R & D in the United States is financed by public rather than private sources.

_____ 9. When productivity growth declines, the consumer loses rather than basic industries or business.

_____ 10. One response to the productivity slowdown is a call for less government—specifically lower taxes and fewer regulations—to provide an incentive for businesses and people to produce more and invest/save more.

Discussion Questions

1. What aspects of the U.S. economy have not been conducive to economic growth? What are the principal arguments used today in favor of rapid economic growth? What are the principal arguments used today against rapid economic growth? What policies can the government adopt to increase the rate of economic growth?

2. Is the United States's technological lead relatively new or something that has existed for a century or more? Is it true that independent inventors play practically no role at all today in the process of technological change? Discuss.

3. Must increases in the rate of technological change result in increases in aggregate unemployment? Why or why not?

4. "There is no good economic reason why the government should subsidize energy research and development rather than textile or machine-tool research and development. All these forms of research and development generate external economies." Discuss and evaluate.

Problem Set

1. Economic growth in Palmerland, the golfer's paradise, is spurred by the production of a new supersonic golf cart. Suppose this technological change results in an increase in full-employment GDP from $1,000 million to $1,100 million.

   a. If the $C + I + G$ line is as shown here, what is the immediate effect on unemployment of this technological change?

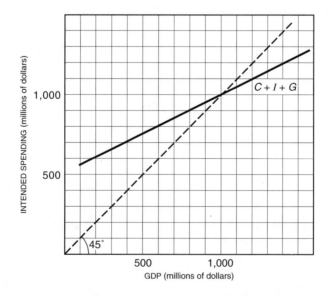

b. In what direction must the $C + I + G$ line be pushed to attain full employment? By how much must it be pushed? Draw the new $C + I + G$ line in the graph.
c. What kinds of policies should the government of Palmerland adopt to push the $C + I + G$ line in the direction indicated in part b?

2. Economy X's productive capacity is growing at 5 percent per year. In 2001, economy X had the capacity to produce $100 billion of GDP. Aggregate demand each year is also shown. All amounts are in billions of constant dollars.

Year	Aggregate demand	Productive capacity	Actual GDP
2001	95	100	____
2002	100	____	____
2003	107	____	____

a. Fill in the blanks.
b. Is the rate of growth of actual GDP between 2001 and 2002 as big as it could have been? Why or why not?
c. Between 2001 and 2002 is the rate of increase of actual GDP as big as it could have been? Why or why not?
d. Between 2001 and 2002 is the rate of increase of actual GDP bigger or smaller than the rate of increase of productive capacity? How is this possible?

3. Suppose that both a haircut (a service) and a watchband (a manufactured good) can be produced by an hour of labor (and for simplicity, no other resources) in 1999. (Assume profits are equal to zero.)

a. What is the cost of a haircut and a watchband in 1999 if the wage rate in both industries is $3 per hour?
b. If technological change is greater in the production of watchbands than in the production of haircuts, with the result that labor productivity increases by 5 percent per year in watchband production but by only 1 percent per year in haircut production, what was the cost of a haircut and a watchband in 2000, if the wage rate in both industries increases by 3 percent per year?
c. If labor productivity and wages increase at these rates, what was the cost of a haircut and of a watchband in 2001?
d. Do you think that this simple model helps explain why the costs of education, local government, and many other services have risen relative to the costs of manufactured goods in recent years? Why or why not?

LESSON REVIEW

If you had difficulty with the Self-Quiz or would like additional assistance, read the following lesson review. It should reinforce and help you understand the content presented in this lesson.

Growth of Per-Capita Output

Early in our history we achieved a high level of economic development and, by 1840, ranked fourth in the world in per capita output (after England, France, and Germany). By 1870, the United States had climbed to second place, and by 1900 to first.

Between 1913 and 1959 our growth slowed somewhat, but we held our lead among industrialized countries because our growth rate continued to exceed theirs (see Table 11.1 in text, page 248). Despite a general upward trend, our growth rate was far from steady. During periods of recession and depression it was low; during recovery and prosperity, it was high.

By the 1950s, the growth rate for the United States was slower than in many other countries. In the 1960s, it accelerated again, but not enough to push us back into the number one position. Overall, our per capita growth rate has held steady at an average of about 2 percent in the 1929 to 1970 period.

But other countries including Canada, France, Germany, and Italy grew at a faster rate in the 1929 to 1970 period. From 1950 to 1980, Japan grew faster than any other country in the world. Though China was growing faster than any other country in the 1990s according to its own data, the United States was growing faster than all other developed countries during that decade.

Factors Contributing to Economic Growth

What factors influence economic growth? The following are likely to have the greatest impact.

1. *Population.* Our population has more than tripled since 1900, partly because of the birth rate and partly because of immigration. Although the birth rate has fallen in recent years, continued growth of the population is anticipated. It is important to recognize, however, that population growth contributes to GDP only so long as it is matched by technological growth; otherwise, it can be a detriment.

2. *Education.* Ours is a country that places relatively high value on public education. By 1980, more than 80 percent of our nation's 17-year-olds could be classified as high school graduates, up from 6.4 percent in 1900. We know that growth in knowledge and skill supports our country's economic growth, and some researchers even believe there are ways to quantify that support. Their evidence suggests that education has been a major contributor to economic growth.

3. *Technological change.* The contributions of technology, like those of education, have been significant. It is difficult, however, to separate education from technology or investment in physical capital (machines and equipment) since these three are interdependent. That is, through education we create the capacity to achieve technology, which in turn can be implemented only if the capital is in place to support it.

   The United States has been a world leader in technology for some time, well over a century. A part of this lead is attributable to the organization of research and development laboratories (the first of which was established in 1876). Prior to the time of the laboratories, technology inched forward one invention at a time. The laboratories allowed talented innovators to pool their knowledge and skills and to market the results more systematically.

4. *Capital formation.* In recent years, we have put about 10 percent of our GDP into capital formation, the generation of new plant and equipment. This priority has given U.S. workers a decided edge; they have more resources with which to work and more up-to-date facilities and equipment than their counterparts elsewhere.

5. *Natural resources.* The United States is fortunate in having an abundance of natural resources, including land and minerals, fertile soil, moderate climate, coal, and oil. Countries with limited natural resources, such as England, Japan, and Switzerland, can import resources or take other productive measures to equalize their opportunities for development, but the costs of such steps can be great.

6. *Environment and values.* American society generally promotes economic growth. For one thing, our value system, which emphasizes work and achievement, supports such growth. In addition, our overall political and economic freedom have encouraged technological development and innovation that might well have been stifled elsewhere. The price system is one of the better devices for allocating resources and discouraging waste and misuse.

During periods when intended spending is too low, however, investment may decline, and many firms may resist new technology, viewing it as a threat to the worker's rightful place in the economy. Such factors can have a negative effect on growth.

The Productivity Slowdown and Its Consequences

The marked slowdown in productivity during the 1970s worried economists for two major reasons:

1. It reflected a possible decrease in the rate of technological change, which could affect future potential for growth.

2. It was seen as a potential contributor to inflation.

In addition, economists were not simply worried about technological slowdown per se but about a reduction in the United States's technological lead over other countries. Too much slowdown could severely impair our ability to compete effectively in world markets.

Causes of the Productivity Slowdown

What causes contributed to the productivity slowdown during the 1970s? Various studies have pinpointed the following factors:

1. Increased proportion of baby-boom teenagers and women participating in the labor force. Because of limited experience and training, these persons had a lower per-capita output rate than workers in general.

2. Reduction in the rate of growth of the capital-labor ratio. Investment in capital was fairly high during the 1950s and 1960s but declined considerably after 1973.

3. Shift from goods to services. Ours had become a more service-oriented economy. Some economists argue that it is more difficult to increase productivity in service industries than in manufacturing industries.

4. Increased government regulation, particularly in the areas of safety and the environment, reduced productivity growth by 0.4 percent per year since 1973.

5. The proportion of GDP devoted to R & D decreased between 1964 and 1978 but recovered partially by 1985. The impact on our technological lead and competitiveness will be felt in the long run.

Has There Been a Decline in the U.S. Innovation Rate?

Innovation (the production of new products and processes) may be declining. The evidence is not overwhelming, but it commands our attention all the same. Essentially it rests on statistics of two types:

1. The decline in the patent rate after 1969. Fewer patents were being granted, but of what significance is each patent? More than statistical analysis is needed before this evidence can be considered conclusive.

2. The decline in the number of major innovations carried out over specified time periods. Again, the number of innovations in an industry, say, pharmaceuticals, may be down, but how important is each innovation and what are its implications for our economy and lifestyle?

The declining rate of innovation has hit some industries harder than others. In part, this results from the fact that certain industries, such as pharmaceuticals, are heavily affected by government regulation, and their rate of growth is thereby impeded. Other industries, however, like microelectronics, are not similarly encumbered, and their rate of growth has been little short of phenomenal during the last decade.

R & D Spending: Another Factor in the Slowdown

Generally, R & D spending has increased dramatically in dollar figures; in 2002, it was over 25 times what it was in 1945. But as a percentage of gross domestic product, R & D spending declined between 1964 and 1978. There were some increases in the late 1970s, but the percentages never approached earlier levels. Several reasons for the slowdown have been proposed: spending in other areas, a winding down of the space program, less emphasis on national defense, and a decline in profitability of R & D. However, in the 1980s, increased spending on military R & D and improved civilian technology increased the proportion of GDP spent on R & D from 2.2 percent in 1978 to 2.7 percent in 1985. The federal government financed about one-third of the R & D in the United States in the 1980s, but because of the rapid increase in private funding, that percentage is now down 28 percent.

- *National defense and space technology.* Because national security and space exploration are public goods (available to all, regardless of their personal financial support), the government must take primary responsibility for research in these areas. Of course, not everyone agrees on the extent to which R & D in these areas benefits the civilian sector.
- *Science.* Because the results of science research are unpredictable, it is unlikely that private investment would be sufficient here to promote an acceptable level of public good; therefore, government plays a major role here too.

In addition to direct support of R & D efforts, the government has other means of supporting civilian R & D. These include the use of R & D tax credits and the proposed use of federal grants and contracts.

R & D Tax Credits

In 1981, Congress passed a 25 percent (later changed to 20 percent) incremental tax credit to encourage R & D. This measure offered the advantage of relatively simple administration, combined with some disadvantages:

1. It rewarded firms for doing the R & D they might have done anyway.
2. It may have tended to encourage ongoing R & D more than innovation.

Federal Grants and Contracts

This approach is already used by the Department of Defense and the National Aeronautics and Space Administration. It has some potential difficulties in

1. Selecting contractors.
2. Determining whether patents resulting from R & D work can remain with the contractor.
3. Selecting projects with potentially high social benefits.

Expanded Responsibility of Federal Laboratories

It has also been suggested that the federal government expand ongoing work through government-run laboratories. This approach would afford the government significant control in selecting which sorts of projects might receive greatest support. But it could also incorporate problems of coordination. R & D is not an end in itself. The results of research must be marketed in such a way that they are both accessible and appealing to potential users. Whether government agencies are as qualified to perform this marketing function as commercial developers is questionable.

EXTENDED LEARNING

This section of the study guide is specifically designed for the two-semester student.

AUDIO

Before Listening
Read Exploring Further of Chapter 11, pages 261–262 in your text.

Next
Listen to the audiotape that accompanies Lesson 11.

After Listening
Answer the following questions:

1. Long-run economic growth can be attributed to three basic categories:

    a. An increase in productive inputs.
    b. An increase in the quality of the inputs.
    c. Better utilization of the inputs.

    Give examples of each category.

2. What has the reduction in the number of farms to do with U.S. growth, and how might agricultural price-support programs hinder growth?

3. How does rapid productivity growth tend to dampen inflation, and what was the relation between productivity and inflation in 1977 to 1980?

4. Were Carter's methods of encouraging greater productivity growth similar to those of Reagan?

5. How could the events of the 1970s and early 1980s have had a dampening effect on investment?

ADDITIONAL READINGS

Bowles, Samuel, David M. Gordon, and Thomas E. Weisskopf. "A Social Model for U.S. Productivity Growth." *Challenge* 27 (March–April 1984): 41–48.

The authors argue that the common explanations for the productivity slowdown are inadequate. They stress changes in worker motivation, conflict in the workplace, and the rate of business innovation. No mathematics or graphs.

Denison, Edward. *Accounting for Slower Economic Growth*. Washington, DC: Brookings Institution, 1979.

Chapters 1 and 2 survey the causes of the productivity slowdown, and Chapter 5 details the effects of the slowing of labor reallocation, pollution control, crime, technology, and economies of scale on productivity growth. The influence the high variation in business activity may have had on productivity is also discussed. No mathematics or graphs.

Heilbroner, Robert L., and Lester C. Thurow. *Economics Explained*. Englewood Cliffs, NJ: Prentice-Hall, 1982.

Chapter 14, "Falling Behind: The Productivity Problem," gives a brief overview of the recent record on productivity for the United States in comparison with other countries and discusses some of the reasons why productivity growth in the United States since the early 1970s has been low. No mathematics or graphs.

Kutscher, R., J. Mark, and J. Norsworthy. "The Productivity Slowdown and the Outlook to 1985." *Monthly Labor Review* 100 (May 1977): 3–8.

The authors summarize the historical record of productivity growth and project the changes in productivity using the factors discussed in the text (composition of the labor force, capital-labor ratio, intersectoral shifts in production, and the effect of pollution abatement and energy costs). No mathematics or graphs.

Mansfield, Edwin. "Basic Research and Productivity Increase in Manufacturing." *American Economic Review* 70 (December 1980): 863–873.

Argues that there is evidence that the rate of productivity increase is directly related to the amount of basic research carried out by the firm or industry. Also describes the changes in the composition of R & D in the 1970s. Difficult mathematics, but the article can be useful without fully understanding the mathematics, no graphs.

ANSWER KEY

Video Questions

1. The factors are numerous and complex, but the most significant are probably these: First, concern over the environment prompted stringent new regulations that made industrial expansion difficult. Innovation was thwarted as industries struggled to survive within the regulations. In addition, money that might have gone for capital investment was diverted into economic restoration. Second, the composition of the labor force was undoubtedly a factor. Many workers were

baby boomers with new or first-time jobs; some had little experience or training. Hence, their output was lower. Third, the oil embargo triggered soaring energy costs that affected both industry and consumers. It became harder for industry to realize a profit, and consumers in turn had less to spend. Moreover, the energy costs were but one part of a larger inflationary picture. Generally higher prices everywhere further discouraged capital investment and made a turnaround seem even more unlikely. A decline in R & D investment put a leash on new technology that might otherwise have spurred new growth. All these factors, working together, brought productivity during the 1970s to less than half the rate during the previous half century.

2. According to economist Richard Gill, these seemingly small numbers (a 1 percent increase in growth or a 2 percent increase) really involve huge changes in output per capita. Although our historic productivity increase hovered just under 2 percent per year, even that rate increased consumers' real incomes—purchasing power, that is—by fivefold within the last few decades. Similarly, even the slightest decline can reduce consumers' purchasing power, decreasing overall demand and slowing productivity in an alarming, self-perpetuating way.

3. New technology is vital to our productivity. It stimulates productivity in several ways. First, it allows the development of new products. Second, it improves the efficiency with which existing products are produced. And third, it induces investment through the promise of increased efficiency and profits. Not least of all, technology has enormous impact on our lifestyles. As a result of space engineering technology, Americans have witnessed unprecedented advances in metallurgy, telecommunications, electronics, and other fields. Technology does much to enrich our lives.

4. Many economists have been critical of too much government involvement, rguing that regulation (particularly that connected to concern for the environment) restricted investment and expansion. Similarly, taxes can inhibit growth or even force shutdowns. On the other hand, although most technology research has been financed by private investment, government can play a role in stimulating research and development through support to private industry, encouragement of innovation, and direct financing of projects that would simply be too costly for private industry.

5. Supply-siders, as they are sometimes called, tend to see government as "the source, not the solution, of our economic miseries." Their philosophy is that private industry should be freed from government interference: Regulation should be held to a minimum, corporate and private taxes should be reduced or restricted, and the free market should be allowed to function without government interference. Supply-siders generally hold that tax cuts encourage productivity by encouraging workers to work harder with the incentive that they get to keep more of what they produce. (Those who oppose this philosophy counter that tax cuts simply encourage more savings, not spending or investment.) Supply-siders had a chance to test their philosophy under the Reagan administration, with massive tax cuts in three successive years of the president's first term. Economists do not agree on the results, however. Some, like Arthur Laffer, believe the

program was enormously successful: more workers working and higher productivity per employed worker. Others are skeptical, admitting a boost in productivity in the long run but attributing this difference to traditional forces of Keynesian economics, through which increased investment improves capital and working conditions, increasing productivity.

Multiple Choice

1. a   Text, 251–253.
2. b   Text, 248, Table 11.1.
3. c   Text, 249, Table 11.2.
4. d   Text, 249.
5. b   Text, 251, Table 11.3.
6. a   Text, 253.
7. c   Text, 254.
8. a   Text, 255.
9. a   Text, 259.
10. d Text, 254.

True-False

1. True   Video.
2. True   Video.
3. False   Video.
4. True   Video.
5. True   Video.
6. True   Video.
7. False   Video.
8. False   Video; Text, 249.
9. False   Video.
10. True   Video; Text, 262.

Discussion Questions

1. The slowdown in growth in the U.S. economy in the 1970s has been attributed to the huge increase in the numbers of inexperienced teenagers and women participating in the labor force, the reduction in the capital-labor ratio, the shift from goods to services, increased government regulation, and the reduced proportion of GDP spent on research and development.

   Proponents of rapid economic growth point to the increased standard of living this growth makes possible. They also point to the need for rapid economic growth if the U.S. economy is to remain a world leader. Opponents of rapid economic growth stress resource depletion and environmental degradation. They argue that economic growth must come without sacrificing our environmental quality.

   The government can alter the rate of growth in the economy by engaging in policies supportive of innovation: Such policies place a premium on education, incentives for industries to engage in research and development, capital accumulation, technological innovation, and the wise use of our natural resources.

2. The United States has since 1900 held a technological lead over the rest of the world. This lead, however, is not as strong as it once was because the U.S. rate of change is slowing and other countries, notably Japan, have economies that are growing at much faster rates than our economy. Technological change comes from both the private sector, where individuals develop new ideas, and the government sector, where government support of research and development creates new techniques and products. Certainly, the space and military complex supported by the U.S. government created a number of new materials that subsequently found uses in the civilian economy.

3. Only if output is held constant do increases in the rate of technological change result in an increase in aggregate unemployment. If output grows at the same rate as or at a greater rate than technological change, then it is possible for unemployment to remain at the same level or even decrease.

4. The government may support one type of research and development over another due to its perception of its comparative advantage in producing goods relative to the comparative advantage of other countries. For instance, it may be more profitable for the government to support research and development in the energy industry relative to the textile industry because the energy industry may pay a higher return and require a higher quality of resources than the textile industry. It would be a more efficient use of resources to employ our higher-quality resources in the energy industry and let another economy, with lower-quality resources (e.g., a less-educated labor force), employ its resources in the textile field. In fact, the historical record of the textile industry supports this point: Over the years, the textile industry has moved from Great Britain to New England to the southern U.S. states to the Pacific Rim. In each of these moves, the textile industry searched out lower-cost, lower-quality labor rather than remain in an economy with relatively higher-cost, higher-quality labor.

Problem Set

1. a. Increased unemployment.
   b. Upward. To the point where it intersects the 45-degree line at $1,100 million.

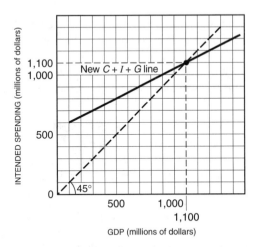

   c. Increase the money supply, reduce interest rates, increase government spending, or reduce taxes.

2. a.

Year	Productive capacity	Actual GDP
2001	100	95
2002	105	100
2003	110	107

  b. No, because, in 2002, actual GDP was less than it could have been if all capacity were utilized.
  c. No, because, in 2003, actual GDP was less than it could have been if all capacity were utilized.
  d. Bigger, because the rate of utilization of capacity was higher in 2003 than in 2002.

3. a. $3.
  b. $3.06 for a haircut and $2.94 for a watchband.
  c. $3.12 for a haircut and $2.89 for a watchband.
  d. Yes, because productivity has not appeared to have risen as rapidly in some of the service industries as in manufacturing.

Audio/Text Questions

1. a. An increase in population of working age, an increase in the capital stock, or the discovery of new resource deposits.
   b. Education or newer plant and equipment.
   c. Improvements in managerial techniques, technological change, or more efficient use of resources.

2. The transfer of labor out of those farms that were only marginally viable to industry raised general productivity. Farm support programs, which keep people on farms that either have low productivity or produce unnecessary or surplus goods, hurt U.S. growth by reducing the average rate of productivity growth and causing an excessive amount of resources to be devoted to agriculture.

3. If wages increase by 5 percent and productivity increases by 5 percent, then the unit labor cost has not changed and the firm need not raise prices to cover the increased wage. In the late 1970s, productivity growth was very low while wage gains were high, so a wage-price spiral was created.

4. The Carter and Reagan programs were somewhat similar in that both favored deregulation and investment tax credits. Carter advocated an active role for government in establishing R & D centers, revision of patent policies, relaxation of antitrust for joint research ventures, and five-year plans for safety, health, and environmental regulations to reduce regulatory uncertainty. Reagan's basic plan was to reduce government involvement and let the private sector innovate without government interference. This was similar to some aspects of Carter's plan, but Reagan tried to carry it out more thoroughly.

5. The oil price shocks, other commodity shortages, and the uncertain and erratic use of fiscal and monetary policies could have held down investment expenditures by making it more difficult to estimate the future stream of returns from an investment. Interest rates were highly variable; this created uncertainty and made it difficult to raise money in equity or bond markets. Long-term investments were particularly affected.

LESSON 12. FEDERAL DEFICITS: CAN WE LIVE WITH THEM?

INTRODUCTION

For most of us, budgeting can be a real challenge in practice, but in theory it seems simple enough: Do not spend more than you take in. In particular, in this age of credit cards, we have had to learn some wariness about building debts to uncontrollable proportions, that is, to the point where we can no longer rid ourselves of those debts.

This desire for balance between income and outgo has traditionally affected the way many persons view government spending as well. However, the government is not bound by quite the same constraints. For one thing, the national debt is not a charge that falls due on a specified date like a bill from a retailer; it can go on indefinitely, declining a bit or—as in recent years—building to increasing proportions. And contrary to what most of us might have thought, during a recession deficits may be necessary or even beneficial to the economy. As it turns out, in fact, it is virtually impossible to deal with unemployment and erase the national deficit at the same time.

Does this mean that the national debt (the net accumulation of past deficits and surpluses) presents no danger? Some economists warn that, while annual budget deficits may have advantages, too large a national debt—just like an overwhelming personal debt—can spell disaster for the future by crippling the economy's ability to produce. In the simplest terms, the danger, these economists argue, lies in increasing the national debt faster than GDP increases, for then we must tax (and spend) inordinate amounts of our national income just to pay the interest on our national debt.

While we know a great deal more about managing fiscal policy now than during the days of the Great Depression, we are still a long way from having all the answers. Under what circumstances is a national deficit desirable? What are the long-range implications for future generations? And how much of a deficit can we reasonably tolerate? These are the questions we address within this chapter.

What You Should Learn

By the end of Lesson 12, you should be prepared to

1. Define what is meant by the terms *federal deficit* and *federal surplus* and explain how a deficit or surplus relates to the national debt.

2. Discuss the relative advantages and disadvantages of a balanced budget during periods of inflation or imminent recession.

3. Explain how public attitudes toward a balanced budget have changed over the past 75 years.

4. Define the *cyclically adjusted budget balance,* and explain how this device has been used by various administrations to measure the stabilization impact of the actual budget.

5. Discuss the effects of various strategies for financing a deficit or using a surplus.

6. Compare the effects of externally held (foreign) and internally held (domestic) national debt.

7. Describe the federal budgetary and the federal tax legislation processes.

8. Discuss the ways in which government has attempted to cope with the national debt under the Carter, Reagan, Bush Sr., Clinton, and Bush Jr. administrations.

KEY TERMS

federal deficit
national debt
surplus
balanced budget
functional finance
crowding-out effect
crowding-in effect

expansionary
contractionary
cyclically adjusted budget balance
federal budget
countercyclical policies

VIDEO

Watch

Economics U$A Program 12, "Federal Deficits: Can We Live with Them?"

Illustrative Events

How the United States managed the huge debt that financed World War II, with Roy Blough, former Treasury Department economist, and Richard Gilbert, former Commerce Department economist.

Eisenhower's attempt in 1958–60 to run a budget surplus despite a recession, a strategy that probably cost Richard Nixon the 1960 election; with Raymond Saulnier, Eisenhower's chair of the Council of Economic Advisers; and Herbert Stein, member of the Committee for Economic Development.

The dangers of Reagan's $200 billion-plus deficits of the 1980s; with former U.S. Representative Barber Conable; Martin Feldstein, former chair of the Council of Economic Advisers; and economist Alice Rivlin of the Brookings Institution. Richard Gill explains the dangers of structural deficits.

After Viewing

Answer the following questions:

1. How did the government use deficits to finance the war effort for World War II, and how did it attempt to pay off that debt?

2. What was the impact of government borrowing on the economy immediately following the war?

3. To what extent will the cost of financing World War II be borne by future generations?

4. How did the fiscal policies of Eisenhower and Nixon differ, and what impact did this difference have on Nixon's presidential campaign?

5. What was happening to the national deficit in the 1980s, and why were some economists concerned that the nature of this deficit might be more serious than in the past? Looking back now, have their concerns come to fruition?

Read

Read Chapter 12, "Surpluses, Deficits, Public Debt, and the Federal Budget," pages 265–285 in your text. After completing your reading, try the Self-Quiz.

SELF-QUIZ

Multiple Choice

1. The *federal deficit* is *best* defined as the

    a. total expenditures by the U.S. government.
    b. difference in expenditures between the actual and full-employment budgets.
    c. amount the government has had to borrow to finance its debts.
    d. difference between federal expenditures and federal revenue.

2. As a percentage of output, the federal deficit in the early 1980s

    a. was about 40 percent of output.
    b. rose considerably but remained below 6 percent.

c. was about the same as it had been in the past 40 years.
d. declined, as it has every year since World War II.

3. Many economists today probably agree that it is legitimate and even desirable for the federal government to run a deficit so long as

   a. it can balance the budget within the fiscal year.
   b. the deficit contributes to the stabilization of the economy.
   c. most of the debts are externally held.
   d. the deficit was incorporated into the annual budget.

4. Which of the following statements is *most* accurate? The idea that the budget should be balanced every year

   a. is new to economics and has never gained wide acceptance.
   b. is generally accepted among U.S. economists today, although it is discounted abroad.
   c. was the prevailing philosophy both here and abroad until the Great Depression.
   d. has been the prevailing philosophy for years in most countries except the United States.

5. Conservative emphasis on the usefulness of a balanced budget rests largely on their desire to

   a. limit government spending.
   b. make the budgeting process more organized and efficient.
   c. make reduction of unemployment the number one fiscal priority.
   d. create a more solid foundation for public welfare programs.

6. The government finances a deficit by

   a. lowering taxes for individuals and corporations.
   b. decreasing the demand for money.
   c. borrowing money.
   d. decreasing the supply of money.

7. Our national debt is the result of

   a. inflation.
   b. government borrowing.
   c. overseas loans.
   d. the Vietnam War.

8. For those born after 1980, Social Security and Medicare

   a. benefits will be great because of the large surpluses accumulated during the working years of the baby boom generation.
   b. will probably not survive until they retire.
   c. will cost more and return less than was true during the generations that preceded them.
   d. will disappear before they graduate from college.

9. If the economy is operating at full employment, a government deficit tends to have which of the following effects?

   a. It shifts the aggregate demand curve to the left.
   b. It shifts the short-run aggregate supply curve to the left.
   c. It shifts the short-run aggregate supply curve to the right.
   d. It shifts the aggregate demand curve to the right.

10. If, under the conditions of question 9, aggregate demand increases, what is the result?

    a. Increased unemployment
    b. Decreased output
    c. A government surplus
    d. Inflation

True-False

____ 1. As a percentage of national output, the national debt has grown steadily since World War II.

____ 2. Over the past 50 years, we learned enough about economics to realize that fiscal policy is virtually ineffectual in resolving modern economic problems.

____ 3. To become law, a tax bill must have the support of both the Senate and the House.

____ 4. During the Reagan years, taxes were cut but government expenditures increased for defense and because of the 1981–82 recession. The result was a dramatic increase in federal government deficits.

____ 5. Most economists support the position that a government's budget should be balanced over the course of each business cycle.

____ 6. The expenditures of World War II were financed largely through taxes.

____ 7. One example of a countercyclical policy is increased spending during periods of recession.

____ 8. Nixon blamed his loss of the 1960 presidential election on the failure of the Eisenhower administration to balance the budget.

____ 9. Most economists tend to agree that the huge deficits incurred under the Reagan administration have actually contributed to the strength of the economic recovery.

____ 10. According to former U.S. Representative Barber Conable, the secret to managing government deficits is to ensure that the economy grows faster than the national debt.

Discussion Questions

1. Is it true that, because of our large national debt, we are in danger of going bankrupt? Why or why not? Is it true that the national debt is a burden that we are transmitting to future generations? Why or why not?

2. If a balanced federal budget is not that important for the economy, why did President Reagan promise to have a balanced budget?

3. Does it make any difference if the government, to finance a budget deficit, borrows from the Fed rather than the general public?

4. During the 1970s and 1980s, there was considerable discussion in the business press of the crowding-out effect. In 1975, when the federal deficit grew to $43.6 billion, the *Wall Street Journal,* among others, worried that the government, when it borrowed the money to meet this deficit, would crowd private borrowers out of the credit markets. Similar feelings were expressed in 1985, when the deficit was far larger than in 1975.

    a. What factors determine the extent to which an increase in government expenditures causes an increase in the interest rate?
    b. Under what conditions does the resulting increase in interest rates result in less private investment?
    c. If this crowding-out effect occurs, does GDP rise by the full amount indicated by the multiplier? Why or why not?
    d. When government expenditures are reduced, can the crowding-out effect work in reverse? Why or why not?

Problem Set

1. The following set of equations defines a model of our basic economy:

    $C_d = 200 + 0.8Y_d$

    $GDP = Y_d$

    $I_d = 160,$

    where C_d equals intended consumption expenditure, I_d equals intended investment, and Y_d equals disposable income. We now add a government sector to this model. In particular, let both government spending (on goods and services) and taxes equal $500 million.

    a. Draw this economy in the following grid.

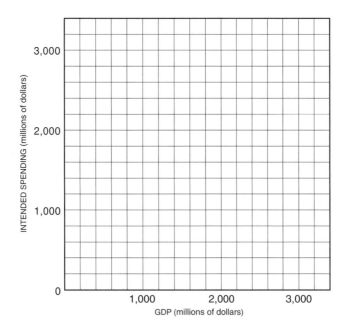

b. Determine equilibrium GDP and show it in your diagram.
c. What is the multiplier for this economy? Demonstrate that your result is correct.
d. Government spending increases to $700 million, while everything else remains constant. What happens to equilibrium GDP?
e. Must intended saving equal intended investment at the equilibrium GDP you determined in part d? Why or why not?

2. The following figures (in millions of dollars) pertain to country Q's economy at various levels of GDP:

Taxes	GDP	Disposable income	Intended consumption expenditure	Intended saving
25	1,000	975	898	77
30	1,100	1,070	983	87
38	1,200	1,162	1,066	96
50	1,300	1,250	1,145	105
67	1,400	1,333	1,220	113
90	1,500	1,410	1,289	121
120	1,600	1,480	1,352	128
158	1,700	1,542	1,408	134
205	1,800	1,595	1,456	139

Suppose that intended investment is $128 million and government expenditures on goods and services equal $27 million.

a. What is the equilibrium level of GDP? What is the status of the government's budget at this value of GDP?

b. Assume full employment to occur at GDP = $1,600 million. If changes in government expenditures are the country's only policy tool, how large must these expenditures be to move the economy to full employment? What is the status of the government's budget once full employment is reached?

3. In the previous problem, suppose that intended investment increases to $143 million and government expenditures on goods and services rise to $37 million.

   a. Is equilibrium GDP the same as it was in the previous problem? What is the new level of equilibrium GDP? What is the status of the government's budget at this equilibrium value of GDP?
   b. Assume full employment to occur at GDP = $1,600 million. How large must government expenditures be to move the country to full employment? When it gets there, does the sum of taxes and intended saving equal the sum of government expenditures and intended investment? Why or why not?

4. You are given the following information about an economy: GDP = $20 billion at full employment, GDP = $16 billion currently, taxes = 0.1(GDP), and government expenditures on goods and services = $1.8 billion.

   a. Is the government running a surplus or a deficit?
   b. Suppose you learn that when GDP = $20 billion, intended saving = $1.8 billion, and intended investment = $1.5 billion. If tax rates cannot be changed and government expenditures are altered to push the economy to full employment, is there a surplus or deficit? How big?

5. Suppose that the government of Erewhon borrows $1 billion at 8 percent interest from U.S. and British banks. The money is invested in irrigation projects that increase Erewhon's national output during the next five years by $300 million per year.

   a. Does this loan result in an increase in Erewhon's national debt? If so, by how much?
   b. Does this loan impose a net burden on the people of Erewhon? Why or why not?

LESSON REVIEW

If you had difficulty with the Self-Quiz, you may wish to go through the following Lesson Review before returning to the text. It should reinforce and help you understand the content presented in this lesson.

Introduction

In the 1980s, the federal deficit (the difference between federal expenditures and revenue) grew to enormous and frightening proportions. To finance the deficit, the government borrowed heavily, partly through the sale of government bonds, thus driving the national debt (the amount owed by the federal government) skyward.

Economists who had previously accepted the concept of a deficit as inevitable and even desirable began to question seriously the limits to which that deficit had grown and ask whether indeed we should once again strive to balance the budget.

Three Perspectives on Balancing the Budget

Three main philosophies regarding balancing the budget merit our attention:

1. *Balance the budget every year.* The idea that the government's budget should be balanced annually was the prevailing attitude in this country until just a few decades ago. The idea enjoyed a strong revival during the early 1980s, as economists and consumers alike became increasingly alarmed about the rate at which the federal deficit was growing. The thing to keep in mind in reviewing this philosophy is that governments are not like families or firms; they are not bound by the same restrictions. There is no specified time, for example, when the money owed by the federal government becomes due. In paying its debts, the federal government borrows additional money, either from the central bank or through the sale of government bonds to citizens. This borrowing can do a great deal to stimulate the economy. If we accept the idea that the budget must be balanced, we in effect make it impossible for government to use fiscal policy to stabilize the economy. The actions required by government to achieve a balanced budget tend, in many cases, to aggravate both unemployment and inflation. For this reason, despite concern over mounting deficits, most economists do not favor the notion of an annually balanced budget.

2. *Balance the budget over the business cycle.* As we have seen, national output goes in cycles, increasing to a peak, then declining until it hits a trough, then mounting again. Unemployment tends to go in cycles as well. This philosophy suggests that the government run a large enough surplus during good economic times to offset its expenditures during down times. Clearly, this approach offers government more flexibility than the annually balanced budget approach. It has a major flaw, however: GDP and employment cycles are anything but regular. A long period of unemployment and low GDP could very well be followed by a short-lived peak of prosperity, then another valley. Under such circumstances, the government could not build sufficient financial resources during prosperity to offset its expenditures during low periods.

3. *Use functional finance.* The idea of living with a deficit to promote optimal combinations of unemployment and inflation is sometimes called *functional finance.* Its proponents hold that the problems created through a moderate growth in deficit are minor compared to the social costs of unemployment and inflation. Of course, the growth in the federal deficit has been anything but moderate in recent years.

The Structural Deficit

The structural deficit is another device for providing perspective about how the deficit affects the economy. The structural deficit shows the difference between tax revenues and government expenditures that would result if we had full employment.

It is quite possible, for example, for an administration to be running a budget surplus under current fiscal policy if GDP is at its potential, even though the actual budget shows a deficit because the economy is experiencing a recessionary gap. Under such circumstances, most economists feel that fiscal policy is not expansionary. Recent administrations have relied heavily on the structural deficit to gauge the impact of fiscal policy on the economy.

How Deficits Are Financed—How Surpluses Are Used

Deficits can be financed in two basic ways. First, the government can borrow from consumers and business firms, increasing the national debt. Such borrowing reduces the amount of money that consumers and firms might otherwise spend, of course; thus, some of the expansionary effect of the deficit is offset by reduced spending.

Second, the government can simply create new money. Since this approach does not affect spending, it tends to enhance the expansionary effects of the deficit more than the first approach.

One way the government can use a surplus is to buy back some of the bonds it sold to the public, reducing the national debt. Or the government can reduce taxes or increase government spending.

Government Debt

The national debt, which results from borrowing, is composed of bonds, notes, and other government IOUs of various kinds. The IOUs are held by individuals (perhaps you have some yourself), firms, banks, and public agencies both in this country and abroad. The market for government bonds is excellent because the risk is very low in comparison to other types of investments.

In 2002, the national debt was $6.2 trillion, the highest it has ever been. The national debt has grown almost every year, with a few exceptions, since the early part of the century. But the most marked increases have been during the years preceding and during World War II and again in the years following 1968, when it began truly to skyrocket. As a percentage of GDP, however, the national debt declined steadily after World War II. The percentage then rose from the early 1980s to the mid-1990s, when it fell again until 2002. In 2002, the percentage started rising again.

Why has the public been so distressed over the size of the national debt? One reason has been concern over placing a burden on future generations. However, we must realize again that the debt never falls due on any specified date. It has become something of a financial reality that we live with to keep the economy moving, somewhat the same way that a family accepts certain expenses like those for rent or groceries or fuel as inevitable. In any event, the primary way that one generation imposes a burden on another is by using up some of the country's productive capacity or failing to add a normal increment to this capacity (through research and development and capital investment). This was the case with the Vietnam War, for example. The borrowing for the war effort has not hurt us as much as that many resources used to produce helicopters and war planes might have been used for other purposes.

Another potentially adverse result of a government deficit is the crowding-out of private investment due to increases in government borrowing, which leads to higher interest rates.

In addition, we must recognize the effects of externally held debt, that is, the debt owed to countries overseas from whom we currently borrow extensively. To repay such debts, we must send goods and services overseas that would otherwise be available to our citizens.

The Federal Budgetary Process: A Brief Review

The federal budget runs for one fiscal year: October 1 to September 30. The steps by which the budget is prepared are, since the Congressional Budget and Impoundment Control Act of 1974, fairly well defined and coordinated. Prior to that time, preparation of federal budgets was a rather haphazard affair.

Budget makers begin their preparations for the budget about 15 months in advance. Briefly, these are the steps involved:

1. Federal agencies submit program proposals to the president and the Office of Management and Budget.

2. The president, together with members of the Office of Management and Budget, reviews these proposals and makes modifications.

3. In January (preceding the fiscal year), the president submits a budget to Congress.

4. Congressional committees review the budget and propose changes.

5. The Congressional Budget Office offers economic analyses to help senators and representatives evaluate alternatives.

6. In May, Congress passes a resolution setting tentative targets for spending and revenues.

7. Before late September, Congress adopts a second resolution, setting limits on both spending and revenues.

Federal Tax Legislation: A Brief Review of the Process

How does the federal government decide how much to tax? Generally, the government begins by looking at the existing tax structure, although periodic changes may be warranted. Here is how they come about:

1. The first initiative often comes from the president, who makes a recommendation in the State of the Union message, budget message, or a special tax message.

(Background information to support this recommendation has already been provided by economic advisers in the Treasury Department, Office of the Tax Legislative Counsel, or Internal Revenue Service.)

2. Representatives of labor, industry, agriculture, and other affected groups voice their views through public forums.
3. A tax bill incorporating the proposed change is submitted to the Ways and Means Committee of the House of Representatives.
4. The committee recommends changes and refers the bill to the House of Representatives.
5. The bill is sent to the Senate, where it is referred to the Finance Committee.
6. A vote is held. If the bill is voted down, that ends the matter.
7. If the bill passes the Senate vote and if it differs from the House version (which is usually the case), it is submitted to a conference committee where differences between the House and Senate versions can be reconciled.
8. The final version is submitted to the president for his or her signature (rarely does a president veto a tax bill).

Fiscal Policy: Carter through Clinton

Briefly, here are a few of the fiscal strategies used by various administrations from Carter's on. Note the emphasis given to tax reduction.

Carter *1978:* $19 billion tax cut (originally $24 billion tax cut proposed by President Carter).

Reagan *1981:* Large tax cut for both individuals and businesses.
1983: A large increase in Social Security taxes.
1986: Revenue-neutral tax reform that eliminated many tax loopholes while reducing tax rates.

Bush *1989–1993:* Reductions in defense spending as a result of the end of the Cold War.
1990: Bush breaks "no new tax" pledge and agrees with Congress to raise taxes on upper-income earners.

Clinton *1993:* Increases the tax rate on upper-income earners again.
1993: Continued reductions in defense spending.

We have learned much about managing the economy over the past 75 years. In particular we learned that solutions are not simple and no single approach serves as a panacea. Our economy is too complex and too changeable for that. Each administration faces a slightly different combination of problems than the previous one. Finding that fiscal policy does not cure all our ills is no reason for abandoning it; used effectively in combination with monetary policy, many economists believe that fiscal policy can stimulate growth and create jobs.

EXTENDED LEARNING

This section of the study guide is specifically designed for the two-semester student.

AUDIO

Listen

Listen to the audiotape that accompanies Lesson 12. There is no additional reading assignment for this lesson.

After Listening

Answer the following questions:

1. In what two major ways can the government can finance a deficit, and what are the effects of each?

2. Henry Wallich of the Federal Reserve Board was quoted as saying, "If we attempted a more stimulative program, business would spend less." Explain what he means and indicate its significance for public policy. Do you agree or not? Why?

3. Why is it important to distinguish between the actual and the full-employment budget?

4. Why didn't the huge deficits of 1985 and 1986 crowd out investment for plant and equipment?

5. Generally speaking, if debt is used to make investments to generate a future stream of payments that will more than pay off the debt, it is wise to go into debt. To what extent is the federal debt used for investments like this?

ADDITIONAL READINGS

Gramlich, Edward M. "How Bad Are the Large Deficits?" In *Federal Budget Policy in the 1980s*, edited by Gregory B. Mills and John L. Poland, 43–65. Washington, DC: Urban Institute Press, 1984.

> An evaluation of how large and persistent the deficits will be in the future and the reasons why these deficits may be harmful to the economy are detailed. The effects on investment and the ability of the economy to maintain present growth rates of consumption are discussed. No mathematics or graphs.

230 | LESSON 12

Mishan, E. J. *Twenty-One Popular Economic Fallacies,* 2d ed. New York: Praeger, 1973.

> Chapter 5, "The National Debt Is a Burden," clarifies the extent to which the national debt could cause a burden on future generations and explains why the common perception of the burden of the debt is erroneous. No mathematics or graphs.

Ritter, Lawrence S., and William L. Silber. *Money,* 5th ed. New York: Basic Books, 1984.

> Chapter 13, "Should We Worry about the National Debt?" discusses the extent to which the national debt reflects a burden on future generations, the distributional consequences of a large national debt, and some of the factors that affect the management of the debt. No mathematics or graphs.

Rabuska, Alvin. "Controlling the Federal Budget." In *To Promote Prosperity*, edited by John H. Moore, 199–216. Stanford, CA: Hoover Institution Press, 1984.

> A leading proponent of a balanced budget amendment discusses why such an amendment is both necessary and feasible. No mathematics or graphs.

Tobin, James. "The Fiscal Revolution: Disturbing Prospects." *Challenge* 27 (January–February 1985): 12–16.

> Provides a brief historical survey of fiscal policy from World War II to the deficits of the Reagan years and argues that the massive Reagan deficits and tight monetary policies are harmful for the long-term growth of the economy. No mathematics or graphs.

ANSWER KEY

Video Questions

1. Tax revenues during World War II paid for less than half of the war effort. The rest was paid for through borrowing, primarily through the sale of government war bonds and stamps. In addition, the government imposed price and wage controls to keep inflation in hand during this period. When the bonds came due, the government paid this debt by incurring another, through more borrowing. This policy caused some economists to refer to the war debt as "a debt that never really went away," although it did shrink in comparison to the GNP.

2. The impact of government borrowing after the war was highly positive. Because so many resources had been devoted to the war effort, the economy was such that luxury items were virtually unobtainable, and even many necessities were scarce. Although people once again had money to spend, there was little to spend it on. For this reason, it would have been virtually impossible to stimulate economic growth without government intervention. The government borrowing drove up

GNP, initiating new business investment and eventually resulting in new jobs and increased consumer spending. Without such borrowing, most economists now agree, the country might well have headed into another severe depression.

3. According to economist Richard Gill, the "basic costs of World War II were borne by the generation that lived and worked during World War II." How is that so? Largely because immediately preceding the war years, unemployment was at its peak in the United States. Resources not being used anyway were employed for the war effort. However, the war did impose one direct cost on the next generation. To the extent that the country used its resources to produce goods that served only the war effort and were not transferable to a civilian, peacetime economy, the nation's future productive capacity was inhibited. In other words, if the country had devoted those same resources to business development, agricultural growth, and so on, its productive capacity in some respects might have been measurably greater.

4. President Eisenhower was determined to leave office with a balanced budget; therefore, in a concerted effort to create a surplus, he opposed tax cuts and government spending in any form. Richard Nixon (Eisenhower's vice president at the time and seeking election to the presidency), on the other hand, wanted to see the economy grow; this was a critical issue for him in an election year. President Eisenhower may have underestimated the depth of the recession that began during the last months of his administration. In any case, Nixon was forced to campaign during increasingly depressed economic times; the economy was slowly grinding down and Senator Kennedy was promising to get things up and moving again. Nixon felt strongly that the recession of 1960, which might have been prevented or moderated through an expansionary fiscal policy (which he advocated), cost him the election.

5. According to Martin Feldstein, former chair of the Council of Economic Advisers, if we continued adding to the national debt at the rate of the mid-1980s (6 percent of GNP), our deficit would grow by more than $1 trillion within five years. This means that taxpayers would have to help finance the interest on that debt through increased tax rates. It also means that the government would need to borrow large portions of national savings, money that might otherwise be used for investment and housing. Over the past 20 years, we have borrowed heavily from other countries—a situation that has many economists worried, since we must repay those debts and, by sending others resources, our own people cannot have them. At the heart of this concern is the realization that once the debt grows faster than GNP, it can quickly become unmanageable. It can grow to a point where any hope of repaying it is lost because it takes all the resources the economy can muster just to cope with a portion of the interest on the debt. Eventually, the validity of the monetary system itself could be threatened. In short, what can work to our advantage in manageable proportions can threaten our very economic existence if allowed to get out of hand.

Multiple Choice

1. d Text, 265.
2. b Text, 266.
3. b Text, 276–278.
4. c Text, 276.
5. a Text, 278–279.
6. c Text, 268–271.
7. b Text, 272.
8. a Text, 278; Video.
9. d Video.
10. d Video.

True-False

1. False Text, 273–274.
2. False Text, 278.
3. True   Text, 279–281.
4. True   Video; Text, 282.
5. False Text, 277.
6. False Video.
7. True   Video.
8. False Video.
9. True   Video.
10. True Video.

Discussion Questions

1. No. Governments can run large debts without fear of going bankrupt. The national debt never falls due on a certain date, and in that sense, it cannot be viewed as a burden we are transmitting to future generations. However, the national debt may impose a burden on a future generation if it represents a decrease in the country's productive capacity or a failure to increase this productive capacity at its normal rate. For example, during times of war, resources are diverted to the production of military equipment; these resources are not available to produce other goods and services.

2. The notion of a balanced federal budget gained momentum during the early 1980s as both economists and consumers became increasingly concerned about the rate at which the federal deficit was growing. Voters do not always understand the mechanism of government finance, nor do they always understand how the government's budget differs from a personal budget. Some of the concern the Reagan administration voiced about the deficit was genuine concern, while some of this concern was election-year politics.

3. When the government borrows from the Fed, the money supply increases and the borrowing may contribute to inflationary pressure in the economy.

4. a. The slope of the supply curve for loanable funds and the extent to which the demand curve for loanable funds shifts out determines the increase in the interest rate. The interest rate may be subsequently affected if the greater government expenditure increases national output, as this results in a shifting out of the supply curve for loanable funds.
   b. The increase in interest rates result in less private investment if the government's demand for loanable funds replaces the private sector's demand for loanable funds. This is easily seen in Figure 12.2.
   c. With crowding out, the increase in government expenditure results in a decrease in investment spending. The multiplier is reduced because financing government expenditures through borrowing results in a decrease in the level of investment, thereby reducing the total change in the level of national output.

d. A reduction in government expenditures causes the demand for loanable funds to shift back to the left by the amount of the decrease in government spending. This reduces the interest rate and results in increased investment spending given that the supply of loanable funds is an upward-sloping curve.

Problem Set

1. a.

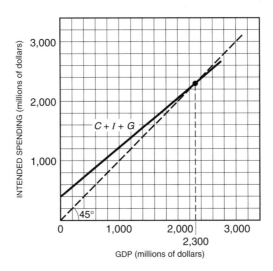

   b. $2,300 million. See part a.
   c. 5. A $1 increase in investment increases GDP by $5.
   d. It increases by $1,000 million.
   e. No. Intended saving plus taxes must equal intended investment plus government spending.

2. a. Since intended investment plus government spending equals $155 million, this should also be the sum of intended saving plus taxes. This is the case when GDP = $1,300 million, so equilibrium GDP is $1,300 million. The government runs a surplus of $23 million.
   b. $120 million. There is a balanced budget.

3. a. No. The new equilibrium GDP is $1,400 million. The government runs a surplus of $30 million.
   b. $105 million. Yes, because this is a necessary condition for equilibrium (if net exports are zero).

4. a. A deficit of $0.2 billion.
   b. A deficit of $0.3 billion.

5. a. Yes. $1 billion.
   b. No, because the extra annual output exceeds the interest cost by $220 million (which, after five years, accumulates to be enough to pay off the amount borrowed).

Audio/Text Questions

1. The government can either sell its bonds (its IOUs) to consumers and corporations or it can sell them to the Federal Reserve. If it sells them to the private sector, it increases the national debt and tends to reduce the private sector's spending on consumption or investment goods. If the Federal Reserve buys them, it is called *monetizing the debt,* because it increases the national money supply just as any open market operations in which the Fed buys bonds cause the money supply to increase. This tends to create inflation (depending in part on how much excess capacity the economy has at the time).

2. Wallich's argument is this: If fiscal and monetary policies are very stimulative when the economy is close to full employment or when inflationary expectations are great, the stimulus tends to raise interest rates, forcing business to curtail its spending for plant and equipment. Every additional dollar of federal spending might crowd out a dollar of private sector spending. The accuracy of Wallich's statement depends on economic conditions. It would tend to be true at full employment or if the economy expects inflation.

3. If the government is running a deficit while the economy is at full employment, it overstimulates the economy and creates inflationary pressures. If the economy is far below full employment, the deficit is not so inflationary. Instead, it is needed to encourage aggregate demand. Therefore, knowledge of whether the deficit would exist if the economy was at full employment or not is necessary to determine whether the deficit should be reduced or increased.

4. Foreign investors, given nominal U.S. interest rates and the outlook for inflation and changes in the exchange rate of the dollar, felt that the United States was a good place to invest. Huge amounts of capital flowed to the United States, permitting investment to take place. The federal deficit was partly financed by foreign funds.

5. A large percentage of federal spending simply transfers money from one person to another. Large percentages are for national defense, the creation of housing, plant and equipment, and education, all of which yield a future stream of returns, although some people value it much less than others. Funds spent for education, research, or maintenance of the health of the population (which transfer payments do in part) could also be considered as investments, although again, it is very difficult to evaluate the stream of returns. Much of federal spending, and therefore a part of the debt, could be considered to be investing in the future productive potential of the country.

LESSON 13. MONETARY POLICY: HOW WELL DOES IT WORK?

INTRODUCTION

How do you determine what portion of your income to put in the bank or invest for the future or just keep in your pocket to spend? While countless factors can influence your decision, chances are that you consider carefully your present level of income, the current state of the economy, and the interest you are likely to draw through savings or investments. These factors, in turn, are determined partially by the quantity of money available in our economy and the current price level.

How is that quantity established? And what is the relationship between the quantity of money in circulation at any given time and the prices we pay for the goods and services we buy? In this chapter, we begin to answer these and related questions. We also take a closer look at the role of the Fed, a role that has not been easy to play. As the major controller of our money supply, the Fed has a responsibility for reviewing and reading the economic indicators that tell us whether the economy is booming or declining. Unfortunately, not everyone agrees on which economic indicators are most reliable. Nor does everyone agree on how our major economic problems should be handled. As we shall see, the Fed has come under heavy criticism from two quarters: from conservatives who believe inflation has not been properly curbed and from liberals who believe the Fed has not attended closely enough to the problems of unemployment.

What You Should Learn

By the end of Lesson 13, you should be prepared to

1. Explain the relationship between the value of money and the price level.
2. Explain the relationship between inflation, unemployment, and the money supply.
3. List three factors affecting the demand for money.
4. Describe the effect of the money supply on interest rates, investment, and equilibrium GDP.

5. Describe the economic conditions under which monetary policy would be described as tight or easy.

6. Discuss the responsibilities and problems faced by the Fed in formulating monetary policy.

7. Summarize and comment on Milton Friedman's proposal that the Fed be governed by a rule specifying the rate of growth for the money supply.

8. Compare the more-sophisticated version of the quantity theory with the crude quantity theory.

KEY TERMS

money supply
precautionary demand for money
investment function
velocity
crude quantity theory
rate of money supply growth
price level
monetarism
transactions demand for money
demand for money

real versus nominal interest rates
monetary base
quantity theory of money
equation of exchange
tight versus easy monetary policy
monetary rule
discretionary monetary policy

VIDEO

Watch

Economics U$A Program 13, "Monetary Policy: How Well Does It Work?"

Illustrative Events

The conflict between Federal Reserve Chair Arthur Burns and Congress over monetary policy during the 1974 recession; with Robert C. Holland, former member of the Federal Reserve Board; U.S. Representative Henry Reuss, former chair, House Banking Committee; and vintage newsclips of the debate between Arthur Burns and Senator William Proxmire.

Then Fed Chair Volcker finally cracks the back of inflation by targeting the money supply but at the terrible cost of the worst recession since the Depression, featuring economist Milton Friedman, senior research fellow of the Hoover Institution, and Frederick H. Schultz, former vice chair of the Federal Reserve Board.

October 20, 1987, the Fed moves quickly to limit the damage from the stock market crash of the day before; newsclips of the crash and interviews with financial analysts and former Fed staff members.

After Viewing

Answer the following questions:

1. How was the economic situation faced by the Federal Reserve Board in the mid-1970s different from that in previous years, and why did it demand a different set of strategies?

2. What was the result of the "hold tough" policy that the Fed clung to so tenaciously under Arthur Burns?

3. How did the Fed depend on the concept of velocity to restructure its approach to monetary policy?

4. Monetarists, like Milton Friedman, advocate what kind of monetary policy? How successful was this policy in subduing inflation in the 1980s when it was put into effect?

5. Under what circumstances is it appropriate for the Fed to deemphasize its long-run goal of fighting inflation?

Read

Read Chapter 13, "Monetary Policy, Interest Rates, and Economic Activity," pages 286–311 and 314–315 in your text. After completing your reading, try the Self-Quiz.

SELF-QUIZ

Multiple Choice

1. Money has value *mainly* because of
   a. gold backing.
   b. the current money supply.
   c. whether a bank has sufficient reserves to back deposits.
   d. people's willingness to accept it for purchases.

2. If the price level increased 100 percent tomorrow, the value of tomorrow's dollar in terms of today's dollar would be
   a. still a dollar.
   b. about fifty cents.
   c. about two dollars.
   d. about zero.

3. The price level has varied most during periods of war. This is *most likely* because

   a. the outcome of a war is always uncertain.
   b. the nature and quantity of goods changes during war.
   c. most wars have simply tended to coincide with periods of price instability.
   d. countries with the least stable economies have been more likely to engage in war.

4. During periods of high inflation, the value of money

   a. doubles.
   b. increases.
   c. decreases.
   d. is more stable than at any other time.

5. When the quantity of money grows too slowly, the result is likely to be

   a. too much growth in GDP.
   b. higher inflation.
   c. lower interest rates.
   d. higher unemployment.

6. The money supply in our country is controlled *mainly* by

   a. the Federal Reserve.
   b. the private sector.
   c. Congress.
   d. commercial banks.

7. As interest rates increase, people tend to

   a. demand less money.
   b. invest more.
   c. sell stocks to augment their cash reserves for emergencies.
   d. use more money for transactions purposes.

8. Monetarists differ from Keynesians in that they believe

   a. nominal GDP is a more significant reflection of growth than real GDP.
   b. the so-called quantity theory of money is flawed.
   c. the velocity of money is highly variable.
   d. the rate of growth in the money supply is the principal determinant of GDP.

9. According to the crude quantity theory of money and prices, a 10 percent increase in the money supply results in a 10 percent

   a. hike in interest rates.
   b. decline in nominal GDP.
   c. reduction in employment.
   d. increase in prices.

10. Most economists would probably agree that, once the economy approaches full employment, most of the increase in GDP reflects

   a. higher output.
   b. better use of resources.
   c. higher prices.
   d. greater circulation of money.

True-False

_____ 1. It is largely the responsibility of the Federal Reserve, under the leadership of its chair, to determine how much money the economy needs to achieve adequate growth without fueling inflation.

_____ 2. The demand for money is affected by the level of GDP and the level of interest rates.

_____ 3. According to the Keynesian model, high interest rates can be due to either a decrease in the demand for money or a decrease in the supply of money.

_____ 4. It is always possible to determine the proper monetary policy by simply following a money supply rule.

_____ 5. The quantity of money necessary to support a given level of GDP does not change from year to year.

_____ 6. The debate between Keynesians and monetarists has centered on how money affects the economy and whether the Fed should try to target the growth in the money supply or the level of interest rates.

_____ 7. Generally, severe inflations have occurred because the government placed far too many limits on the supply of money.

_____ 8. There is often a long, and highly variable time lag between an action by the Federal Reserve and its effect on the economy.

_____ 9. Some monetarists, led by Milton Friedman, believe that monetary policy would be improved if discretionary policy were replaced by a rule that the Fed should increase the money supply at a fixed rate each year.

_____ 10. The crude quantity theory is a useful predictor during periods of runaway inflation and works reasonably well in predicting long-term trends in price level.

Discussion Questions

1. Describe the way an increase in the money supply affects economic activity, according to the Keynesian model.

2. Explain precautionary and transactions demand for money.

3. How does the amount of money people hold (cash and checking accounts) vary with changes in interest rates and the level of national income?

4. What does the supply for money have to do with the price level and nominal GDP?

5. Explain how the public, which begins to increase the speed with which it spends money, can create inflation without any increases in the money supply.

Problem Set

1. In nation A, the price level during various years was as follows:

Year	Price level
1960	36
1970	47
1980	100
1990	159
2000	209

   a. Plot the relationship between price level and time in this graph.

   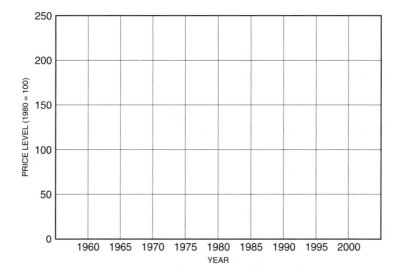

   b. By what percentage did the value of money decline in nation A from 1970 to 1980? From 1960 to 2000?
   c. If your grandfather had invested in a 40-year, $1,000 bond in nation A in 1960 and held it until maturity in 2000, how much did he receive in principal in 2000 dollars? In 1960 dollars?
   d. If nation A had indexed its bonds to the inflation rate, how much would your grandfather have received in principal in 2000 dollars? In 1960 dollars?

2. Suppose that, in the nation of South Isthmus, the relationship between the interest rate and the quantity of money demanded, holding GDP constant, is

   $$i = 20 - 2M,$$

   where i is the interest rate (in percentage points) and M is the quantity of money (in trillions of dollars).

a. What is the name often given to this relationship?
b. What is the interest rate in South Isthmus if the quantity of money demanded equals $5 trillion?
c. Suppose that GDP in South Isthmus increases. Does the relationship between i and M remain constant? If not, in which direction does it shift?

3. a. In South Isthmus, suppose that the quantity of money increased considerably during 1990. The following graph shows two investment functions, one of which was the one that existed before the increase in the money supply, the other the one that existed after the increase in the money supply. According to the Keynesian model, which one is which?

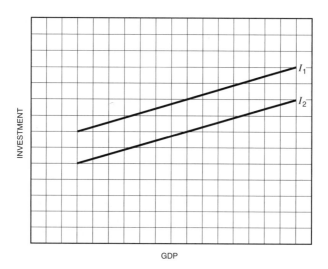

b. After the increase in the money supply, it was discovered that the crude quantity theory of money was applicable. The money supply was increased by 10 percent. How much did the price level increase during 1990?

4. A bond pays interest of $100 per year (forever). The following table shows the price of the bond at selected interest rates. Fill in the blanks.

Interest rate (percent)	Price of bond (dollars)
1	____
2	____
____	2,500
____	2,000
10	____
12.5	____

5. Suppose that the quantity of money (denoted M) demanded in country X is related in the following way to nominal GDP (denoted Y) and the interest rate (denoted i):

$$M = \frac{Y(30 - 2i)}{50},$$

where *M* and *Y* are in trillions of dollars and *i* is in percentage points.

a. Is the demand curve for money in this country a vertical line?
b. Does an increase in GDP from $1 to $2 trillion affect the slope of the demand curve for money? If so, what is its effect?
c. If the interest rate exceeds 15 percent, do you think that this equation holds? Why or why not?

LESSON REVIEW

If you had difficulty with the Self-Quiz or would like additional assistance, read the following lesson review. It should reinforce and help you understand the content presented in this lesson.

The Value of Money

How is the value of money determined? It is not a matter of gold backing or of intrinsic value. Our money can no longer be exchanged for gold, and precious metals have not been used as currency in the United States for many years. Currency and demand deposits are really just IOUs, debts of the government and the banks. Money has value because *people are willing to accept it in payment for goods and services.*

How valuable is our money? Its value depends on what it buys. If prices double tomorrow, the value of our money is cut in half. Throughout our nation's history, the price level has fluctuated in irregular cycles, the greatest fluctuations resulting from wartime and postwar economies. Since World War II, however, prices have soared. In fact, the price level increased 84 percent from 1913 to the end of 1945, but from the end of 1945 to April of 2000 it increased by *851* percent.

The value of money is inversely related to the price level. In other words, during periods of inflation, the value of money drops; when prices fall, the value of money rises.

Inflation and the Money Supply

Generally, severe inflation occurs when the government increases the money supply at a rapid rate. Runaway inflation can actually undermine a country's money and eventually its entire economic system. Once inflation becomes severe enough, consumers resort to a barter system, because they no longer depend on the value of money; hence, it has no value. The only way the government can guard against such an economic catastrophe is through careful management of the money supply to keep the value of the money relatively stable.

Unemployment and the Money Supply

The quantity of money can also grow too slowly, causing spending to become sluggish and national output to stagnate. The result is an increase in unemployment. Economists now blame a decrease in the money supply for many of the recessions our economy has suffered in recent years.

The Demand for Money: What Determines It?

What makes people want to hold onto their money rather than to put it into capital investments, land, or other holdings? Several factors are significant:

1. *Transactions demand for money.* People like to keep some money readily accessible so that they can buy things. The higher is a person's income level, generally, the more she or he keeps for transactions. And the higher is the level of GDP, the greater the quantity of money demanded by consumers overall for transactions.

2. *Precautionary demand for money.* People hold onto a certain amount of money as a precautionary measure in case of unforeseen emergencies, for example, health problems and needed repairs. As GDP goes up, the amount held for precautionary purposes tends to increase.

The Interest Rate and the Demand Curve for Money: Keynesian Model

If GDP is constant, the amount of money demanded by individuals and firms is inversely related to the interest rate. In other words, the higher is the interest rate, the lower the quantity of money demanded; the lower is the interest rate, the greater the quantity of money demanded. As interest rates decline, the appeal of savings and investment drops and the appeal of having ready cash to spend rises. As interest rates go up, the cost of holding onto money (when it could be earning interest) rises. The higher is the level of GDP, the greater the quantity of money demanded.

What happens when the money supply increases according to the Keynesian model? Given a constant demand for money, the increase in the supply of money causes a surplus of money to develop. Interest rates drop due to competition among lenders. In other words, people compete for financial instruments such as bonds and commercial paper, causing these financial assets to increase in price. When the price of a bond that pays $100 per year in interest increases, the yield the investor earns on that investment drops. For example,

If the bond price is $900,

$$\frac{\text{Interest}}{\text{Price of security}} = \frac{\$100}{\$900} = 11.1 \text{ percent.}$$

If the bond price is $1,000,

$$\frac{\$100}{\$1,000} = 10 \text{ percent.}$$

With the lower interest rates that will exist in the money market after the increase in the supply of money, businesses should be more willing to borrow money to invest in new plants and equipment. Investment then increases, the $C + I + G$ line shifts upward, and through the multiplier process, equilibrium GDP rises.

If the supply of money is decreased, the reverse process occurs. The shortage of money created causes interest rates to rise and the higher rates discourage borrowing and investment.

Suppose the money supply decreases. What then? First, the interest rate increases as people demand more money than is being supplied. Having less money than they want, they sell stocks, bonds, and other assets to raise more cash, with the result that the prices for such assets decline *at a rate equivalent to the increase in the interest rate*. Since it is more costly for firms and individuals to invest with the higher interest rates—and more difficult to obtain credit—the investment function shifts downward. With a decrease in consumer spending and investment, the $C + I + G$ line shifts downward, and equilibrium GDP falls.

Monetarists: The Quantity Theory of Money

Some economists, led by Milton Friedman, differ in their analysis and reasoning from the Keynesians (and new Keynesians). Many of the differences between these groups is summarized in the next chapter, but for now, we focus on their views concerning the effects of the money supply on GDP.

The monetarists' analysis is based on the *quantity theory of money*. Further, they hypothesize that the demand curve for money has a somewhat different shape than that hypothesized by the Keynesians.

Basically, monetarists believe that the *rate of growth of the money supply* is the principal determinant of nominal GDP (money GDP). As Friedman said, "The rate of change of the money supply shows well-marked cycles that match closely those in economic activity in general and precede the latter by a long interval."

Velocity of Money

Underlying the quantity theory of money is a concept termed the *velocity of circulation of money*. Simply defined, it means the number of times each dollar is used during a year to purchase final goods and services. In other words, suppose that $10,000 is in circulation and each dollar is used twice to make purchases of final goods and services. The velocity is 2 for the period, and the total amount *spent* on goods and services for the period is $20,000:

$$\$10,000 \times 2 = \$20,000.$$

Velocity is calculated this way:

$$V = GDP/M,$$

where V is velocity, GDP is the nominal gross domestic product, and M is the money supply.

The nominal gross domestic product can also be expressed as the product of real gross domestic product (Q) and the price level (P). Therefore, a second equation for determining velocity is

$$V = PQ/M.$$

Equation of Exchange

The equation of exchange restates the definition of velocity of circulation of money in different terms. By multiplying both sides of the preceding equation ($V = PQ/M$) by M, we get

$$MV = PQ.$$

Here, the right-hand side equals the amount received for final goods and services, and the left-hand side equals the amount spent on final goods and services. This equation forms the basis for the crude quantity theory of money used by the classical economists—and in a somewhat different way, for more recent theories posed by the monetarists. Let us see how.

Crude Quantity Theory of Money and Prices

The classical economists made two important assumptions:

1. They assumed V (velocity) was constant, given consumers' stable habits of holding money.
2. They assumed Q (real GDP) would remain constant at its full-employment value.

Given these two assumptions, we see from the equation that if V and Q are always constant, then P (price level) must be (as just discussed) proportional to M (money supply):

$$MV = PQ$$

In other words, if V on the left-hand side and Q on the right-hand side are constants, then the value of M depends on the value of P, since the two sides of the equation must balance. Given this conclusion, the crude quantity theorists would say that, for example, if there were a 10 percent increase in the quantity of money (M), there would eventually, following an increase in aggregate demand, also be a 10 percent increase in P (price level).

Quantity Theory: A More-Sophisticated Version

A more sophisticated version of the crude quantity theory can be derived by relaxing the assumption that the real gross domestic product (Q) remains fixed. According to this version, nominal GDP is proportional to the money supply, and velocity (V) is represented by a constant, a. Hence,

$$GDP = aM.$$

According to this formula, if the money supply (M) increases by 10 percent, nominal GDP also increases by 10 percent, since velocity is assumed to be constant. (Price may rise by less than 10 percent since Q may also rise.) The problem is this: Research based on the circulation of money from 1920 to the present indicates that velocity is not constant, although its rate of variation is not great. We can conclude from this that even the sophisticated version of the quantity theory equation cannot be used to make precise predictions about GDP in the short run. However, the theory is useful in validating an important and accurate assumption: Increases in the money supply are likely to increase nominal GDP, while decreases in the money supply are likely to decrease nominal GDP.

The Monetarists' View (and the Keynesians' View)

The crude quantity theory is just a close approximation to reality. From the monetarists' point of view (and that of most modern economists), it has two basic weaknesses, its assumptions that velocity and full employment are constant. The economy, in fact, is not always at the full-employment level, and as it turns out, elocity is not constant.

The theory is a useful predictor, however, during periods of runaway inflation and works reasonably well in predicting long-term trends in the price level.

The monetarists and Keynesians agree on a basic point reflected in the crude quantity theory: *Increases in the money supply are expected to increase nominal GDP, and decreases are expected to decrease nominal GDP*. Further, both groups agree that, as the economy approaches full employment, an ever-larger share of the increase in nominal GDP occurs in the form of price increases, not growth in output.

Short-Term Interest Rates: The Keynesians' Indicator

In reading the current state of the economy, Keynesians look carefully at interest rates. Their thinking is generally as follows. High interest rates tend to discourage investment, eventually lowering GDP. Low interest rates, on the other hand, encourage investment, increasing GDP. High interest rates then are taken as a sign of a tight monetary policy, low interest rates as a sign of an easy monetary policy.

Many economists take the theory a step further, saying that it is the real interest rate that counts, not the *nominal* rate. The real interest rate is adjusted for inflation. So, for example, if the interest rate is 12 percent, and inflation is running at 4 percent, then the *real* interest rate is 8 percent.

The Rate of Increase: The Monetarists' Indicator

Monetarists look at the rate of increase in the money supply to determine whether monetary policy is tight or easy. If the money supply is growing relatively slowly (less than 4 or 5 percent per year), they say that monetary policy is tight. When it grows much faster than 5 percent a year, they say monetary policy is easy.

Monetarists also look closely at the monetary base, member bank reserves plus urrency outside member banks. Again, growth much under the 5 percent level is taken as a sign of tight policy, while growth much over the 5 percent level is considered a sign of easy monetary policy.

The Fed: Decisions and Difficulties

As we see, interest rates and the rate of growth in the money supply are principal indicators economists rely on in analyzing monetary policy. But, since these factors are inversely related to one another, the Fed may be confronted with some difficult—if not irreconcilable—choices.

For example, the Fed can control interest rates by increasing or decreasing the money supply. If the money supply is increased, interest rates go down; if decreased, they go up. Economists who favor the current interest rates as the chief economic indicator may argue that, unless those rates are lowered, a recession results. But economists who look at the rate of growth as the chief indicator counter that, if the money supply is increased at too rapid a rate (to combat recession), inflation results.

During the 1950s, 1960s, and 1970s, the Fed attended more to interest rates than increases in the money supply. That picture changed dramatically in the late 1970s and 1980s, however, because of the growing influence of the monetarists.

Three Responsibilities of the Fed

The Fed is faced with three major kinds of responsibilities; its decisions about these points play a very significant role in our economy:

1. It must continually check the economy for signs of inflation or recession and forecast the economy's short-term movements.
2. It must decide to what extent it should tighten or ease money.
3. Having decided whether to tighten or ease money, it must determine how this should best be done.

These decisions are made particularly difficult by two factors:

1. The lag time between action by the Fed and its impact on the economy (which some economists consider to be about 12 to 14 months and other economists about 9 months).
2. Disagreement among experts about which indicators best measure how tight or easy monetary policy is.

Review of the Fed's Performance

How well has the Fed performed? We consider several critical factors:

1. *Forecasting.* Here, most economists would likely agree, the Fed seems to have done a good job of recognizing changes in the economy.
2. *Recognition of lags.* If the Fed takes action to combat inflation but the policies begin to have impact months later, when the economy is in recession, the results can be detrimental rather than helpful. Improvement is needed here, but even expert economists do not agree on what can be done to better this situation.
3. *Coordination.* The Fed gets fairly high marks for its coordinated efforts with the Treasury and the Council of Economic Advisers.
4. *Emphasis.* If there is one area of the Fed's performance on which economists disagree most, this is it. Often the Fed has been criticized for placing too much emphasis on preventing inflation and too little on preventing unemployment. Conservatives are likely to counter that short-term measures to relieve unemployment lead to worse problems in the long run. This is an issue that cannot be resolved, and one's perspective depends heavily on one's personal political views.

A Fixed Rate Rule: Good or Bad?

Some monetarists, notably Milton Friedman, feel strongly that some of our economic difficulties would be relieved if the Fed were governed by a fixed rate rule specifying the amount by which the money supply should grow annually, say, 4 or 5 percent. The Fed's job then would simply be to ensure that the money supply grew by just this amount. The Fed would no longer need to worry about the problem of lag time. The rule would also eliminate the problems of constantly adjusting to ever-fluctuating economic indicators, which monetarists feel is ineffective and actually makes business fluctuations more disruptive.

EXTENDED LEARNING

This section of the study guide is specifically designed for the two-semester student.

AUDIO

Before Listening

Read Exploring Further of Chapter 13, pages 311–314 in your text.

Next

Listen to the audiotape that accompanies Lesson 13.

After Listening

Answer the following questions:

1. Why does the relationship between the money supply and economic activity change from one year to the next?

2. How do the changes in the velocity of money make it more difficult to conduct monetary policy? What is a recent example of that problem?

3. Why does the crude quantity theory of money seem to be more useful for explaining hyperinflation than for conducting monetary policy under more normal times?

4. Economist Allen Meltzer was quoted in 1976 as saying, "Given anticipations, the level of capacity utilization in the economy makes little difference. An increase in the money supply in the 1930s would have had the same impact on prices as a

similar increase in the 1960s." What does he mean? Why does this statement conflict with the Keynesian model?

5. What is the major problem with using interest rates as an indicator of monetary policy tightness, and the major problem with the use of money supply growth rates as an indicator?

ADDITIONAL READINGS

Blinder, Alan S. "Monetarism is Obsolete." *Challenge* 24 (September–October 1981): 35–41.

> Blinder argues that proponents of anti-inflationary, tight money policy should focus on underlying inflation rates, recognize that fiscal policy should also be used, and avoid a sudden deceleration of money growth. No mathematics or graphs.

Friedman, Milton. "Monetary Policy for the 1980s." In *To Promote Prosperity*, edited by John H. Moore, 23–60. Stanford, CA: Hoover Institution Press, 1984.

> Provides a brief overview from a monetarist perspective of Federal Reserve policy since 1914 and a more-detailed analysis of recent years. Argues that economic instability is largely due to monetary instability and notes that Volcker's monetarist-type policy is not monetarist, in that the Fed generated more variability in monetary growth rates than ever. No mathematics or graphs.

Kaufman, Herbert M. *Financial Institutions, Financial Markets, and Money.* New York: Harcourt Brace Jovanovich, 1983.

> Chapter 19, "The Money Supply Process and the Strategy of Monetary Policy," is a brief review of how the Federal Reserve has conducted monetary policy since 1951, and the rationale for its policies. Moderately difficult, some mathematics and graphs.

Modigliani, Franco. "The Monetarist Controversy or, Should We Forsake Stabilization Policies?" *American Economic Review* 67 (March 1977): 1–19.

> A well-known discussion of the degree to which government efforts to stabilize the economy were successful. Modigliani maintains that, although the economy is not as inherently unstable as the early Keynesians argued and improper macropolicies can destabilize, we should not adopt a passive constant growth rate rule for money supply policy. No mathematics or graphs.

Simpson, Thomas. "Changes in the Financial System: Implications for Monetary Policy." *Brookings Papers on Economic Activity* 1 (1984): 249–265.

> Simpson discusses how changes in the financial system have caused the demand for money to change, leading the Federal Reserve to be more tight in its monetary policy than it had intended, and he argues that uncertainty regarding the demand for money will continue for many years. Simple mathematics, no graphs.

ANSWER KEY

Video Questions

1. During periods of inflation, the Fed, which has responsibility for controlling the money supply, typically tightens funds, giving banks less to lend. During periods of recession, the Fed generally loosens the money supply, making loans easier to get and encouraging investment and growth. During the mid-1970s, the country was faced with a new sort of problem: high inflation coupled with high unemployment; in other words, recession in the midst of inflation. Clearly, a new approach was needed since the old approach called for contradictory actions. Federal Reserve Board Chair Burns blamed the problem on the low velocity of money and favored a policy that would allow the monetary supply to grow, but at a very modest, very controlled rate.

2. Under Burns, the Fed refused to "turn on the spigot," to increase the money supply with one swift, decisive action. The fear was that, although such an action might have the short-term effect of boosting employment, it could lead to long-term disaster in the form of runaway inflation. With inflation already at 6 percent and threatening to go higher, the Fed did not want to take the chance. So it held to a tight monetary policy, despite pressures from all sides. Very gradually, the economy did recover. Best of all, the policies of the Fed did not lead to new inflation. Easing the money supply and urging higher velocity seemed to have done the trick for this time around. Unemployment was also eased, and the country pulled itself out of the recession and into a new period of economic growth.

3. In the formula $MV = PQ$, M is the basic money supply, V the velocity of money (the number of times in a year that a dollar circulates), P is the price level, and Q is real GDP. One way to increase Q, so the theory goes, is to increase M. Burns and other members of the Fed Board argued that it could be equally effective to increase V. In other words, we would need less money in circulation if each dollar were spent more times, if we could maintain the flow. The tricky question was, How could we be sure that we would increase Q (output) and not P (prices)? Burns and others hoped that a slow influx of money would stem the tide of inflation and cause productivity to expand without a great upswing in prices. The overall result of combining a gradual expansion in the money supply with great emphasis on increasing velocity was the stabilization of consumer spending. And in fact, productivity did rise without an increase in inflation. Inflation actually receded during this period.

4. The monetarists, under the leadership of Milton Friedman, advocate setting a target for a fixed growth rate of the money supply. They wish to keep the rate of growth in the money supply at a level consistent with zero inflation. Critics charge that the result would be totally unpredictable interest rates, a condition that would not be good for the economy as a whole. All the same, the Fed did follow what was essentially a monetarist policy for a period of time, focusing on the money supply, rather than interest rates, which has proven to be at best an imprecise measure of economic conditions. The result of this policy was a sharp

drop in inflation but at the cost of rising unemployment. As a result of that experience, many economists concluded that monetary policy cannot be counted on as a force to eliminate short-term economic difficulties but that, with continued effort and education, we may well learn to control inflation by controlling the money supply. The emphasis for now is on long-term stabilization, although increasingly we are coming to recognize that any economic good is bought at a cost.

5. The answer to this question depends on your economic viewpoint. Keynesians argue that inflation can be fought successfully primarily through demand policies (i.e., adjusting the levels of consumer, government, and/or investment demand) and secondarily through manipulation of the money supply. Monetarists argue that adherence to a constant rate of money supply growth eliminates inflationary tendencies. A third group of economists, like Martin Feldstein, argue that policy at best is about coarse adjustment rather than fine-tuning. This group would advocate intervening in the economy only when substantial and unusual levels of unemployment or inflation occur.

Multiple Choice

1. d   Text, 287.
2. b   Text, 287.
3. b   Text, 287–288.
4. c   Text, 281.
5. d   Text, 289–290.
6. a   Text, 290.
7. a   Text, 292.
8. d   Text, 299–300.
9. d   Text, 302.
10. c   Text, 303.

True-False

1. True   Text, 290.
2. True   Text, 290–291.
3. False   Text, 292.
4. False   Text, 310–311.
5. False   Text, 302–304.
6. True   Text, 306–311.
7. False   Text, 289, 302–304.
8. True   Text, 308–310.
9. True   Text, 310–311.
10. True   Text, 303–304.

Discussion Questions

1. According to the Keynesians an increase in the money supply lowers the interest rate and results in an excess supply of money if the demand for money is constant. This surplus leads to a drop in interest rates. As interest rates fall, investment increases and the $C + I + G$ line shifts upward, resulting in a higher level of equilibrium GDP.

2. The precautionary demand and transactions demand are two explanations given for why people hold money. The transactions demand for money is the demand for money to make purchases or transactions. The precautionary demand for money is the demand for money as a precautionary measure in case unforeseen emergencies arise. As GDP increases both the precautionary demand and the transactions demand for money increase so that people demand a greater quantity of money.

3. Holding GDP constant, as interest rates drop, the appeal of holding extra cash increases due to the reduced opportunity cost of holding money. In contrast,

when the interest rates rise, people demand less money since they wish to earn the higher interest rate. When GDP increases, the demand for money also increases to facilitate increased purchases of goods and services.

4. The crude quantity theory of money suggests that, as the money supply increases, the price level increases proportionately. This is due to the underlying assumptions that both real output and velocity are constant. A more-sophisticated version of the crude quantity theory suggests that nominal GDP is proportional to the money supply: This version relaxes the assumptions that real output and velocity are constant. This theory supports the idea that increases in the money supply are likely to increase nominal GDP, while decreases in the money supply are likely to decrease nominal GDP.

5. If the velocity of money is not constant but increasing, this indicates that, in a given time period, each dollar of the money supply is being spent more times. With a fixed level of output and no change in the money supply during the time period, this faster spending leads to greater pressure on prices to increase. Even though the money supply and the output level have not changed, the increase in velocity results in inflationary pressure.

Problem Set

1. a.

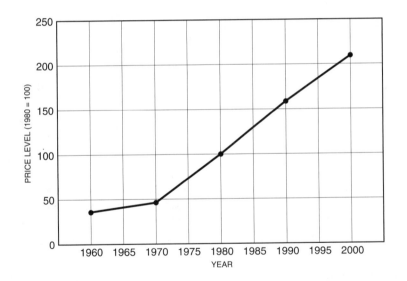

   b. 53 percent. 83 percent.
   c. $1,000. $172.25.
   d. $5,805.56. $1,000.

2. a. The demand curve for money.
   b. 10 percent.
   c. No. It shifts upward and to the right.

3. a. The higher one (I_1) is after the increase in the money supply; the lower one (I_2) is before the increase in the money supply.

b. 10 percent.

4. The complete table is

Interest rate (percent)	Price (dollars)
1	10,000
2	5,000
4	2,500
5	2,000
10	1,000
12.5	800

5. a. No. There is a negative relationship between the quantity of money demanded and the interest rate. That is, the demand curve slopes downward and to the right.
   b. Yes. The slope changes from –25 to –12.5.
   c. No, because if this equation holds, M is negative if i is greater than 15.

Audio/Text Questions

1. The number of economic transactions a given supply of money "finances" varies from year to year because of changes in individuals' or firms' willingness to hold a large amount of liquid assets relative to the number of transactions they make (due to changes in interest rates, fear of being caught illiquid, or structural changes in methods of conducting financial transactions) *or* because the number of economic transactions has changed so quickly that people have not yet reorganized the way they hold their assets to keep the same ratio of money to transactions as before (this would happen if something other than monetary forces caused a sudden contraction in economic activity).

2. Unpredictable changes in the velocity of money mean that it is difficult to know how large a money supply is necessary to support a targeted, or hoped for, level of economic activity. Therefore, if velocity falls sharply, the number of transactions or income per dollar's worth of money supply falls, then the Fed has a much more deflationary effect than it planned when it decided what the money supply should be. In 1982, velocity fell drastically, and the Fed therefore contributed to a much deeper recession than it wanted to create.

3. The way an increase in the money supply is split between increases in prices and increases in real output, or the way velocity can change, is hard to predict accurately, weakening the usefulness of the quantity theory. With hyperinflations, the exact magnitudes are not such a great concern, and the changes in velocity or the level of prices are going to be small relative to the changes in the money supply and prices.

4. Meltzer meant that increasing the money supply may initially drive interest rates down, but the community's awareness of how the increased money supply would lead to inflation would cause interest rates to rise because of the inflationary premium.

Keynesians would argue that people would not anticipate higher inflation, because they would not automatically assume that higher money supply growth leads to higher inflation, particularly in a deep depression.

5. Interest rates may mislead because of the inflationary premium. The market interest rates may be high even when the money supply is expanding rapidly, because people expect that the greater money growth will lead to higher inflation.

The variability of the velocity of money makes it difficult to use money supply growth rates as a guide. If velocity falls, a given money growth will be very tight, even if one would expect it to be expansionary.

LESSON 14. STABILIZATION POLICY: ARE WE STILL IN CONTROL?

INTRODUCTION

Economists are unable to agree on what causes economic fluctuations in output, employment, and prices. Traditionally, the Keynesians have placed their faith in the government's ability to control the economy through fiscal policy. The monetarists, by contrast, are highly skeptical of reliance on the government, placing more emphasis on the Fed's control of the money supply and the natural capacity of the economy to stabilize itself through the interplay of business growth and consumer spending, saving, and investment.

Today the focus of this long-standing controversy has shifted somewhat, but the strength of the disagreement continues. And new perspectives have been added: those of the rational expectation theorists and the supply-side economists. Which of these groups, if any, has the answers? Although we may not come close to resolving that question in this chapter, we make a start by examining these diverse perspectives in closer detail to see what each group suggests as the proper approach to stabilizing our economy.

What You Should Learn

By the end of Lesson 14 you should be prepared to

1. Explain how economic conditions during the Great Depression of the 1930s provided support for Keynesian economics.

2. Contrast the views of the Keynesians and monetarists with regard to business fluctuations and economic stability.

3. Discuss the current state of the Keynesian-monetarist debate with respect to the stability of private spending, flexibility of prices, and rules versus activism.

4. Define the theory of rational expectations, and explain the role it plays in work by today's economists.

5. Discuss the theory of supply-side economics, and explain why modern economists feel this theory is insufficient as a basis for current policy.

6. Contrast the views of Keynesians and supply-siders regarding the economic recovery of 1983 and 1984.

7. Describe the disagreements between the new classical macroeconomists and the new Keynesians.

KEY TERMS

stabilization policy
Keynesian
monetarist
new classical macroeconomics
new Keynesians
menu costs
time inconsistency
policy activism
rational expectations theory

supply-side economics
demand management
real business cycle models
implicit contracts
policy rules
supply shocks
rigid policy rules
feedback policy rule
discretionary policy

VIDEO

Watch

Economics U$A Program 14, "Stabilization Policy: Are We Still in Control?"

Illustrative Events

The role of expectations in the painful recession of 1982 and its relation to the Fed's efforts to lick inflation; with Frederick Schultz, former vice chair of the Federal Reserve Board.

The 1985 economic summit conference in Bonn and the attempt to coordinate international economic policies, featuring Beryl Sprinkel, chair of the Council of Economic Advisers, and economist Robert Gordon.

A recap of the government's efforts to control the economy over the past 25 years, with Keynesian Walter Heller championing fiscal policy, Milton Friedman arguing the monetarist perspective, and Martin Feldstein advocating coarse-tuning over fine-tuning. Richard Gill summarizes the main currents in macroeconomic thought in mid-1985.

After Viewing

Answer the following questions:

1. Describe the difficulties the U.S. government had in using monetary and fiscal policy to fine-tune the economy during the 1970s.

2. During the early 1980s, our foreign trade more than doubled. How did this affect our economy in both positive and negative ways, and what strategies were urged to counter the negative effects?

3. How did economists in the 1980s respond to the issue of fine-tuning the economy through monetary and fiscal policy?

Read

Read Chapter 14, "Controversies over Stabilization Policy," pages 316–338 in your text. After completing your reading, try the Self-Quiz.

SELF-QUIZ

Multiple Choice

1. In attempting to identify what determines the level of output, employment, and prices, the Keynesians have emphasized reliance *primarily* on

    a. fiscal policy.
    b. monetary policy.
    c. fiscal and monetary policies.
    d. the private sector.

2. The dominant economic view of the 1940s, 1950s, and 1960s, both here and abroad, was

    a. classical economics.
    b. Keynesian economics.
    c. monetarist policy.
    d. supply-side economics.

3. The theory that a decrease in the money supply helped perpetuate the Great Depression of the 1930s is attributable to the

    a. classical economists.
    b. monetarists.
    c. Keynesians.
    d. rational expectations theorists.

4. The Keynesians generally oppose a rule regulating the growth of the money supply. The *main* reason for their opposition is their belief that such a rule
    a. is entirely too difficult and costly to enforce.
    b. eliminates any justification for the Fed's existence.
    c. triggers a general downward trend in nominal GDP.
    d. limits the use of discretionary policy.

5. Real business cycle theorists believe that
    a. supply shocks are important causes of business fluctuations.
    b. prices and wages respond flexibly to changing economic conditions.
    c. both business fluctuations and economic growth stem from factors that shift the long-run aggregate supply curve.
    d. all of the above.

6. The new Keynesians believe that prices or wages tend to adjust slowly because of
    a. menu costs.
    b. long-term contracts.
    c. implicit contracts.
    d. all of the above.

7. Supply shocks are
    a. shifts to the left of the aggregate supply curve.
    b. shifts to the right of the aggregate supply curve.
    c. emphasized by real business cycle theorists.
    d. all of the above.

8. Milton Friedman's suggestion that the money supply be set so that it grows at a fixed, agreed-on percentage rate is
    a. a rigid policy rule.
    b. a feedback policy rule.
    c. a discretionary policy.
    d. all of the above.

9. The supply-side economists believe that the *best* way to deal with inflation is to
    a. lower consumer demand.
    b. hold the demand for money steady.
    c. raise taxes.
    d. increase output.

10. Economists who do not support policy activism believe
    a. business and consumer spending is a substantial source of economic instability.
    b. prices are relatively inflexible.
    c. implementing policy rules would stabilize the economy.
    d. all of the above.

True-False

_____ 1. According to the new classical macroeconomists, prices can be sticky because of the existence of menu costs.

_____ 2. The new classical macroeconomists believe that fluctuations in aggregate demand are due principally to erratic and unpredictable government policy.

_____ 3. According to Robert Lucas, excess unemployment is essentially voluntary.

_____ 4. Critics claim that the new classical macroeconomics neglects the inertia in wages and prices and is inconsistent with the evidence.

_____ 5. Expectations that the government will reverse an anti-inflation policy increase its potential for success.

_____ 6. Rational expectations may keep a stimulative policy from lowering unemployment because individuals and firms may simply demand higher wages and prices.

_____ 7. Supply-side economics is concerned primarily with stimulating the rightward shift in the aggregate supply curve through the use of various financial incentives, particularly tax cuts.

_____ 8. Supply-side policies should be viewed as a replacement for demand management.

_____ 9. Real business cycle models assume that prices and wages are flexible.

_____ 10. The new classical macroeconomists argue that a big problem stemming from discretionary policy is time inconsistency.

Discussion Questions

1. How does the rigidity or flexibility of wages and prices affect the debate between the new classical macroeconomists and the new Keynesians?

2. Do you think that "any conceivable output shock could explain why output fell one-third in the Great Depression of the 1930s"? Why or why not?

3. In what respects do Keynesians tend to place more importance on changes in interest rates than monetarists?

4. If no one believes the government will "stick to its guns" in an anti-inflationary policy, how effective will that policy be? What does this imply for the level of unemployment necessary to reduce the inflation rate substantially?

5. Where does your own economic philosophy fit? Chances are, even with a developing knowledge of economics, your perspective does not fit neatly into any single category. Neither does that of most economists today. They tend to borrow from several philosophies and to reshape the traditional views of the past to fit new times and circumstances. Try to define your economic philosophy at this point in your life with the knowledge you have gained thus far in this course.

Problem Set

1. Suppose that the quantity of money demanded (M_d) depends on GDP and the interest rate (i) in the following way:

   $$M_d = 0.4\text{GDP} - 2i,$$

   where M_d and GDP are measured in billions of dollars and i is measured in percentage points.

   a. If GDP = $100 billion and $i = 8$, what is the quantity of money demanded?
   b. If the quantity of money demanded equals the quantity of money supplied when GDP = $100 billion and $i = 8$, what does the velocity of money equal?
   c. Suppose that the monetary authorities increase the money supply from $24 billion to $30 billion, with the result that GDP increases to $110 billion and the interest rate falls to 7 percent. What now is the quantity of money demanded? Does the quantity of money demanded equal the quantity of money supplied?
   d. Under the circumstances described in part c, what change, if any, occurs in the velocity of money?
   e. Suppose that the fiscal authorities carry out an expansionary fiscal policy, with the results that GDP increases to $115 billion and the interest rate rises to 8 percent. The money supply remains at $30 billion. What now is the quantity of money demanded? Does the quantity of money demanded equal the quantity of money supplied?
   f. Under the circumstances described in part e, what change, if any, occurs in the velocity of money?
   g. A Keynesian economist claims that the velocity of money is not constant in this economy. Is she correct?
   h. A monetarist economist claims that the velocity of money is predictable in this economy. Is he correct? If so, how can it be done?
   i. Why is it useful to try to predict the velocity of money?

LESSON REVIEW

If you had difficulty with the Self-Quiz or would like additional assistance, read the following lesson review. It should reinforce and help you understand the content presented in this lesson.

Controversies over Stabilization Policy

Historically, the debate as to what constitutes a stable economy has been between the Keynesians and the monetarists. The Keynesians, traditionally, placed more emphasis on fiscal policy than the monetarists, believing that discretionary government intervention was the key to economic stability. The poor economic conditions of the

1930s provided much support for Keynesian economics. We did not have to wait for inherent forces within the economy to push us toward recovery; the government could step in and speed things along. And indeed, this philosophy predominated through the 1940s, 1950s, and 1960s, when the government turned to tax reform and increased government spending as major economic stabilization policies.

By the mid-1960s, the Keynesian theories were being seriously challenged by the monetarists, who held that monetary policy, not fiscal policy, was the key to stabilization. The monetarists gained many followers during the late 1960s, in large part because the enormous delays in enacting tax legislation—and the subsequent failure of the 1968 tax increase to have much restrictive effect on GDP anyway—made many economists begin to doubt the efficacy of fiscal policy.

Supply-Side Economics

Since World War II, economic policy has been dominated largely by attention to aggregate demand. In the 1970s and 1980s, however, the supply-side economists suggested that greater attention be given to aggregate supply. Actually, this is not a new theory; major economists of the last two centuries have been concerned with aggregate supply. But the difference now is that pushing the aggregate supply curve to the right, rather than holding back the aggregate demand curve, is seen as a potentially effective means of combating inflation.

How do we effect this shift? The supply-siders favor the use of financial incentives, primarily tax cuts. Tax cuts, they say, can have the following effects:

1. They stimulate people to work longer and harder, increasing full employment output.

2. They encourage firms to take risks in investment and research, expand, and replace plant and equipment more rapidly.

3. They increase savings. The supply-siders tend to see savings as a boon to investment, which augments the nation's productive capacity. But, remember that the Keynesians viewed an increase in savings as a loss to spending, resulting in a decline in aggregate demand.

Not all economists agree, of course, that tax incentives do all that the supply-siders promise. Some studies show, for instance, that tax reductions have a great influence on personal savings. But these research findings are widely debated, and no final conclusion has yet been reached.

New Classical Macroeconomics

The new classical macroeconomists, like Robert Lucas, also came to prominence in the 1970s. On the basis of their assumptions, the new classical macroeconomists conclude that the government cannot use monetary and fiscal policies to close recessionary and inflationary gaps in the ways described in Chapters 6 and 13, because the models presented in those chapters do not recognize that the expectations of firms and individuals concerning their incomes, job prospects, sales, and other relevant variables are influenced by government policies. If firms and individuals formulate their expectations rationally, they will tend to frustrate the government's attempts to use activist stabilization policies.

According to real business cycle models put forth by some new classical macroeconomists like Edward Prescott, business fluctuations are due largely to shifts in the aggregate supply curve. Among the most important factors shifting the aggregate supply curve are new products, new methods of production, new sources of raw materials, and good or bad weather. Real business cycle theorists tend to ignore monetary policy and believe that changes in real GDP result in changes in the money supply, rather than the other way around.

New Keynesians

The new Keynesians, like the old Keynesians, assume that prices and wages tend to be rigid in the short run, with the result that the quantity of output, more than price, tends to adjust to changes in aggregate demand. But, whereas the old Keynesians merely assumed that wages and prices are sticky, the new Keynesians have developed theories that help to explain why such wage and price stickiness can be expected, given the rational behavior of individuals and firms.

According to the new Keynesians, prices tend to be sticky because of menu costs (costs incurred by firms when they change prices), and wages tend to be sticky because of long-term labor contracts. On the basis of the theory of implicit contracts, they conclude that wages are set on the basis of long-term considerations. (Responding to workers' aversion to risk, firms maintain relatively rigid wages.)

EXTENDED LEARNING

This section of the study guide is specifically designed for the two-semester student.

AUDIO

Listen

Listen to the audiotape that accompanies Lesson 14. There is no additional reading assignment for this lesson.

After Listening

Answer the following questions:

1. How do monetarists and Keynesians differ over the effect of interest rates on economic activity?

2. Why does the monetarist interpretation of the effect of interest rates make them more concerned with crowding out, than Keynesians?

3. How does the degree of wage and price rigidity affect the validity of the rational expectations hypothesis?

4. How do long-term union contracts affect the validity of the rational expectations hypothesis?

5. What are supply-side policies? Are they useful for short-run stabilization, for long-run growth, or for short- or long-run anti-inflationary efforts?

ADDITIONAL READINGS

Fellner, William. "The Credibility Effect and Rational Expectations: Implications of the Gramlich Study." *Brookings Papers on Economic Activity* 1 (1979): 167–190.

> Provides clear definitions of the credibility effect and the rational expectations hypothesis and discusses how these concepts differ from standard Keynesian theory. Technical and moderately difficult; no mathematics or graphs.

Gordon, Robert J. "Postwar Macroeconomics: The Evolution of Events and Ideas." In *The American Economy in Transition*, edited by Martin Feldstein, 101–158. Chicago: University of Chicago Press, 1980.

> The monetarist and Keynesian positions (and the changes in those positions in response to events) are evaluated according to their ability to explain the economic record from 1946 to 1979. Moderately difficult, no mathematics, simple graphs.

Marris, Stephen. "Why the Dollar Won't Come Down." *Challenge* 27 (November–December 1984): 19–25.

> Discusses how the U.S. macroeconomic stance of tight monetary and easy fiscal policy in the 1982 to 1985 period was in conflict with European policies of easy money and a close rein on spending. This caused the dollar to strengthen, the U.S. trade balance to worsen, U.S. recovery to be uneven, and high worldwide interest rates. Argues the need for the coordination of macroeconomic policies. No mathematics or graphs.

Ritter, Lawrence S., and William L. Silber. *Money,* 5th ed. New York: Basic Books, 1984.

> Chapter 4, "The Monetarists versus the Keynesians," gives a clear exposition of how the two schools of thought differ. No mathematics or graphs.

Tobin, James. "Stabilization Policy Ten Years After." *Brookings Papers on Economic Activity,* Tenth Anniversary Issue (1980): 19–90.

> A thorough survey of macroeconomic policy from 1970 to 1980 from a prominent Keynesian's point of view. Tobin discusses the evolution of Keynesian theory in response to the economic events of the decade, and the current Keynesian attitude toward monetary policy and the problems of stagflation. Technical and moderately difficult; no mathematics, simple graphs.

ANSWER KEY

Video Questions

1. In the years immediately following the Great Depression, almost all economic efforts were directed toward building and maintaining high employment. But, beginning with the late 1960s and increasingly through the 1970s, inflation came to be seen as the number one economic issue of the times. Unfortunately, this shift in emphasis did not signify an end to problems of unemployment. On the contrary, just at the time that inflation was skyrocketing, unemployment problems were mounting as well. The dilemma faced by the Nixon, Ford, and Carter administrations was this: How do you deal with problems of inflation and unemployment simultaneously? Previous experience with monetary and fiscal policy had taught us no satisfactory strategies for countering these two problems at the same time. We might, for example, tighten the money supply to deal with inflation or loosen it to encourage growth and employment; we could not do both. Again, a choice was inevitable. And for some time, concerns over unemployment ultimately won out. Each administration in turn took serious measures to deal with inflation, but as unemployment again threatened to get out of hand, policy makers would back off, fearing that their interference was making things worse. As a result, inflation continued to grow virtually unchecked until the early 1980s, when the Reagan administration (with advice from Fed Chair Paul Volcker) determined to take a hard and fast stand against inflation, even at the potential risk of boosting unemployment. Eventually, inflation was—with consistent, unrelenting measures—brought under control. The lesson is clear: Managing the economy through manipulation of monetary and fiscal policy is not so simple or straightforward a task as we believed during the 1960s.

2. As inflation was brought under control, prices dropped, unemployment was eased slightly, confidence in the economy was restored to a great extent, and spending increased. Unfortunately, too many of consumers' dollars began going overseas, rather than back into the U.S. economy. On the one hand, this heavy

foreign trade helped hold the value of the dollar down to a degree and encouraged the open market and free trade concepts which most economists support. At the same time, however, it restricted domestic economic growth and ultimately increased our trade deficit. Eventually, because our trade deficit increased to monumental proportions and monetary values were subject to flexible, variable exchange rates, the value of the dollar began to grow, making competition against foreign markets ever more difficult. In a summit among major economic powers during the early 1980s, the United States was urged to get its deficit under control; we in turn urged other economies to expand to create new markets for U.S. goods. Coordinated efforts to reduce the value of the U.S. dollar have proven relatively successful. Generally, economists view international cooperation as a promising approach to keeping world markets open; most agree that everyone benefits from free trade so long as exports and imports can be kept in some sort of balance.

3. Economists disagree generally about the relative success of monetary and fiscal policy, as well as the approach that should be taken. Monetarists, for example, believe that steady monetary growth offers the best solution to combating inflation and unemployment. Given such an approach, they suggest, recessions will be mild, short lived, and self-correcting. Things will not be perfect, but the economy will be more stable than in the past. Other economists favor an occasional countercyclical policy when extreme economic conditions seem to require it. In other words, we might follow a general hands-off policy, but we would not be restricted by that policy if severe inflation or unemployment occurred. Economists like Walter Heller who strongly supported a countercyclical policy during the 1960s fear that a hands-off policy limits our options, that we must learn as we go, remaining responsive to the ever-changing conditions of the economy. Perhaps fine-tuning every week or month is too destabilizing, but such economists argue strongly for at least a review of economic policy each business cycle. Overall, most economists are less hopeful than they once were about our capabilities to control the economy. Too many factors, they suggest, work against it: the interdependency of economies throughout the world, the fact that unemployment seems—beyond a certain, limited point—resistant to virtually any measures designed to reduce it, and the fact that consumers' expectations have a marked effect on the economy. In conclusion, it appears as if we are not so much in control of things as we once thought.

Multiple Choice

1. a Text, 316–317.
2. b Text, 316–317.
3. b Text, 227.
4. d Text, 311.
5. d Text, 323–324.
6. d Text, 326–331.
7. d Text, 323–324.
8. a Text, 332.
9. d Text, 318.
10. c Text, 332.

True-False

1. False Text, 318–323.
2. True   Text, 320.
3. True   Text, 320.
4. True   Text, 322.
5. False Text, 318–321.
6. True   Text, 318–321.
7. True   Text, 318–319.
8. False Text, 318–319.
9. True   Text, 323–326.
10. True Text, 332–333.

Discussion Questions

1. If wages and prices are rigid and not flexible, then the market will not automatically correct itself and return to full employment. Instead, it is conceivable that recessions will last a long time due to the slow adjustment of the market. New Keynesians believe that wages and prices are inflexible, particularly in a downward direction; hence, they advocate the need for government intervention to maintain full employment through activist policies. The new classical macroeconomists, on the other hand, believe that wages and prices are flexible and economies not producing at the full-employment level of output will quickly return to that level of production.

2. The real business cycle models believe that business cycles can be best explained by looking at shocks to the aggregate supply curve. In using this model for the Great Depression, one would look for events that altered the amount and availability of resources, the production processes used to produce goods and services, or weather-related disruption to the productive processes. In the case of the Great Depression, it is unlikely that a single supply shock created the entire depression.

3. Monetarists are more interested in the growth rate of the money supply and changes in that growth rate. Keynesians, in contrast, look at the interest rate as being more important because of its influence on the level of investment spending and, hence, aggregate demand.

4. If the general belief is that the government is not serious with regard to its anti-inflationary policy, then that policy will not be effective. If the inflation rate is relatively high, this implies that high unemployment must be tolerated to reduce inflation significantly.

5. This is an opinion question. Most students will find it helpful to compare each perspective presented in the chapter. It would also be helpful for each student to look at each perspective's weaknesses and strengths in deciding on his or her own economic philosophy.

Problem Set

1. a. $24 billion.
   b. 4.17.
   c. $30 billion. Yes.
   d. Velocity drops to 3.67.
   e. $30 billion. Yes.
   f. Velocity increases to 3.83.
   g. Yes.
   h. Yes. So long as the quantity of money demanded equals the quantity of money supplied, velocity (= GDP/M_d) equals $GDP/(0.4GDP - 2i)$.
   i. Because if we know the velocity and the quantity of money, we can predict nominal GDP.

Audio/Text Questions

1. Monetarists generally feel that the real interest rate has a strong, pervasive effect on the economy. Keynesians argue that it has a strong effect only if it is very high. The national income, or GNP, has such a strong effect on expenditures, such as investment, that the interest rate effect usually is overshadowed by changes in income and business executives' expectations of the level of future economic activity.

2. If interest rates increase with government efforts to stimulate the economy and rising interest rates have a strong negative effect on various components of final demand, then government efforts to stimulate may be totally offset by interest rate effects. Every additional dollar of demand due to, say, deficit spending is offset by a fall in private sector demand because of the higher interest rates.

3. Prices and wages must be relatively flexible upward and downward for the rational expectations hypothesis to hold true. Expansionary policies must be met with upward movements of wages and prices, and deflationary policies (which are credible) must generate a rapid easing of wages and prices.

4. They tend to invalidate the theory because they imply some rigidity to nominal wages. Real wages may change, however, and indexing and reopening clauses in labor contracts may tend to support the theory.

5. Policies that encourage more output by reducing costs or increasing the after-tax incentive to produce are supply-side policies. Investment tax credits, reduction in corporate or personal income taxes, reducing environmental or workplace health and safety costs, and deregulation in general are supply-side policies. They tend to work over a long period of time only, so they help long-run growth but are of little use for short-run stabilization or anti-inflation efforts.

LESSON 15. THE FIRM: HOW CAN IT KEEP COSTS DOWN?

INTRODUCTION

Great importance is attached to those who manage the United States's 23 million plus business firms. Within certain guidelines, their decisions determine where, when, how, and to what extent various resources are used. Motivations of these business managers are sometimes complex, and arguably a number of businesses devote some energy to improving the environment or bettering our lives. By and large, though, businesses exist to make a profit. How do they do it? Although this is by no means a simple question, we begin to answer it in this chapter by examining

- The kinds of firms common in the United States today.
- The motivations that drive those firms.
- Factors, like technological development, that enhance or constrain business growth.
- The process by which firms determine which production technique yield the greatest profits.

What You Should Learn

By the end of Lesson 15, you should be prepared to

1. List the pros and cons of proprietorships, partnerships, and corporations.
2. Explain how a firm's potential for profit relates to technology, inputs, and the production function.
3. Distinguish between fixed inputs and variable inputs, and explain how this distinction relates to short-run and long-run profits.
4. Define the *law of diminishing marginal returns,* and explain why marginal products do *not* tend to increase beyond a certain point.
5. Use figures for marginal product and price of input on two variables to calculate what input combination minimizes total costs.

KEY TERMS

proprietorship
partnership
corporation
stock
maximizing profits
technology
input
production function
fixed input
profits
variable input

short run
long run
average product of an input
marginal product
law of diminishing marginal returns
optimal input
planning horizon
limited liability

VIDEO

Watch

Economics U$A Program 15, "The Firm: How Can It Keep Costs Down?"

Illustrative Events

The 1979 decision by Coca-Cola to substitute high fructose corn sweetener for sugar, a formula switch achieved without the kind of protests seen in 1985 against "New Coke," with Jesse Meyers, publisher of *Beverage Digest,* and Robert Barry, economist at the USDA.

The demise of the Studebaker company, which finally lost the struggle to operate without the benefit of economies of scale enjoyed by the Big Three; with Ray Burnette, former advertising director of the Studebaker Company, and Lester Fox, vice president of UAW, Local 5.

The multimillion dollar success story of *The Asbury Park Press,* which achieved profitable growth through computerization; with Jules Phangere Jr., publisher of the *Asbury Park Press,* and Tom Jobson, managing editor of the *Asbury Park Press.*

After Viewing

Answer the following questions:

1. What factors cause a manufacturer of a successful product like Coca-Cola to change production inputs?

2. What factors led to the demise of the Studebaker Corporation?

3. What does the impact of computerization on the publishing industry teach us about competition in a free economy?

Read

Read Chapter 15, "The Business Firm: Organization, Motivation, and Optimal Input Decisions," pages 341–358 and 360–362 in your text. After completing your reading, try the Self-Quiz.

SELF-QUIZ

Multiple Choice

1. The way in which resources are used in our economy is determined largely by

    a. government regulation.
    b. firms' desire to benefit the community.
    c. the profit motive.
    d. fluctuations in foreign markets.

2. The organizational structure Alfred Sloan imposed on General Motors proved more effective than that established by founder William Durant *mainly* because

    a. although divisions retained much autonomy, Sloan retained a strong central control.
    b. Sloan, unlike Durant, allowed GM to diversify.
    c. Durant cared only for profits, while Sloan worked hard to improve products.
    d. under Durant, GM had grown large and unwieldy but Sloan reduced total firm size.

3. In general, one could say that General Motors is typical of U.S. firms in

    a. structure but not in size.
    b. size but not in structure.
    c. both size and structure.
    d. neither size nor structure.

4. Probably the *main* advantage of a proprietorship is

    a. limited liability.
    b. access to numerous resources.
    c. unlimited life.
    d. simplicity.

5. One of the *main* disadvantages to a corporation is

    a. double tax liability.
    b. limited resources.
    c. limited life.
    d. limited growth potential.

6. As a firm adds variable inputs to a fixed input, average output per variable resource

   a. grows consistently and without limit.
   b. grows without limit but at an inconsistent rate.
   c. grows up to a point, then declines.
   d. generally remains unchanged, other inputs being equal.

7. Given a period of one week, which of the following would *most likely* be a fixed input for a farm?

   a. Labor
   b. Land
   c. Fertilizer
   d. Seed

8. To make all inputs variable for the farm (question 7), we would need to change the

   a. period of time under consideration.
   b. amount of labor used.
   c. desired productivity level.
   d. acceptable profit level.

9. The law of diminishing marginal returns is applicable only assuming that

   a. technology increases steadily.
   b. all inputs are variable.
   c. production is variable.
   d. at least one input must be fixed and at least one can be varied.

10. Given two inputs, fertilizer and land, the optimal input combination occurs at the point where the ratio of the marginal product of fertilizer to the marginal product of land is equal to the ratio of

    a. units of fertilizer to units of land.
    b. price of fertilizer to price of land.
    c. price of fertilizer to total input cost.
    d. price of land plus fertilizer to total input cost.

True-False

_____ 1. A corporation has many advantages over other types of business firms, primarily limited liability, unlimited life, and greater ability to raise large sums of money.

_____ 2. The relationship between the output of a commodity and the mix of inputs used to produce it per period of time is called the *production function*.

_____ 3. An *input* is a factor, such as labor, machinery, or land, that contributes to production.

_____ 4. Even though the production function embodies a given technology, a change in that technology does not affect the relationship between inputs and output.

_____ 5. In the case study involving Coca-Cola, the technology for producing the beverage remained constant, but the substitution of a low-cost sweetener for sugar reduced costs and shifted the production function favorably for the firm.

_____ 6. A firm can minimize costs by combining inputs in such a way that the marginal product of a dollar's worth of any one input equals the marginal product of a dollar's worth of any other input used.

_____ 7. Inputs that can be changed more easily than others in response to a change in demand are called *fixed inputs*.

_____ 8. In the case of Studebaker, economies of scale could not be achieved because the company lacked the time and money to renovate or replace their major fixed cost liability, a very old and archaic assembly plant.

_____ 9. If more of an input is added, while technology and other inputs are held constant, and successive additions to output decrease, the input is subject to *diminishing marginal returns*.

_____ 10. The use of technology to cut the costs of production, as illustrated by the Asbury Park Press, can also result in a favorable shift of the production function for a business firm.

Discussion Questions

1. One prominent economist has said that the only social responsibility of business is to make profits for its stockholders. Comment on that assertion.

2. Is the production function for an automobile firm the same in the long run as in the short run? Why or why not?

3. What is the significance of diminishing marginal returns?

4. Do firms take their production functions as given or do they engage in various kinds of activities to alter their production functions? If the latter is the case, what names are commonly used to designate activities of this sort?

5. Suppose that capital and labor are a firm's only inputs. If the price of capital and the output of a firm are held constant, how can we determine how many units of labor the firm hires at various prices of labor? Show that the amount of labor the firm hires is inversely related to the price of labor.

Problem Set

1. The Uphill Corporation is a small firm manufacturing bicycle pedals. Suppose that its production function is as follows:

Number of workers hired per month	Number of bicycle pedals produced per month
0	0
1	200
2	400
3	600
4	700
5	800

   a. How many additional pedals can be manufactured when the company increases its workforce from three to four workers? Does the addition of each extra worker result in the same addition to output?
   b. Suppose that all workers at the Uphill Corporation are paid $500 a month. At what level of employment is the labor cost per unit of output highest?

2. Suppose that the production function for a 1-acre wheat farm is as follows:

Number of years of labor	Bushels of wheat produced per year
1	50
2	90
3	120
4	145
5	165

   a. What is the average product of labor when one year of labor is used?
   b. What is the marginal product of labor when between two and three years of labor are used?
   c. Does the law of diminishing marginal returns seem to hold? Why or why not?

3. Suppose that the marginal product of labor is as shown here.

Quantity of labor per day	Marginal product of labor	Total output per day
0		0
1	3	—
2	5	—
3	8	—
4	—	23
5	2	—

   a. Fill in the blanks
   b. Does this case conform to the law of diminishing marginal returns? Why or why not?

4. Suppose that the average product of capital is as follows:

Quantity of capital used per day	Average product of capital	Marginal product of capital
1	3	___
2	8	___
3	8	___
4	6	___
5	4	___

a. Fill in the blanks.
b. What is the maximum amount of capital that this firm uses per day? Why?

5. A firm uses two inputs, labor and capital. The price of capital is $5 per unit, the price of labor is $7 per unit, and the marginal product of capital is 15.

a. Does the firm minimize cost if the marginal product of labor is 20? Why or why not?
b. If the firm does not minimize cost, should it use more or less labor relative to capital? Why?

6. A firm has two plants, A and B, producing the same product. The price of capital and the price of labor are the same at both plants. The marginal product of labor is 6 at plant A and 15 at plant B.

a. Can you tell whether each plant minimizes cost? Why or why not?
b. If the marginal product of capital is 20 at plant A and 40 at plant B, does each plant minimize cost? Why or why not?
c. If the marginal product of capital is 40 at plant A and each plant minimizes cost, what must the marginal product of capital be at plant B?
d. If the marginal product of capital is 40 at plant A and each plant minimizes cost, can you tell what the price of capital and the price of labor are?
e. If the marginal product of capital is 40 at plant A, what is the ratio of the price of labor to the price of capital?

LESSON REVIEW

If you had difficulty with the Self-Quiz or would like additional assistance, read the following lesson review. It should reinforce and help you understand the content presented in this lesson.

Characteristics of U.S. Firms: Some Salient Facts

Most U.S. business firms are small, independently owned organizations. These small firms control only a small portion of the nation's productive capacity; the large firms wield the economic power.

In addition, economic power is centered in manufacturing. Even though manufacturing firms constitute only about 4 percent of all U.S. business firms, they account for more than a third of all business receipts.

We look more closely at three common business structures. The United States's businesses can be categorized as proprietorships, partnerships, and corporations. How is each structured, and what are the relative pros and cons from the perspective of the business owners and managers?

Proprietorships

About 70 percent of the nation's business firms are proprietorships. A proprietorship is a firm owned and managed by a single individual. Most businesses fall into this category, although very few are of any great size. Why have proprietorships been so popular? And why are they generally limited to smaller firms? To understand this better, consider the relative advantages and disadvantages of this particular business structure.

Advantages

1. *Control.* Owners of proprietorships have complete control over their own businesses. They make their own decisions and answer to no one but themselves; the appeal of working under these conditions is undeniable.

2. *Simplicity.* A proprietorship is easy and inexpensive to establish. You need only declare that you are in business.

Disadvantages

1. *Lack of finances.* It is hard for one person to scrape together the financial resources needed to run a business of any size. Therefore, a shoe store, corner grocery, or pet shop may exist as a proprietorship; an automobile manufacturing plant cannot.

2. *Liability.* A proprietor reaps all the profits of the firm but is also liable for all debts and can lose all personal assets to creditors if the business does not do well.

Partnerships

A partnership is a business organization in which two or more people agree to own and manage a business. Each partner agrees to contribute some portion of the financial capital and labor required and take responsibility for some portion of profits or losses. In some cases, a firm may have one or more "silent partners," who contribute money but have little or nothing to do with the day-to-day management of affairs. Partnerships are common in some industries, such as law, but are generally less numerous in the United States than either proprietorships or corporations.

Advantages

1. *Easy startup.* Like a proprietorship, a partnership is relatively inexpensive and simple to start, although partners are wise to seek legal counsel in drawing up the papers by which their roles and responsibilities are defined.

2. *More resources.* A proprietor must contribute everything to the business. A partnership offers the advantage of more financial resources, more labor, and a broader range of expertise, often increasing the likelihood that the business succeeds.

Disadvantages

1. *Liability.* Liability in a partnership is no less than in a proprietorship. Every partner is liable without limit for the debts of the firm, and if one partner cannot pay, another can be held fully responsible, even if that means confiscation of personal property.

2. *Limited life.* Each time a partner dies or leaves or a new partner wishes to be admitted to the firm, a new partnership agreement must be drawn.

3. *Limited capital.* The partnership offers more resources than the proprietorship, to be sure; but even these combined resources are generally insufficient to generate major production capability. As a result, partnerships are practical only with relatively small firms.

Corporations

The corporation is a fictitious legal person created by the state, separate and distinct from its owners. It is formed by having a lawyer draw up the appropriate legal papers to state what sorts of activities the owners of the corporation will engage in. Owners can issue stocks, each share entitling its owner to one vote in the selection of members for the corporation's board of directors. This board generally has responsibility for establishing corporation policy.

Advantages

1. *Limited liability.* The extent of liability is determined by the numbers of stocks held and does not exceed the value of those stocks. In other words, if a corporation goes broke, stockholders lose their shares in that corporation but nothing more. They have no further responsibility for debts.

2. *Unlimited life.* Stockholders in a corporation may sell their stocks without disrupting corporate management or profit.

3. *Better financing.* The corporation, because it involves many stockholders, stands the best chance of the three business structures of raising the money required to finance a large-scale business operation.

Disadvantages

1. *Double taxation*. Corporations themselves pay income taxes on their profits. Then, when those profits are returned to stockholders in the form of dividends, the stockholders are taxed again.

2. *Legal expense*. Drawing a corporate charter requires expenses and efforts perhaps inappropriate to some small firms.

Production Function

What motivates the business firm? Economists assume that firms are generally motivated by the desire to maximize profits. This is clearly a simplification. Firms have other motives too and may claim to exist for the purpose of improving the community or the environment in some way. These claims are very likely valid, but whether one accepts them or not, the overriding consideration for business firms is desire for profit since without it, they cannot exist.

A firm's capacity to make a profit is limited by the current state of technology. If, for example, current technology dictates that it requires 250 person-hours of labor to construct an automobile, a firm cannot increase its production beyond what these constraints dictate, regardless of motivation.

To construct a model that represents the current state of technology, economists consider all *inputs* required to manufacture a product. Inputs are anything at all used in the production process: labor, raw materials, machinery, tools, facilities, whatever.

The relationship between each input and creation of the final product (output) is termed the *production function*. The production function is pictured as a table or graph that shows how increments in an input over a specified period of time change the total output.

Types of Inputs

Keep in mind throughout this discussion that our purpose here is to discover the optimal production technique—technique, in this context meaning combination of resources, or inputs. In other words, we search for the combination that boosts production to a given level at the lowest cost, maximizing profits. For the purposes of this discussion, the production level is always assumed to be fixed. Given this understanding, we make some distinctions that help us work through the process.

Inputs can be classified as *fixed* or *variable*. A fixed input is one whose quantity cannot change during the time under consideration. For example, a book publisher can readily change editors within a six-month period. Or she can order new paper stock or different ink, or she can change the work schedule. She cannot very easily install new presses within that period, however. Therefore, the presses are a fixed input; other inputs are variable. Similarly, a farmer may vary the equipment he uses, the number of workers he hires, or the amount of fertilizer used. But over a six-month period, the amount of land worked is likely to remain fixed. If we extend the period to six years, however, everything changes. In that scenario, no inputs are likely to be fixed. As a general rule, the longer is the period of time under consideration, the greater the number of inputs that are variable rather than fixed.

We can now make an additional distinction based on time. The *short run* is taken to mean any period in which at least one of the firm's inputs is fixed. In the case of the farm, for instance, six months would likely be a short run, assuming that the amount of land being worked would not change within that time. The *long run* is that period in which all inputs are variable. For the farm that might mean a year or two years or whatever period would likely witness a change in all inputs, land included.

Short run and long run have important consequences for planning. Before a firm decides to add a new product to its line, it is in a long-run situation, because everything is variable, including any new equipment or resources required to develop the product. But, once an investment is made, the firm is in a short-run situation, since certain factors (notably equipment and major resources like land) cannot readily be altered.

Average Product of an Input

Every input is a resource that contributes in some way to the manufacture of a product. To find out how much each contributes (the average product of an input), we divide total output by the units of input used to produce it. For example, suppose a 1-acre wheat farm produces 100 bushels of wheat per year. If two person-years of labor are required to produce the 100 bushels, the average product of labor is 50 bushels per person-year. If four person-years of labor are required, the average product of labor is 25 bushels per person-year.

Marginal Product of an Input

As noted earlier, adding more resources or inputs increases production, up to a point. The amount by which each additional unit of input increases production is called the *marginal product of an input*. In calculating this figure, we assume that other inputs are held constant. To see more clearly how this works, look at this table.

Number of person-years of labor	Total output (bushels per year)	Marginal product (bushels per person-year)	Average product (bushels per person-year)
0	0		—
		30	
1	30		30
		40	
2	70		35
		30	
3	100		33 1/3
		25	
4	125		31 1/4
		20	
5	145		29

Note that, as we go from 0 to 1 person-year of labor, the total output of wheat in bushels goes up by 30. As we add a second person-year of labor, total output increases by 40 bushels (to 70 total). Therefore, 40 bushels is the marginal product of input for the second person-year of labor. Again, note that the marginal product does not increase indefinitely. In this case, it increases for only a very short time, and with the addition of the third person-year of labor, begins to decline. Similarly, the average product of the variable input (in this case, labor) also reaches a peak then begins to decline. Note that average production is lower with five person-years of labor than with one.

This decline that we observe in the table is referred to by economists as the *law of diminishing marginal returns*. Simply put, this law states that, *if equal increments of an input are added, other inputs being held constant, the marginal product of input decreases beyond a certain point*. Why does this occur?

Suppose you were a cook in a busy restaurant. It might be very difficult for you to keep up with lunch orders. To make things easier, you might hire a second cook to assist you. Now you could do twice the work, right? This might very well be so with just two cooks, depending on the size of the facilities, the supplies available to you, and the equipment involved. Say your kitchen is just large enough and has just enough equipment to keep two cooks busy. Now suppose you hire a third cook. What happens? You bump into one another. You have to wait to use the grill. There is confusion about who is responsible for what, and a lot of time is wasted just in trying to sort out responsibilities and take turns. Total output might increase, all right, but average output per person certainly declines, and the amount by which production increases with every new cook added likely goes down steadily after cook number 2. The problem is that variable resources, cooks (i.e., labor), increased but fixed resources did not. Now, if you could provide comparable facilities (additional kitchen space with sufficient equipment) for each cook added, the law of diminishing marginal returns would not apply.

The law of diminishing marginal returns depends on several points:

1. It is assumed that technology remains fixed. In other words, if technology expands and a firm grows more efficient in its production, the law of diminishing marginal returns does not apply in the same way because the firm uses resources more effectively.

2. It is assumed that one input is varied while other inputs are held constant. If there are proportional increases in all inputs (e.g., a new stove and unlimited food supplies for each new cook), the law does not apply.

3. It must be possible to vary the proportions in which various inputs are utilized.

Optimal Input Decision

We return now to our question about which combination of resources or inputs is best. Each firm should select the production technique (combination of inputs) that maximizes profits or minimizes costs. How do we determine that technique?

$$MP_L/P_L = MP_K/P_K$$

In simple terms, *the firm minimizes the cost of producing a given amount of output by combining inputs in such a way that the marginal product of a dollar's worth of any* one input equals the marginal product of a dollar's worth of any other input used. In other words, all resources should contribute equally to productivity. This is quite logical if one thinks about it for a moment. Take the case of the farm, for example. Suppose we combine resources in such a way that labor contributes significantly to productivity, and its marginal product per input is high. But, at the given level of productivity, other resources (say, farm equipment) are not being used so effectively. Maybe there are more tractors and tillers than the laborers can use and half of them stand idle most of the time, so the marginal product per input is low for equipment. What is gained on the efficient use of labor is lost on the inefficient use of a second resource (input), equipment. If one resource has to make up for another, we cannot hope to maximize profits. Therefore, some other combination must be optimal in this case. This optimal combination is reached when

$$MP_L/P_L = MP_K/P_K.$$

Another way of looking at the same thing is to say that *the firm minimizes cost by combining inputs in such a way that, for every input used, the marginal product of the input is proportional to its price*. In other words, if we must spend so much to add extra inputs (more labor, more equipment) that the expense cannot be recovered by increased productivity and profits, then there is no point in expanding.

Now we look at a specific example to see how the optimal input combination is calculated. First, to determine the marginal product of a dollar's worth of any input, we must divide the marginal product of the last unit of an input used by the cost of hiring that last unit. For instance, if the marginal product of a person-year of labor is 40 units of output and the price of labor is $4,000 per person-year, the marginal product of a dollar's worth of labor is

$$40/\$4{,}000 = 0.01 \text{ units of output.}$$

In other words, $1 purchases 0.01 unit of output at this level of productivity. If this ratio holds for every input, not just person-years, then we have discovered the optimal input level:

Amount of input used		Marginal product		Marginal product ÷ price of input		Total cost
Labor (person-years)	Land (acres)	Labor	Land	Labor	Land	(dollars)
0.5	7.0	50	5	50 ÷ 4,000	5 ÷ 1,000	9,000
1.0	4.1	40	10	40 ÷ 4,000	10 ÷ 1,000	8,100
1.5	3.0	30	30	30 ÷ 4,000	30 ÷ 1,000	9,000
2.5	2.0	20	50	20 ÷ 4,000	50 ÷ 1,000	12,000

In the table, we have two inputs to consider: labor and land. To find the optimal input combination for a given level of output, we must determine at what point the marginal product for labor divided by the price of labor equals the marginal product of land divided by the price of land. Assume the price for one person-year of labor is $4,000 and the price for 1 acre of land is $1,000. The right combination is 1.0 person-year of labor and 4.1 acres of land. We know this because looking across the table, we see that

$$\frac{40}{\$4{,}000} = \frac{10}{\$1{,}000}$$

$$\frac{\text{Marginal product of labor}}{\text{Price of labor}} = \frac{\text{Marginal product of land}}{\text{Price of land}}$$

$$\frac{MP_L}{MP_K} = \frac{P_L}{P_K}.$$

On the basis of this rule, we can also say that the ratio of input A's marginal product to input B's marginal product must equal the ratio of input A's cost to input B's cost. To see the significance of these ratios, consider a real example. Suppose that a pound of fertilizer costs 0.003 times as much as an acre of land. We know from our formula that the cost ratio must equal the marginal product ratio. Now look at this table.

Amount of input used

Fertilizer (pounds)	Land (acres)	Marginal product of fertilizer / Marginal product of land
0	1.19	0.0045
20	1.11	0.0038
40	1.04	0.0030
60	0.99	0.0019
80	0.96	0.0010
100	0.95	0.0003

Source: E. Heady and L. Tweeten, *Resource Demand and Structure of the Agricultural Industry* (Ames: Iowa State University Press, 1963), p. 111.

The ratio we are looking for (0.003) occurs with the combination 40 pounds of fertilizer and 1.04 acres of land. Thus, that is the optimal combination in this case.

EXTENDED LEARNING

This section of the study guide is specifically designed for the two-semester student.

AUDIO

Before Listening

Read Exploring Further of Chapter 15, pages 358–360 in your text.

Next

Listen to the audiotape that accompanies Lesson 15.

After Listening

Answer the following questions:

1. Textbooks often use agriculture as an example of diminishing marginal returns because it is easy to see how the addition of more and more fertilizer or more and more labor to a given amount of land results in diminishing returns. What about manufacturing, however? Once the assembly line for automobiles is in place, doesn't it take a fixed amount of workers to run the plant? Is marginal analysis valid in such a situation?

2. Explain why a firm minimizes cost by combining inputs in such a way that the marginal product of a dollar's worth of any one input equals the marginal product of a dollar's worth of any other input used.

3. What is the difference between average product and marginal product, and why do economists focus on marginal product?

4. "The production function of an electronics firm in Japan is the same as the production function of an electronics firm in Mexico, since all firms must become acquainted with the latest technology to remain competitive." Comment.

5. In the early 1980s, Chrysler Corporation announced that it had reduced the breakeven point; that is, the number of cars it had to sell per year at prevailing prices to break even was much lower than previously. Why was this adjustment necessary? What does this imply for the levels of the firm's fixed costs? Would the reduction of the breakeven point be a long-run adjustment or a short-run adjustment?

ADDITIONAL READINGS

Fisher, Stanley, and Rudiger Dorbusch. *Introduction to Microeconomics,* 2d ed. New York: McGraw-Hill, 1988.

> Chapter 7, "Production, Costs, and the Firms Output Decisions," discusses production functions, economies of scale, and long- and short-run cost functions. No mathematics, moderately difficult graphs.

Friedman, Milton. "The Social Responsibility of Business Is to Increase its Profits." *New York* magazine (September 13, 1970): 122–126.

> Considers the meaning, logic, morality, and politics of the idea that corporations should forgo profits to act in a socially responsible manner. No mathematics or graphs.

Haveman, Robert H., and Kenyon A. Knopf. *The Market System,* 3d ed. New York: John Wiley & Sons, 1978.

> Chapter 4, "The Competitive Business Firm—A Decision-Making Unit," details how a firm chooses a cost-minimizing mix of inputs for production, and the cost and supply curves that result. Technical presentation, simple mathematics, difficult graphs.

Scherer, F. M. *Industrial Market Structure and Economic Performance,* 2d ed. Boston: Houghton Mifflin Company, 1980.

> Chapter 4, "The Determinants of Market Structure," gives a thorough discussion of the presence of and effect of economies of scale. Scale economies in production, advertising, finance, transportation, and so on are described. No mathematics, simple graphs.

Wonnacott, Paul, and Ronald Wonnacott. *Economics,* 3d ed. New York: McGraw-Hill Book Company, 1986.

> Chapter 21, "Costs and Perfectly Competitive Supply," discusses the production function, and an appendix to that chapter details how a firm is encouraged to choose the lowest cost mix of inputs. No mathematics, moderately difficult graphs.

ANSWER KEY

Video Questions

1. Even a successful company like Coca-Cola must consider sales and profits continuously. How can the company generate more sales and make more profits? This became a critical issue for Coca-Cola during the mid-1970s, when Pepsi Cola began gaining a larger share of the market and thus cutting into Coke's profits. One way of increasing profits, other than enlarging one's market, is to cut production costs. By using corn sweetener (less costly to bottlers than cane or beet sugar), Coke could develop a comparable product—one consumers could not distinguish from the original—at a lower cost. Such an opportunity could not be passed by. In a free market economy, a firm must cut production costs wherever it can so long as it does not jeopardize the quality of its products by doing so.

2. A number of factors contributed to the downfall of Studebaker. Among them was poor decision making—or perhaps one should say, a failure to stay in touch with what consumers wanted. Once car ownership became more common, consumers grew increasingly choosy about what they would buy. They wanted the latest designs and features responsive to their needs and whims. Studebaker did not provide these. Why not? Part of the reason was probably lack of knowledge about consumer interests. In addition, Studebaker fell victim to its own inability to take advantage of economies of scale. That is, it could not afford to mass produce its product in the numbers GM and Ford could handle with ease.

Changes in design were relatively routine with these larger companies, which could afford to experiment with a certain percentage of their product. With its smaller-scale production, Studebaker could not afford to take those risks, and its very uniformity and conservatism made it less appealing in the public eye. Further, small size restricted Studebaker's advertising and marketing, thus its competitiveness. Dealers making little profit to begin with could not afford to trim prices; therefore, consumers were being asked to pay more for a product they did not find as attractive (as other cars) in the first place. In addition, Studebaker had maintained relatively high wages to avoid costly shutdowns during its boom years. When sales began to slip, it could not afford to cut those wages, or it might have had to close its plants even sooner. These factors together eventually made it impossible for Studebaker to compete and finally to survive.

3. It is fair to say that computerization has revolutionized the publishing industry. Work that used to take painstaking hours is now accomplished within minutes or seconds, often with superior results. Page layout, writing and editing, and even typesetting have all been simplified. What does this mean for the industry as a whole? First, it means increased efficiency and potential for greater profits. In addition, it means a shifting of resources. Money that might once have gone for a typesetter's wages, for example, is now diverted into the purchase and maintenance of electronic equipment. Some jobs are lost, others created, and new skills are required of employees who wish to remain with the industry. New technology has other implications as well. When one company within an industry gains efficiency through some major technological change, others must follow suit or risk losing their capacity to compete. Thus, the ramifications are far reaching. Resistance to change can threaten the very survival of a firm, particularly a small firm with limited diversity. Successful businesses learn quickly that they must cut costs wherever possible to provide the resources necessary to take risks and take advantage of new technology; only then can they remain competitive.

Multiple Choice

1. c   Video; Text, 348.
2. a   Text, 343.
3. d   Text, 344.
4. d   Text, 345.
5. a   Text, 347–348.
6. c   Text, 352–355.
7. b   Text, 351.
8. a   Text, 351.
9. d   Text, 354–355.
10. b Text, 356–358.

True-False

1. True   Text, 347.
2. True   Text, 349.
3. True   Text, 349.
4. False   Video; Text, 349.
5. True   Video; Text, 355.
6. True   Text, 350.
7. False   Text, 350.
8. True   Video; Text, 344.
9. True   Text, 352–355.
10. True   Video.

Discussion Questions

1. This is an opinion question. In a very narrow sense, one can agree with this quote and note that stockholders do have the right to purchase stocks that they

expect to provide financial benefits, and almost all people who buy stock do so to make money, not to make a contribution to a charity. Also, by focusing on profits, firms make sure that resources are used efficiently and allocated to where they are most needed. However, in a broader social sense, there may be a problem with this attitude. The corporation whose stock someone owns might be involved in production activities that create pollution, for example. Here, the business might be serving the economic best interest of their stockholders and yet act in a manner that some people might not consider socially responsible.

2. No, the production function for an automobile firm is different in the long run, because in the long run, there are no fixed inputs and technology can change.

3. Diminishing marginal returns suggest that adding more and more of a variable input to a fixed input eventually results in output increasing at a decreasing rate. It suggests there are limits to how much extra variable input you can economically use when at least one input is fixed.

4. Firms consider producing a given level of output using different combinations of inputs. After determining the different combinations of inputs that can produce a given level of output, the firm then looks at the prices of inputs and determines which production option results in a minimum cost of production for that level of output. Engineering studies can provide information on possible combinations of inputs to produce output. In addition, innovations based on technological improvements can alter the relationship between inputs and outputs.

5. The firm hires the amount of labor such that the marginal product of labor divided by the price of labor equals the marginal product of capital divided by the price of capital. For a given marginal product of capital and price of capital, a firm can hire more units of labor if the price of labor declines. This can be seen by inspecting the formula

$$MP_K/P_K = MP_L/P_L.$$

Problem Set

1. a. 100 units of output per month. No.
   b. Five workers per month.

2. a. 50 bushels of wheat per year of labor.
   b. 30 bushels of wheat.
   c. Yes, because as more labor is used, the marginal product of labor declines.

3. a.

Marginal product of labor	Total product per day
	0
3	3
5	8
8	16
7	23
2	25

b. Yes, because marginal product eventually falls as more labor is applied.

4. a. *Marginal product of capital*

    13
    8
    0
    −4

   b. Three units, because capital's marginal product is not positive when more capital is used.

5. a. No, because the ratio of the marginal product of capital to its price does not equal the ratio of the marginal product of labor to its price.
   b. It should use less labor because the ratio of labor's marginal product to its price is lower than the ratio of capital's marginal product to its price.

6. a. You cannot tell because not enough information is given.
   b. No, because the prices of capital and labor are the same at both plants, and the ratio of the marginal product of labor to the marginal product of capital must be the same at both plants if each plant minimizes cost.
   c. 100.
   d. No.
   e. 3/20.

Audio/Text Questions

1. Usually a manufacturing plant locks in a capital-labor ratio that can be changed only slightly after the plant is built. There is still some flexibility, however, and if the relative prices of labor and machinery change radically, the firm may retool to minimize costs. In addition, for society as a whole, new plants are being built continuously, so the economy responds to changes in relative prices of inputs. Marginal analysis is generally valid, although in specific firms or markets it may take a long time to adjust to changes in prices.

2. If an additional dollar's worth of machinery can add more to output than an additional dollar's worth of labor, the firm produces at minimum cost if it increases its machinery, not its labor force. At some point, however, the diminishing returns to increasing machinery causes the marginal product of machinery to fall. If the firm continues to add machinery so that the additional dollar's worth of machinery added less to production than an additional dollar's worth of labor, it would not minimize costs.

3. The average product is calculated by dividing *total* output by the *total* amount of the input, whereas the marginal product is the *additional* output due to the *addition* of the last unit of the input. Marginal product is used because that better represents the value to the firm of expanding the use of the input. The value then can be balanced against the cost to determine how much of that input to use.

4. A firm may purposely decide to use an outdated technology if the local cost of inputs, of labor, capital, land, and so on, are such that the outdated technology enables it to produce at a competitive cost.

5. Chrysler realized that it would not be able to sell the volume of cars that it had previously sold because of the stiff foreign and domestic competition, and because it lacked the ability to mount a major competitive effort. Therefore, it decided to reduce its fixed costs so it could cover those costs with fewer units and still keep prices down. This is a long-run adjustment, because the size of Chrysler's plant was changed. Investment in fixed plant and equipment is the least variable of inputs, and the long run is defined as the period of time in which all inputs are variable.

LESSON 16. SUPPLY AND DEMAND: WHAT SETS THE PRICE?

INTRODUCTION

How do you, as an individual consumer, decide which goods and services to buy? Seems like a simple enough question, yet the answers are not always easy, for they depend on many factors. First is the question of taste. What you do with $100 of extra income likely is very different from what your cousin Mildred or your neighbor George does. Other factors include your present circumstances and lifestyle: whether you are working or attending school, whether you are married or single, whether you have children or parents to support, and so on. In addition, you must consider your income and the prices of the goods and services you want and need. For most of us, there are numerous differences between what we like and what we can afford to buy.

Economists measure the level of satisfaction consumers derive from various combinations of goods and services they might purchase in units called *utils*. Comparing the utility value of one combination to another is a useful way of predicting what consumers will purchase and how much of a good or service they are likely to want at a given income level. This information, in turn, is highly useful to suppliers in setting price. More than any other single factor, price determines how much of a given commodity is purchased. Understanding the laws of consumer demand helps suppliers set prices that equate a supply and demand. As we have seen before, the price system, left to its own devices, is a powerful tool for helping us to use resources efficiently; in other words, to produce precisely what we want to consume. When that price system is tampered with, however, the results for the economy can be problematic, as we will see.

What You Should Learn

By the end of Lesson 16, you should be prepared to

1. Describe the factors an economist considers in constructing a model of consumer behavior.

2. Explain the meaning of *utility,* and describe how this measure determines the ways in which a consumer spends money.

3. Given figures for the total utility of a commodity at various amounts, derive the marginal utility for any given amount.

4. Explain the *law of diminishing marginal utility* and its likely effect on price.

5. Describe how economists calculate the equilibrium market basket.

6. Explain how the market demand curve is derived from individual consumers' demand curves.

7. Explain the difference between implicit costs and explicit costs.

8. Explain how a firm calculates its profits.

9. Explain the difference between a short-run and long-run period of time when considering the production of a good or service.

10. Explain the relationship between average cost and marginal cost.

11. Explain the impact of diminishing returns on the total variable cost, average variable cost, average cost, and marginal cost.

12. Explain the reasons behind the U-shaped long-run average cost function.

KEY TERMS

model of consumer behavior
utility
marginal utility
law of diminishing marginal utility
individual demand curve
market demand curve
opportunity cost
implicit costs
explicit costs
short run
long run
total fixed cost
total variable cost

law of diminishing marginal returns
total cost
average fixed cost
average variable cost
average total cost
marginal cost
long-run average cost function
increasing returns to scale
decreasing returns to scale
constant returns to scale
specialization

VIDEO

Watch

Economics U$A Program 16, "Supply and Demand: What Sets the Price?"

Illustrative Events

The drought in northern California in the middle and late 1970s illustrating the law of diminishing marginal utility, with Dietrich Stroeh, then manager of the Marin Municipal Water District; Pamela Lloyd, board member and Marin County resident.

The 1970 Arab oil boycott, skyrocketing fuel prices, and the attraction of new suppliers to the market; with James Schlesinger, former secretary of energy; economist Ike Kerridge, Hughes Oil Company; and oil wildcatter William Rutter Jr.

The fabulous success story of Jordache jeans and the designer jean craze of the 1970s, with Joe Nakash, president of Jordache; advertising executive Erwin Ephron; and Brenda Gall, apparel research consultant at Merrill Lynch. Richard Gill demonstrates shifts in the demand curve.

After Viewing

Answer the following questions:

1. What factors determine the value of a resource like water?
2. What impact did the water shortage have on other segments of the economy? Did anyone benefit?
3. What factors led to government imposed ceilings on oil prices in the 1970s, and then later to decontrol?
4. What factors lead to the rise and decline of fads in the United States?

Read

Read Chapter 16: "Getting behind the Demand and Supply Curves," pages 363–391 in your text. After completing your reading, try the Self-Quiz.

SELF-QUIZ

Multiple Choice

1. Which of the following influences what consumers purchase in the marketplace?
    a. Consumers' taste
    b. Consumers' income
    c. Product prices
    d. All of the above

2. In analyzing consumer behavior, economists generally make the assumption that an individual consumer's choices tend to be

   a. rational and fairly consistent.
   b. varied and impulsive.
   c. wholly unpredictable.
   d. pretty much like those of any other consumer.

3. Americans in general spend about which percent of their income on goods and services?

   a. About 95 percent
   b. About 80 percent
   c. About 50 percent
   d. About 10 percent or less

4. Utility is a measure of

   a. consumer satisfaction.
   b. product usefulness.
   c. efficient use of resources in production.
   d. cost to price ratio.

5. Suppose the total utility for 1 gallon of ice cream is 12, and the total utility for 2 gallons of ice cream is 15. What is the marginal utility for the second gallon of ice cream?

   a. 15
   b. 27
   c. 13.5
   d. 3

6. The law of diminishing marginal utility states that beyond some point additional

   a. output results in a decrease in quality.
   b. output results in inefficient use of resources.
   c. units of a good yield less satisfaction than previous units of the good.
   d. consumption cannot be generated regardless of price.

7. Suppose that a consumer has an equilibrium market basket containing only three items: food, clothing, and books. She spends all her income consistently on these three items. Which one of the following assumptions could we make about this equilibrium market basket?

   a. The marginal utility for food is the same as for the other items at all price levels.
   b. The marginal utility derived from the last dollar spent on food is the same as that for the last dollar spent on clothes and on books.
   c. The per-unit price for food is identical to the per unit price for clothing and books.
   d. The consumer spends the same percentage of her income on food as she spends on clothing and on books.

8. The individual demand curve shows
   a. to what extent a consumer prefers one product over another.
   b. what portion of income a consumer devotes to each of several products.
   c. how consumer demand shifts with changes in taste.
   d. what quantity of a product a consumer demands at each price level.

9. Which of the following statements is *most* accurate?
   a. Market demand curves slope downward to the right, but their shapes and locations differ.
   b. Market demand curves slope downward to the right and have about the same shape and location.
   c. Few market demand curves slope downward to the right, and each has its own shape and location.
   d. Market demand curves slope upward to the right and tend to have the same shape though different locations.

10. In the short run, which of the following does *not* change as output increases?
    a. Total fixed cost
    b. Average fixed cost
    c. Average variable cost
    d. Average total cost

True-False

_____ 1. If the marginal utility of a first hamburger is 10 utils and the marginal utility of the second hamburger is 12 utils, the total utility of the first two hamburgers is 22 utils.

_____ 2. On the basis of the information in question 1, the typical consumer would be very *unlikely* to purchase a second hamburger.

_____ 3. If a consumer buys three beach balloons on July 1 when the price is $1 apiece and then buys four beach balloons on August 1 when the price is $0.75 apiece, we can conclude that there has been a change in her demand for balloons between July and August.

_____ 4. According to the theory of consumer behavior, the consumer's equilibrium market basket would be the one that yields maximum utility, given the constraints of income and prices.

_____ 5. According to the law of diminishing marginal utility, the extra satisfaction from consuming an extra unit of a commodity declines only if the price remains constant.

_____ 6. The experience of Marin County residents during the 1975–77 drought suggests that, during severe shortages, people tend to reduce their use of even essential goods when the price of consuming an additional unit of the good skyrockets.

_____ 7. The marginal utility of a third automobile reflects the satisfaction the consumer derives from that automobile *over and above* whatever satisfaction she derives from her first two automobiles.

_____ 8. Total cost changes at the same rate as total variable cost.

_____ 9. Firms tend to produce in the decreasing returns to scale portion of their long-run average total cost curve.

_____ 10. As producers expand production, the economies of scale initially experienced grow even larger, and the cost of producing each additional unit decreases.

Discussion Questions

1. "Since no one can measure a person's utility, the theory of consumer behavior cannot provide an adequate basis for decision making. Furthermore, since a person cannot tell whether he will like something until he has bought and tried it, no one knows what utility to attach to a good until it is too late to be of any use in decision making." Discuss and evaluate this point of view.

2. If the marginal utility of one good is 3 and its price is $1, while the marginal utility of another good is 6 and its price is $3, is the consumer maximizing his satisfaction, given that he is consuming both goods? Why or why not?

3. Universities frequently ask for student opinion about instructors and courses. The usual method is to distribute a questionnaire in class toward the end of a term. What are the costs of such surveys? Be sure to think through what economists mean by costs. Try to formulate an actual dollar cost at your institution. Do you think such surveys are worth the costs?

4. Why does the marginal cost curve intersect both the average variable cost curve and the average total cost curve at their minimum points? Can there be cases where this is not true?

5. Suppose that two firms have exactly the same marginal cost curves, but their average fixed cost curves are not the same. Will their average variable cost curves be the same?

Problem Set

1. Suppose that Bill Smith's utility can be regarded as measurable and the utility he gets from the consumption of various numbers of hot dogs per day is as follows.

Hot dogs consumed per day	Total utility (utils)
0	0
1	5
2	11
3	16
4	20
5	23

a. What is the marginal utility of the third hot dog per day to Bill Smith? What is the marginal utility of the fourth hot dog?

b. Plot Bill Smith's marginal utility curve for hot dogs in the following graph:

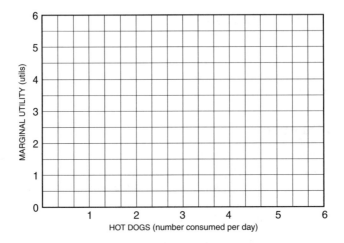

c. Suppose that Bill Smith divides his income entirely between hot dogs and Hershey bars in such a way as to maximize his satisfaction. His marginal utility from an extra Hershey bar is 2 utils, and the price of a Hershey bar is $0.60. If the price of a hot dog is $1.20, how many hot dogs does he consume per day?

2. You are given the following information about Sue, who spends all of her income of $700 on clothing and food in a way that maximizes her total utility:

| Food price | Quantity (units) | |
(dollars per unit)	Food	Clothing
40	5	_____
30	10	_____
10	20	_____

a. Fill in the last column of the table. (Clothing costs $50 per unit.)
b. What is the ratio of the marginal utility Sue gets from the fifth unit of food to the marginal utility she gets from the 20th?

3. Suppose that you are given the production function, the price of the variable input, and the total fixed costs of the ABC Company. These data follow. Use this formula in figuring out marginal cost:

$$MC = \text{change in total cost}/\text{change in output}.$$

But since in this problem *change in total cost* = price of unit of variable input, and *change in output* = marginal product (*MP*),

$$MC = 2/MP.$$

Fill in the blanks in the following table (costs and prices in dollars).

Units of variable input	Units of output produced	Average product	Marginal product	Unit of variable-input price	Total variable cost	Average variable cost	Total fixed cost	Total cost	Average total cost	Marginal cost
0	0	—	—	2	—	—	100	—	—	—
1	4	—	—	2	—	—	100	—	—	—
2	9	—	—	2	—	—	100	—	—	—
3	15	—	—	2	—	—	100	—	—	—
4	22	—	—	2	—	—	100	—	—	—
5	30	—	—	2	—	—	100	—	—	—
6	37	—	—	2	—	—	100	—	—	—
7	43	—	—	2	—	—	100	—	—	—
8	48	—	—	2	—	—	100	—	—	—
9	52	—	—	2	—	—	100	—	—	—

4. Farm A is a profit-maximizing, perfectly competitive producer of wheat. It produces wheat using 1 acre of land (price = $1,000) and varying inputs of labor (price = $500 per month of labor). The production function is as follows:

Number of months of labor (per month)	Output per month (in truckloads)
0	0
1	1
3	2
7	3
12	4
18	5
25	6

Show that the production of farm A is subject to increasing marginal cost.

5. Firm S hires a consultant to estimate its long-run total cost function. The consultant, after a long study, concludes that for firm S long-run total cost equals $2 million + $4Q, where Q is annual output.

   a. What does this equation imply about the long-run total cost of producing nothing? Is this reasonable? Why or why not?
   b. What is the minimum value of long-run average cost?
   c. What size of plant results in the minimum value of long-run average cost? Is this reasonable? Why or why not?

LESSON REVIEW

If you had any difficulty with the Self-Quiz, read through the following Lesson Review before returning to the text. It should help clarify key concepts within the textbook discussion.

Consumer Spending and Market Demand

How do consumers spend their income? Economists find this a particularly significant question since consumers are in a very real sense "the masters of the economic system." What you and your fellow consumers purchase each day determines what goods and services are available for purchase tomorrow and, in part, what those goods and services are likely to cost.

Recent government figures indicate that the typical U.S. family spends about 80 percent of its income on goods and services, much of it for housing, food and transportation. Personal taxes account for another 15 percent on average. Considerably smaller amounts are spent on furniture, clothing, gasoline, and various miscellaneous goods and services.

A Model of Consumer Behavior

In constructing a model of consumer behavior, the economist must consider the tastes of the consumer (some people like opera, some football) as well as income levels and prices. In addition, the economist makes an assumption that the consumer makes rational choices, acting in his or her own best interests.

In determining what these best interests might be, economists rely on a utility index, which is to say a measure of the satisfaction a consumer derives from the purchase of particular goods and services. That satisfaction might come from the purchase of a product, such as food, to meet a particular need or from the purchase of a product, say, a stereo or a VCR, to satisfy some other desire.

- *Marginal utility*. The total utility of a market basket (some hypothetical combination of goods and services) reflects its overall level of satisfaction for the consumer. Therefore, a market basket containing 2 pounds of food and four items of clothing might have a utility value of 10, while a market basket with 1 pound of food and three items of clothing might have a utility value of 6. Marginal utility measures, for each commodity in the basket, the additional satisfaction that a consumer derives from one additional unit of the commodity. Hence, if the total utility of 3 pounds of food is 9 and the total utility of 2 pounds of food is 7, the marginal utility of the third pound of food is 2 (= 9 − 7).

- *The law of diminishing marginal utility*. People do not buy unlimited amounts of products. There is a limit to how much food one family can consume or how many television sets its members wish to own. Beyond some point, then, there is a decline in the extra satisfaction derived from the last unit of the commodity consumed. If a family typically consumes 20 pounds of food in a week, the marginal utility for the first pound may be fairly high, and it will be lowest for the 20th pound. This decreased satisfaction will also affect the price that the consumer is willing to pay for each additional pound of food. Briefly, the law of diminishing marginal utility states that, as a person consumes more and more of a given commodity (the consumption of other commodities being held constant), the marginal utility of the commodity eventually tends to decline.

Equilibrium Market Basket

The equilibrium market basket is that combination of goods and services which maximizes consumer satisfaction. But which is the optimal market basket? The one that offers the highest utility index? It turns out that it is the one where the consumer's income is allocated among commodities so that, for every commodity purchased the marginal utility of one commodity relative to the marginal utility of another in the basket is proportional to the price of the first commodity relative to the price of the second. This is a way of quantifying the assumption that consumers will not purchase new stereos when they do not have enough eggs and milk; on the other hand, they will not continue to stock up on eggs and milk once basic demands are met.

The optimal market basket can be identified in another way. Briefly, we can say that *the rational consumer chooses a market basket where the marginal utility of the last dollar spent on all commodities purchased is the same*. The marginal utility of the last dollar spent is calculated by dividing the marginal utility for a given commodity by the per-unit price of that commodity. Thus, if the marginal utility of the last pound of food is 4 and food costs $2 per pound, then the marginal utility of the last dollar spent is 2. The formula is as follows:

$$MU_f/P_f,$$

In this case it is 4/2 = 2, where MU_f equals the *marginal utility of food* and P_f equals the *price of food*.

Deriving the Market Demand Curve

In analyzing consumer behavior, economists use the concept of an individual demand curve. This curve shows how much of a commodity is demanded by the individual consumer at various prices. To derive the market demand curve, we horizontally sum all the individual demand curves (add up the quantities demanded at various prices) and plot that. In real life, of course, economists cannot construct demand curves for every consumer in a market; they can, however, construct sufficient numbers of curves for representative samples of the consumer population in question. In this way, they can gauge very accurately what consumer demand is at various price levels. Market demand curves almost always slope downward and to the right because quantity demanded falls as price rises. This is less true for some commodities than others, though—milk prices tend to have less effect on quantity demanded than, say, stereo prices—so every demand curve looks a little different in terms of shape and location.

Cost Functions: Short Run and Long Run

We begin our discussion of costs with some clarifying definitions. According to the opportunity cost doctrine, the cost of a certain course of action (or a certain use of resources) is the value of the next best alternative course of action (or use of resources) that could have been adopted. Thus, the cost of building a condominium is the value of the goods and services that could have been produced in some other way if the condominium had never been built.

Costs for an individual firm can be either explicit or implicit. If the firm's owner pays some outside laborer or supplier for resources used, that payment constitutes an explicit cost. But if the firm's owner provides the resources (as in the case of the local grocery store owner who stocks shelves and waits on customers without paying himself a direct salary), the costs of these owner-supplied resources are implicit costs.

Short-Run Cost Functions

The short run, as you recall, is that period during which at least one of the firm's inputs (resources) is fixed. Usually, it is plant or equipment. Three kinds of costs are important in the short run:

1. *Total fixed cost* is the total expenditure by the firm for fixed inputs during the time in question. Examples of short-run fixed costs are property taxes or interest payments.

2. *Total variable cost* is the firm's total expenditure on variable inputs for the time period in question. For a farm, such inputs would include seed, fertilizer, water for irrigation, fuel, small equipment parts, labor, and so on.

3. *Total cost* is the sum of total fixed cost and total variable cost.

Law of Diminishing Marginal Returns

This law states that if equal increments of an input are added, the quantities of other inputs being held constant, the resulting increments of product decrease beyond some point. Take the farm as an example. At first, if we increase the amount of seed provided to the farm, holding all other inputs (fertilizer, labor, water) constant, the marginal output increases. Eventually, however, marginal product declines. There will be too little labor to handle the planting and harvesting, enough water to irrigate all that is planted, enough fertilizer to maintain as high a yield per acre. Thus, it will take more seed to obtain the same increment in output as was yielded by smaller additions of seed earlier. The result is that the total variable cost first increases at a decreasing rate, then increases at an increasing rate.

Average Costs in the Short Run

The *average cost* tells how much a product costs per unit of output. There are three average cost functions, and they are derived from the total cost functions outlined in a preceding section. The three average cost functions are

1. *Average fixed cost*, the total fixed cost divided by output. Since it equals a constant (fixed cost by definition does not change), it must decline with increasing output.

2. *Average variable cost*, the total variable cost divided by output. Like average fixed cost, average variable cost at first declines with increases in output, but after some point, increases with increases in output.

3. *Average total cost*, the total cost divided by output. Because average total cost is a function of average fixed and average variable costs, it follows the same pattern as average variable cost. However, for a time, the increases in the average variable cost are more than offset by continuous decreases in the average fixed cost. Therefore, the average variable cost hits a minimum and begins to increase at a lower output than average total cost.

Marginal Cost in the Short Run

The law of diminishing marginal returns states that, since increases in variable inputs result in less and less extra output, it follows that a larger and larger quantity of variable inputs must be added to produce an extra unit of output. Thus, the cost of producing each extra unit of output must increase.

Marginal cost is the addition to total cost resulting from the addition of the last unit of output. In other words, suppose it costs $50 to produce one bushel of wheat, and $60 to produce two bushels. The marginal cost for one bushel is $50 (the difference between $0 and $50), and the marginal cost for the second bushel is $10 ($60 – $50).

The marginal cost varies according to a firm's output level. At first, the marginal cost tends to decrease with increases in output. This is logical if we stop to think that at first a firm uses resources very efficiently. It may be nearly as easy for our hypothetical farm to produce 12,000 bushels of wheat as 10,000 bushels. Beyond some point, however, it becomes more and more costly for the firm to produce yet another unit of output. Resources become stretched to the limit. Consider the farm again. There are only so many workers, so many acres, so many units of machinery that can be effectively supervised and coordinated under one farm manager. If the farm attempts to expand output beyond this level, inefficiency results. Output increases somewhat, but at an ever-higher cost.

Relating Marginal Cost to Average Cost Functions

The marginal cost curve intersects both the average variable cost curve and the average total cost curve at their minimum points. The reason for this is that, if the marginal cost is higher than the average variable cost (or average total cost), it causes that cost to rise. This is clearer, perhaps, if you keep in mind that the marginal cost is the cost of producing the last unit. And the average cost is the cost, on average, of producing all units. If the marginal cost is lower than the average cost, then it causes average cost to decline. Therefore, the average cost hits its minimum only when it equals the marginal cost.

Long-Run Average Total Cost Function

In the long run, the firm can vary all inputs. It can bring in new equipment, expand, build a new plant. Therefore, the long-run average total cost function shows the minimum average total cost of producing each output level when any desired type or scale (scale referring essentially to the size of the plant and the level of other inputs used in production) of plant can be built.

The shape of the long-run average total cost function depends on the production function, which shows the most output existing technology permits from each quantity of inputs. Basically, one of three situations can occur:

1. *Increasing returns to scale.* In this situation, the output increase is proportionally greater than the input increase.

2. *Constant returns to scale.* In this situation, the output increase is directly proportional to the input increase.

3. *Decreasing returns to scale.* Here, the output increase is proportionally smaller than the input increase.

What causes these variable situations? Simply put, expansion alone is not always the answer to greater efficiency, even when all inputs, including plant and equipment, expand simultaneously. Consider the farm again. Suppose Farmer Jones has 1,000 acres to farm, and suppose he has a chance to double this acreage. Would it be more efficient for him to have 2,000 acres in one parcel or two parcels 10 miles apart? You need not be an expert in agricultural management to envision many of the problems and expenses the second situation could create. At the same time, there can be a definite managerial advantage in keeping units small, particularly if specialization is involved. Every case is different. Consider a few of the factors that affect efficiency of scale:

1. *Indivisibilities.* Certain types of equipment are more efficiently used on a large scale because they cannot be adapted to smaller scales. The grocery chain uses computerized checking efficiently, for example; but the corner grocery that averages three customers an hour will not likely find it a wise or feasible investment.

2. *Specialization.* As more people and machines are used, it becomes easier to subdivide tasks. If the farm employs only five laborers, it may be essential that everyone know how to do everything. But if it employs 20, each person may develop a specialty shared by only one or two others.

3. *Coordination.* The difficulty of coordinating a large enterprise can result in decreasing returns to scale. Communication breaks down in larger organizations. Employees may feel lost or isolated. Advancement can be difficult. Because of such difficulties, the potential efficiency of a larger organization can be impaired.

An individual organization can experience increasing, then constant, then decreasing returns to scale, resulting in a U-shaped long-run average total cost function. This pattern is not found in all industries, but it is very common. The important point to remember is that each firm is different, and each case must be analyzed individually to determine what organizational structure, in the long run, results in the most efficient use of resources.

EXTENDED LEARNING

This section of the study guide is specifically designed for the two-semester student.

AUDIO

Listen

Listen to the audiotape that accompanies Lesson 16. There is no additional reading assignment for this lesson.

After Listening

Answer the following questions:

1. What do prices have to do with consumers' efforts to maximize utility, and what does that imply for the shape of the demand curve?

2. How does the concept of diminishing marginal utility explain the apparent paradox in which diamonds (which are not necessary to support life) are expensive, and water (which is so important to survival) is cheap?

3. How can consumers maximize the total amount of utility they get from spending their money?

4. Since consumers obviously do not calculate how much utility they derive from consuming a product, how can the utility maximization principle be correct?

5. If, in the long run, when all costs are variable, one plant can produce enough to serve the entire market and still not exhaust scale economies, how competitive will that industry be? Is this common? What are some examples?

ADDITIONAL READINGS

Alchian, Armen A. "An Introduction to Confusion." In *No Time to Confuse*, edited by Morris A. Adelman et al., 1–25. San Francisco: Institute for Contemporary Studies, 1975.

> Criticizes a study that failed to take the effect of prices into account when projecting energy needs and devising policy options. No mathematics, moderately difficult graphs.

Arrow, Kenneth J., and Joseph P. Kalt. *Petroleum Price Regulation*. Washington, DC: American Enterprise Institute, 1979.

> Pages 9–21 summarize the history of petroleum price regulation since Nixon's wage and price controls and discuss the effect of price controls on the efficient use of petroleum and the incentive to search for more petroleum domestically. Simple mathematics and graphs.

Baumol, William. "The Empirical Determination of Demand Relationships." In *Microeconomics: Selected Readings*, 2d ed., edited by Edwin Mansfield, 55–72. New York: W. W. Norton & Company, 1975.

> Discusses the problems in actually determining the demand curve for a product quantitatively. Covers various approaches, notes need to include all important variables, and discusses the statistical problems associated with explanatory variables correlated with each other and with simultaneity. Moderately technical, moderately difficult mathematics and graphs.

Dorfman, Robert. *Prices and Markets,* 3d ed. Englewood Cliffs, NJ: Prentice-Hall, 1978.

> Chapters 2 and 5 provide a concise and clear discussion of the theory of consumer demand and the theory of the firm. Simple mathematics, moderately difficult graphs.

Riddell, Tom, Steve Stamos, and Jean Shackelford. *Economics,* 3d ed. Reading, MA: Addison-Wesley Publishing Company, 1987.

> Chapter 10, "The Theory of Markets," discusses the factors that affect the supply and demand curves. Numerical examples are used and an analysis is given of how the principles of supply and demand can be applied. Simple mathematics and graphs.

ANSWER KEY

Video Questions

1. One major factor is its relative scarcity. When water is plentiful, people take it for granted. As Marin County, California, residents discovered during the severe drought of the 1970s, people may be willing to pay up to 500 times the usual

going price for something they require that is in short supply. In addition, the value of a resource depends on its uses. Water has multiple uses, obviously, although we may be unaware of many of them unless faced with a shortage. In addition to its relative scarcity, the value of water is established by the values consumers put on its various uses. Ultimately, life depends on it. As the price of water increases, people are willing to let their gardens die, not wash their cars, and take fewer showers, but they are prepared to pay almost any price to sustain their lives.

2. Even in the most dire economic circumstances it is rare for no one to benefit. When demand is high, there is always a profit to be made somewhere. Thus, those who had water available to sell stood to benefit. And those who could make water available (well drillers, for example) benefited as well. It is not stretching things much either to say that the residents of Marin County themselves ultimately benefited from the experience in one respect, since their perspective about the need to protect resources shifted considerably. As a result of their experience, bond issues were passed that probably would not have stood a chance prior to the shortage, and the water supply for the future was thus assured so far as current technology and conservation strategy would permit.

3. The price ceilings were imposed by the Nixon administration in 1971 in an effort to curb inflation. Prices had been rising steadily, but with oil supplies generally plentiful over the preceding decades and prices fairly stable, the real cost of oil had been declining in previous years, with the result that there had been little incentive for domestic drillers to seek new sources. The ceilings further dampened that incentive because oil is a high-risk industry with many failures. In 1972, the U.S. industry was offered an important incentive: Oil found after 1972 could follow the higher world price. Additional research and exploration were stimulated greatly, particularly given that OPEC had quadrupled the price of oil in 1973 and oil prices worldwide were climbing steadily and rapidly. The boom, however, was short-lived. Fearing that consumers would suffer the pinch of dramatic oil price hikes, President Ford imposed ceilings on all domestic oil. Again, domestic production was squelched, and the dependence on foreign suppliers was felt more strongly than ever. Then, in December 1978, Iran curtailed oil production. Faced with the prospect of a new energy crisis, oil suppliers pressured the government to decontrol gas and oil prices; in June 1979, President Carter announced a gradual phaseout of all domestic oil controls. Predictably, the result was an immediate return to U.S. oil rigs.

4. Probably the single biggest factor in the creation of fads is advertising. Once consumers become aware of a product and are persuaded of its advantages—regardless of whether those advantages are real or created by the producer—they feel compelled to purchase the product. The designer jeans fad is a case in point. Certainly jeans are a useful item of clothing. But the consumers who purchased designer jeans were not concerned with practicality; they were concerned with style, trends, having what everyone else had. These are created by advertising and peer pressure. What caused the jeans fad to die? Essentially, saturation of the market. When everyone had designer jeans, they were no longer so appealing. They were not a sign of status or a symbol of any particular lifestyle. They

became ordinary, and like the plentiful water of Marin County before the drought, they were taken for granted. Then consumers would no longer pay designer jean prices, and the fad was over.

Multiple Choice

1. d Text, 38–41, 361.
2. a Text, 364–365.
3. b Text, 363.
4. a Text, 365.
5. d Text, 365.
6. c Text, 366.
7. b Text, 367–368.
8. d Text, 369.
9. a Text, 370–372.
10. a Text, 373–384.

True-False

1. True   Text, 365–366.
2. False Text, 365–366.
3. False Text, 367–370.
4. True   Text, 367–368.
5. False Text, 366–367.
6. True   Video; Text, 368.
7. True   Text, 365–367.
8. True   Text, 373–378.
9. False Text, 385–386.
10. False Text, 385–386.

Discussion Questions

1. Utility cannot be measured. Economists have used this concept to build a model of the consumers' behavior. If it explains consumer behavior well and makes good predictions about it, then it does not matter that utility cannot be measured or that consumers do not understand the theory involved. Furthermore, comparing utilities of goods is not that far from what we do all the time. We constantly make choices about which television programs to watch, which music CDs to buy, which clothes to buy and wear. It is obvious that some things give us more satisfaction than others, we just cannot measure how much. It is true that when we decide on something, we make the decision on the basis of what we expect the utility to be. If we are mistaken in a negative way, we are unlikely to repeat that decision. The fact that all self-help books and time management courses encourage us to set goals and make lists of things we want to accomplish and to set priorities shows that this theoretical model is used, knowingly or not, for decision-making purposes.

2. To maximize total utility, this consumer should decrease the amount purchased of the second good and increase the amount purchased of the first good until such point as the marginal utility per dollar's worth of each good is equal. This happens because of the law of diminishing marginal utility.

3. There are the readily apparent costs represented by the paper cost, copying cost, printing machine cost, and the distribution and collection costs. There is also the opportunity costs that entail what each student must give up to fill out the questionnaires. These opportunity costs can be quite sizable if the class is large: Often, in a class of 300 students, the distribution and collection of these forms takes at least half the class period. To evaluate if the surveys are worth the costs, one must also consider the benefits gained by using the surveys. Is the information gathered useful? Is the information accurate? Is the information revealing

about the quality of the course and its instruction? Is the amount of poor instruction reduced? Does the student, the instructor, or the university benefit from the information gathered?

4. The marginal cost must always intersect both the average variable and average total cost curves at their minimum points. The marginal cost curve represents the additional cost of producing one more unit of the good. When marginal cost is greater than the average variable cost or average total cost, the marginal cost causes the average variable cost or average total cost to increase. When marginal cost is lower than the average variable cost or average total cost, the marginal cost causes the average variable cost or average total cost to decrease. The average variable cost and average total cost must hit their minimum when the marginal cost equals average variable cost and average total cost, respectively.

5. Yes.

Problem Set

1. a. 5 utils. 4 utils.

   b.

   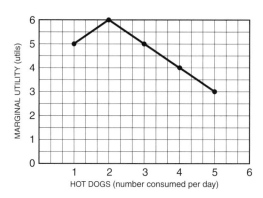

   c. Four hot dogs.

2. a. *Clothing (dollars per unit)*

   500/50 = 10
   400/50 = 8
   500/50 = 10

   b. 4 to 1.

3.

Average product	Marginal product	Total variable cost	Average variable cost	Total cost	Average total cost	Marginal cost
—		0	—	100	—	
	4					0.50
4		2	1/2	102	25 1/2	
	5					0.40
4 1/2		4	4/9	104	11 5/9	
	6					0.33
5		6	6/15	106	7 1/15	
	7					0.29
5 1/2		8	8/22	108	4 10/11	
	8					0.25
6		10	1/3	110	3 2/3	
	7					0.29
6 1/6		12	12/37	112	3 1/37	
	6					0.33
6 1/7		14	14/43	114	2 28/43	
	5					0.40
6		16	1/3	116	2 20/48	
	4					0.50
5 7/9		18	18/52	118	2 14/52	

4. Since the services of each worker cost $500 per month, the total variable cost of each output level is (per month; cost in dollars):

Output	Total variable cost	Marginal cost
0	0	
		500
1	500	
		1,000
2	1,500	
		2,000
3	3,500	
		2,500
4	6,000	
		3,000
5	9,000	
		3,500
6	12,500	

5. a. It implies it equals $2 million. No, because there are no fixed costs in the long run.
    b. $4.
    c. An infinite size of plant. No, because one would expect that eventually the long-run average cost function would turn up.

Audio/Text Questions

1. The higher is the price of a good relative to other prices, the more likely consumers get more satisfaction (utility) by purchasing less of that good and more of others. This implies that the demand curve for an individual good slopes downward to the right.

2. The first unit of water per day is very dear, worth much more that the "first unit" of diamonds. But the 200th unit of water has much less value to the consumer. Because water is so plentiful, it is easy to get as much as one wants, and the price reflects the valuation of the 200th unit. Diamonds, however, are relatively scarce, so the price reflects the valuation of the "first unit."

3. They should not spend a dollar on anything that gives them less added satisfaction than some other possible use of the dollar. They should allocate their spending over all the goods they consume in such a way that the utility of the last dollar's worth of food purchased equals the utility of the last dollar's worth of clothes and the last dollar's worth of everything else they consume.

4. Consumers implicitly weigh the price they pay for something against the value (or satisfaction or utility) they derive from it, and they have a rough idea of what else they could spend the money on that might give them more satisfaction. They may make mistakes from time to time or be misinformed as to the quality of the goods they purchase, but in general, the utility maximization principle simply states a commonsense rule of behavior.

5. Unless the government prevents it, the industry is likely to become a monopoly as the larger plant can produce at a lower cost and drive the smaller firms out of the market. There are few cases of economies of scale continuing up to the point of fulfilling total market demand. Utilities (gas, water, electricity, telephone) and other services that serve a local market are the most common examples.

LESSON 17. PERFECT COMPETITION AND INELASTIC DEMAND: CAN THE FARMER MAKE A PROFIT?

INTRODUCTION

As we see in this lesson, demand not only determines what is produced in a free market system, its sensitivity to price changes also affects business firms' revenues and profits. Demand for some products, like automobiles, is much more sensitive to price increases or decreases than for other products, like bread. In other words, as prices of cars rise and fall, the number of cars consumers purchase changes dramatically. Bread sales, by contrast, tend to be less flexible. What makes the difference? Again, the question is complex, and to answer it, we must look at the nature of price elasticity (sensitivity to price changes), the relationship between demand and income level, and the relationship between demand for one product and demand for another.

What You Should Learn

By the end of Lesson 17, you should be prepared to

1. Describe the relationship between price and quantity demanded illustrated in the market demand curve for a given commodity.

2. Define the *price elasticity of demand,* and distinguish among price elasticity, price inelasticity, and unitary elasticity.

3. List and explain the determinants of the price elasticity of demand.

4. Explain the relationship between price changes and total money expenditures for different types of price elasticity.

5. Explain why the demand curve for farm products is relatively price inelastic.

6. Define income elasticity of demand, and describe its effect on various common products.

7. Define *cross elasticity of demand*, and describe its effect on commodities classified as substitutes or complements.

KEY TERMS

market demand curve
direct market experiment
price elasticity of demand
price elastic
price inelastic
unitary elasticity
income elasticity of demand
cross elasticity of demand

substitutes
complements
concept of parity
Agriculture and Consumer Protection Act of 1973
arc elasticity of demand

VIDEO

Watch

Economics U$A Program 17, "Perfect Competition and Inelastic Demand: Can the Farmer Make a Profit?"

Illustrative Events

The plight of U.S. farmers following the collapse of the agricultural market in the 1920s, revealing the age-old farm problem of inelastic demand, featuring farmer Kenneth Litton and Wayne Rasmussen, chief historian for the USDA.

The violent dairy strike and milk dumping episodes of the Farm Holiday Association in the 1930s, illustrating the farmers' desperate effort to get a fair price for their products; with Herbert Forest, former director of the Dairy Division of USDA, and Iowa journalist George Mills.

The failure of government farm subsidy programs to solve the farmers' dilemma from Roosevelt to Kennedy, featuring New Deal Senator William Jennings Randolph; Don Paarlberg, assistant secretary of agriculture under Eisenhower; and John R. Block, Reagan's secretary of agriculture.

After Viewing

Answer the following questions:

1. Why is the story of the U.S. farmer considered one of the great ironies of modern economics?

2. What factors underlie the financial difficulties farmers have faced since the 1920s?

3. What message has the price system consistently given to farmers?

4. Why were the strikes of dairy farmers during the 1930s unsuccessful?

5. What has been achieved in U.S. agriculture as a result of pressures from the price system?

Read

Read Chapter 17, "Market Demand and Price Elasticity," pages 392–405 and 416–418 in your text. After completing your reading, try the Self-Quiz.

SELF-QUIZ

Multiple Choice

1. When a new product such as the Edsel automobile fails, the *main* reason is usually that

   a. the product is misrepresented in advertising.
   b. the market demand for the product is too small.
   c. supply cannot keep pace with market demand.
   d. consumers devalue a product for which there are no ready substitutes.

2. The market demand curve for a commodity shows

   a. how much of the commodity is purchased during a particular period at various prices.
   b. how much is purchased during a particular period at a given price.
   c. how much the demand changes over time at a given price.
   d. the current equilibrium price for a given commodity.

3. Probably the quickest and easiest way to estimate a market demand curve for a particular commodity is to interview consumers about their spending habits and intentions. This particular technique has been

   a. the single most effective way of estimating market demand to date.
   b. relatively effective for luxury items but of limited effectiveness for nonluxury items.
   c. highly effective for current products, although it tells us nothing about products yet to come.
   d. relatively ineffective overall since consumers often misjudge their own intentions.

4. The percentage change in the quantity demanded resulting from a 1 percent change in price is known as

   a. the market demand curve function.
   b. the estimated demand curve.
   c. the price elasticity of demand.
   d. unitary elasticity.

5. Suppose the price elasticity of demand for airline travel is 2.4 and the price elasticity of demand for corn is 0.49. We can conclude from this that

   a. there are a lot more substitutes for corn than for airline travel.
   b. if the price of airline travel is reduced, the total amount spent on airline travel decreases.
   c. if the price of corn goes up, the total amount spent on corn increases.
   d. price changes affect consumer demands for airline travel and corn about equally, although demand for one will go up, and for the other down.

6. Farm incomes vary a great deal between good times and bad, more so in fact than nonfarm incomes. The *main* reason for this is that

   a. farm prices tend to vary widely, while output tends to be stable.
   b. both agricultural prices and output tend to vary a great deal.
   c. the government tends to be highly irregular in its farm supports.
   d. agricultural technology has tended to grow in highly irregular spurts.

7. If the demand for a product is price elastic and the equilibrium price increases, the result will be a(n)

   a. relatively greater change in price than quantity.
   b. relatively smaller change in price than quantity.
   c. equal change in price and quantity.
   d. equal percentage change in price and quantity.

8. Probably the *best* way to measure the impact of price changes on the quantity demanded of a given commodity is to

   a. calculate the price elasticity of demand.
   b. conduct a consumer survey to determine buying habits.
   c. conduct a direct market experiment to see what happens when prices are altered.
   d. estimate the demand curve on the basis of past performance of the commodity in the market.

9. A main contributing factor to low farm income has been that

   a. consumer demand is highly variable year to year.
   b. there are too many resources devoted to farming.
   c. farmers have opposed the storing of surpluses.
   d. farmers have been unwilling or unable to increase supplies.

10. When farm surpluses drove market prices down following World War I, the result was

   a. a substantial rise in consumer demand.
   b. an economic situation in which only the most efficient farmers could compete.
   c. an unforeseen shortage of resources within the farming industry.
   d. decreased production but overall higher profits for farmers.

True-False

_____ 1. Market pressures that force competitive firms to use the least costly method of production and expand production to the point at which the marginal cost of production equals the market price tend to result in an inefficient allocation of resources.

_____ 2. If the price elasticity of demand is very low, only minor changes in price occur when there is a sudden increase or decrease in supply.

_____ 3. The degree of elasticity generally is smaller if firms and consumers are given more time to respond.

_____ 4. The government attempted to support agricultural prices by subsidizing foreign demand for U.S. agricultural products, buying part of the "surplus," and encouraging farmers not to produce.

_____ 5. The financial difficulties experienced by farmers are due primarily to a lack of productivity.

_____ 6. According to Dr. Gill, government subsidies to farm families have assisted in the necessary flow of farm families into other occupations.

_____ 7. The demand for most agricultural products tends to be inelastic.

_____ 8. As dairy farmers learned in the 1930s, voluntary agreements to limit production are difficult to maintain for an extended length of time in a competitive environment.

_____ 9. A competitive industry or market is one in which there are many independent buyers and sellers, so no one firm or consumer can affect a large percentage of the market.

_____ 10. Luxury items are generally assumed to have higher income elasticities of demand than necessities.

Discussion Questions

1. An evening TV news program reported the following: "Watch out Starbucks! Coffee drinking is not as popular as it once was. Over the past year, per capita consumption has dropped from 3.2 cups a day to 2.2 cups a day. Paradoxically this decline in consumption has not kept prices down. Even though charges of price gouging have been denied by coffee distributors, prices have more than

doubled in the same time period." Does the information given here prove that there has been a shift to the left in the demand curve for coffee and that the market is not functioning properly as is implied?

2. In fall 1973, there was talk of a beef shortage; in winter 1974, there was a gasoline shortage. Why did government officials talk more about rationing gasoline to solve the latter problem than about rationing beef to solve the former?

3. How could a state government use the information that the price elasticity of demand for cigarettes is about 0.4 when considering an increase in the state cigarette tax as a means of providing additional revenue for the state? How might the information that New Hampshire has a per-capita sale of cigarettes twice that of any neighboring state affect your decision to use the number 0.4 as your estimate of price elasticity in your calculations?

4. What are some ways that market demand curves can be measured? According to results obtained by Professor William Vickrey, the demand for passenger service on the New York subways is price inelastic. Does this mean that fare increases would result in greater revenues for the New York subways?

5. According to estimates made by agricultural economists, the price elasticity of demand for cotton is about 0.12. If this is the case, to what extent does the quantity demanded of cotton increase if the price of cotton is reduced by 1 percent?

Problem Set

1. Suppose that the relationship between the price of aluminum and the quantity of aluminum demanded is as follows:

Price (dollars)	Quantity
1	8
2	7
3	6
4	5
5	4

    What is the arc elasticity of demand when price is between $1 and $2? Between $4 and $5?

2. Suppose that the price elasticity of demand for gasoline is 0.50. About how big a price increase is required to reduce the consumption of gasoline by 1 percent?

3. If a 1.5 percent reduction in the price of Nike running shoes results in a 3.0 percent reduction in the quantity demanded of New Balance running shoes, what is the cross elasticity of demand for these two commodities? Are they substitutes or complements?

4. Suppose that the market demand curve for mink coats is as follows:

Price (dollars)	Quantity of mink coats
500	500
1,000	300
1,500	200
2,000	100

   a. What is the price elasticity of demand for mink coats when the price is between $1,500 and $2,000?
   b. What happens to total expenditures on mink coats when the price is raised from $500 to $1,000 per coat?
   c. Using only your answer to part b, is the price elasticity of demand between $500 and $1,000 elastic or inelastic?

5. Suppose that the Brazilian government destroys a substantial portion of its coffee harvest to increase its revenue from coffee exports. What conditions are essential to make this type of policy economically beneficial for the country? Why would the conditions you identify increase export revenue?

LESSON REVIEW

If you had difficulty with the Self-Quiz or would like additional assistance, read the following lesson review. It should reinforce and help you understand the content presented in this lesson.

Market Demand Curves

As you may recall from Lesson 2, a commodity's market demand curve shows how much of the commodity is purchased during a particular period of time at various prices. The demand curve tends to slope downward and to the right, because as the price goes up, the amount purchased tends to decline. The degree of response is very different for different products, however. Consumers may balk at a price hike for home theaters but (within limits) continue to use electricity at the same rate despite a price increase. In one case, the commodity is a luxury most feel they can do without; in the other, it is an integral part of everyday life and work.

The market demand curve, simply put, reflects what consumers are willing to pay for. What happens when it shifts? A shift upward and to the right indicates that consumers want more of a commodity at all prices. Producers see an opportunity for more sales and higher profits, and prices *tend to rise*.

Similarly, a shift downward and to the left in the market demand curve tells producers that consumers want less of a commodity at all prices. This response by consumers tends to generate decreased production and lower prices.

Measuring Market Demand Curves

Market demand curves can be measured in several ways, some more useful and practical than others. One way is through a consumer survey, simply asking consumers about their buying habits and preferences. This method is relatively inefficient, however, because no one can be sure that consumers' responses are accurate.

Another method is through direct market experiments. Under this approach, producers actually change the price of a commodity to see the consumer response.

A third technique is to estimate a demand curve by plotting the level of quantity demanded for various periods in the past. This method is useful for observing general trends over time and, in that respect, offers insights about consumers' habits. It is not especially accurate, however, because it does not reflect shifts in the market demand curve over time. Fortunately, we have a more statistically reliable method of calculating changes in demand termed *price elasticity*.

The Price Elasticity of Demand

For some commodities, changes in price have a great impact on the quantity demanded by consumers. With other commodities, the impact may be very slight. This sensitivity to price changes is measured through something called the *price elasticity of demand,* defined as the percentage change in quantity demanded resulting from a 1 percent change in price (note that the change in price could signify either an increase or decrease).

As we discuss price elasticity, you should keep two important points in mind:

1. *Price elasticity* is defined in terms of percentage changes, not absolute changes. In other words, it makes no sense to ask what the effect on consumer demand is if shoelaces go up $0.50. It makes sense to ask only what the effect is if shoelace prices go up 25 percent.

2. The price elasticity of demand is likely to vary from one point to another on the market demand curve. In other words, if shoelaces already cost $5 a pair, an increase or decrease in price may have more effect (because it reflects a percentage of total cost) than if they cost only $0.75 to begin with.

Calculating the Price Elasticity of Demand

We can calculate the price elasticity of demand if we know what changes have occurred in the price of a commodity and the quantity demanded over a specified period of time. Consider, for instance, the following shortened example from the text:

Farm price of wheat (dollars/bushel)	Quantity of wheat demanded (million bushels)
2.00	700
2.20	675

As this short table shows, the quantity demanded during the 1960s was 700 million bushels at a price of $2.00 per bushel, and 675 million bushels at a price of $2.20 per bushel. To calculate the arc price elasticity of demand for this particular change, the formula is

$$\frac{\text{Percentage change in quantity demanded}}{\text{Percentage change in price}} = \frac{(Q_{D_2} - Q_{D_1})/(Q_{D_2} + Q_{D_1})/2}{(P_2 - P_1)/(P_2 + P_1)/2}$$

We can see by looking at the table that

- The change in quantity demanded is 700 – 675 = 25.
- The average of quantity demanded is (675 + 700)/2 = 687.5.
- The change in price is $2.20 – $2.00 = $0.20.
- The average price is ($2.20 + $2.00)/2 = $2.10.

Therefore, the price elasticity of demand equals

$$\frac{25/687.5}{0.20/2.10},$$

which is the same as 0.036 divided by 0.095, which equals 0.38 (rounded to the nearest hundredth). According to our definition, then, every 1 percent change in the price of wheat (at this particular point on the market demand curve) results in a 0.38 percent change in the quantity demanded.

Factors That Determine Price Elasticity of Demand

According to estimates, the price elasticity for women's hats is 3.0. The price elasticity for newspapers is 0.1, for gasoline 0.2, and for potatoes about 0.3. What factors do you suppose create these differences? Three are particularly important.

1. *Number and closeness of available substitutes.* If a commodity has many close substitutes, its price elasticity is likely to be high. In other words, price shifts affect the quantity demanded greatly. This is so because, if consumers can readily turn to a substitute when prices rise, they will; similarly, when prices fall, consumers who presently buy substitutes turn to the cheaper commodity. The closeness of the substitutes depends on how narrowly the commodity is defined. For example, take the generic category of *cars;* as one would expect, there are few substitutes. You might buy a truck or a motorcycle or a bike instead, but generally speaking, if a car is what meets your needs, you will be less than content with something else. If we narrow the category to *Fords,* however, the number of substitutes increases; maybe you would be just as happy with a Chevrolet or an Oldsmobile. The point is that, the narrower is the definition of the product, the larger the number of substitutes (potentially) and the higher the price elasticity (sensitivity to price changes). If a product is so narrowly defined that it has perfect substitutes, its price elasticity approaches infinity. For example, if Write-Along Company makes ballpoint pens that, in consumers' views at least, are no different from hundreds of other ballpoint pens on the market, then a price increase by Write-Along could plunge its sales to zero.

2. *Importance of the commodity in consumers' budgets.* The price elasticity for some commodities (like salt, sugar, and potatoes) is likely to be quite low,

because in the first place, consumers spend a relatively small portion of income on these items and, in the second place, consumers purchasing them may see them as "basic necessities," quite different from, say, RVs, home theaters, or trips to Europe.

3. *Length of the period the price change has been in effect.* The time involved is important too. The quantity demanded is likely to be more sensitive to price change over a long period than over a short period, because the longer consumers have, the easier it is to substitute one commodity for another. If the price of oil rises, for instance, some consumers may want to change to gas heat or electric heat. But making such a change is not like buying shoes. It takes time and planning. It may be a very long time before consumers' response to oil increases is reflected in demand for gas furnaces.

Price Elasticity and Total Money Expenditure

Firms and government agencies look closely at the price elasticity for various commodities. In general, they divide commodities into three categories. We define each, keeping in mind that a commodity may fall into one category at one time but another category at another time.

1. *Demand is price elastic.* The demand for a commodity is said to be price elastic if its price elasticity of demand is greater than 1. For such a commodity, a reduction in price spells an increase in the total amount spent on that commodity. Remember that the total amount spent equals the quantity demanded times the price, so if the quantity demanded goes up by more than 1 percent, the total amount spent must rise too. At the same time, a rise in price means a decrease in the total amount spent on the commodity.

2. *Demand is price inelastic.* The demand for a commodity is said to be price inelastic if its price elasticity of demand is less than 1. For such a commodity, a decrease in price means a decline in the total amount spent on that commodity (quantity demanded times price). An increase in price means an increase in the total amount spent.

3. *Demand is unitary elastic.* The demand is said to be of unitary elasticity if its price elasticity of demand equals 1. For such commodities, the total amount spent remains the same. Why? Because the percentage change in price shifts offsets the percentage change in quantity demanded.

Industry and Firm Demand Curves

The market demand curve for a commodity is not the same as the market demand curve for the output of a single firm producing that commodity, unless that is the only firm in the industry. Why? Because generally products of various firms tend to be close substitutes for one another. One breakfast cereal may be much like another—or at least close enough so that if the cost of your favorite doubles, you quickly switch loyalties. But a cereal lover may not feel like shifting from cereal to eggs. So the demand curve for breakfast cereals as a whole is different from that for Cheerios or Wheaties or Special K or any of the dozens of other varieties. In short, the demand curve for the output of a particular firm is generally *more price elastic* than that for the commodity as a whole.

If numerous firms sell a homogeneous product, the individual firm's demand curve becomes horizontal, or essentially so. This is because, when many competitors make virtually comparable products, an increase in output or sales by one firm has an imperceptible change on total industry output. Therefore, for all practical purposes, a firm in this situation must assume that its output has no real impact on market price.

Income Elasticity of Demand

While price is important, it is not the only factor influencing the quantity demanded. Of great significance is consumers' income. As your income rises or falls, the number of goods and services you purchase together with the nature of those goods and services is likely to change significantly.

The sensitivity of quantity demanded to the *total money income of all consumers in the market* is measured by the *income elasticity of demand*. The income elasticity of demand is *the percentage change in the quantity demanded resulting from a 1 percent change in total money income* (all prices being held constant).

A commodity's income elasticity of demand can be positive or negative. This is another way of saying that, as consumers' money income rises, they tend to buy more of some items but less of others. For example, perhaps they buy more steak but less margarine, for now they can afford butter. On the other hand, consumers at the lower end of the pay scale may buy more margarine than before, because perhaps they could not afford either butter or margarine previously. As a general rule, luxury items tend to have higher income elasticities of demand than necessity items.

Cross Elasticity of Demand

The quantity demanded of one commodity may depend on the price of other commodities. This relationship, known as the *cross elasticity of demand,* is defined as *the percentage change in the quantity demanded of one commodity resulting from a 1 percent change in the price of another commodity.*

The way in which demand is affected depends on how the two commodities are related. Economists classify commodities that are interchangeable as *substitutes* and commodities that tend to be used together as *complements*. For example, butter and margarine are substitutes. If the price of butter goes up, the quantity of margarine demanded tends to rise because people turn to the less-expensive substitute. On the other hand, hot dogs and hot dog buns are complements. If the price of hot dogs goes up, the quantity of hot dog buns demanded likely declines since one is rarely used without the other.

Economists can define these relationships statistically, a matter of great interest to producers. For instance, the cross elasticity of demand for butter and margarine is 0.81. This is another way of saying that a 1 percent increase in the price of butter means a 0.81 percent increase in the quantity of margarine demanded. If you were head of a firm that produced margarine, such information could be invaluable to you in predicting sales.

Exploring the Farm Problem: A Study in Price and Income Elasticity

The size of the agriculture industry has been decreasing steadily for over a century. It now employs fewer than 3 million Americans. Technologically, it has been among our most successful industries; per-capita output has grown faster in agriculture than in any other major sector of the U.S. economy.

At the same time, farm incomes have tended to be about 20 percent lower than nonfarm incomes. To be sure, agriculture has seen some good years, short-lived periods with bumper crops. But overall, the prosperity seen in other sectors of the economy tends to elude farming. The first two decades of the twentieth century were good ones for the farmers, but the industry never really recovered from the depression of 1920, and the 1930s were disastrous. Despite some recovery following World War II, farm incomes continued to run steadily below nonfarm incomes, and that generalization holds true today.

To understand the reasons behind the economic difficulties experienced by agriculture, we need to examine the characteristics of the demand and supply curves for farm products.

- *The demand curve*. The shape of the demand curve (sharply angled, nearly vertical) reflects the fact that food is a necessity, almost immune to variations in price. In other words, the demand curve is *price inelastic*. Some food items, like steak or lobster, are purchased in greater quantities of course if prices decline, but other food items see little change in quantity purchased then, there is just so much that one family can consume, regardless of price or income. So overall, remembering that the farm demand curve reflects the demand for all food products, quantity demanded is little affected by price changes. In addition, the farm demand curve is not likely to shift to the right much as per-capita income rises because, as noted, consumption is necessarily limited. We may eat a little differently as our income goes up; few of us eat a great deal more. In other words, consumption of food is also income inelastic.

- *The supply curve*. The supply curve is also quite sharply angled because the quantity of farm products supplied tends to be relatively price inelastic (insensitive). Once they have planted, farmers have only limited control over output. Weather, irrigation costs, insects, and numerous factors over which producers have no control at all influence what can be supplied. In the long run, the supply curve has been shifting rapidly to the right because of advanced technology that makes production faster and cheaper.

- *Equilibrium price*. What is the result of these combined characteristics and shifts? Essentially, because both curves are inelastic and in the long run the demand curve shifts very slowly and the supply curve very rapidly, the equilibrium price of food (marked by the point where the two curves intersect) tends to fall steadily. With a fall in prices, farm income declines as well. The situation is particularly insidious given the technology that makes supply ever easier to produce.

- *Immobility of resources.* Another factor that contributes to the problem has been the reluctance of farm families to move out of agriculture. Fewer families (producers) would mean higher per-capita income. And the price system has given an unmistakable message that current demand levels do not support the number of producers, but the exit has been slow. The change is notable, all the same. In 1930, the farm population represented about 25 percent of the total population; by 1981, that figure had dropped to 3 percent.

Government Aid to Agriculture

Agriculture has had considerable influence in Congress. Small wonder, considering that food production is essential to our very lives as well as to our economic structure. Added to that realization is the strength of the argument posed by many agriculture spokespersons that we owe it to ourselves to preserve the qualities and values inherent in rural culture; and the overwhelmingly positive response to that argument is a fixture in U.S. tradition.

The Concept of Parity

In the Agricultural Adjustment Act of 1933, Congress announced that the concept of parity would be a major objective of U.S. farm policy. Essentially, this concept affirms that a farmer should be able to exchange a given quantity of his or her output for just as much in nonfarm goods and services as at some designated time in the past.

For the concept of parity to hold, farm prices must therefore increase at the same rate as the average prices of the goods and services farmers buy. Of course, these goods and services do not increase in price at a steady rate. Interestingly, for years the period of 1910 to 1914 (a time of relatively high farm prices) was used as the basis for parity.

The concept of parity was the base for government price supports up until 1973. From 1933 to 1973, Congress periodically enacted bills saying that the government would provide support amounting to a percentage of parity. But the principle remained the same, to provide government support that would raise farm prices above what they would normally be in a free market.

Because the support price was always above the free market price, consumers bought less farm goods but paid more for them. At the same time, because the quantity supplied exceeded the quantity demanded at the support price, surpluses developed. And these were purchased—and stored—by the government, at great expense.

Policies to Cut Surpluses

Because the surpluses represented, in the eyes of many people throughout the world, a great waste of precious resources, the government sought ways to get rid of them. Essentially, two techniques were followed:

1. *The government tried to restrict output of farm products.* Through an acreage allotment program, the government limited the number of acres farmers could

plant. This had only moderate impact, however, since farmers used their technological know-how to increase output per acre.

2. *The government tried to shift the demand curve for farm products to the right.* Some antipoverty programs used extra farm supplies to feed the poor. In addition, the government tried to expand markets abroad, in Europe, Japan, Russia, and elsewhere. Developing countries were permitted to buy farm surpluses with their own currency rather than U.S. dollars. Overall, surpluses dwindled during the late 1960s and early 1970s.

Recent Developments

Largely because of great increases in foreign demand (triggered partly by poor harvests during the early 1970s in the Soviet Union), farm prices rose markedly during the early and mid-1970s, and surpluses disappeared. Congress passed a new farm bill in 1973, the Agriculture and Consumer Protection Act of 1973, intended to reduce government involvement in agriculture and a return to free markets. The bill stipulated, however, that the government would pay farmers if prices fell below target levels; such levels were lower, generally, than those established through parity.

In 1976 and 1977, bumper crops pushed farm prices down again, and again farmers clamored for government support. The expressed policy of the Reagan administration opposed government intervention, but the pressures to maintain growth within the agricultural sector of the economy were great and the controversy was far from resolved.

The Food Security Act of 1985 continued the income support policies. Even with large subsidies in 1986, 11 percent of all farms were in serious financial trouble. During the late 1980s, the situation on the nation's farms improved. By the mid-1990s, optimism spread among many parts of U.S. agriculture, and the government tried to wean farmers from federal aid by passing the Crop Insurance Reform Act of 1994 and the Federal Agriculture Improvement and Reform Act of 1996. In 1996, net farm income hit a record of $57.8 billion, but the Asian financial crises of 1997–98 reduced the demand for farm products and farm income dropped to $46.2 billion in 1998.

By 2001, net farm income was up to $50.6 billion. But in 2002, in the aftershock of the terrorist attacks of September 11, 2001, farm income plummeted to $35.3 billion. As a result, Congress extended the 1996 Farm Bill from 2002 through 2007 at the cost of around $20 billion per year.

EXTENDED LEARNING

This section of the study guide is specifically designed for the two-semester student.

AUDIO

Before Listening

Read Exploring Further of Chapter 17, pages 405–416 in your text.

Next

Listen to the audiotape that accompanies Lesson 17.

After Listening

Answer the following questions:

1. Describe two ways the federal government has tried to keep farm prices up by reducing the amount of goods brought to market, and two ways it has sought to increase demand.

2. Explain why, in terms of price elasticity of demand, it was in Henry Ford's best interest to *lower* prices, whereas it is in OPEC's interest (in the short run at least) to *raise* prices.

3. Why isn't it contradictory to say, on the one hand, that an individual farmer loses all of his sales if he raises his price above the market price (i.e., the farmer faces a "perfectly elastic" demand curve) but, on the other hand, demand curves for farm goods as a whole are very inelastic?

4. If a family budgets a fixed amount of money for food and clothing, say, $400 for food and $100 for clothing, what is that family's price elasticity of demand for food and clothing?

5. How, in the absence of government farm programs, does the low price elasticity of demand for farm products help cause farm income to fluctuate so much?

ADDITIONAL READINGS

Fite, Gilbert C. *American Farmers: The New Minority*. Bloomington: Indiana University Press, 1981.

> Chapters 4 and 6 discuss technological and economic pressures on farmers in the 1920s, 1930s, and 1950s and the government policies developed in the 1930s and 1950s to help them. No mathematics or graphs.

Haveman, Robert H., and Kenyen A. Knopf. *The Market System,* 3d ed. New York: John Wiley & Sons, 1978.

> Chapter 5, Section 3, "The Elasticity of Supply and Demand," gives a concise description of elasticity and numerous examples. Moderately difficult mathematics and graphs.

Houthakker, Hendrik S., and Lester D. Taylor. *Consumer Demand in the United States: Analysis and Projections*. Cambridge, MA: Harvard University Press, 1970.

> Describes how demand elasticities are estimated in practice and the evolution of the pattern of demand in the United States. Moderately difficult mathematics and graphs.

Suits, Daniel B. "Agriculture." In *The Structure of American Industry*, 3d ed., edited by Walter Adams. New York: Macmillian Company, 1961.

> An excellent theoretical analysis of the reasons for the problems farmers had in the twentieth century. The interaction of competition, technology, long- and short-run supply and demand elasticities, and the reluctance of farmers to shift to new occupations is detailed, and the effects of the farm programs of the 1930s and 1950s are discussed. Simple mathematics, moderately difficult graphs.

Weiss, Leonard W. *Case Studies in American Industry*, 2d ed. New York: John Wiley & Sons, 1971.

> Chapter 2, Sections 3 and 4, discuss the problems that the various agricultural elasticities (the price elasticity of demand, and the short- and long-run price elasticity of supply) create for U.S. agriculture and the effect of government programs on farm income. Simple mathematics, moderately difficult graphs.

ANSWER KEY

Video Questions

1. It is ironic that an industry characterized by such efficient use of resources and advanced technology should suffer such financial hardship. The fact is that, while most countries in the world have struggled to reach a production level sufficient to satisfy demand, the problem in the United States has been quite different, bringing demand up to match unprecedented supply. Food shortages in this country are virtually unheard of.

2. In part, the financial difficulty has stemmed from a tendency to expand production during times of peak demand (World War I and World War II) then to try to maintain that production and its accompanying price levels despite declines in demand that followed the war efforts. In large part, the demand for food is limited because as income grows, people may buy higher priced items, but they do not tend to buy a great deal more. In addition to rapid increases in supply brought about by improved technology, in the 1980s, farmers began to contemplate another problem: The predicted slowdown in population growth for both the United States and the world. Despite these difficulties, some farmers have been reluctant to leave the industry since they can stave off bankruptcy with government subsidies. This, of course, compounds the problems financially healthy and efficient farmers already face.

3. The price system has consistently given farmers the message that there are too many of them in the market. Farmers have been reluctant to heed this message; yet, increasing competition has forced many out. Currently, farmers represent only 3 percent or so of the total U.S. labor force, and that figure is expected to decline further.

4. In large part the strikes failed because dealers and sellers could obtain milk supplies elsewhere. In perfect competition, it is hard for a producer or even a handful of producers to have much influence because there are so many sources of supply. In addition, it is hard to make such strategies work in a competitive environment because of the total cooperation required. If any producers do not wish to go along, they can make things difficult for the others. Once supplies are down, prices go up. Then, remaining on strike or continuing to deplete supplies may appear less attractive because the promise of profits is high. So, some producers may relent and begin supplying products once again. Voluntary agreements seldom last.

5. Despite a generally dismal picture for many U.S. farmers, some of whom actually have been forced out of the industry altogether, there have been some social benefits to increased agricultural productivity. For one thing, our agriculture has become extremely efficient. That is, we can produce more using fewer resources than any country in the world. Given that many resources, like land, are limited, this efficiency offers us an enormous economic advantage. It also means more food for more people, not only here in the United States but in many countries throughout the world; the social benefits of this are hard to dispute. In addition, our society has shifted from an agrarian to an industrial and service-oriented economy. This increased total GDP and potential for employment for our citizens.

Multiple Choice

1. b   Text, 390.
2. a   Text, 390–391.
3. d   Text, 391–392.
4. c   Text, 393.
5. c   Text, 398–400.
6. a   Text, 399.
7. b   Text, 393–398.
8. a   Text, 393–400.
9. b   Video.
10. b   Video.

True-False

1. False   Video.
2. False   Text, 399.
3. False   Text, 397.
4. True   Video.
5. False   Video.
6. False   Video.
7. True   Video; Text, 399.
8. True   Video.
9. True   Video.
10. True   Text, 402.

Discussion Questions

1. A decrease in the amount purchased and an increase in the price point to a shift in the supply curve not the demand curve (see Figure 2.13 in Chapter 2 of the textbook). So there was a movement up and to the left along the demand curve, not a shift in it to the left. The information given allows us to make a rough estimation of coffee's price elasticity of demand. It would be approximately 0.3

(0.5 using the arc elasticity of demand formula)—as we would expect, rather inelastic.

2. The demand for beef is more price elastic than the demand for gasoline. There are many close substitutes for beef and very few, if any, close substitutes for gasoline. Also the time period to adjust demand is much shorter for beef than for gasoline. Of course, there was an actual shortage of gasoline but not of beef because the wage and price controls imposed by President Nixon in 1971 had been removed from beef and many other items by 1973 but not from oil and gasoline even by 1974.

3. The state could use this number and the planned tax to estimate the new price with the tax and the expected revenues from such a cigarette tax. In evaluating the effect of a tax increase, the price of cigarettes in adjacent states would need to be considered because consumers would purchase their cigarettes out of state if the difference between in-state and out-of-state prices got too large. This is particularly true for relatively small states (like New Hampshire), where travel costs to adjacent states are small.

4. Demand curves can be measured by using consumer surveys, direct market experiments, or plotting the level of quantity demanded for various periods in the past. If demand is price inelastic, increases in fares result in greater revenues.

5. By 0.12 percent.

Problem Set

1.
$$\frac{Q_2-Q_1}{\frac{Q_1+Q_2}{2}} \div \frac{P_2-P_1}{\frac{P_1+P_2}{2}} = \frac{-(7-8)}{\frac{8+7}{2}} \div \frac{2-1}{\frac{1+2}{2}} = \frac{3}{15} = 0.20.$$

$$\frac{Q_2-Q_1}{\frac{Q_1+Q_2}{2}} \div \frac{P_2-P_1}{\frac{P_1+P_2}{2}} = \frac{-(4-5)}{\frac{5+4}{2}} \div \frac{5-4}{\frac{4+5}{2}} = \frac{9}{9} = 1.00.$$

2. 2 percent.

3. 2. Substitutes.

4. a.
$$\frac{200-100}{150} \div \frac{1,500-2,000}{1,750} = \frac{100}{150} \div \frac{500}{1,750}$$

$$= \frac{2}{3} \div \frac{2}{7} = \frac{2}{3} \times \frac{7}{2} = \frac{7}{3} = 2\frac{1}{3}$$

   b. When the price is $500, total expenditure is $250,000; when it is $1,000, total expenditure is $300,000. Total expenditures rise when the price is raised from $500 to $1,000 per coat.
   c. The price elasticity of demand is inelastic between $500 and $1,000.

5. The price elasticity of demand must be less than 1, Brazil must supply a substantial part of the world market in coffee, and other countries must not have

substantial amounts of coffee beans in their inventories. Export revenue would increase, because if the price elasticity of demand is less than 1, increases in price (and reductions in quantity) increase revenue.

Audio/Text Questions

1. Supply reduction, government payments to reduce acreage and government purchases of crops at a support price. Demand increase, food stamps and Food for Peace.

2. The price elasticity of demand for automobiles was greater than 1 in the early 1900s, so a given percentage reduction in price led to greater percentage increase in sales. Total revenue would have increased with the lower price. For petroleum, the price elasticity (in the short run) is much less than 1, so OPEC's total revenue is lower when prices fall, higher when prices rise.

3. If one farmer raises his prices above that of the market, all buyers seek out a lower-priced seller. But if all sellers have a higher price (either through cartelization or total market supply and demand conditions change and result in a higher price), then each seller loses only a small fraction of sales, and that fraction is determined by how many buyers drop out of the market because of the higher price.

4. If this family's money expenditures on food and clothing remain unchanged even if the price of food and clothing change, then the family's price elasticity of demand for both food and clothing is 1.

5. A low price elasticity implies that the quantity demanded is unresponsive to price; that is, the price must fall a great deal before the quantity sold increases much. If a harvest is good, the large supply cannot be sold until prices fall very low, and if the harvest is bad, the prices are driven way up because consumers continue to purchase only slightly less as the price increases. These large fluctuations in price lead to large changes in farm incomes.

LESSON 18. ECONOMIC EFFICIENCY: WHAT PRICE CONTROLS?

INTRODUCTION

It is usual to think of the United States as a competitive society. Competition pervades most aspects of our lives, from sports to education, and certainly affects the way businesses operate. Not all businesses compete in the same way, however. As we see in this chapter, different forms of market organization promote different styles and degrees of competition; further, as it turns out, certain forms of market organization encourage more efficient use of resources than others.

Here, we take a particularly close look at one market structure, *perfect competition,* the way in which prices are determined, and hence, how resources are allocated within this structure. Interestingly, it turns out that, under perfect competition, price depends in part on the efficiency with which resources are used. For this reason, many economists prefer perfect competition as a form of market organization for society.

What You Should Learn

By the end of Lesson 18, you should be prepared to

1. Distinguish among *perfect competition, monopoly, monopolistic competition,* and *oligopoly* according to the following criteria:

    a. Number of producers.
    b. Type of product.
    c. Power of the firm over price.
    d. Barrier to entry.
    e. Nonprice competition.

2. Describe two methods for determining a firm's maximum profit output rate.

3. Describe the circumstances under which it may be better for a firm to produce nothing at all.

4. Explain how a perfectly competitive firm's individual supply curve is determined.

5. Explain how a perfectly competitive market's supply curve is derived.

6. Describe the effects of price ceilings and price supports on the economy.

7. Explain the conditions under which equilibrium is achieved in a perfectly competitive market.

KEY TERMS

perfect competition
monopolistic competition
monopoly
oligopoly
total revenue
total cost
profit
market supply curve
entry
exit
rationing
average variable cost
average total cost

marginal cost
long-run average cost function
short run
long run
golden rule of output determination
economic profits
firm's supply curve
firm's demand curve
price floors
price supports
price ceilings

VIDEO

Watch

Economics U$A Program 18, "Economic Efficiency: What Price Controls?"

Illustrative Events

Richard Nixon's attempt to curb inflation through imposition of a price freeze and the market distortions that resulted, with Herbert Stein, economic adviser to President Nixon, and J. Dawson Ahalt, former member of the Cost of Living Council.

The implementation of wage and price freezes during World War II and why they were unusually successful; featuring John Kenneth Galbraith, President Franklin Roosevelt's "price czar."

The controversial impact of longtime rent control in New York City: how it was installed and why it persists in spite of strong opposition, featuring former New York City Mayor Abraham Beame, a builder, a landlord, and a tenant.

After Viewing

Answer the following questions:

1. When President Nixon instituted the price controls on beef, pork, and lamb, what was the administration gambling would happen? What really occurred?

2. How did cattle ranchers react to the price controls? What was the effect of their strategy?

3. Describe the potential negative effects of price controls as summarized by presidential economic adviser Herbert Stein and economist Richard Gill.

4. How did price controls work to the benefit of the nation during World War II?

Read

Read Chapter 18, "Economic Efficiency, Market Supply, and Perfect Competition," pages 419–440 in your text. After completing your reading, try the Self-Quiz.

SELF-QUIZ

Multiple Choice

1. Which of the following statements is *most* accurate? Perfect competition is

    a. a useful economic model even though it has no precise counterpart in the real world.
    b. not a very useful economic model because it does not exist in the real world.
    c. the one market model that has real-life counterparts.
    d. a useful model for describing the auto industry, although it has little application to other industries.

2. The market model characterized by many producers, differentiated products, and some power of the firm over price would be classified as

    a. perfect competition.
    b. monopolistic competition.
    c. monopoly.
    d. oligopoly.

3. Multiplying price times total output yields a firm's

    a. total profit.
    b. average long-term profit.
    c. maximum profit.
    d. total revenue.

4. Consider the following figures for *output* and *total cost* (in dollars):

Output per week (pianos)	Price	Total revenue (price × output)	Total fixed cost	Total variable cost	Total cost	Total profit
0	1,000	0	1,000	0	1,000	-1,000
1	1,000	1,000	1,000	200	1,200	-200
2	1,000	2,000	1,000	300	1,300	700
3	1,000	3,000	1,000	500	1,500	1,500
4	1,000	4,000	1,000	1,000	2,000	2,000
5	1,000	5,000	1,000	2,000	3,000	2,000
6	1,000	6,000	1,000	3,200	4,200	1,800
7	1,000	7,000	1,000	4,500	5,500	1,500
8	1,000	8,000	1,000	7,200	8,200	-200

According to these figures, the *marginal cost* when output is between 0 and 1 is

a. $1,000.
b. $2,000.
c. $1,500.
d. $200.

5. Based on figures from question 4, the *average total cost* when production is at 5 units would be

a. $600.
b. $2,000.
c. $15,000.
d. $200.

6. Hang Tight Staple Company is in trouble. Despite the best technology available, Hang Tight is unable to realize a profit from its staples, regardless of level of output. In the *short run*, Hang Tight should probably continue production only if

a. the cost of liquidating exceeds the cost of production.
b. the cost of diverting resources into manufacture of some other product exceeds the cost of production.
c. there is an output rate where price exceeds average variable cost.
d. there is an output rate where price exceeds average fixed cost.

7. In the short run, a perfectly competitive firm can usually maximize profits by choosing an output level at which price is equal to

a. marginal cost.
b. total revenue.
c. average total cost.
d. average variable cost.

8. For prices above the minimum value of average variable cost, a firm's supply curve is exactly the same as its

   a. demand curve.
   b. average variable cost curve.
   c. marginal cost curve.
   d. price axis.

9. Assume that the supply curve of each firm in industry X is a vertical line. If no firm can enter or leave the industry, we can infer that the market supply curve is

   a. also a vertical line.
   b. a horizontal line.
   c. upward sloping to the right.
   d. downward sloping to the left.

10. Suppose 1,000 firms manufacture scissors. Output in the scissors industry does not affect the price of resources. For each firm, the marginal cost of producing five pairs of scissors per month is $2, the marginal cost of producing six scissors per month is $3, and the marginal cost of producing seven scissors per month is $5. If the price of a pair of scissors is $3, the industry output is

    a. 5,000 pairs of scissors per month.
    b. 6,000 pairs of scissors per month.
    c. 7,000 pairs of scissors per month.
    d. well over 7,000 pairs of scissors per month.

True-False

____ 1. Firm B, a perfectly competitive firm, produces at an output rate where its marginal cost is $1 under its per unit price. To increase its profit, firm B should increase its output rate.

____ 2. If the short-run supply curve of every firm in an industry slopes upward and to the right, the industry's market supply curve must also slope upward and to the right.

____ 3. Profits are negative at all points where the total revenue curve lies below the total cost curve.

____ 4. If the supply curve were vertical, then any decrease in demand, however slight, would lower price.

____ 5. If price is fixed, a firm's profits are not affected by changes in output.

____ 6. Under perfect competition, the product of each seller is a little different from the products of all other sellers.

____ 7. In long-run equilibrium, a perfectly competitive firm has an economic profit of zero.

____ 8. One defining characteristic of perfect competition is that resources can be reallocated to other uses.

_____ 9. If there is only one output rate at which price exceeds average variable cost, a firm is better off to cease production than to operate at a loss.

_____ 10. Price controls are virtually always detrimental to the economy.

Discussion Questions

1. Show why a firm continues to produce in the short run so long as the price exceeds the average variable cost, even if the price is lower than the average cost.

2. "There is a learning curve in many industries; that is, unit costs go down as more units are produced. This is a major reason why supply curves slope downward to the right." Do you agree? Why or why not?

3. Distinguish between (a) diminishing marginal returns and (b) diseconomies of scale.

4. Explain why in the long run under perfect competition equilibrium requires that price must be equal to the lowest value of long-run average total cost.

5. "Competition is all very well in theory, but in practice it generally is a disaster, leading to low profits and eventual government intervention. Agriculture is a case in point." Comment and evaluate.

Problem Set

1. Suppose that the total costs of a perfectly competitive firm are as follows:

Output rate	Total cost (dollars)
0	40
1	60
2	90
3	130
4	180
5	240

   a. If the price of the product is $50, what output rate should the firm choose?
   b. What is the firm's total profit?

2. Suppose that the total cost curve of the Rem Sofa Company is as follows:

Output (sofas per month)	Total cost (dollars per month)
1	1,000
2	1,100
3	1,200
4	1,300
5	1,500
6	1,700
7	2,000
8	2,500

   a. If the price of a sofa is $300, how many sofas does Rem produce per month?

b. Suppose that Rem's fixed costs increase by $100 per month. What effect does this have on the optimal output?

c. If its fixed costs increase by $100 per month, what is the maximum profit rate that the Rem Sofa Company can earn?

d. Does the Rem Sofa Company exhibit increasing marginal cost? What is the value of marginal cost when between seven and eight units of output are produced per month?

3. Data are provided here concerning the Allied Peanut Company, a firm producing peanut brittle.

   a. Supposing that this firm is a member of a perfectly competitive industry, complete the following table (amounts in dollars):

Daily output of peanut brittle (tons)	Price per ton of peanut brittle	Total revenue	Total cost	Marginal cost	Profit
0	200	—	100		—
1	—	—	200		—
2	—	—	310		—
3	—	—	500		—
4	—	—	700		—
5	—	—	1,000		—

b. If the price of a ton of peanut brittle falls to $50, does Allied continue producing or shut down?

c. What is the minimum price at which Allied continues producing (assuming that it cannot produce fractions of tons of output)?

d. If the price of a ton of peanut brittle is $200, what output rate does Allied choose? Does price equal marginal cost at this output rate?

4. You are the owner of a firm currently losing $1,000 per month, with fixed costs per month of $800. A management consultant advises you to cease production. Should you accept the advice? Why or why not?

5. Suppose that a perfectly competitive firm has this short-run total cost function:

Output	Total cost (dollars)
0	10
1	12
2	16
3	22
4	30
5	40

a. If the firm can produce only integer amounts of output, what output level does it choose when the price of its product is $3? $5? $7? $9?
b. What are the firm's profits when the price of its product is $3, $5, $7, $9?
c. If 1,000 firms are in this industry and all have the cost function just shown, the market supply curve follows. Fill in the blanks.

Price (dollars)	Quantity supplied
3	_____
5	_____
7	_____
9	_____

d. If the market demand curve is as follows, what is the equilibrium price of the product?

Price (dollars)	Quantity supplied
3	3,000
5	2,000
7	1,500
9	1,000

e. What is the output of each firm?
f. How much profit does each firm make?
g. Will firms tend to enter or leave this industry in the long run?

LESSON REVIEW

If you had any difficulty with the Self-Quiz, read the following Lesson Review before returning to the text. It should help you in understanding the textbook discussion and identify key concepts.

Market Structure and Economic Performance

Economists have found it useful to classify markets into four broad types: perfect competition, monopoly, monopolistic competition, and oligopoly. We consider each in light of several distinguishing characteristics.

- *Number of firms.* In perfect competition and monopolistic competition, there are many sellers, each producing only a small portion of total industry output. Monopoly, by contrast, has only one seller. Oligopoly has a few. The auto and computer industries are examples of oligopolies.

- *Control over price.* A firm under perfect competition has no control over price at all because so many other firms produce essentially the same thing; if one producer raises prices, buyers just go to another. A monopolist, on the other hand, has considerable control over price because consumers have only two choices, buy from the monopolist or do without. A firm under monopolistic competition or oligopoly has some control over price but not so much as the monopolist.

- *Type of product.* Perfectly competitive firms produce essentially identical products (one ear of corn is about like another, one gallon of milk about the same as another). In a monopolistically competitive industry, like dressmaking, firms produce somewhat different products. In an oligopolistic industry, firms sometimes produce identical products but not always, and some differences may be largely created through advertising. In a monopolistic industry, there can be no substitutes since there is but one firm.

- *Barriers to entry.* It is easy to enter into perfect competition or monopolistic competition. Members of the market do not oppose entry by others, and the investment is relatively small. In oligopolies, entry is more difficult largely because it is expensive. And in a monopoly entry is extremely difficult because of government barriers to entry.

- *Nonprice competition.* Nonprice competition refers to advertising or product differentiation. There is no nonprice competition in perfect competition. In monopolistic competition and oligopolies, nonprice competition is important. And there is some nonprice competition by monopolists too since, even though they have no competitors in the industry, they are always working to broaden their markets.

Perfect Competition

We take a closer look now at the characteristics that distinguish perfect competition. A market is considered perfectly competitive if it satisfies these three conditions:

1. *Homogeneity of product.* That is, the product of one seller is essentially the same as the product of any other seller.

2. *Many buyers and sellers.* So many buyers and sellers must be in the market that no one has any real influence over price. A firm under perfect competition faces a horizontal demand curve. That is, variations in its output have no effect on market price. And changes in the price an individual firm charges can have a huge effect on the quantity demanded of its output.

3. *Mobility of resources.* All resources must be able to switch readily from one use to another. For example, if consumer tastes shift from corn to wheat, the industry must be able to divert some resources used for corn production into wheat production.

No industry now or at any time in the past has completely satisfied all three conditions. However, agricultural markets come very close.

Determining the Firm's Output in the Short Run

In the short run, the firm can vary output by increasing or decreasing use of its variable inputs. For this discussion, we assume that the product price is a given. The first step, then, is to calculate the total revenue: price times output. To use the text's example of the Allegro Piano Company, if the price of a piano is $1,000 and output is two pianos per week, then revenue for the week is $2,000.

The next step is to determine total costs: variable costs (for supplies such as wood, ivory, and metal for the pianos; labor to build the pianos; and so on) plus fixed costs (rent, utilities, and so on).

Next, subtract the total costs from the total revenue to determine the total profits at each output rate.

These data for the Allegro Piano Company are summarized (in dollars):

Output per week (pianos)	Price	Total revenue (price × output)	Total fixed cost	Total variable cost	Total cost	Total profit
0	1,000	0	1,000	0	1,000	−1,000
1	1,000	1,000	1,000	200	1,200	−200
2	1,000	2,000	1,000	300	1,300	700
3	1,000	3,000	1,000	500	1,500	1,500
4	1,000	4,000	1,000	1,000	2,000	2,000
5	1,000	5,000	1,000	2,000	3,000	2,000
6	1,000	6,000	1,000	3,200	4,200	1,800
7	1,000	7,000	1,000	4,500	5,500	1,500
8	1,000	8,000	1,000	7,200	8,200	−200

Note that total profits rise for a time, peak at $2,000, then decline. Why does this occur? Because, at some point, the total variable costs begin to rise at a rate faster than the rate at which total revenues rise. As in earlier discussions, increasing resources indefinitely does *not* increase efficiency of output indefinitely; in fact, quite the opposite occurs. To provide a very simple illustration, imagine yourself working 40 hours per week. If you worked 80 hours per week, could you produce twice as much? Three times as much if you worked 120 hours? As this very simplified example suggests, there is a point of diminishing returns with the use of any combination of resources. We return to the piano company. According to this table, Allegro maximizes profits at an output rate of four to five pianos a week. If it makes any more or any fewer than this number, it will make less money and may even lose money.

As an alternative to this method, we can calculate maximum profit by looking at the price and marginal cost. Recall that the marginal cost is the additional cost involved in adding the last unit of output. On the basis of the figures from the total cost column in the table, we can derive the following table:

Output per week (pianos)	Marginal cost (dollars)	Price (dollars)
0		1,000
	200	
1		1,000
	100	
2		1,000
	200	
3		1,000
	500	
4		1,000
	1,000	
5		1,000
	1,200	
6		1,000
	1,300	
7		1,000
	2,700	
8		1,000

As it turns out (on the basis of what we know from looking at the table), the maximum profit is achieved at an output rate where the price equals the marginal cost. This, in fact, summarizes the golden rule of output determination for a perfectly competitive firm: *Choose the output rate at which the marginal cost is equal to the price.*

What If You Cannot Turn a Profit?

Sometimes, even doing its best, a firm is unable to make a profit. What then? The firm attempts to minimize losses. In the short run, the firm cannot expand or alter its equipment or plant. In the short run, a firm must pay its fixed cost even if it is producing nothing. If the loss resulting from production is greater than those fixed costs, the firm is better off shutting down. If it can cover the variable costs, it is better off producing at a loss for a while. The rule is this: *If there is an output rate where the price exceeds the average variable costs, it will pay the firm to produce, even though price does not cover the average total cost.* If there is no such output rate, the firm is better off producing nothing at all.

Market Supply Curve

From our discussion thus far we know that

1. The firm's price is a given.

2. The firm chooses the output level at which the price equals the marginal cost.

3. If the price is below the average variable cost at *every output level,* the firm produces nothing.

Now consider this figure.

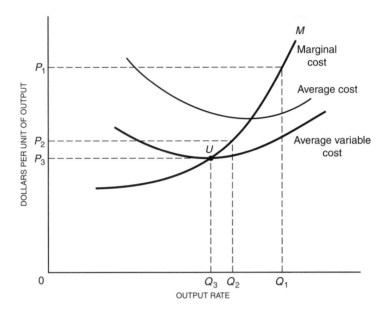

Note that the marginal cost curve intersects the average variable cost curve at the latter's lowest point, U. If the price is below this level, it does not pay the firm to produce (point 3).

If the price is higher than $0P_3$, then the firm sets its output rate at the point where the price equals the marginal cost (point 2). Hence, if the price is $0P_1$, the firm sets its output at $0Q_1$. If price is $0P_2$, the firm sets its output at $0Q_2$.

In other words, *the firm's supply curve is exactly the same as the firm's marginal cost curve for prices above the minimum value of average variable cost ($0P_3$).*

Deriving the Market Supply Curve

Assume for now that increases or decreases in market supply do not affect input prices (in real life, this is not always a valid assumption, but we make it here for the sake of our illustration). In that case, *the market supply curve can be regarded as the horizontal summation of the supply curves of all the firms producing the product.*

In other words, if each producer supplies a hundred units of a product at a per unit price of $2 and there are 1,000 producers, the market supply curve shows a total production of 100,000 units at a per unit price of $2. (This is a highly simplified illustration in which production is the same for all firms; in real life, of course, outputs differ firm to firm.)

Since marginal cost curves (as we saw in the preceding section) determine the firms' supply curves, the *location and shape of each marginal cost curve depend on the size of a firm's plants, the level of input prices, and the state of technology.* Further, the location and shape of the market supply curve in the short run are determined by the number of firms in the industry. The more firms, the farther to the right the supply curve is. Generally, the market supply curve in the short run slopes upward and to the right, because marginal cost curves in the short run slope upward and to the right.

Price and Output: The Short Run

In the short run, the market supply curve in a perfectly competitive industry slopes upward and to the right because each firm in the market faces the law of diminishing returns. The market demand curve slopes downward and to the right because each consumer in the market faces the law of diminishing marginal utility.

The equilibrium price in the market is determined by the intersection of the demand and supply curves. This price rations the quantity available to consumers and determines the amount of the good firms find it most profitable to produce.

The price determined in the market can result in the typical firm in the market making above-normal, normal, or below-normal economic profits.

Price and Output: The Long Run

In the long run, a firm can change its plant and equipment, expand, even liquidate. This means that a firm may leave an industry if it has below-average profits or enter an industry if there is a promise of above-average profits.

Equilibrium is achieved in the long run when exactly enough firms are in the industry that economic profits are zero. Economic profits are defined as the excess of a firm's profits over what it could make in other industries. So long as economic profits are anything more or less than zero, firms enter or exit an industry, and resources continue to be shifted and reallocated until equilibrium is achieved.

Recalling that the market supply curve is the sum of the firms' supply curves (assuming no changes in input prices), we can see that the long-run market supply curve shifts to the left if firms leave the industry (because total production declines) and shifts to the right if firms enter the industry (because total production increases). The long-run supply curve is stable only if the number of firms remains constant and there is no improvement in production technology.

Remember that economic profits cause firms to enter or leave an industry. If economic profits are being earned, firms come in; if economic losses are occurring, firms exit. Stability is achieved only when economic profits are zero. This occurs at the point where long-run average total costs equal price. Therefore, long-run equilibrium occurs at the point where long-run average total costs equal price.

Allocation of Resources under Perfect Competition

In a perfectly competitive economy, resources shift as consumer tastes change and technology improves. Suppose, for instance, that consumers determine they like wheat better than corn. What happens?

In the short run, the price of wheat rises a bit and output may go up a bit too in response to demand, but output cannot expand very much, because in the short run, firms cannot alter their production processes greatly; that is, they cannot expand capacity. What of the corn producers? At first their output declines just slightly. Again, shifts in resources take time. Firms continue producing for a while so long as they can cover variable costs.

As time goes on, changes in the relative prices of wheat and corn signal producers that reallocation of resources is called for. Resources that can be used as effectively to produce wheat as to produce corn are reallocated. This happens in various ways. New farms may enter the industry, or a farmer may simply shift from raising one crop to raising another. Eventually short-run equilibrium is attained; but the reallocation of resources is not yet complete.

In the long run, adjustments in production tend to be greater than in the short run; adjustments in price tend to be smaller. If the consumer demand pressures continue, some corn-related resources are liquidated or even abandoned. As a result, the supply curve shifts to the left, pushing prices up. The transfer of resources out of corn production stops when *the price has increased to the point where losses are avoided.*

Meanwhile, the wheat industry is gaining resources. New firms are entering the industry. Farmers are growing more wheat, using more equipment, labor, land, and other resources. The price of wheat is depressed because the supply curve shifts to the right as more producers enter the market. Entry ceases when economic profits are no longer being earned; at this point, no more firms enter the market, and the supply curve stabilizes. Long-run equilibrium is finally achieved, and the shift in resources stops.

EXTENDED LEARNING

This section of the study guide is specifically designed for the two-semester student.

AUDIO

Listen

Listen to the audiotape that accompanies Lesson 18. There is no additional reading assignment for this lesson.

After Listening

Answer the following questions:

1. "Competition is all very well in theory, but in practice it is generally a disaster, leading to low profits, and eventual government intervention. Agriculture is a case in point." Comment and evaluate.

2. Why are profits maximized if a firm expands production up to the point at which the additional cost of the last unit produced per week (or year) is equal to the additional revenue that unit brings in. Why is that the same as "the marginal cost equals the price" for a competitive firm?

3. Explain why a firm continues to produce in the short run so long as price exceeds average variable cost, even if price is lower than average total cost.

4. In long-run equilibrium, economic profits are zero. Does that mean that the owners or managers of the firm lose money?

5. For most of the 1970s, petroleum prices were partially controlled by the government. Why was this done, why did it cause problems, and what would have been a more efficient way to solve the problem that the price controls were meant to solve?

ADDITIONAL READINGS

Dorfman, Robert. *Prices and Markets,* 3d ed. Englewood Cliffs, NJ: Prentice-Hall, 1978.

> Chapters 3 and 7 cover the theory of the perfectly competitive firm and the concept of economic efficiency in a technical but concise way. Simple mathematics, difficult graphs.

Gill, Richard T. *Economics and the Private Interest,* 2d ed. Pacific Palisades, CA: Goodyear Publishing Company, 1976.

> Chapter 7, "Interdependence and Efficiency," provides clear diagrams and explanations of the interrelationships of supply and demand for goods and factors that determine prices, and how, under certain assumptions, the market leads to an economically efficient method of allocating scarce resources. Simple mathematics and graphs.

Haveman, Robert H., and Kenyon A. Knopf. *The Market System,* 3d ed. New York: John Wiley & Sons, 1978.

> Chapter 6, "The Performance of a Market System," explains the concept of economic efficiency by first describing general equilibrium and tracing out how changes in tastes or technology have repercussions throughout the market system. Then, the way the general equilibrium solution tends to maximize welfare given scarce resources is discussed. No mathematics, moderately difficult graphs.

Kristof, Frank S. "Housing Economics, Facets of New York City's Problems." In *Agenda for a City,* edited by L. G. Fitchand and A. H. Walsh. Beverly Hills, CA: Sage Publications, 1970.

> Kristof discusses all the factors, including rent control, that led to the abandonment of thousands of housing units in New York City in the late 1960s. No mathematics or graphs.

Schultz, George P., and Kenneth W. Dam. *Economic Policy beyond the Headlines.* New York: W. W. Norton & Company, 1977.

> Chapter 4, "The Life Cycle of Wage and Price Controls," describes the rationale for limited controls during the Nixon administration but argues that controls can never work for extended periods. No mathematics or graphs.

ANSWER KEY

Video Questions

1. The gamble in this case, as in many parallel cases, was that prices for other commodities (particularly the resources or inputs required to produce the commodities in question) would hold fairly steady. In fact, this did not happen. A drought destroyed huge portions of that year's winter wheat crop, and suddenly cattle ranchers were faced with soaring feed prices at a time when they could not raise the price of their product. Eventually, things got so bad that many ranchers felt they simply could not take their animals to market.

2. Some cattle ranchers banded together, determined not to sell their cattle at controlled prices that were below their costs of raising their livestock. The effect was a beef shortage that was caused by the government setting beef prices below the equilibrium price. This shortage did not last very long because the cattle ranchers faced a big problem. Their herds still had to be fed and cared for. If the cattle ranchers sold their cattle at controlled prices, they lost money. If they did not sell, they lost even more money. So suddenly the cattle ranchers sold almost all of their herds to try to avoid bankruptcy. This sudden increase in the supply of beef kept prices down. However, because many cattle ranchers did go bankrupt and the ones that survived did not rebuild their herds, there was a tremendous decrease in supply for years after this. After price controls were removed, this ironically caused much higher prices of beef than would have prevailed if the government had not intervened in the first place.

3. Government price controls can lead to reductions in supply by forcing producers out of the market. They can also contribute to inflation after the controls are removed by pushing prices up so that the quantity demanded is brought into equilibrium with the reduced quantity supplied. According to Herbert Stein, the controls may be necessary in emergencies, but for extended periods during peacetime, their effects can be devastating.

As Richard Gill explains, price is typically determined by equilibrium supply and demand. When the government intervenes and establishes a price lower than this equilibrium level, some producers are driven out of the market because they cannot make a profit. At the same time, additional consumers are pulled in because more consumers can afford the product at the lower price. While controls are in place, these two responses create a situation of excess demand in which people want to buy more than is being offered for sale at the controlled price.

One can speculate too on the effects this situation might have on product quality, since producers must find some way to maximize profits without expanding price.

4. Price controls can be necessary and even beneficial in an emergency situation. This was the case in World War II, where price controls worked quite successfully, but under very special circumstances. First, we must recognize that the war involved a tremendous transfer of resources from civilian production to military production. The demands on the economy were such that, without price controls, the inflation resulting from an upward spiral of prices and wages could have damaged the war effort considerably. Second, people understood the reasons behind the controls, and accepted them as a wartime measure essential for dealing with a special situation. This moral support for the price controls undoubtedly contributed to their success.

Multiple Choice

1. a   Text, 416.
2. b   Text, 417. Table 18.1.
3. d   Text, 420.
4. d   Text, 421–422.
5. a   Text, 380–381.
6. c   Text, 425.
7. a   Text, 423.
8. c   Text, 427.
9. a   Text, 427–428.
10. b Text, 423, 427.

True-False

1. True   Text, 423–424.
2. True   Text, 427–428.
3. True   Text, 420–423.
4. True   Text, 428–429.
5. False Text, 421–424.
6. False Text, 419.
7. True   Text, 429–431.
8. True   Text, 419.
9. False Text, 425.
10. False Video.

Discussion Questions

1. If the firm shut down, its losses would equal its fixed cost, since in the short run, the firm cannot reduce its fixed cost even if output is reduced to zero. If price exceeds average variable cost but is less than average total cost, a firm's revenue covers more than its variable cost but does not cover its total cost. The firm loses money in this situation, but its losses would be less than if it shut down.

2. No. Supply curves typically slope upward, implying that, as the price rises, firms supply more of the good or service. There is a learning curve to producing goods in the sense that there is an optimal size of plant and use of resources such that unit costs are minimized when producing at this combination. This topic was

covered in Chapter 16 under the discussion of returns to scale: The firm as it moves along its long-run average cost curve goes from increasing returns to scale to constant returns to scale; unit costs fall as output is increased. But the unit costs expressed in the average cost curve do not provide the firm's supply curve; that is found by using marginal cost data.

3. a. Diminishing marginal returns occur as more and more of a variable input is used with at least one fixed input. Initially, output may expand at an increasing rate, but as more and more of the variable input is used, output eventually expands at a decreasing rate due to the limitations the fixed input places on production.
   b. Diseconomies of scale refers to the upward-sloping portion of the long-run average cost curve. This portion of the long-run average cost curve indicates that unit cost increases as output increases.

4. Long-run equilibrium in perfectly competitive industries occurs when economic profits equal zero. This occurs only when price equals marginal cost equals minimum average total cost. If economic profits are greater than zero, this acts as a signal for more resources to come into the industry: New firms enter the industry. If economic profits are less than zero, this acts as a signal that resources need to exit the industry: Some firms no longer produce the good or service.

5. Perfect competition as discussed in this chapter does not exist in the real world; it is instead a model of how such a market structure would work and how efficient allocation of resources could occur through market forces. First, perfect competition results in zero economic profits in the long run, but zero economic profits in the context of economics means that all resources are paid a return equal to their opportunity cost. There is no underpayment or overpayment to any resource. If the average profit rate made by firms in all other industries were 15 percent, then a firm's economic profit would be zero if its profit rate, as calculated by accountants, is also 15 percent. Second, markets where the government has intervened often are beset with problems that either are not resolved through government intervention or are made even worse through government intervention. One strength of the model of perfect competition is the idea that markets can allocate resources well and efficiently if there is no intervention and no externalities or public goods are present.

Problem Set

1. a. Three or four units of output per period of time.
   b. $20.

2. a. Six or seven units per month.
   b. No effect.
   c. Zero profits.
   d. Yes. $500.

ECONOMIC EFFICIENCY | 345

3. a.

Daily output of peanut brittle (tons)	Price of a ton of peanut brittle	Total revenue	Marginal cost	Profit
0	200	0		−100
			100	
1	200	200		0
			110	
2	200	400		90
			190	
3	200	600		100
			200	
4	200	800		100
			300	
5	200	1,000		0

b. It shuts down.
c. $100.
d. Either 3 or 4 tons per day. Yes, as shown in the answer to part a, marginal cost is $200 when output is between 3 and 4 tons per day. Price also equals $200.

4. Yes. Because you lose less money ($800) if you cease production than at present.

5. a. 1. 2. 3. 4.
   b. −$9, −$6, −$1, +$6.
   c. Quantity supplied

   1,000
   2,000
   3,000
   4,000

   d. $5.
   e. 2.
   f. −$6.
   g. They will leave it.

Audio/Text Questions

1. Agriculture is indeed the most competitive industry, but it is a special case. The extremely low short-run price elasticity of demand and supply, the rapid increase in productivity, and the reluctance of people to look for jobs outside of the agriculture sector have made that industry subject to instability. Most industries can be competitive without such instability. Low profits do not mean everyone in a firm is not making a good wage. The profit is what is left over after managers and other operating costs have been paid, and even low profits are

likely to be sufficient to earn a "normal" rate of return on capital.

2. As output expands, costs per unit increase. If the firm expands production past the point of $MC = MR$, then it clearly reduces net revenue, that is, profits, because the additional revenue is less than the additional cost. Marginal revenue is the money the last unit brings in when sold. For competitive firms, that is the going market price.

3. If a firm can in any way continue to cover part of its fixed costs by remaining in operation, then it would be in its interest to do so unless it feels it will never make a profit again. If the revenue is greater than the average variable costs, then part of the fixed costs are covered, even though the firm is taking losses.

4. No, economic profit is defined as profit in excess of the salaries of the managers of the firm (as well as all other costs of operation) and in excess of a "normal" rate of return on the capital invested in the firms by its owners.

5. Oil price controls were meant to help people who had little alternative to using petroleum products from being subjected to rising prices. The main problems were that the controls and the threat of new controls tended to keep supply from expanding as much as it might have and they reduced efforts to conserve petroleum. If poor people who had to use gasoline were hurt, a more economically efficient way to help these people would have been a rebate on or reduction in their income taxes or special cash assistance.

LESSON 19. MONOPOLY: WHO IS IN CONTROL?

INTRODUCTION

One reason we have confidence in our economic system is that it is based, for the most part, on competition. Industries must vie with one another for their respective shares of the market and, in so doing, must use resources efficiently, must heed consumers' demands, and must keep pace with modern technology. Otherwise, their competitive edge rapidly dulls.

When an industry is dominated by a monopoly, there is only one seller. Yet, monopolies are not without competition. In an age of rapidly changing technology, he foundations of monopolies are shaky. Still, history warns us that monopolies are powerful, that they can, under the right circumstances, control an industry for many years, regulating output and setting prices to suit themselves. Overall, do the potentially damaging economic effects of monopolies outweigh any potential benefits? This is a question economists still debate, and one we explore in greater detail in this lesson.

In addition, we examine the ways in which monopolies get their start, the methods by which they determine output and price, and the effects of attempted regulation.

What You Should Learn

By the end of Lesson 19, you should be prepared to

1. Describe the characteristics of a monopoly and list four factors that can contribute to the formation of a monopoly.

2. Describe how the monopolist calculates price and output in the short run.

3. Compare monopoly and perfect competition in terms of price and output.

4. Discuss the effects of monopoly on resource allocation.

5. Describe the case against monopoly from the economists' standpoint.

6. Explain the reasons for and effectiveness of public regulation of monopoly.

KEY TERMS

monopoly	economies of scale
natural monopoly	historical cost
marginal revenue	social value
reproduction cost	social welfare
golden rule (profit-maximizing rule) of output determination (for a monopoly)	patent
	public regulation
	deregulation
total revenue	technological change

VIDEO

Watch

Economics U$A Program 19, "Monopoly: Who's in Control?"

Illustrative Events

The dramatic making and breaking of the Standard Oil monopoly and the development of U.S. antitrust laws, with Ruth Sheldon Knowles, author of *The Greatest Gambler;* Thomas L. Krattenmaker, professor of law at Georgetown University; and Dallas oil executive Robert L. Goddard. Richard Gill explains how monopolies keep output low and prices high.

The government-authorized "natural" monopoly of AT&T and how new technology finally broke it up, featuring Pic Wagner, AT&T executive; Henry Geller, former general counsel of the FCC; John Goeken and William McGowan, founder and board chair of MCI.

How patents helped establish the Eastman Kodak monopoly and the challenge it faces in today's competitive technological world; featuring Brenda Landry, industry analyst at Morgan Stanley, and Peter Carstensen, professor of law at University of Wisconsin.

After Viewing

Answer the following questions:

1. How do monopolies like Standard Oil so often result in low production and high prices?

2. How does a monopoly create barriers to entry that keep other competitors out?

3. The video presentation suggests that technology maintained the Bell Systems monopoly—and then technology ended it. What is meant by this, and what implications does it have for the development of technology by monopolies?

4. Why is it important to regulate so-called natural monopolies?

5. In 1997, the Justice Department filed an antitrust suit against Microsoft Corpora-

tion. It claimed that Microsoft was abusing the monopoly (90 percent of the market share) it enjoyed in the market for operating system software for desktop personal computers. How was Microsoft damaging consumers according to the Justice Department's Antitrust Division?

Read

Read Chapter 19, "Monopoly and Its Regulation," pages 441–460 and 464–466, in your text. After completing your reading, try the Self-Quiz.

SELF-QUIZ

Multiple Choice

1. A monopoly may *best* be defined as a market where there exists
   a. only one seller who has no direct competition.
   b. one seller with direct but no indirect competition.
   c. only one seller with no direct or indirect competition.
   d. one seller who has both direct and indirect competition.

2. The purpose of the patent system is to
   a. create monopolies.
   b. prevent monopolies.
   c. control the use of resources by monopolies.
   d. encourage innovation.

3. Suppose that firm X develops a new process for finishing cars. The finish is scratchproof, rustproof, and never needs waxing. Firm X could probably become a monopoly by
   a. continuing to keep supply below demand.
   b. applying for a patent on the finishing process.
   c. setting the price well above market levels.
   d. making the finishing process as cost-efficient as possible.

4. A *natural* monopoly tends to occur in situations where the
   a. total cost of production declines as output increases.
   b. average total cost of production declines throughout the relevant range of market production.
   c. total cost of production rises as output increases.
   d. average total cost of production rises as output increases.

5. The market demand curve for a monopolist tends to be
   a. horizontal.
   b. vertical.
   c. downward sloping to the right.
   d. downward sloping to equilibrium, then vertical.

6. Suppose that a firm manufactures and sells 600 kites per year at an average cost of $6 per kite. Kites are priced at $10 apiece. The firm's total revenue is

   a. $4.
   b. $2,400.
   c. $3,500.
   d. $6,000.

7. Assume that the kite firm (question 6) is a monopoly with a typical demand curve. On the basis of the information given, we can assume that the marginal revenue

   a. is $10.
   b. is less than $10.
   c. is more than $10.
   d. cannot be determined from the information given.

8. If a monopolist is free to maximize profits, it chooses a price and output rate where the difference between total

   a. revenue and total cost is zero.
   b. revenue and total profit is maximized.
   c. revenue and total cost is maximized.
   d. cost and total profit is maximized.

9. For the monopolist, short-run equilibrium occurs at the point where the marginal cost equals the

   a. total revenue.
   b. average cost.
   c. average profit.
   d. marginal revenue.

10. Comparing a monopoly to a perfectly competitive industry, we can generally assume that, under the monopoly, output is

    a. smaller and the price higher.
    b. greater and the price higher.
    c. about the same but the price is higher.
    d. smaller and the price may or may not be higher.

True-False

_____ 1. Monopolies never have to worry about competition, direct or indirect.

_____ 2. The monopolist's demand curve is often horizontal.

_____ 3. In times of high inflation, most regulatory commissions rely on replacement cost to value a firm's assets.

_____ 4. Compared to a seller in perfect competition, a monopolist is more interested in profit maximization.

MONOPOLY | 351

_____ 5. Like perfect competition, monopoly seldom corresponds exactly to real life, but it is a useful economic model nevertheless.

_____ 6. A natural monopoly may actually work to the advantage of the consumer provided that regulation keeps prices in check.

_____ 7. A firm may gain and hold monopolistic power for years through the acquisition of patents.

_____ 8. The public generally opposes government regulation of natural monopolies.

_____ 9. One way that both monopolies and perfectly competitive firms can maximize profits is to limit output to the point where price equals marginal cost.

_____ 10. A monopolist tends to push prices up as high as the market allows.

Discussion Questions

1. Define what is meant by monopoly. Is a monopolist free of all indirect and potential forms of rivalry? What are the most important conditions for monopoly?

2. "Even if a monopolist earns no economic profits whatsoever, it may harm society." Do you agree? If so, how does the harm come about? Be specific.

3. Prove that a monopolist, to maximize profit, should choose an output rate such that the marginal revenue equals the marginal cost.

4. How do the price and output set by a monopolist compare with those that would prevail if the industry were perfectly competitive? Why do many economists argue that the allocation of resources under perfect competition is likely to be more socially desirable than under monopoly? Use diagrams to illustrate your arguments.

5. What are some criticisms directed at the regulatory commissions and the principles they use? Why did Congress require in 1962 that new drugs be proven effective as well as safe to be approved by the Food and Drug Administration?

Problem Set

1. The Uneek Corporation is the only producer of battery-powered soup ladles. Suppose that the demand curve facing the firm is as follows:

Quantity of soup ladles demanded per day	Price (dollars per soup ladle)
1	30
2	20
3	10
4	6
5	1

a. Using the data on the preceding page, fill in the following table for the Uneek Corporation (revenue in dollars):

Quantity	Total revenue	Marginal revenue
1	___	
2	___	___
3	___	___
4	___	___
5	___	___

b. Suppose that the Uneek Corporation has a horizontal cost curve, with a marginal cost of $9 per soup ladle (see the following graph). Its fixed costs are zero.

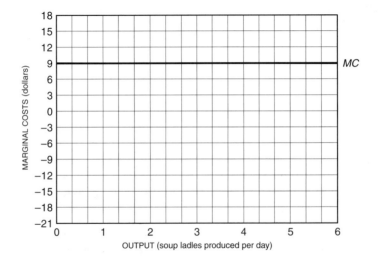

If the Uneek Corporation's costs are as described, and it produces one unit of output, how much does a second unit of output (that is, a second ladle) add to its costs? How much does it add to its revenue? Is it profitable to produce a second unit?

c. On the basis of the data given, what price should the Uneek Corporation charge?
d. What output should it choose to profit maximize?
e. What is the Uneek Corporation's profit if it produces at the optimal output rate?

2. In a particular industry the minimum value of the average cost is reached when a firm produces 1,000 units of output per month. At this output rate, the average cost is $1 per unit of output. The demand curve for this product is as follows:

Price (dollars per unit of output)	Quantity (produced per month)
3.00	1,000
2.00	8,000
1.00	12,000
0.50	20,000

    a. Is this industry a natural monopoly? Why or why not?
    b. If the price is $2, how many firms, each of which produces an output such that average cost is at a minimum, can the market support?

3. Suppose that a hypothetical monopoly has the following demand curve and total costs (price, revenue, and costs in dollars):

Output sold (per month)	Price	Total revenue	Marginal revenue	Total cost (per month)	Marginal cost	Profit
0	50	—		40		—
1	45	—		50		—
2	40	—		70		—
3	35	—		95		—
4	30	—		125		—
5	25	—		165		—
6	20	—		225		—

    a. Fill in the blanks.
    b. What output (or outputs) maximize the monopolist's profits?
    c. What price does the monopolist choose?

4. A monopolist's demand curve is as follows:

Price (dollars)	Quantity demanded
20	0
15	1
10	2
5	3

The monopolist's total cost (in dollars) equals $3 + 20Q$, where Q is its output rate. What output rate maximizes the monopolist's profit?

5. Suppose that a firm is producing quarks and it has a complete monopoly over quarks. The following information is given:

Marginal revenue = $1{,}000 - 20Q$
Total revenue = $1{,}000Q - 10Q^2$
Marginal cost = $100 + 10Q$

where Q = output of quarks and P = price of a quark. How many quarks would be sold and at what price if

a. The firm sets price as a monopoly?
b. The industry (firm) behaves perfectly competitively?

LESSON REVIEW

If you had any difficulty with the Self-Quiz or would like additional assistance, read the following lesson review. It should help you understand the content presented in this lesson.

What Is a Monopoly?

A *monopoly* is a market with one and only one seller. Like the perfect competition model, the monopoly model tends only to approximate real-life situations and, as we shall see, has become harder to maintain as a market structure in recent years because of rapid technological advances. For the purposes of our discussion, however, we view the monopoly as a price maker and sole supplier, a firm with no direct competitors. Keep in mind, however, that a monopoly can have indirect competitors. Suppose a monopoly controls the manufacture of automobiles and all are priced beyond your purchasing power. You may choose to buy a used car or a motorcycle, ride the bus, or pay a fee to Sam Smith, who just started his own car pool agency for you and the thousands of others like you who can no longer afford new automobiles. The point is, competition occurs in many forms. The monopolist is safe from direct competition only in the form of product or service duplication, and even that isolation may be short-lived, given the potential for product improvement.

How Do Monopolies Get Started?

Monopolies arise through several different circumstances.

1. *Government franchise.* A firm sometimes becomes a monopolist because a government agency awards it a franchise, a license to provide a service (such as provision of electricity) to consumers within a particular area. In exchange for this right, the firm agrees to government regulation.

2. *Patents.* A firm may acquire a monopoly because it holds a patent for its product or for one or more vital procedures required to make that product. Patents run for 20 years, and during that time, an innovative company may build on the technology of the original patented product and develop something new for which it also seeks a patent. In this way, a firm can hold its technological edge for some

time, given sufficient dedication. The patent serves two purposes: (1) it encourages innovation and (2) it discourages industrial secrecy.

3. *Control of inputs.* A firm may become a monopolist by obtaining control over most or all of some basic input required to manufacture a product.

4. *Declining average cost of production.* A natural monopoly can arise in a situation where average total cost tends to decrease with increased production. This is the case in the electric power industry, for example, where there are great economies of scale. That is to say, it is more efficient for one large power plant to provide electric service than for many small plants to do so. In such a case, the *average total costs of producing the product reach a minimum at an output rate large enough to satisfy the entire market (at a price that is profitable).* In other words, one producer can satisfy everyone. If more producers enter the market, each gets a smaller market share and production costs necessarily rise. Thus, each producer spends more and uses more resources to produce the same product at a higher cost to consumers. This means that there are advantages for the consumer in the natural monopoly. Often, however, government regulation is essential to keep production at sufficiently high levels to ensure the market is satisfied and to keep costs at a "fair return rate."

Demand Curve (Average Revenue) and Marginal Revenue under Monopoly

Because the monopolist is the only supplier of its product, the demand curve it faces is the market demand curve for the product, which usually slopes downward to the right. This contrasts with perfect competition, in which the market demand curve is horizontal.

To calculate marginal revenue, we must first know the firm's *total revenue*. *Total revenue,* or total dollar sales volume, is defined as the quantity produced of the product times the price. If a firm produces 100 lawnmowers at a price of $50 apiece, the total revenue for the firm is $5,000. The *marginal revenue* is defined as *the addition to the total revenue attributable to the addition of one unit to sales.* The marginal revenue always is less than the price if the firm's demand curve slopes downward. This is so because, as the price declines, the quantity demanded rises; in other words, the lower is the price, the more consumers enter the market. Or to put it another way, if the firm wishes to expand its market, it must lower the price not only on the additional unit sold but on all previous units sold too. Therefore, the marginal revenue brought in by selling one more unit is less than the price for which the last unit sold.

Price and Output in the Short Run

If the monopolist is free to maximize profits (that is, if it is not controlled by government regulation), it chooses the price and output rate at which *the difference between the total revenue and the total cost is greatest.* As the following table from the text shows, for the firm in question, both the total revenue and total cost (in dollars) rise with output; however, the cost rises faster.

Quantity	Total revenue	Total cost	Total profit
1	100	140	−40
2	180	170	10
3	240	210	30
4	280	250	30
5	300	300	0
6	300	360	−60
7	280	450	−170
8	240	550	−310

The difference between the revenue and the cost is greatest at an output of between three and four units. Therefore, *profit* is maximized at this output rate.

How much does a monopolist charge? It *charges the price that results in its selling the profit-maximizing output*. Recall that the revenue is the product of output and price. Therefore, to find the price, we simply divide the revenue by the output. At three units per day, the price would be 240/3, or $80. At four units per day, the price would be 280/4, or $70. Therefore, the firm maximizes profits by charging between $70 and $80 per unit.

This brings us to the golden (profit-maximizing) rule of output determination for a monopoly: *Set the output rate at the point where the marginal revenue equals the marginal cost*. In other words, the rate where the extra revenue taken in by selling one more unit is equal to the extra cost required to produce one more unit. If the marginal revenue (extra intake) exceeds the marginal cost, the firm can make a higher profit by producing more. If marginal revenue is lower than marginal cost (that is, the extra cost of producing an additional unit is higher than the extra profit to be made), then it pays the firm to cut back on production. Profits are maximized only when the marginal revenue equals the marginal cost. Hence, the short-run equilibrium occurs at the output where the marginal cost curve intersects the marginal revenue curve.

Price and Output in the Long Run

If a monopolist earns an economic profit in the short run, chances are it will not have competitors in the long run, unless it ceases to be a monopoly. The monopoly, in contrast to the firm under perfect competition, can earn economic profits in the long run too. (Recall that long-run equilibrium can be achieved only under perfect competition, when there are no economic profits; this is so because economic profits bring new competitors into the market and the short-run equilibrium is then lost.)

A monopolist that incurs a short-run economic loss may leave the market or explore the possibility of expansion or other alterations to scale. Perhaps, a larger or smaller plant, for example, makes better use of the firm's resources. If all possibilities are explored and none enables the firm to avoid economic losses, it leaves the industry.

Because a monopoly is free to restrict output, output tends to be smaller and prices generally higher than under perfect competition.

Monopoly and Resource Allocation

Economists generally believe that allocation of resources is socially more desirable under perfect competition than under monopoly. Firms under perfect competition must cater more to consumers' desires, and because their prices are influenced by supply and demand curves rather than their own decisions regarding output, they must be more careful how they use resources if they are to maximize profits. Prices tend to be higher under a monopoly. And, most economists agree, a monopoly can impose a burden on society by misallocating resources by restricting output to maximize profits and hence by using fewer resources than is socially optimal.

Economists have other criticisms to make of monopolies as well. They include the following:

1. *Income distribution.* Under a monopoly, income is distributed in favor of monopolists. Although it is a little difficult to prove objectively that this is wrong or harmful, it is also difficult to justify it.

2. *Efficiency.* Because monopolists face no direct competition, they may be less careful about managing resources and costs. After all, a certain amount of waste can be covered by price increases.

3. *Technological change.* Some economists charge that monopolists are lethargic about instituting new methods and developing new products. Again, the problem is lack of direct competition. Innovation requires risk, a change in the status quo. A monopolist taking in a healthy profit is not likely to look favorably on new ideas that could rock the golden boat. We return to this question in a later section.

In Defense of Monopolies

Some economists, notably Joseph Schumpeter and John Kenneth Galbraith, believe that the rate of technological change is likely to be higher under imperfect competition (monopoly or oligopoly) than under perfect competition. They suggest that firms under perfect competition have fewer resources to devote to research and development and, further, given their minimal control over the market, they have little incentive to innovate, since they do not directly reap the rewards. The large monopolies have the money and the facilities to support major research, and indeed some economists believe that research and development could not grow at the same rate under perfect competition.

Available studies cast doubt on these assertions. There is little evidence that research and development expenditures in most industries would decrease if the largest firms were replaced by smaller firms. What the evidence does indicate, however, is that diversity of firm size is advantageous. Some large firms offer the capital to support research not otherwise affordable. Further, the large firms can focus on large-scale production, marketing, or technical resources; and the smaller firms on specialization. How much monopoly power is optimal? This is a question economists cannot fully answer. It is quite possible that *some* monopoly power advances technological research, as Galbraith and others suggest; it is also quite possible that balance between monopoly and other market structures is preferable.

Public Regulation of Monopoly

Public regulation is intended to reduce the harmful effects of monopoly. It is one answer to a natural monopoly, a market in which competition is not feasible and consumers must be protected.

Regulatory commissions often set the monopolist's price (or maximum price) at the point where *the demand curve intersects the average total cost curve*. This results in a price that tends to be higher than under perfect competition but lower than what the monopoly would charge without such regulation (see Figure 19.6, page 454 of the textbook). The commission tries to achieve for the monopoly a so-called fair rate of return, generally defined as somewhere around 8 to 10 percent. But on what is this percentage based? This has not been an easy question to answer. A company's assets can be valued at either *historical cost* (what the firm paid at the time of purchase) or at *reproduction cost* (the cost of replacing those assets). Most commissions now use historical cost because, with inflation, reproduction cost rapidly grows prohibitive.

The commissions have been widely criticized for acting as agents of the very firms they are intended to regulate. Although regulation probably has lowered average prices somewhat, the evidence in support of this position is weak enough to make us question the effectiveness of regulation from the consumers' perspective.

EXTENDED LEARNING

This section of the study guide is specifically designed for the two-semester student.

AUDIO

Before Listening

Read Exploring Further of Chapter 19 in your text, pages 460–464.

Next

Listen to the audiotape that accompanies Lesson 19.

After Listening

Answer the following questions:

1. "Whether one considers a firm a monopolist all depends on how the relevant market is defined. If the market is very narrow, many firms would be classified as monopolists; using a very broad definition, there may be no such thing as a monopolist." Explain.

2. "Monopoly prices do not reflect true opportunity costs to society." Explain.

3. Is the trucking industry a natural monopoly? Why has the trucking industry been regulated by the Interstate Commerce Commission? What advantages are probably accruing from deregulation of the trucking industry? Why did some trucking companies oppose such deregulation?

4. State the arguments for monopoly power put forth by Joseph Schumpeter and John Kenneth Galbraith, and describe the extent to which the available evidence seems to support these arguments.

5. According to Milton Spencer, the makers of methyl methacrylate used to sell it at $0.85 per pound for commercial purposes. However, for denture purposes, it was sold to the dental profession for $45 per pound. Assuming that there was no difference in quality, why would the producers of methyl methacrylate, DuPont and Rohm and Haas, find it profitable to charge different prices? In which of these markets (the commercial market or the dental market) do you think that the price elasticity of demand was lower?

ADDITIONAL READINGS

Caves, R. E. *American Industry: Structure, Conduct and Performance,* 6th ed. Englewood Cliffs, NJ: Prentice-Hall, 1987.

> Chapter 4, "The Promotion of Competition and Control of Monopoly," surveys the history of antitrust laws and enforcement and discusses natural monopolies and the problems involved in regulating such monopolies. No mathematics or graphs.

Dorfman, Robert. *Prices and Markets,* 3d ed. Englewood Cliffs, NJ: Prentice-Hall, 1978.

> Chapter 6, "Monopoly and Oligopoly," describes why some industries came to be dominated by one or a few firms, and how monopolists and oligopolists behave to maximize their profits. Simple mathematics, moderately difficult graphs.

Douglass, Elisha P. *The Coming of Age of American Business*. Chapel Hill: University of North Carolina Press, 1971.

> Chapter 33, "Standard Oil and Its Competitors," gives a lively account of the creation of Standard Oil and how it came to dominate petroleum refining in the late 1900s. The various practices Rockefeller used to consolidate his power are objectively evaluated. No mathematics or graphs.

Kahn, Alfred E. *The Economics of Regulation: Principles and Institutions.* Vol. 2, *Institutional Issues*. New York: John Wiley & Sons, 1971.

> On pages 113–151, Kahn discusses the concept of a natural monopoly and the degree to which the telephone industry can be considered a natural monopoly. Some moderately difficult mathematics.

Waverman, Leonard. "The Regulation of Intercity Telecommunications." In *Promoting Competition in Regulated Markets*, edited by Almarin Phillips. Washington, DC: Brookings Institution, 1975.

> On pages 201–240, Waverman surveys the history of the telecommunications regulation from 1937 to 1971, discusses the role of the FCC, defines a natural monopoly, and discusses how technical change can erode the position of a natural monopoly. Uses regressions to support the argument, but the article is useful even if the reader is unfamiliar with regression analysis. Moderately difficult mathematics, simple graphs.

ANSWER KEY

Video Questions

1. The power of a giant firm like Standard Oil tends to keep competitors out of the market (for reasons discussed in answer 2). Thus, the demand curve faced by the monopolist is the same as the industrywide market demand curve but with this difference: The monopolist need *not* take the market price as a given. It can set that price well above the equilibrium supply and demand level and does so, often, by restricting output. In this way, the monopolist makes not just ordinary profits but excess profits. The low output creates, in effect, an artificial shortage that works to support the higher price. But without competition, the monopolist has no incentive to keep quality high or use resources effectively. It may use more resources than needed to manufacture its product, pushing output yet farther below what it would be under perfect competition.

2. The profits of most monopolies can look very attractive to would-be competitors, but entry into their markets is not easy. For one thing, those high profits give the monopolist capital to expand, creating capabilities that are ever harder to duplicate. It gets more and more expensive, in other words, just to start competition against a monopoly. Further, the monopolist can afford to undercut competitors because profits are already high. Some monopolists just buy their competitors out, while others keep profits from going too high to create the image of the huge industrial giant making only a modest profit. Potential competitors reason that if profits are that hard to come by even with access to significant technology and research, perhaps they would be wise to look elsewhere.

3. For many years, only Bell could offer long distance service. This was a system Bell technology had created and Bell controlled. Under the Kingsbury agreement of 1914, Bell agreed to stop buying up competitors and provide long distance connections to independent phone companies, but these companies still had to work through the Bell system since the expense precluded the establishment of numerous long distance networks (economies of scale). Then, during World War II, Bell developed microwave technology, and a whole new potential for cross-country communications was born. Suddenly, through computers, microwaves, and satellites (no wires, no installation expense, no maintenance),

revolutionary communication systems were available to many competitors. Ironically, however, many consumers still choose Bell over the competitors. Some economists speculate this is so because they view the regulated monopoly as their best buy.

In this technological age, monopolies tend to be rather short-lived as compared to those of the past. Century-long domination of a market is not likely to be achievable again because no single product can hold sway over a market for that length of time. Something easier, better, simpler, cheaper inevitably is developed to take its place. This fact puts pressure on monopolies to maintain developmental technology and makes possible the creation of new monopolies to dominate a transient market for a short while.

4. Remember that a natural monopoly occurs where there are declining average costs; in other words, the higher is the output, the lower the average cost. Thus, it pays the monopoly to expand to a certain point. But as we have seen, the monopoly can also keep prices above natural market levels by restricting output. This can be a particularly serious problem in the case of a service like communications, where the market is enormous; virtually everyone wants and needs local telephone service for convenience, safety, business transactions, and a host of other purposes. Regulation provides a means of ensuring that the product (telephone service, for instance) is made available to a community or metropolitan area at an affordable cost. Regulation allows the monopoly a "fair rate of return," although this can be difficult to establish.

5. The Justice Department accused Microsoft of acting in a way that hurt its competitors. This would ultimately hurt consumers because, without competition, higher prices, shoddy products, and less innovation might result. In particular, the Justice Department focused on the battle between Netscape's Internet browser, Navigator, and Microsoft's browser, Explorer. Netscape was the first to the market with its product by several years. The Justice Department claimed that Microsoft was illegally using its near monopoly in the operating system software for desktop personal computers to destroy the market for Netscape Navigator. According to the Justice Department, this would be bad for consumers because the Internet browser held out the possibility of offering a platform to operate software (like word processing, spreadsheet, and database software) that could cause competition for Microsoft's operating system. Whether there is any validity to this possibility or not, Microsoft introduced its browser by offering it for free. Netscape at that time was asking $60 for its browser. In addition, Microsoft gave discounts on its operating system software to personal computer manufacturing companies like Dell and Gateway if the icon for Explorer would be shown on the desktop of the computer screen when a new computer was first turned on.

Multiple Choice

1. a   Text, 441.
2. d   Text, 442.
3. b   Text, 442.
4. b   Text, 443.
5. c   Text, 444.

True-False

1. False   Video; Text, 441.
2. False   Text, 444–445.
3. False   Text, 454.
4. False   Text, 444–445.
5. True   Text, 438.

6. d Text, 445.	6. True Text, 443.
7. b Text, 444–445.	7. True Video; Text, 442.
8. c Text, 446–450.	8. False Video; Text, 443.
9. d Text, 447–448.	9. False Text, 451–452.
10. a Text, 451–452.	10. False Video.

Discussion Questions

1. A monopoly is a market in which there is only one seller of the good. A monopoly does not face any direct competition but does face indirect competition. Monopolies arise because of government franchise, patents, control of essential inputs, or massive economics of scale (the case of natural monopolies).

2. Yes, because the monopoly misallocates society's resources since it does not produce the optimal level of output, where the marginal cost equals the marginal revenue equals the price. Monopolies produce too little of the good because the price consumers are willing to pay for the last unit sold is greater than the marginal cost of producing that last unit of the good.

3. If the monopolist produces at an output where the marginal revenue is greater than the marginal cost, it can increase its profits by producing a higher level of output because the additional output contributes more to total revenue than it contributes to total cost. Similarly, when a monopolist produces an output where the marginal cost is greater than the marginal revenue, it can increase its profits by producing less output because reductions in output decrease the total cost more than they decrease the total revenue.

4. The perfectly competitive industry produces more of the good at a lower price than the same industry organized as a monopoly would produce. The resources under perfect competition are allocated more efficiently than the resources under monopoly, because the value consumers place on the last unit produced (its price) is equal to the marginal cost of producing this last unit.

5. It is argued that regulatory commissions are often captured by the monopolies they are to regulate. Such capture implies the regulatory commission is not altogether successful in setting price at its appropriate level. The FDA in regulating effectiveness as well as the safety of drugs seeks to protect the consumer and provide helpful information that will not necessarily be provided by the market.

Problem Set

1. a.

Total revenue (dollars)	Marginal revenue (dollars)
30	
	10
40	
	–10
30	
	–6
24	
	–19
5	

b. The second ladle adds $9 to its costs and $10 to its revenue. Yes.

c. $20.
d. 2 soup ladles per day.
e. $22.

2. a. No. If the price is $1, 12 firms of optimal size can exist in the market.
   b. Eight.

3. a.

Output sold (per month)	Total Revenue	Marginal cost	Marginal revenue	Profit
0	0			−40
		45	10	
1	45			−5
		35	20	
2	80			10
		25	25	
3	105			10
		15	30	
4	120			−5
		5	40	
5	125			−40
		−5	60	
6	120			−105

   b. Two or three units per month.
   c. $40 or $35.

4. The marginal cost equals $20. The marginal revenue from the first unit of output is $15, from the second unit $5, and from the third unit −$5. Therefore, the monopolist should produce nothing.

5. a. Since marginal revenue = marginal cost,

   $$1{,}000 - 20Q = 100 + 10Q;$$

   this means that $900 = 30Q$, or $Q = 30$.
   Since $PQ = 1{,}000Q - 10Q^2$, the demand curve must be

   $$P = 1{,}000 - 10Q.$$

   And if $Q = 30$, P must equal 700.

   b. Since the industry's supply curve is the same as the monopolist's marginal cost curve, the supply curve is

   $$P = 100 + 10Q.$$

   As pointed out in part a, the demand curve is

   $$P = 1{,}000 - 10Q.$$

In a competitive market,

$$100 + 10Q = 1{,}000 - 10Q$$
$$20Q = 900$$
$$Q = 45.$$

And $P = 1{,}000 - 10(45) = 550$.

Audio/Text Questions

1. If we define the market of computer operating systems as that for desktop personal computers that use Motorola processors, then Apple with around 100 percent of that market looks very much like a monopolist. But if we define the market as that for all computers (super, mainframe, server, personal, workstation, game station, and more), then even Microsoft, not to mention Apple, does not look like a monopoly. Of course, some economists do not use market share as the exclusive measure of monopoly power. They are interested in whether a firm with a large market share uses its dominance to harm consumers by restricting output, increasing prices, and retarding innovation.

2. Monopolies distort prices. In perfect competition, the additional cost of expanding production by one more unit is the basis of the price. The resources required to expand production by that additional unit have to be "bid away" from some other productive use, and that other use is the opportunity cost of the resource. The price, by reflecting the marginal costs, also reflects the opportunity costs. In a monopoly, the price is not closely related to the marginal costs, so the price does not reflect the opportunity cost of producing the good. The opportunity cost is lower than the price.

3. No. It was regulated because it competed with a natural monopoly, the railroads, which were regulated by the ICC, and the ICC regulated trucking to protect the railroads from competition. Prices are more likely to reflect costs, and costs are likely to fall under competitive pressures. Companies opposed it because they had a secure, low-risk situation when they were regulated, and they were allowed to make good profits under regulation.

4. They argue that technical change is likely to be faster under monopolies since the competitive pressures in nonmonopolized industries will tend to squeeze out any research and development work being performed by the firm in a competitive industry. Also, the competitive firm does not have sufficient control over the market to reap all the benefits of an innovation.

   However, there may be less incentive for monopolistic firms to develop new techniques since they have no competition and they may have a bias in favor of keeping their current equipment profitable. Also, it may be better for many small entrepreneurs to wrestle with the problem, than one organized research department. The evidence does not support the Schumpeter-Galbraith argument in general, although there are some cases in which it holds.

5. If a firm facing an elastic demand curve sets its price too high, it drives sales down by more than it increased the price. If it faces an inelastic demand curve, then a price increase raises the firm's revenue. The price elasticity of demand is lower in the dental market.

LESSON 20. OLIGOPOLIES: WHATEVER HAPPENED TO PRICE COMPETITION?

INTRODUCTION

The U.S. economy is built on competition. Or is it? As we are finding out, economic competition can be a complex blend of spirited rivalry and profit-motivated cooperation. Sometimes, the consumer benefits from this interplay, sometimes not. Either way, however, we can sharpen our skills as consumers and potential business entrepreneurs through a better understanding of how firms truly function in today's economy.

The models of perfect competition and monopoly that we already examined are helpful in promoting this understanding, but seldom do such models reflect reality. What we are more likely to see in the United States today is a combination of monopolistic competition and oligopoly. In this chapter, we see how these business models evolved, and what implications they have for consumers individually and the economy as a whole.

What You Should Learn

By the end of Lesson 20, you should be prepared to

1. Define *monopolistic competition* and explain the conditions under which it occurs.
2. Define *oligopoly* and contrast it with *monopolistic competition*.
3. Explain what is meant by *product differentiation,* and discuss its significance using a real-life example of monopolistic competition.
4. Describe how price and output are determined under monopolistic competition.
5. Name three factors said to be responsible for the evolution of oligopoly.
6. Define *collusion,* and explain the relationship between *collusion* and *cartel*.
7. Name three barriers to collusion, and discuss the implications of each for modern business.

8. Describe what is meant by *price leadership,* and distinguish between the *dominant firm model* and the *barometric firm model.*

9. Discuss two methods of *nonprice competition* and their implications for the consumer.

10. Contrast perfect competition with oligopoly.

11. Contrast perfect competition with monopolistic competition.

12. Explain the intent and the impact of the major antitrust laws.

13. Describe what is meant by the *rule of reason,* and explain its implications for the Supreme Court Decision affecting U.S. Steel.

KEY TERMS

product differentiation
product group
long-run equilibrium
cartel
price leadership
barometric firm
rule of reason
dominant strategy
advertising
production development
Clayton Act
Federal Trade Commision Act
tying contract
Celler-Kefauver Anti-Merger Act
trust busting

monopolistic competition
oligopoly
pure oligopoly
differentiated oligopoly
monopoly power
zero economic profit condition
collusion
trust and antitrust
dominant firm model
payoff matrix
theory of games
player
rules of the game
payoff
Sherman Antitrust Act

VIDEO

Watch

Economics U$A Program 20, "Oligopolies: Whatever Happened to Price Competition?"

Illustrative Events

The beginnings of oligopoly in the auto industry, when GM's shrewd styling and advertising beat out the lower-priced Ford Model T, featuring Richard Strout, *Christian Science Monitor*; and historian Leo Ribuffo. Richard Gill explains product differentiation under oligopoly.

Conspiracy and price fixing in the electrical industry of the 1950s, showing how far business will sometimes go to avoid price competition, with Julian Granger of the *Knoxville News Sentinel,* who exposed the collusion; and Robert Bicks, former assistant attorney general of the U.S. Department of Justice.

After Viewing

Answer the following questions:

1. What big differences in philosophy distinguished Henry Ford, founder of Ford Motor Company, and Alfred Sloan, head of General Motors?

2. The economist Richard Gill calls Ford and GM "monopolists in a limited sense." What does Gill mean by this phrase?

3. According to Gill, what is the primary reason that big businesses engage in price fixing or illegal manipulation of sealed bids?

Read

Read Chapter 20: "Monopolistic Competition, Oligopoly, and Antitrust Policy," pages 467–491 in your text. After completing your reading, try the Self-Quiz.

SELF-QUIZ

Multiple Choice

1. Oligopoly occurs in markets where there are

    a. many sellers.
    b. few sellers.
    c. many buyers.
    d. few buyers.

2. The best example of a pure oligopoly would be the market for

    a. automobiles.
    b. computers.
    c. cement.
    d. televisions.

3. For an industry to qualify as a case of monopolistic competition, how many competitors must there be?

    a. Any number at all
    b. Fewer than 10
    c. 50 to 100 or more
    d. Over 1,000

4. Which of the following is a condition for long-run equilibrium in monopolistic competition?

   a. Firms must be making a profit.
   b. Entry into the monopolistic group must be relatively easy.
   c. Prices must be flexible.
   d. Each firm must be making no economic profits or losses.

5. A monopolistically competitive firm maximizes profits at the point where the

   a. marginal cost equals the marginal revenue.
   b. marginal cost equals the long-run average cost.
   c. demand equals the output.
   d. per-unit cost equals the marginal cost.

6. Unlike perfect competition, monopoly, and monopolistic competition, oligopoly has no single, unified model to demonstrate precisely how it works. The *main* reason for this is that

   a. the importance of oligopoly in the U.S. economy has diminished greatly since the 1930s and 1940s.
   b. oligopoly is such a new market structure that many economists are just now beginning to recognize it.
   c. economists still cannot agree on what an oligopoly is.
   d. no one has yet been able to devise a model that covers all relevant cases of oligopoly adequately.

7. Prices within an oligopoly are *most* likely to

   a. stay very rigid.
   b. decline gradually because of competition among rivals.
   c. go up slightly with the struggle for profits.
   d. go up and down irregularly as a barometer of the economy in general.

8. Collusion occurs when firms get together and agree to

   a. share technology.
   b. set limits on price and output.
   c. set common goals for research and development.
   d. increase competition with one another.

9. Other things being equal, which of the following industries would likely spend the *highest* percent of gross revenues on advertising?

   a. Cigarettes
   b. Automobiles
   c. Computers
   d. They would probably spend about the same percentage.

10. Oligopolists generally prefer to compete through advertising and product differentiation than price reductions. The *main* reason for this is that

    a. they fear cutting into their profit margins.
    b. most have agreements with rivals *not* to cut prices.

c. price reductions can easily be matched by rivals.
  d. advertising and research are the most proven methods for market expansion.

True-False

____ 1. Monopolistic competition occurs in markets where there are many sellers whose products are somewhat different.

____ 2. The firm is likely under monopolistic competition to produce more and charge a lower price than under perfect competition.

____ 3. Firms under monopolistic competition offer a wider variety of styles, brands, and qualities than firms under perfect competition.

____ 4. Oligopolies are characterized by a small number of firms with a great deal of interdependence, actual and perceived.

____ 5. Oligopolists tend to compete more aggressively through advertising and product differentiation than through direct price reduction.

____ 6. Prices in oligopolistic markets tend to fluctuate more than prices under perfect competition.

____ 7. As a result of the Sherman Antitrust Act of 1890, collusive business arrangements no longer exist in any form in the United States.

____ 8. The deregulation of the airline industry decreased competition among air carriers, increased the cost of travel for the consumer, and is an example of monopolistic competition.

____ 9. Ford Motor Company and General Motors are examples of firms operating under perfect competition.

____ 10. The impact of antitrust laws depends not only on interpretation in the courts, as in the case of AT&T and IBM, but the vigor with which the Antitrust Division of the Justice Department prosecutes cases.

Discussion Questions

1. Suppose your economics professor states publicly that he grades on a curve (the top 10 percent of the students get an A, the next 20 percent a B, the next 40 percent a C, the next 20 percent a D, and the lowest 10 percent fail). The whole class could save itself a lot of work then by agreeing privately not to study at all for the final exam and just to let the rankings thus far determine the final grades. Why might such an agreement be difficult to maintain and enforce?

2. "U.S. Steel Corporation's abrupt decision to cancel the 4.5 percent price increase on flat-rolled products that it had announced for October 1 is an encouraging reminder that . . . [the] market still has the last word. Where supply is ample and demand moderate, the market's decision will be: No price increase." Is this statement in accord with oligopoly theory? Why or why not?

3. In the middle 1970s, there was considerable debate in Congress and elsewhere concerning the desirability of breaking up the major oil firms. Do you consider such a step socially desirable? Why or why not?

4. "A cartel merely redistributes income. It takes from the cartel's customers and gives to the cartel members. So long as the latter are as worthy as the former, there are no adverse social consequences." How valid do you think this statement is?

Problem Set

1. The cost curves and demand curve of the Jones Manufacturing Company, a monopolistically competitive firm, follow.

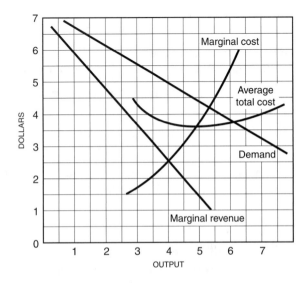

   a. What output rate does this firm choose?
   b. What price does it charge?
   c. How great are its profits?
   d. Is this a long-run equilibrium situation?

2. The India Company and the China Company are duopolists. A duopoly is an industry with only two sellers. Each firm has two possible strategies. The payoff matrix is as follows:

Possible strategies for the China Company	Possible strategies for the India Company	
	Strategy A	Strategy B
Strategy 1	China's profit: $6 million India's profit: $5 million	China's profit: $7 million India's profit: $6 million
Strategy 2	China's profit: $5 million India's profit: $6 million	China's profit: $6 million India's profit: $7 million

   a. Does the China Company have a dominant strategy?
   b. Does the India Company have a dominant strategy?
   c. Which strategy does the China Company choose?

d. Which strategy does the India Company choose?
3. Suppose that an industry is composed of 20 firms, each with a horizontal marginal cost curve. In particular, each firm can produce at a marginal cost of $2 per unit of output. Variation in industry output does not affect the cost curve of the individual firms.
   a. If the industry is cartelized, what does the marginal cost curve of the cartel look like?
   b. The marginal revenue for the cartel is $3 when it produces 100 units of output, $2 when it produces 200 units of output, and $1 when it produces 300 units of output per month. Does it produce more or less than 100 units of output per month?
   c. Does it produce more or less than 300 units per month?
   d. Can you tell what output level it chooses? If so, what is it?

LESSON REVIEW

If you had difficulty with the Self-Quiz or would like additional assistance, read the following lesson review. It should reinforce and help you understand the content presented in this lesson.

Monopolistic Competition and Oligopoly: Major Characteristics of Each

A market characterized by *monopolistic competition* features many sellers (as in perfect competition) and *product differentiation*. This means that there are either really differences (technical or stylistic) among products or consumers *perceive* differences among products.

In a market characterized by *oligopoly*, there are few sellers, and products may be either alike (e.g., as in the steel, cement, or tin can industries) or different (e.g., as in the automobile, cigarette, and airline industries).

Characteristics of Monopolistic Competition

The *key* feature of monopolistic competition is product differentiation. Firms can achieve product differentiation by

- Changing the style of a product.
- Technologically improving or altering the product.
- Creating an image for the product.
- Making advertising claims about differences that are real or contrived.

Through these product differences, competing firms gain a *degree* of monopolistic power, but it remains limited by the fact that, consumer beliefs and product images aside, their products are similar.

The other three features of monopolistic competition are as follows:

1. The product group must include a large number of firms, 50 to 100 at least.
2. In fact, the number of firms needs to be large enough that one firm can take action without retaliation by others. (Contrast oligopoly with this condition.)
3. Entry into the product group must be relatively easy, and there must be no collusion (e.g., price fixing, market sharing) among members.

Price and Output under Monopolistic Competition

In the *short run*, a firm maximizes profits by setting its output and hence its price at a level where the marginal cost equals the marginal revenue. Economic profits are earned because the price charged exceeds average total cost at this output rate.

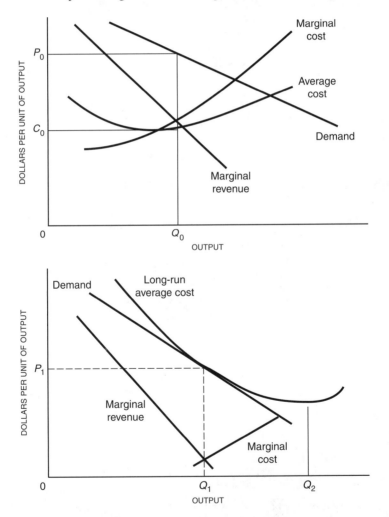

In the *long run*, a firm also sets its output and hence its price where the marginal cost equals the marginal revenue, but now no economic profits are realized. Competition in the long run forces profit to a level equal to the average cost. No entry or exit of firms occurs.

Probable Characteristics of Firms under Monopolistic Competition

The firm under monopolistic competition is likely to

1. Produce less and charge more than under perfect competition.
2. Have greater output, lower profits, and a lower price than a monopoly.
3. Be somewhat inefficient.
4. Offer a wider variety of styles, brands, and qualities than firms under perfect competition and spend heavily on advertising and other selling expenses.

Oligopolies

Both monopolies and oligopolies exert a major influence on markets, but the characteristics of each are, to a knowledgeable observer, quite different.

Characteristics of Oligopoly

Simply put, oligopoly is a market structure in which a few firms dominate. The key characteristic of an oligopoly is the interdependence—real and perceived—of the member firms. An oligopoly contains only a small number of firms; therefore, changes in price or output by one firm influence the sales and profits of all other members.

The following factors contribute to the evolution of oligopoly:

1. In some industries, a firm can achieve low production costs only by producing output equal to a substantial portion of the total available market. (For example, an auto manufacturer that controlled only 0.5 percent of the U.S. market probably could not survive.)
2. Economies of scale may make it unprofitable for many firms to enter an industry. If per-unit costs tend to fall with increases in production, the industry is unfavorable to large numbers of competitors.
3. Entry into the industry may be blocked by the need for a firm to build a large, expensive plant, obtain patents, or obtain scarce raw materials. Some potential competitors simply are unable to meet the costs of these undertakings.

Game Theory

A game is a competitive situation where two or more players pursue their own interests and no player can dictate the outcome. The relevant features of a two-person game can be shown by constructing a payoff matrix. In some games, each player has a dominant strategy (a strategy that is best regardless of what strategy the other player chooses).

Collusion and Cartels

Collusion occurs when firms get together and agree on price and output. A cartel is an open, formal collusive arrangement. The advantages to the firm of collusion are these:

- Increased profits.
- Greater certainty about future price levels, profits, and market shares.
- Greater opportunity to prevent entry by other firms.

In the United States, most collusive arrangements, both covert and open, were declared illegal by the Sherman Antitrust Act, passed in 1890. Nevertheless, they continue to exist.

Barriers to Collusion

Oligopolies tend to promote collusion because of their makeup: A few interdependent rival firms sharing common interests and profit incentives. Yet, there are several significant barriers to collusion:

1. *Legal problems.* The antitrust laws forbid outright collusion and price fixing. However, the power of the law depends on judicial interpretation and the willingness of the political party in office and the Justice Department to prosecute.

2. *Technical problems.* Collusion may be difficult to maintain if an oligopoly contains more than a handful of firms, if their products differ considerably, or if their cost structures are different. For example, if one firm discovers an extremely cost-effective production strategy, it may be more appealing to that firm to slash prices than to collude on price with member firms.

3. *Cheating.* In hard economic times, the temptation to cut prices below the agreed-on level may be more than some firms can resist. And if one firm cheats, others tend to follow.

Price Leadership

How can firms coordinate prices without collusion? The answer is to designate a price leader. There are essentially two types of price leadership:

1. The dominant firm model, in which a single large firm sets prices that smaller member firms follow.

2. The barometric firm model, in which the firm best able to gauge public demand and expectations, regardless of that firm's size or power, sets prices that others feel they will profit by following.

Nonprice Competition

We have seen that, within an oligopoly, firms tend to cooperate on price setting, whether through collusion or price leadership and prices tend to be very rigid. How then do these firms compete?

In both oligopoly and monopolistic competition, firms use nonprice competition to differentiate their product from that of their rivals. There are essentially two means by which firms can compete aggressively without direct price reductions:

1. *Advertising.* Interestingly enough, the less product differentiation there is, the more firms are likely to spend on advertising. Although advertising can be considered socially desirable, since it can acquaint consumers with products they might otherwise never hear of, it may also be more misleading than informative. Much advertising aims to convince the consumer that she or he cannot live comfortably without the product or that one product is better than another.

2. *Product development.* Firms can also conduct research and development to make real (not just advertised) changes in their products. If improvements result, then this R & D can be considered socially desirable.

Comparing Oligopoly with Perfect Competition

1. Prices are higher and output less under oligopoly than under perfect competition, assuming similar production costs.

2. Firms spend more on advertising and product differentiation under oligopoly than under perfect competition.

3. Profits, on average, are higher under oligopolies than under perfect competition.

Antitrust Laws

Public policy in the United States has tended to promote a competitive economy, and the antitrust laws have helped in this effort. Still, monopolies exist, and certain court decisions have permitted, even promoted, monopoly.

Sherman Act

The Sherman Act was passed by Congress in 1890. The act outlaws conspiracy to restrain trade or commerce among states or with foreign nations, as well as conspiratorial attempts to monopolize trade or commerce.

Clayton Act

General dissatisfaction with the ineffectiveness of the Sherman Act led to the passage of two additional laws: the Clayton Act and the Federal Trade Commission Act. The Clayton Act was intended to be more specific in forbidding practices that would "substantially lessen competition or tend to create a monopoly." Specifically, the Clayton Act outlawed

- Unjustified price discrimination, in which one buyer is charged more than another for the same product.
- Use of a tying contract, which forces a buyer to purchase additional items to get the item he or she wants.

Federal Trade Commission Act

This law was intended to prevent undesirable and unfair competitive practices by creating a commission with the power to investigate these practices and issue cease-and-desist orders. Because it became difficult to define what was meant by *unfair,* the commission eventually lost much of its power, but it retains

- The function of outlawing untrue or deceptive advertising.
- The authority to investigate the structure and conduct of U.S. business.

Role of the Courts

The interpretation of the antitrust laws has changed markedly over time. During the early part of the century, and even into the 1920s and 1930s, the Supreme Court based its decisions on what came to be known as the rule of reason: the idea that only unreasonable combinations in restraint of trade (those that engaged in overt coercion or predatory practices) should be prosecuted under the Sherman Act. In 1911, under this rule of reason, Standard Oil and the American Tobacco Company were forced to give up large shares of holdings in other companies. But later, in the 1920s and 1930s, the Court applied the rule of reason in quite another way, holding that U.S. Steel had not violated the antitrust laws despite its attempt to monopolize the industry. Similarly, Eastman Kodak and International Harvester, both near-monopolies, were found innocent of any violation because they had not used coercion to achieve their dominant positions.

Then, late in the 1930s, the Supreme Court reversed direction with its decision against Aluminum Company of America. Alcoa was innocent of any wrongdoing according to the rule of reason, but the focus had now shifted from market conduct to market structure. Alcoa controlled nearly all the industry's aluminum output, and that, the Court determined, was unacceptable. The Alcoa case also reversed the earlier decisions in the U.S. Steel and International Harvester cases. In other words, what had once been interpreted as reasonable was now viewed as a violation of the antitrust laws.

Role of the Justice Department

The impact of the antitrust laws depends not only on interpretation in the courts but also on the vigor with which the Antitrust Division of the Justice Department prosecutes cases. The tendency to prosecute varies greatly with the philosophy of the political party in power and has ranged from virtual inactivity (under Grover Cleveland, Calvin Coolidge, and Ronald Reagan) to frenetic heights (under Theodore Roosevelt, Franklin Delano Roosevelt, John F. Kennedy, and Bill Clinton).

In 1982, two of the biggest antitrust cases in history were decided, with different outcomes:

1. American Telephone and Telegraph was forced to divest itself of 22 companies that provide most of the nation's local telephone service, keeping its Long Lines division, Western Electric, and Bell Laboratories.

2. A large case against IBM was dropped by the government because it was considered to be without merit.

Both cases continue to be widely debated; not everyone agrees with the logic or justice of either decision. So, generally, how effective have the antitrust laws been? They have been effective insofar as industry giants like AT&T or IBM can be held accountable for monopolistic tendencies. Yet, most economists would likely agree that such laws have been less effective than they might have been because they lack sufficient public support and no politically powerful pressure group pushes for enforcement.

EXTENDED LEARNING

This section of the study guide is specifically designed for the two-semester student.

AUDIO

Listen

Listen to the audiotape that accompanies Lesson 20. There is no additional reading assignment for this lesson.

After Listening

Answer the following questions:

1. Why is a firm's market power related to entry barriers and the price elasticity of demand for its product?

2. Why are firms in an oligopolistic industry more likely to avoid price competition than firms in a perfectly competitive industry? What are some of the ways firms in an oligopoly compete?

3. What are some of the factors that cause an industry to be composed of only a few firms?

4. Describe why an oligopolistic firm may gain very little by lowering its price below that of its competitors and lose a great deal by raising its price.

5. How does a high cross elasticity between the products of two firms in a monopolistically competitive industry restrict each firm's monopoly power?

6. What are some of the ways, legal and illegal, that firms in an oligopolistic industry keep price competition from occurring?

7. Theoretically, how is the optimum price of a profit-maximizing cartel determined, and what must the members of the cartel agree on if that price is to be maintained?

8. Distinguish between monopoly, oligopoly, and monopolistic competition in terms of how much higher the price is than in perfect competition and whether the firm(s) in the industry can earn economic profits.

ADDITIONAL READINGS

Brozen, Yale. "Entry Barriers: Advertising and Product Differentiation." In *Industrial Concentration: The New Learning*, edited by Harvey J. Goldschmid et al., 115–136. Boston: Little, Brown, and Company, 1974.

> Argues that advertising makes markets more competitive rather than less, by making entry more likely. No mathematics or graphs.

Caves, R. E. *American Industry: Structure, Conduct, and Performance,* 6th ed. Englewood Cliffs, NJ: Prentice-Hall, 1987.

> Chapters 1 and 2 discuss the effect of various market structure characteristics, such as seller concentration, product differentiation, entry barriers, growth of demand, price elasticity of demand, and buyer concentration, on the market performance of firms. No mathematics, simple graphs.

Caves, R. E. "The Structure of Industry." In *The American Economy in Transition*, edited by Martin Feldstein, 501–545. Chicago: University of Chicago Press, 1980.

> A good overview of the extent of market concentration in the United States and its effects on the economy. Industrial concentration, size, merger and acquisition activity, and multinational firms are discussed; the way market concentration influences pricing, output, productivity, R & D, and profits are also covered. No mathematics or graphs.

Dorfman, Robert. *Prices and Markets*. Englewood Cliffs, NJ: Prentice-Hall, 1967.

> Chapter 6, "Monopoly and Oligopoly," pp. 137–164, is a good short survey of the forces that lead to the establishment of monopolies and oligopolies, the optimum pricing rule for a monopoly, and the interdependence of oligopolistic decision making. Moderately difficult mathematics and graphs.

White, Lawrence J. "The Automobile Industry." In *The Structure of American Industry,* edited by Walter Adams, 136–190, 6th ed. New York: Macmillan Co., 1982.

> Discusses market structure and conduct of the auto industry in the 1970s and early 1980s and includes a thorough discussion of how all aspects of public policy (i.e., safety regulation, pollution regulation, fuel economy, import limitations, the Chrysler loan guarantees, and antitrust) affected the auto industry. No mathematics or graphs.

ANSWER KEY

Video Questions

1. Ford wanted to develop a product that every working American could afford, and he wanted to improve it every year so that it would never wear out. He counted on the combined quality and practicality of his product to make sales and keep the sales rate high. But with a product that seldom wears out, and therefore

seldom has to be replaced, Ford would have to count on an ever-expanding market to succeed. Alfred Sloan took a different tack. He felt Americans wanted something more from their cars than practicality. He guessed they might want choices, options, sleeker styling. Sloan was right. He emphasized the car's appearance more than its function, and virtually stole the market from Ford. What were the implications? No longer was it essential that the product hold up indefinitely. In fact, it became desirable that consumers be motivated to replace products at regular intervals, either because they had worn out or because they went out of style. And this philosophy became a model for countless U.S. industries.

2. Gill refers to the fact that every car is a little different from every other car or at least is perceived to be different by the public. Two cars may share an identical engine and may even have similar body styles, but certain details differentiate them sufficiently that one will appeal to market A and one to market B. In this sense, one can say that a car manufacturer has an exclusive product: Only Ford can sell Thunderbirds, only General Motors can sell Cadillacs, and so on.

3. There are many reasons, including company loyalty, but probably the most significant reason is the desire for security. Oligopolies are by nature interdependent structures that depend on cooperation for survival. If one member cuts prices, for example, the resulting price war could be devastating to all. Cooperation, even if it occurs in illegal forms like price fixing, offers an appealing sense of stability and security. Each member firm knows what its share of the current market will be, what prices it will charge, and how much profit it will realize. The risk of having to outguess others is gone.

Multiple Choice

1. b   Text, 468.
2. c   Text, 468.
3. c   Text, 469.
4. d   Text, 469–470.
5. a   Text, 469.
6. d   Text, 472–473.
7. a   Text, 480.
8. b   Text, 475.
9. a   Text, 480–483.
10. c Text, 480.

True-False

1. True   Text, 468.
2. False Text, 471.
3. True   Text, 471.
4. True   Text, 472.
5. True   Text, 480–484.
6. False Text, 479–480.
7. False Text, 475.
8. False Video.
9. False Video.
10. True. Text, 483–488.

Discussion Questions

1. A student could improve her or his grade by studying if all the other students maintained the agreement and did not study. Because this is true for all students (except the top student), there is an incentive to cheat on the agreement and the agreement will break down.

2. Oligopoly theory suggests that prices are relatively rigid and that oligopolistic firms use nonprice competition primarily. A price change, however, might be reflective of price leadership by the dominant firm or an attempt to mask cartel behavior.

3. This is an opinion question. If the breakup of the major oil firms results in greater competition with lower prices and greater output, then this is socially desirable. The oil industry, however, may be characterized as one in which low production costs can be achieved only if output for each firm is a substantial part of the total market, economies of scale can be realized only in relatively large-scale plants, or entry into the industry is prohibitively expensive.

4. It overlooks the social costs of misallocating resources. The cartel, when successful, produces too little of the good at too high a price from a social viewpoint.

Problem Set

1. a. Four units of output.
   b. $5.
   c. $5. The cost per unit is around $3.75 according to the graph of the average total cost curve, so the profit per unit is $1.25. Four units are produced and sold, so the firm's profit is $5.
   d. No.

2. a. Yes.
   b. Yes.
   c. Strategy 1.
   d. Strategy B.

3. a. A horizontal line at $2 = MC$.
   b. More.
   c. Less.
   d. Yes. 200 units of output if it maximizes profit.

Audio/Text Questions

1. The likelihood that a firm earns monopoly or economic profits depends on its ability to restrict the total market output of a specific product and how difficult it is for consumers to use substitutes or go without using the product. If a new firm can enter easily, the output cannot be restricted by the firm trying to earn monopoly profits. And if consumers can easily switch to a close substitute or forbear consuming the product altogether (which implies a large price elasticity of demand for the product), the firm cannot raise prices significantly.

2. When there are few firms in an industry, it is easy for each firm to see that, if it lowers its price, all other firms will also lower prices, so it cannot increase its market share through price competition. Instead, all firms will probably be worse off because all will be selling at lower prices. Therefore, implicit (or explicit) collusion becomes likely. To increase the market share, firms in an oligopoly compete by trying to make their product slightly different from that of other firms (or make the consumer think the product is different) through advertising, style changes, or small quality differences.

3. Economies of scale in production and sales, which make it difficult for a small firm to price competitively, and other barriers to entry, such as large financial requirements, limited access to necessary raw materials, or patents.

4. If a firm lowers its price, the other firms quickly realize it and lower their prices as well. Therefore, the first firm to lower its prices gains very little if any sales. If sales change little at a lower price, the total revenue falls. If the firm raises its price and the other firms do not follow, then that firm loses many of its customers to those competitors and its revenues fall.

5. If one firm tries to restrict output and force up the price of its product the way a pure monopolist would do, some buyers decide that the difference between that firm's product and the similar product of a firm that has not raised its price is not enough to justify paying the higher price. The buyers purchase the other firm's product, sharply reducing the sales of the initial firm. The higher is the cross elasticity of demand for its product, the less power the firm has in controlling its market.

6. Price leadership, in which one firm, usually the largest in the industry, sets a price and the others implicitly agree to follow is a common legal way to avoid price competition. Another is an agreement to use markup pricing, so that an increase in the cost of materials or labor is a signal for all firms to increase their prices to cover the higher costs. A third is the practice of disciplining a price-cutting firm by underpricing it. The dominant firm may lower prices to the point of running losses temporarily, in the hope that the small, price-cutting firm suffers such a loss of its market position and revenue that it raises its prices and avoids price competition in the future. Firms may also avoid price competition by dividing markets geographically. Explicit collusion in setting prices, such as the creation of a cartel, is an illegal method of avoiding price competition.

7. The rule for maximizing the total profits of all members of a cartel is the same as that of a monopoly. The members must agree to restrict output and thereby force up the price, until the point is reached at which the reduction in sales totally offsets the gain of a higher selling price. The members of the cartel have to agree how to share the output restriction. There is a strong incentive for each member of a cartel to cheat and sell more than its quota, but if all firms did that, the price would be driven down by the increased supply.

8. A monopoly, because it controls the market for a product for which there are no close substitutes, usually sets the price much higher than in perfect competition, and it earns monopoly profits. An oligopoly, unless the firms illegally band together in a cartel and act like a monopoly, tends to have a slightly lower price than a monopoly because of the need to keep price discipline in the industry and discourage new firms from coming in, and it earns less economic profit than a monopoly. Monopolistic competition is close to perfect competition, with little if any economic profit in the long run, but prices and costs are likely to be higher because the firm tends to carry excess capacity and spends a great deal on marketing and product differentiation.

LESSON 21. POLLUTION: HOW MUCH IS A CLEAN ENVIRONMENT WORTH?

INTRODUCTION

Have you wondered whether water from the kitchen tap is safe to drink? Would you be willing to pay a penny a glass to know for certain that the water is safe? A nickel? How about a quarter? A dollar? At some point, you would likely say that your concern about the water is no longer sufficient to justify the cost of the guarantee. As this simple example suggests, costs are involved in living with pollution as well as in controlling it. Striking the right balance between the two can be a tricky matter.

Most scientists and social observers today feel that environmental pollution is one price we pay for economic growth. But is that pollution inevitable? How much should we (can we) tolerate, and what does it cost us as a society to try to eliminate pollution?

These are not easy questions to answer. As a first step, we consider the nature of external diseconomies and their contribution to environmental pollution, the relationship between pollution and technology, and various efforts by government to control pollution.

What You Should Learn

By the end of Lesson 21, you should be prepared to

1. Describe some of the major factors contributing to air and water pollution.

2. Explain what role external diseconomies play in contributing to pollution, and suggest how that role might be altered.

3. Contrast private cost and social cost, and explain how the differences between the two help explain the pollution problem.

4. Discuss the relationship between pollution and economic growth, especially with respect to this central question: Is pollution inevitable if the economy continues to grow?

5. Present arguments for and against zero economic growth.

6. List and discuss three major ways in which government can intervene to control pollution.

KEY TERMS

external diseconomy
private cost
social cost
economic growth
zero economic growth
direct regulation

effluent fee
Water Quality Improvement Act
transferable emission permits
tax credits

VIDEO

Watch

Economics U$A Program 21, "Pollution: How Much Is a Clean Environment Worth?"

Illustrative Events

The federal court case against the Reserve Mining Company of Duluth, Minnesota, for dumping taconite tailings into Lake Superior, illustrating externalities, with environmentalist Alden Lind, EPA official Dr. Philip Cook, and Silver Bay residents. Richard Gill explains the government's role in managing externalities.

The difficult social choices posed by attempts to enforce the 1970 Clean Air Act in congested Los Angeles; featuring William Ruckelshaus, first director of the Environmental Protection Agency, and Kenneth Hahn, Los Angeles County Supervisor.

The government decision to employ cost-benefit analysis to measure the social and private costs of environmental regulation, focusing on the EPA's order that oil companies reduce the amount of lead in gasoline; with Dr. Vernon Houk, Center for Disease Control; James Miller, chair of the FTC; and Dr. Joel Schwartz, EPA.

After Viewing

Answer the following questions:

1. What does the experience of the Reserve Mining Company in Minnesota illustrate about the important balance between environmental and economic concerns?

2. Why do most economists generally oppose an all-out "war" on pollution or other factors that threaten the environment?

3. Discuss the different perspectives on global warming presented by economists as opposed to environmentalists in the video.

4. What are the limitations of cost-benefit analysis, according to the video presentation and economic analyst Richard Gill?

Read

Read Chapter 21, "Pollution and the Environment," pages 492–509 in your text. After completing your reading, try the Self-Quiz.

SELF-QUIZ

Multiple Choice

1. One thing we learned from trying to enforce the 1970 Clean Air Act in congested Los Angeles is that

    a. pollution is not so serious a problem as an energy shortage.
    b. the easiest way to reduce pollution is to reduce demand for energy.
    c. decreased use of automobiles would have little impact on pollution.
    d. cleaning up the environment would be costly in many ways.

2. The nature of pollutants in the atmosphere suggests that

    a. air pollution is an inevitable by-product of economic productivity.
    b. much air pollution results from natural causes that cannot be controlled.
    c. in large cities automobile exhaust is a major source of air pollution.
    d. air pollution is an exaggerated problem.

3. When someone engages in a pollution-causing activity, the social cost of that activity exceeds the private cost of the activity by the

    a. cost of the external diseconomy.
    b. average cost of the activity.
    c. opportunity cost of the activity.
    d. marginal cost of the activity.

4. The competitive model assumes that

    a. everyone uses and benefits from resources equally.
    b. the producer should pay production costs, the consumer social costs.
    c. private and social costs are always equal.
    d. the full cost of using any resource is not borne by the person or firm that uses it.

5. In a market economy, resources tend to go to those individuals and firms that

    a. have no competitors.
    b. create no pollution.

c. find it worthwhile to bid the most for the resources.
d. find a way to make social costs exceed private costs.

6. Polluters find it tempting to dump wastes into streams and rivers *mainly* because

   a. this method of disposal is cheap.
   b. no government regulation prevents this action.
   c. consumers do not complain enough about pollution.
   d. they recognize that the consequences are not as serious as many people think.

7. Zero population growth may not be the answer to pollution problems because

   a. population is not related in any way to pollution levels.
   b. zero population growth is not achievable within this century.
   c. the cost of achieving zero population growth would be greater than the cost of living with pollution.
   d. some individuals and societies contribute more to the pollution problem than others.

8. The costs for the Reserve Mining Company of Babbitt, Minnesota, to construct a new dumping facility (following court action regarding the pollution of Lake Superior) were borne by the

   a. company alone.
   b. public alone.
   c. company and the public.
   d. government.

9. Suppose that Bounceback Rubber Company is required to pay a monthly fee to the government, based on the estimated amount of pollution it adds to a nearby water supply. This is an example of

   a. an external economy.
   b. direct government regulation.
   c. an external diseconomy.
   d. an effluent fee.

10. Most economists would probably say that this approach to controlling the pollution of Bounceback Rubber (question 9) was

    a. extremely effective since it would cause private costs to approximate social costs.
    b. theoretically sound but impractical since no one can estimate the true costs of pollution.
    c. totally ineffective because fee-based regulations are not enforceable.
    d. adequate, though less effective than tax credit approaches.

True-False

_____ 1. The price system is not likely to allocate resources efficiently in the presence of significant external diseconomies.

_____ 2. If polluters do not pay the true cost of waste disposal, they tend to produce too little.

_____ 3. Rising pollution levels are inextricably tied to rising levels of national output.

_____ 4. Although the United States has only about one-twentieth of the world's population, it is responsible for about one-third of the world's pollution.

_____ 5. A customer deposit fee on bottles and cans requires the consumer to pay part of the cost for disposal.

_____ 6. One way to halt pollution would be to halt all technological growth.

_____ 7. If we could achieve zero population growth in all countries worldwide, we could also achieve zero pollution growth.

_____ 8. Pressures to clean up our environment are stronger in the United States today than at any other time.

_____ 9. Economists believe that the goal of environmental policy should be to reduce pollution to zero regardless of how much this would cost given the obvious benefits.

_____ 10. It is likely that one day, given sufficient technology, we will rid ourselves of pollution.

Discussion Questions

1. Show how too much pollution, from society's point of view, is likely to arise if the private costs of water and air for waste disposal are less than the social costs. Is it likely that the output rate of heavy polluters is too high, from a social point of view? Why or why not? Show how, once cans and no-deposit bottles were introduced, an external diseconomy arose with regard to disposal of these items.

2. The optimal amount of pollution is not zero; we are quite sure of that. However, if some pollution is necessary for a social optimum, how do we know that we currently have too much pollution? Is it possible that we do not have enough pollution yet? Is more, not less, the direction in which we should be moving?

3. Must economic growth necessarily result in increased pollution? Should the rate of technological change be slowed to reduce pollution? Explain.

4. Can you utilize your understanding of cost-benefit analysis, opportunity costs, and other economic principles to analyze how one would decide whether a particular state should pass legislation to ban throwaway or disposable bottles and cans for soft drinks and beer? Should manufacturers also be forbidden to use throwaway containers for macaroni? Detergents? Baby food? Should consumers have to pay a deposit on egg cartons?

5. Explain how effluent fees can be used to reduce pollution. What are their advantages? Why do many economists prefer them over direct regulation or tax credits for pollution control equipment?

Problem Set

1. Suppose that the demand and supply curves for gasoline are as follows. The curve S_P represents the supply curve when only private costs are considered. The curve S_S represents the supply curve when social costs are considered as well.

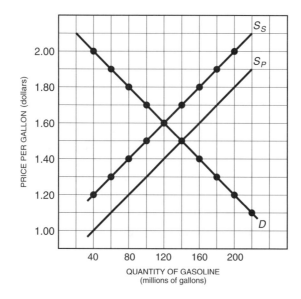

   a. Since social costs are private costs plus the cost of the external diseconomies (if any), how much is the cost of the external diseconomies here per gallon?
   b. If only private costs are taken into consideration, what is the equilibrium price and equilibrium quantity produced and consumed?
   c. If this market were to take into consideration social costs, what would be the equilibrium price and quantity?
   d. If only private costs are considered, how much more than the socially optimal amount is being consumed?

2. Suppose that the demand and supply curves for fuel are as follows:

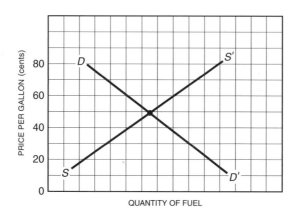

a. If a tax of 20 cents per gallon is imposed on fuel, draw the new supply curve in the graph.
b. Indicate on the graph how much the consumption of fuel is reduced by the tax.
c. Is the tax be paid entirely by consumers or do producers have to bear some of it? Explain.

3. Some states, such as Oregon and Vermont, have passed laws that all carbonated beverage containers must carry a minimum refundable deposit.

   a. According to the director of communications services for American Can Company, "What is happening in Oregon is that consumers are paying $10 million more a year for beer and soft drinks than they did before the bottle bill became law. Retail price increases . . . have far exceeded those in neighboring states." Why do you think that this was true?
   b. According to this executive of American Can Company, "Oregon (and Vermont) consumers are denied their free choice of container." Is this true? According to William Baumol and Wallace Oates, this amounts to "a denial of . . . the freedom to pollute unpenalized." Do you agree?

4. According to one study of the Delaware River, the extra social costs involved in going from one level of pollution abatement to another are shown in the table (in millions of dollars). Also shown are the extra benefits to society (in millions of dollars) in going from one level of pollution to another.

Transition	Extra cost	Extra benefit
From abatement level 1 to 2	35	200
From abatement level 2 to 3	20	30
From abatement level 3 to 4	130	10
From abatement level 4 to 5	245	25

   a. If abatement level 1 is currently achieved, is it socially worthwhile to advance to abatement level 2? Why or why not?
   b. Is it socially worthwhile to advance to abatement level 4? Why or why not?

5. In July 1979, the Commerce Committee of the U.S. House of Representatives approved a plan that would have given the president of the United States standby authority to ration gasoline.

   a. Suppose the government wants to cut gasoline consumption to a certain number of gallons per day. Is it possible to do this without resorting to rationing? How?
   b. Suppose the government wanted to cut gasoline consumption by 10 percent. Do you think that this could be accomplished by a 10 percent increase in price? Do you think that a 20 percent price increase would suffice?

LESSON REVIEW

If you had difficulty with the Self-Quiz or would like additional assistance, read the following lesson review. It should reinforce and help you understand the content presented in this lesson.

Environmental Problems

Pollution occurs in many forms and affects many aspects of the environment. In recent years, those concerned with maintaining a healthy physical environment have even touched on the negative effects of visual pollution (through the proliferation of billboards, for instance) and noise pollution. For purposes of this discussion, we focus on two of the most serious forms of pollution: air pollution and water pollution.

Chemical wastes are released by industrial plants and mines as well as by farms and homes in the form of fertilizers, pesticides, and detergents. In addition, tankers, sewage systems, oil wells, and other sources spill oil into the waterways. Some wastes are dumped directly into streams and rivers. Others are picked up by rain and washed into watersheds. No major water source is immune to the effects of pollution in some form.

Major cities in the United States and around the world are affected by air pollution. Although we cannot measure precisely the effect of this air pollution on human health, rough estimates suggest that a 50 percent reduction in air pollution might reduce deaths from respiratory diseases by up to 25 percent.

Most air pollution in the United States results from the combustion of fossil fuels, and much of it is attributable to the use of impure fuels or inefficient burning techniques. It is estimated that our nation pumps over 200 million tons of waste into the atmosphere annually, about 40 percent of it from automobiles.

External Diseconomies

When one person's or firm's use of a resource causes damage to others who are not properly compensated, an external diseconomy is said to occur. To function properly, the price system requires that those who use resources bear the full cost of that use. Only then will those resources be used in their most socially valuable way. If others must bear the cost of replacing or repairing damaged resources or the cost of cleaning up pollution resulting from mismanagement of resources, the price system does not operate efficiently. Too many resources are used because they are too cheaply priced, and the products resulting from those resources tend to be priced lower than is socially optimal.

The *private cost* of resources is the actual financial cost to a firm or individual for using those resources. The *social cost* is the cost to society for the use of those resources, and this cost can encompass environmental restoration if the use of resources results in pollution. If firms and individuals take sufficient responsibility for their actions to ensure environmental preservation or restoration, then the private and social costs match. If they do not match, too much of a good may be produced, and it may be sold at too low a price. For example, since owners of automobiles do not pay the full cost of disposing of automobile waste, they actually pay an *artificially* low price for operating their automobiles, and they own and operate more automobiles than is socially desirable.

Pollution and Economic Growth

Economic growth (defined as *increases in total economic output per capita*) has been closely associated with pollution. This is not surprising, considering that much of our pollution comes from industry and the automobile, both products of technology.

Correlation does not imply causation, however. We must keep in mind that economic growth need not inevitably result in pollution. Technology, an important part of economic growth, provides us strategies for combatting pollution.

Recently, some critics have suggested *zero economic growth* as a means of addressing problems of pollution. Economists and the public at large do not seem to favor this policy. First, it would curtail the very technology that may eventually alleviate many of our problems. Second, it would entail such drastic alterations to our present standard of living that most economists and social observers doubt it could be readily accepted barring national emergency. In addition, we must recognize that economic growth per se is not the villain here. Pollution is the result of *choices,* decisions we make regarding the way in which we use or abuse resources and the effort and money we are willing to expend to reduce pollution.

Some suggest zero population growth as an answer. Pollution and population size also show a correlation, but the relationship is not a simple one. The rate at which individuals in one society consume resources (and generate pollution) can be quite different from the rate for individuals in another society. For example, it has been estimated that the United States, with less than one-twentieth of the world's population, is responsible for about one-third of the world's pollution. Our standard of living and per capita use of electric power, combustible fuels, detergents, and so on make the difference. In large part, this level of consumption reflects choices made by individuals and firms.

Public Policy toward Pollution

Essentially, the government can intervene to help control pollution in four ways:

1. *Direct regulation.* The government can issue enforceable rules for waste disposal; prohibiting the use of incinerators or dumping certain materials in the ocean, for instance. It can ban the use of pesticides like DDT or require that cars meet emission control standards. This is currently the most common means by which our government seeks to control pollution.

2. *Effluent fees.* An effluent fee is a fee a polluter must pay to the government for discharging wastes. The more firms pollute, the more they must pay. The idea is

to bring the private cost of waste disposal nearer to the true social cost. Many economists believe this is the best way to deal with pollution.

3. *Transferable emissions permits.* The government issues permits allowing each holder of a permit to generate a certain amount of pollution. These permits are limited in number and sold to the highest bidders.

4. *Tax credits.* Government can offer tax credits to firms that introduce pollution control equipment or use pollution-free production methods. Of course, the development and installation of pollution control devices can be very expensive; hence, this method will work only if the tax credits are sufficient in the firm's view to offset considerable costs. For this reason, this method is somewhat less effective overall than the use of effluent fees in achieving a balance between private and social costs.

Pollution Control Programs in the United States

The 1970 Water Quality Improvement Act authorized grants to establish training programs to demonstrate new methods and techniques in water control management. States have set standards for allowable pollution levels, and many state governments have provided matching grants to help municipalities construct treatment plants.

In 1969, Congress established the Council on Environmental Quality, whose responsibility it is to oversee and plan the nation's pollution control programs. This council is charged with gathering information on environmental trends, evaluating federal programs related to pollution control, developing appropriate national policies, and conducting research.

In 1970, the federal government established the Environmental Protection Agency (EPA), whose job is to set standards for clean air and water and devise rules by which firms can meet established goals.

In 1990, major changes were made in the Clean Air Act. The George H. W. Bush administration seemed more interested in new environmental initiatives than the Reagan administration.

How Clean Should the Environment Be?

It might seem at first that the goal of public policy should be to eliminate all pollution. Unfortunately, this is not economically feasible. To achieve zero discharge of pollutants would cost, by current estimates, some $320 billion. What *is* achievable?

The rational approach is to consider the cost of cleaning up the environment together with the cost of pollution. If we could plot these two costs on a graph, we could identify the point at which *the sum of the two costs* is minimal and select that point as representing the level of pollution we tolerate. The problem is that the costs of pollution are very hard to estimate. We can talk about the dollar costs of removing so many tons of chemical X from river Y, but what about the costs of relocating an entire community whose very health is threatened by that chemical? What of those persons who become ill or die as a result of pollution?

Pollution control has hidden costs too. Stringent controls may put firms out of business, raise unemployment, and threaten the economic welfare of entire communities. Clearly, both sides of the question involve human costs as well as financial costs.

Even if we cannot know the precise costs or determine as yet just what the minimal-cost level of pollution might be, one thing is certain: We have to live with *some* level of pollution in the foreseeable future because we cannot rationally or economically do otherwise.

Recent Political Directions

Demand for better control of pollution and more attention to the environment mounted during the 1960s and early 1970s. Then, in the late 1970s and 1980s, policy makers became concerned that regulatory agencies like the EPA were not attending sufficiently to the costs of such controls. The disagreement between environmentalists and those who favor a more conservative approach continues. The Reagan administration, according to its spokespersons, claimed it was "trying to promote and restore balance between environmental objectives and economic growth." Further deadlines for achieving pollution levels were postponed due to the inability of cities to comply. In the George H. W. Bush administration, major changes were made in the Clean Air Act. But the George W. Bush administration rejected the Kyoto global warming treaty. Achieving realistic pollution control has proven to be a politically taxing goal.

EXTENDED LEARNING

This section of the study guide is specifically designed for the two-semester student.

AUDIO

Listen

Listen to the audiotape that accompanies Lesson 21. There is no additional reading assignment for this lesson.

After Listening

Answer the following questions:

1. The Clean Water Act of the early 1970s had a "zero discharge" provision that forced municipalities, regardless of their situation, to use expensive tertiary

treatment procedures before dumping the effluent into a waterway. Does the "zero discharge" make economic sense?

2. The optimal amount of pollution is not zero. What about the optimal amount of crime? Should we expand police forces and police powers until the crime rate is reduced to zero?

ADDITIONAL READINGS

Crandall, Robert W. *Controlling Industrial Air Pollution: The Economics and Politics of Clean Air*. Washington, DC: Brookings Institution, 1983.

> Chapter 3, "The Efficiency of the Current Standards," evaluates the methods used to control air pollution, balancing incremental costs against benefits, and concludes that there would have been less costly ways to achieve the same benefits. He argues, however, that it is possible that even the excessive cost controls may have resulted in benefits greater than the costs. The data are insufficient to perform an overall cost-benefit assessment. No mathematics, simple graphs.

Edel, Matthew. *Economies and the Environment*. Englewood Cliffs, NJ: Prentice-Hall, 1973.

> Chapter 5, "Environmental Fine Tuning," gives an excellent summary of the application of marginal analysis to problems of pollution. Moderately difficult mathematics and graphs.

Lave, Lester B. *The Strategy of Social Regulation: Decision Frameworks for Policy*. Washington, DC: Brookings Institution, 1981.

> Three of the chapters of this book are particularly useful: Chapter 2, "Eight Frameworks for Regulation," pages 8–28; Chapter 5, "Health Safety, and Environmental Regulation," especially pages 103–114; and Chapter 6, "The Benefits and Costs of Benefit-Cost Analysis," pages 129–135. Moderately difficult mathematics, simple graphs.

Lave, Lester B., and Gilbert S. Omenn. *Clearing the Air: Reforming the Clean Air Act*. Washington, DC: Brookings Institution, 1981.

> In this short book, the authors argue that the Clean Air Act has not lead to a significant amount of pollution abatement because Congress used administrative and legal procedures rather than economic principles and incentives. No mathematics or graphs.

Mishan, E.J. *Cost-Benefit Analysis,* 3d ed. New York: Praeger, 1982.

> Chapter 11, "Opportunity Cost," and Chapters 25 to 34 on investment criteria cover the most important aspects of cost-benefit analysis, although other sections of the book provide concise explanations of other concepts of cost-benefit analysis (shadow pricing, valuation of externalities, uncertainty, etc.). Moderately difficult mathematics and graphs.

ANSWER KEY

Video Questions

1. The Reserve Mining Company in northern Minnesota found a way to extract valuable iron ore from a substance called *taconite;* however, the residue from this process ("tailings") had to be disposed of. For years, the simplest, cheapest means of disposal was simply dumping the tailings into Lake Superior. Environmentalists grew increasingly concerned about the social costs and health costs of this practice. Was the water safe to drink? Would it support marine life? What about the tourist industry in the area? Duluth built a new filtration system to purify the water, but public protest continued to mount. People felt concerned, frightened, angry; something clearly had to be done. But, while some were citing the potential dangers of pollution, other equally concerned citizens were worried about the future of their area should Reserve Mining be forced out of business. In what was essentially a one-business economy, they saw little hope for the future. Meanwhile, the environmentalists produced witnesses who claimed the tailings were dangerous; Reserve Mining countered with its own witnesses. The battle continued in court for several years, finally terminating with a federal court decision requiring Reserve Mining to pay for the effects of its pollution through construction of a new disposal sight 7 miles inland from the lake.

   The point is this: Pollution can be controlled to an extent, but pollution control has a cost. Pollution control is not free, either economically or socially. Business profits must sometimes be restricted, jobs suspended or lost, and local economies reshaped to accommodate the costs and effects of pollution control. In this case, the problem was resolved—albeit at great financial cost to Reserve Mining. But under different circumstances, things might not have worked out so well. The company might have been forced to close altogether, putting hundreds of local residents out of work in an area that had no other way to support them. Or, without government intervention, Reserve Mining might have continued to pollute the waters of Lake Superior unchecked, perhaps with disastrous social and financial consequences for the local and regional economies in years to come.

2. Most economists today feel that "perfecting" the environment is an unrealistic goal in a highly industrialized society such as ours, given current technologies. The costs are simply too high. True, we have the technology available right now to remove numerous pollutants from our air and water. But economists point out that the costs of doing so are often staggering. In Los Angeles, for example, strict enforcement of the Clean Air Act in the early 1970s would have meant an 80 percent decrease in road traffic. People would not have been able to get to work or school. Jobs would have been lost, the economy would have bogged down, education and social life would have suffered, and the general quality of life would have dwindled, despite the advantages of breathing cleaner air. Economists argue, therefore, for a balance of costs and benefits.

At first, the benefits of cleaning up the air, for example, are very great. Health risks are reduced and virtually everyone enjoys a higher standard of life. Therefore, the initial costs of a clean-air program (to cite one example) are reasonably easy to justify within limits. However, improving the quality of air beyond a certain point becomes ever costlier and more difficult and produces increasingly smaller benefits given the financial investment required. Once health standards are met and people feel quite comfortable, does it make sense to use exorbitant quantities of resources (that might be diverted elsewhere) to improve air quality still further? Economists do not oppose environmental improvements but do suggest that the benefits to be derived be carefully weighed in balance with their costs (including the costs of those benefits that will be lost when resources are expended).

3. In the video, the different perspectives of environmentalists and economists are subtly developed. The environmentalists warn that, in the near future and over the next century, absolute, irreversible calamity will face the world if something is not done now to stop global warming. They imply that cost should not be an obstacle, since the consequences of not doing something are so dire. The economists in the video are much more cautious. They admit that there is no consensus on global warming or its consequences, and they question the reliability of the apoplectic future scenarios. The economists want to ascertain as best as possible what the cost of doing something now will be and what benefits those costs are likely to deliver.

4. Cost-benefit analysis is not perfect, as Richard Gill points out. It is simply the best means we have so far for balancing our environmental and economic interests. A pollution-free environment is desirable without doubt. But what will it do to our standard of living, realistically, if achieving such an environment threatens the economy? Loss of work can be both socially and economically disastrous, as seen in earlier chapters. At the same time, we must recognize that certain factors are difficult or impossible to measure in strictly economic terms. Children's health is such a factor. We can discuss medical costs and other such indicators, but we must acknowledge that these give us only a limited picture of the true costs. At the same time, it is important to recognize that the loss of a healthy economy entails hard-to-measure social costs too: people out of work, businesses unable to make a profit, loss of morale, loss of buying power, loss of hope, possibly increases in crime and the social and financial costs that accompany it.

In summary, we can use cost-benefit analysis as one efficient means of weighing alternatives, recognizing that certain factors simply cannot be measured in any equitable way. In addition, we must remember that the social costs of one decision (quite apart from the financial costs) are often offset by the social costs of any alternative decision; for example, pollution entails serious social costs, but so, on the other hand, does the unemployment that often results from reducing pollution. Cost-benefit analysis is, in short, a highly complex and controversial issue.

Multiple Choice

1. d   Video.
2. c   Video; Text, 493.
3. a   Text, 493–494.
4. c   Text, 493–494.
5. c   Text, 493–494.
6. a   Text, 494.
7. d   Text, 497.
8. c   Video; Text, 496.
9. d   Text, 497.
10. a   Text, 497–498.

True-False

1. True   Text, 493–494.
2. False   Text, 494.
3. False   Text, 495.
4. True   Text, 497.
5. True   Text, 497.
6. False   Text, 495–496.
7. False   Text, 495–496.
8. False   Text, 498–499.
9. False   Text, 498–502.
10. False   Text, 497–502.

Discussion Questions

1. Whenever the divergence between the private and social costs of production is not corrected, there is an externality: When the social costs exceed the private costs of production, an external diseconomy exists and the market produces too much of the good at too low a price. In both examples in the question, there is a divergence between the private costs and social costs of production: In both cases, an external diseconomy exists and the market does not correct the over-production of the good.

2. To decide the optimal level of pollution, we know to look at the costs of cleaning up the environment and the social cost of pollution. The optimal amount of pollution occurs where the sum of these two costs is minimized.

3. Economic growth and technological change do not necessarily result in more pollution. Technology may provide improved methods for reducing pollution. Pollution inherently reflects the choices we make regarding the way we wish to use or abuse resources.

4. In evaluating packaging requirements, one needs to look at the costs of providing landfill space and the social cost of increased use of land for garbage disposal. If the prices of these packaged goods reflected their true disposal cost, this cost would be borne by the consumer. Higher prices, everything else being the same, would result in lower consumption. The market, by internalizing the disposal costs of these goods, could eliminate or greatly reduce the externalities represented by these goods.

5. An effluent fee is a charge levied on producers for each unit of pollution they produce. As firms pollute more they pay a higher fee. Effluent fees are preferable to direct regulation because they more nearly equate the private cost of waste disposal to the true social cost of waste disposal. Effluent fees are preferred to tax credits for pollution control equipment because tax credits may be prohibitively expensive, since firms are reluctant to develop and install expensive pollution control devices if they are not given sufficient financial incentive.

Problem Set

1. a. $0.20.
    b. $1.50 a gallon and 140 million gallons.
    c. $1.60 a gallon and 120 million gallons.
    d. 20 million gallons.

2. a.

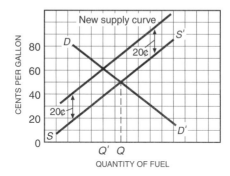

   b. Consumption will be reduced from $0Q$ to $0Q'$ in the graph shown in the answer to part a.
   c. The producers have to bear some of it. Producers now sell fewer units and receive a net price (net of the tax) equal to 40 cents per gallon.

3. a. The law resulted in increased costs of handling, sorting, washing, returning, and refilling bottles; and these higher costs have been partially shifted on to the consumers of the carbonated beverages.
    b. The issue is too complex to permit a very brief answer, but many economists would agree with Baumol and Oates. Consumers should consider the costs of their activities that cause pollution.

4. a. Yes, because the extra benefit exceeds the extra cost.
    b. No, because the extra benefit is less than the extra cost.

5. a. Yes, by raising the price of gasoline. This could be achieved by taxing gasoline at a higher level.
    b. It depends on how sensitive gasoline consumption is to price changes. To see how much the price of gasoline must change to reduce consumption by 10 percent, we need information about the demand and supply curves for gasoline.

Audio/Text Questions

1. No, it prevents any balancing of costs and benefits. Some municipalities discharge effluents into a high flow or tidal waterway where the danger of pollution is low. Natural removal would keep the river safe; then there are zero benefits of reducing that pollution. The increase in taxes needed to pay for the treatment facility would have no benefit.

2. No. There are incremental costs to society of reducing crime, and incremental benefits of each additional reduction in the crime rate. Although crime victims would favor it, society at large would be reluctant to give up some of its other benefits to devote a huge amount of its resources to crime prevention. Resources should continue to be allocated to the police up to the point at which the additional cost is greater than the additional benefit.

LESSON 22. LABOR AND MANAGEMENT: HOW DO THEY COME TO TERMS?

INTRODUCTION

Have you ever wondered why a professional basketball player might earn $1 million a year, a surgeon $300,000, a teacher $40,000, and a grocery clerk $20,000? We can make all sorts of speculations about their relative talents and the importance of their job. We can ask how many persons qualify for each job or could be trained to do it. In other words, how hard is it to replace a grocery clerk, teacher, surgeon, or basketball player? How much education, training, talent, or experience is required for each position? And how hard would it be to get along without them?

Perhaps you are willing to stock, price, and package your own groceries at the supermarket. But you cannot take out your own appendix. And perhaps you can teach yourself history and geography and entertain yourself on Saturday night if there is no professional basketball game to attend, but within a certain price range, you may prefer to have someone else educate or entertain you. The value that you and other consumers attach to the products of labor determines how wages are set. This is another way of saying that wages (*the price of labor*) are set like any price by the interaction of supply and demand. In a perfectly competitive market, wages go up when demand is high and supply is limited. The demand for surgeons, for example, is very great and the supply is small. The demand for grocery clerks may be moderate but the supply is relatively high: If one clerk quits, usually a dozen applicants or more are ready to fill the job.

As we shall see, however, the supply and demand picture is not quite so simple as our example with the surgeon and grocery clerk might suggest. Since the 1930s, many industries have felt the increasing influence of labor unions in determining wage levels and labor supply. The labor unions were organized to protect the union members and give them a collective voice that, until the 1930s, they did not have. Gradually these unions grew in power until they were capable of manipulating the industry supply and demand in ways that had real impact on what we could buy and what we had to pay for it.

In this lesson, we take a closer look at the ways unions affect wage levels and at the ways wages are determined under perfect competition.

What You Should Learn

By the end of Lesson 22, you should be prepared to

1. Distinguish between money wages and real wages.
2. Explain how to determine the profit-maximizing quantity of labor employed.
3. Discuss the concept of *derived demand* and the way it applies to labor.
4. Discuss the reasons for the backward-bending supply curve for labor.
5. Explain how the wage rate is determined under perfect competition.
6. Distinguish among closed shop, union shop, and open shop.

KEY TERMS

labor
money wages
real wages
firm's demand curve for labor
marginal product of labor
market demand curve for labor
derived demand
market supply curve
noncompeting groups
labor union
labor force
value of the marginal product of labor

check-off
collective bargaining
closed shop
union shop
open shop
strike
injunction
yellow-dog contract
featherbedding
market supply curve for labor
national unions
local unions

VIDEO

Watch

Economics U$A Program 22, "Labor and Management: How Do They Come to Terms?"

Illustrative Events

The 1909 strike of ladies' garment workers (ILGWU), a landmark in labor organization, featuring Leon Stein, former editor of *Justice*, the ILGWU newspaper, and author of *Out of the Sweatshop*.

The death of the *New York Herald Tribune* under pressure from labor union demands and strikes; featuring columnist Jimmy Breslin; Clay Felker, former editor of *New*

York magazine; Bertram Powers, president of Local 6, Typographical Union; and *New York Times* labor reporter, A. H. Raskin.

The unprecedented concessions made by the UAW to help Chrysler get its historic government bailout; featuring Douglas Fraser, former president, United Auto Workers; Harley Shaiken, automobile industry analyst at MIT; and labor economist Jack Barbash, University of Wisconsin. Richard Gill analyzes changes in labor-management relations.

After Viewing

Answer the following questions:

1. Unions have resulted in numerous benefits to workers and some costs as well. Explain.

2. What factors contributed to the "death" of the *Herald Tribune?*

3. Why do some observers feel that labor-management negotiations at Chrysler might have signaled the beginning of a new era in union-management relations?

Read

Read Chapter 22, "The Supply and Demand for Labor," pages 513–534 in your text. After completing your reading, try the Self-Quiz.

SELF-QUIZ

Multiple Choice

1. From the economist's point of view, the term *labor* refers to
   a. output.
   b. all persons belonging to trade unions.
   c. the output of persons belonging to trade unions.
   d. the work of all employed persons.

2. Which of the following statements is *most* accurate? In the period since 1960,
   a. money wages have risen significantly faster than real wages.
   b. both money wages and real wages have risen significantly.
   c. real wages have risen significantly, but money wages have declined.
   d. both real wages and money wages have declined.

3. A graph showing the amount of labor that a given firm uses at each level of wages is the
   a. market demand curve for labor.
   b. firm's demand curve for labor.
   c. market supply curve for labor.
   d. firm's supply curve for labor.

4. The following table shows the output rate for Wheelbye Roller Skate Company:

Number of workers per day	Total output per day
0	0
1	5
2	9
3	12
4	15

What is the marginal product of labor resulting from hiring the second worker?

a. 14
b. 5
c. 9
d. 4

5. If roller skates sell for $10 a pair and workers must be paid $40 a day, how many workers does Wheelbye (question 4) hire?

a. 1
b. 2
c. 3 or 4
d. None

6. Under perfect competition, a firm maximizes profits when the value of the marginal product is equal to

a. the product's price.
b. total revenue.
c. the price of labor.
d. average cost of inputs.

7. A single perfectly competitive firm's demand curve for labor is the same as its

a. market supply curve.
b. value of marginal product curve.
c. marginal cost curve.
d. individual firm supply curve.

8. If the demand for automobiles is highly price elastic, then the market demand for auto workers

a. tends to be highly price elastic also.
b. tends to be somewhat inelastic.
c. tends to be highly inelastic.
d. is not be determinable since these two variables are not related.

9. According to the following figure, the equilibrium price of labor for the market shown is

a. precisely 0*P*.
b. precisely 0*Q*.

c. somewhere above 0P.
d. PQ.

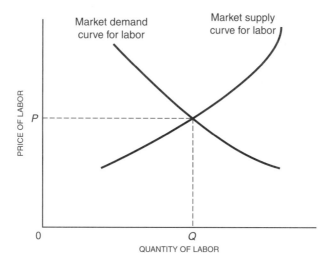

10. The *main* reason that surgeons tend to receive far higher wages than unskilled laborers is that

   a. they have been more successful in negotiating higher wages in the marketplace.
   b. they work harder than unskilled laborers.
   c. surgeons are members of a noncompeting group, which unskilled laborers are not.
   d. relatively fewer people are qualified to be surgeons relative to demand.

True-False

____ 1. If a technological change occurs that increases the marginal productivity of labor and at the same time the supply curve of labor shifts to the right, the price of labor must fall.

____ 2. If a union shifts the supply curve of labor to the left, the price of labor falls.

____ 3. If the value of the marginal product is greater than the input's price, the perfectly competitive firm can increase its profit by decreasing its use of the input.

____ 4. Union growth was most rapid during the 1930s and early 1940s.

____ 5. A firm's demand curve for an input shows, for each price, the amount of that input the firm uses.

____ 6. The *main* reason for the backward-bending supply curve is that the higher wages go the fewer is the number of qualified persons to fill a given position.

_____ 7. The wage for surgeons is higher than for unskilled laborers because the demand curve for surgeons is farther to the right and the supply curve for surgeons is farther to the left than the corresponding curves for unskilled laborers.

_____ 8. Beyond some point, increases in wages may actually result in smaller amounts of labor being supplied.

_____ 9. Wage differences between noncompeting groups are gradually erased as people move from lower-paying jobs into higher-paying jobs.

_____ 10. Under perfect competition, the supply curve of labor for an individual firm is a horizontal line.

Discussion Questions

1. According to *USA Today,* May 1, 2000, the average player in major league baseball makes $2 million a year. The highest paid was a pitcher who made $15.7 million that year. In general, pitchers make much more than players at other positions. Why would this disparity exist? Baseball players make twice as much on average as football players. What accounts for this difference?

2. How might a consumer boycott of grapes or lettuce work to the detriment of farm laborers in California?

3. Why is the Wagner Act often called U.S. labor's Magna Carta?

4. One study suggests that union workers over the last several decades have earned wages that are 10 to 20 percent higher than the wages paid to nonunion labor. Does that imply that wages in the United States would, on average, be lower if there were no unions?

Problem Set

1. Suppose that the Ace Manufacturing Company is a member of a perfectly competitive industry. Suppose that the relationship between various amounts of labor input and output is as follows:

Product price (dollars)	Units of labor	Units of output	Marginal product of labor	Value of marginal product (dollars)
10	0	0		
10	1	2½	___	___
10	2	5	___	___
10	3	7	___	___
10	4	8	___	___

a. Fill in the blanks.

b. If you are told that the Ace Manufacturing Company is hiring three units of labor, you can establish a range for the value of the wage rate prevailing in the labor market (assuming that the firm maximizes profit). What is this range? Specifically, what is the maximum value that the wage (for a unit of labor) may be? What is the minimum value? Why?

c. Suppose that the Ace Manufacturing Company must pay $20 for a unit of labor. How many units of labor does it hire? Why?

2. Suppose that the demand curve for lawyers is as follows:

Annual wage (thousands of dollars)	Quantity of labor demanded (thousands of person-years)
20	200
30	180
40	160
50	140
60	120
70	100
80	80

a. What is the equilibrium wage for lawyers if the market is perfectly competitive and 140,000 person-years of labor is supplied at any wage?

b. Suppose that lawyers form a union and that the union forces the wage up to $70,000 a year. How many person-years of labor will be supplied but unable to find work?

3. Suppose that the relationship between the number of laborers employed per day in a car wash and the number of cars washed per day is as follows:

Number of laborers	Cars washed
1	15
2	40
3	50
4	55

Suppose that the owner of the car wash receives $2 for each car wash and the price of labor is $20 per day. How many laborers will the owner hire per day?

4. A perfectly competitive firm has the following value-of-marginal-product curve:

Number of units of labor per day	Value of marginal product (dollars)
1	
2	52
3	47
4	42
5	37
6	32

a. If there are 1,000 firms, all of which have the same value-of-marginal-product curve, the market demand curve for labor is as follows:

Price of labor per day (dollars)	Number of units of labor demanded per day
50	_____
45	_____
40	_____
35	_____

Fill in the blanks. (Assume that only integer numbers of units of labor can be used.)

b. The supply curve for labor is as follows:

Price of labor per day (dollars)	Number of units of labor supplied per day
35	3,000
40	4,000
45	5,000
50	6,000

What is the equilibrium price of a unit of labor per day?

c. What is the total amount of labor demanded in the market? What is the amount demanded by each firm?

d. What is the extra cost that a firm would incur if it added an extra unit of labor per day?

e. What is the value of the marginal product for the last unit of labor hired for this firm?

f. If a minimum wage of $45 per day is established, what is the total amount of labor demanded in the market?

LESSON REVIEW

If you had difficulty with the Self-Quiz or would like additional assistance, read the following lesson review. It should reinforce and help you understand the content presented in this lesson.

The Labor Force and the Price of Labor

To the economist, labor is the work or service provided by any employed person, whether that employee is a truck driver, teacher, surgeon, astronaut, or car seller. Recent figures suggest that almost two-thirds of the people employed in the United States today are white-collar workers (sellers, doctors, secretaries, managers) or service workers (servers, bartenders, cooks). Only about one-third are either blue-collar workers (carpenters, mine or factory workers, laborers) or farm workers.

In 1999, data showed that service workers made up the largest group of workers by major industry at 30.5 percent of nonagricultural employment. Those employed in mining made up the smallest at 0.8 percent. The federal government, a category unto itself, was the largest single employer with 2.3 percent. If you add employees of state and local governments to the employees of the federal government, one out of every six workers is employed by government.

Average weekly earnings vary considerably from one industry to another, and also from one period to another. Recent statistics show that between 1960 and 1999, average weekly earnings in many industries grew between 300 and 500 percent. This does not mean, however, that the average U.S. worker has experienced enormous leaps in buying power. In any discussion of wages, we must distinguish between the *money wage* (the actual salary figure that appears on a worker's paycheck) and the *real wage* (what that money buys in goods and services). So, while money wages have grown considerably over the past several decades, real wages have not. In the following discussion, we assume that product prices are constant; hence, our discussion focuses on real wages.

Equilibrium Wage and Employment under Perfect Competition

A firm's demand curve shows, for each price, the amount of labor that firm hires. Assume for this discussion that labor is the only variable input. If we know the production function (output of each worker per day), we can determine the marginal product of labor when various numbers of workers are employed. (Recall that the marginal product of labor is *the additional output resulting from each extra unit of labor*.)

Number of workers per day	Total output per day	Marginal product of labor	Value of marginal product (dollars)
0	0		
		7	70
1	7		
		6	60
2	13		
		5	50
3	18		
		4	40
4	22		
		3	30
5	25		

According to the table, the firm shown achieves a daily output of seven units when it hires its first worker. This is seven units over what it has with no workers; in other words, the marginal product of labor with one worker is 7. If the firm's product is priced at $10, the firm's value of the marginal product (*VMP*) is 7 × 10, or $70.

Suppose it costs the firm $50 to hire the worker. If its value of the marginal product is $70 and it must pay the worker $50, it is profitable for the firm to hire this first worker. It is also, as it turns out, profitable to hire the second worker. For the second worker,

$$\text{Marginal product of labor} = 6$$
$$\text{Value of marginal product} = 6 \times 10, \text{ or } \$60$$
$$\text{Worker's wage} = \$50$$
$$\text{Additional revenue minus worker's wage} = \$60 - \$50 = \$10.$$

So the firm adds $10 to its total profits by hiring the second worker.

Note what happens with the fourth worker, however. For the fourth worker,

$$\text{Marginal product of labor} = 4$$
$$\text{Value of marginal product} = 4 \times 10, \text{ or } \$40$$
$$\text{Worker's wage} = \$50$$
$$\text{Revenue minus worker's wage} = \$40 - \$50 = -\$10.$$

So the firm reduces its total profits by $10 when it hires the fourth worker.

How many workers should the firm hire? It should continue to hire workers as long as the extra workers add as much to revenue as they do to costs. When additional costs outweigh additional revenue, the firm has gone too far. When additional revenue outweighs additional costs, the firm has not hired enough. And, *to maximize profits, the firm should hire enough workers that the value of the marginal product is equal to the price of labor*. In the example shown in the table, this occurs with the hiring of the third worker, since the *VMP* of labor at this level is 5 (5 × 10 = $50) and equals the cost of hiring the worker (wage of $50). And, since the profits are maximized at a level where the value of the marginal product is equal to the price of labor, the *firm's demand curve for labor is the same as its value-of-marginal-product curve*.

Market Demand Curve for Labor

The market demand curve shows *the relationship between the price of labor and the total amount of labor demanded in the market*. In other words, it shows, for each price, the amount of labor demanded in the entire market, not just by one firm.

The demand for labor and other inputs is a *derived demand*. That is, it results from the market demand for products and services produced by those inputs. Demand for auto workers depends on the demand for cars; demand for teachers depends on the number of students who attend school. This means that the greater is the price elasticity of demand for a given product, the greater is the price elasticity of demand for an input used to produce that product.

Market Supply Curve for Labor

The market supply curve is the *relationship between the price of labor and the total amount of labor supplied in the market*. Labor is a little different from other sorts of inputs. A worker who provides labor provides something he or she could use personally (leisure time). Therefore, beyond some point, the worker may not be willing to provide more of this input to someone else, regardless of increases in price. If you are working 40 hours per week and you can make double your usual wage by working an extra 10, you may agree to do it. Perhaps you will even agree to an extra 20 hours if you are very ambitious. But if you get an across-the-board raise for your basic 40 hours, you may not even wish to work the extra 10; you may prefer to spend those hours in recreation. This is a typical pattern with workers in the United States, and in fact, the average workweek has tended to decline. So, beyond some point, increases in price may actually result in *smaller* amounts of labor being supplied, and the market supply curve for labor bends backward (see Figure 22.2 on page 514 of your text).

Remember that the supply curve of labor or other inputs to an individual firm may be horizontal under perfect competition (that is, an individual firm may have access to all the labor it needs at the equilibrium price determined in the labor market). Yet the *market* supply curve for the input (in this case, labor) is never horizontal.

Equilibrium Price and the Quantity of Labor

The price of labor tends toward equilibrium at the level where the quantity of labor demanded equals the quantity of labor supplied. The equilibrium amount of labor used is *also shown by the intersection of the market supply and demand curves*. But what factors affect this demand?

In part, it is the value we place on the goods or services provided. We tend to value the skills of a surgeon, for example, very highly. We also place high value on the talents of a professional athlete, for very different reasons. We place generally less value on the work of an unskilled laborer, largely because the laborer would be much easier to replace than the surgeon or the athlete. Not everyone can be an Olympic star. Not everyone can perform neurosurgery, regardless of training, education, or opportunity. Professional athletes and unskilled laborers are examples of noncompeting groups. That is, a worker cannot move readily from a low-paid job as a laborer to a high-paid job as a baseball player.

Labor Unions

About 1 in 10 nonfarm workers in the United States belongs to a union, and the perfectly competitive model does not apply to the way wages are set for these workers. To understand how unions work, we take a closer look.

How Unions Increase Wages

Basically, unions have three methods for increasing wages.

1. *The union may try to shift the supply curve for labor to the left.* A union can do this, for instance, by forcing employers to hire only union members, then restricting union membership through high initiation fees or reduction in new membership. Unions have also favored restrictions on immigration and shorter working hours, two other means for holding down the natural labor supply.

2. *The union may bargain with employers to secure a higher wage, even though this results in fewer job openings and some unemployment.*

3. *The union may try to shift the demand curve for labor upward and to the right.* One way it does this is by featherbedding or trying to define the job so narrowly that it takes numbers of people to perform what could be performed by one. Unions can also try to shift the demand curve by helping employers compete against other industries or encouraging Congress to pass legislation protecting employers from foreign competition. A further method would be to increase labor productivity and the *VMP,* hence the demand curve.

Collective Bargaining

Collective bargaining is a negotiation process between labor unions and management. Its purpose is to determine the wage level and working conditions satisfactory to both sides. It is usual in collective bargaining for each side to ask for more than it expects to get, anticipating that compromises are required to reach agreement. An agreement generally specifies these elements:

- The extent and kind of recognition given by management to the union.
- The level of wage and fringe benefits for each job involved.
- The length of the workweek.
- The rates for overtime.
- The rights of seniority (particularly when layoffs occur) and job security.
- Management's prerogatives.
- Steps for handling grievances.
- Working conditions.

Historically, firms have accepted one of three arrangements: the closed shop, union shop, or open shop.

1. *The closed shop* is an arrangement by which workers must be union members to be hired. The closed shop was banned by the Taft-Hartley Act.

2. *The union shop*, which offers the union less power than the closed shop, allows employers to hire nonunion members, so long as they become union members after they are hired. The union shop is legal under the Taft-Hartley Act unless outlawed by state laws. In about 20 states "right-to-work" laws make the union shop illegal.

3. *The open shop* allows the employer to hire any worker, union or nonunion, and nonunion workers need not join the union after hiring. Open shops are a threat to union power and are hence opposed by unions, as are "right-to-work" laws.

Collective bargaining is affected by the basic laws of supply and demand. During periods of high demand (and potentially high sales), an employer is likely to give in to demands for higher wages because the costs of disagreement and loss of production are greater during this period than the costs of settlement. During periods of low consumer demand, the costs of settlement may seem to outweigh the costs of disagreement, and the employer tends to hold ground. Of course, the real strength of the employer is measured by ability to withstand a strike, and the real strength of the union by its ability of its members to survive the loss of income during a strike.

EXTENDED LEARNING

This section of the study guide is specifically designed for the two-semester student.

AUDIO

Listen

Listen to the audiotape that accompanies Lesson 22. There is no additional reading assignment for this lesson.

After Listening

Answer the following questions:

1. Indicate how, under perfect competition, the firm's demand curve for labor can be derived, given the firm's production function and the price of the product.

2. Describe three ways that unions can increase wages and give examples.

3. What are some of the ways a union can damage productivity?

4. What are some of the ways a union can enhance productivity?

5. What trade-offs face labor unions when a firm wants to automate? Who gains and who loses? Describe the difference between the attitude of the New York typographical union's response to new technology and the UAW's attitude in the 1980s.

ADDITIONAL READINGS

"Beyond Unions." *Business Week* (July 8, 1985): 72–77.

> Describes the trend away from union protection of workers toward an expansion of laws and court rulings that define workers' rights. No mathematics or graphs.

Duncan, G. J., and F. P. Stafford. "Do Union Members Receive Compensating Differentials?" *American Economic Review* 70 (June 1980): 355–371.

> Investigates various explanations for the union-nonunion wage differential including the degree to which the workplace is structured, overtime-hours flexibility, repetitiveness, and so on. Technical discussion, moderately difficult mathematics, no graphs.

Freeman, Richard B. "The Evolution of the American Labor Market, 1948–1980." In *The American Economy in Transition*, edited by Martin Feldstein. Chicago: University of Chicago Press, 1980.

> An excellent survey of the changes in the labor market in the postwar era. The author identifies and discusses the seven most important changes, including a slowdown in the rate of growth of real wages, a change in the composition of jobs, and a decline in trade unionism. No mathematics or graphs.

Freeman, Richard, and James L. Medoff. *What Do Unions Do?* New York: Basic Books, 1982.

> Chapter 1 and the concluding chapter of the book summarize the authors' viewpoints regarding the economic effects of today's unions. They argue that unions can increase economic efficiency because the benefits of a better workplace are largely public goods and the ultimate value of unions for society depends on the management-union interaction in each specific case. No mathematics or graphs.

Galenson, Walter, and Robert S. Smith. "The United States." In *Labor in the Twentieth Century*, edited by John T. Dunlop and Walter Galenson. New York: Academic Press, 1978.

> A survey of the major trends and events in the history of labor from 1900 to 1975. Sections on the demographic changes, trade unionism, the rise in real wages, the evolution of labor legislation, and current problems provide good brief overviews of those topics. No mathematics or graphs.

ANSWER KEY

Video Questions

1. Through union negotiations, workers have won higher wages, greater benefits, better working hours and conditions, and sometimes additional benefits like profit sharing. But these benefits are gained at some cost—sometimes minimal, sometimes substantial. At the very least, the employment of workers at a higher wage means that fewer workers can be employed. This may require some workers to transfer to another industry entirely to find work. Great declines in the ranks of the UAW in recent years are a case in point. In other cases, as with the *New York Herald Tribune*, the costs can be far greater. If workers are able to hold out longer than the industry, a labor strike can actually spell the end of a corporation.

2. Labor unions at the *Herald Tribune* and other New York papers felt threatened by the new computer technology, which among other things, greatly simplified and speeded the typesetting process. The fear was, of course, that jobs would be lost as skills workers had traditionally done by hand became computerized and automatic. (In fact, computerization typically creates other new jobs, but this is a

separate issue.) The union did not directly refuse to automate but instead spelled out conditions for automation that made the entrance of any new technology exceedingly difficult. In effect, the Typographical Union had "veto power" over computerization. Profitable papers could afford the excessive costs of the new technology. The *Herald Tribune,* however, could not. In an effort to stay alive, the *Herald Tribune* merged with other struggling papers, forming the *World Journal Tribune.* It was not to be long for the world. Even though the new paper signed a contract with Big 6 (the International Typographical Unions local member), other unions refused to sign, and the *World Journal Tribune* was picketed. Printers, following tradition, refused to cross the picket line. And the struggling new paper, already stretched tight on limited resources, simply could not survive another crisis. The factors contributing to its demise were weakness that was a result of the unprofitability of its three founding partners, the intransigence of the labor unions epitomized by their willingness to let a firm their members worked for go bankrupt rather than compromise their bargaining position, and the development of a new technology that was perceived by the unions as a threat.

3. The experience of the Chrysler Corporation in the late 1970s stands in sharp contrast to that of the *Herald Tribune* more than a decade earlier. Again, the existence of a corporation was on the line, and again, advancing technology was playing a key role: this time in the form of mileage-efficient foreign cars that swept the market out from under Chrysler. To remain functioning, Chrysler would need capital, new plant and equipment, and time. Even with government assistance, these requirements could not be met without the extensive commitment and cooperation of the firm's workers. Union workers at Chrysler agreed to more than $450 million worth of pay cuts, in exchange for which they received profit-sharing opportunities, assurances against additional plant closings, a greater voice in decision making, and the promise of better wages later. The temporary pay cuts bought the company the time it needed to use government funds effectively and turn its production and marketing around. Chrysler stayed alive because of cooperation between labor and management—what Douglas Fraser (former president of the UAW) called "equality of sacrifice." Some observers feel that the success of the Chrysler negotiations and the subsequent success of the company itself go a long way toward demonstrating the importance of shelving antagonisms for purposes of survival. The question is one of cooperation between the union and management of the firm so both can achieve a common goal, self-preservation in their competition with other firms for a share of the automobile market.

Multiple Choice

1. d   Text, 513–514.
2. a   Text, 515.
3. b   Text, 515–517.
4. d   Text, 516.
5. b   Text, 517.
6. c   Text, 517.
7. b   Text, 517.

True-False

1. False   Text, 515–521.
2. False   Text, 526–527.
3. False   Text, 517.
4. True   Text, 523.
5. True   Text, 515.
6. False   Text, 518–519.
7. True   Text, 520–521.

8.	a	Text, 518.	8.	True	Text, 518–519.
9.	a	Text, 520.	9.	False	Text, 521.
10.	d	Text, 520–521.	10.	True	Text, 519.

Discussion Questions

1. The wage differential between pitchers and players of other positions reflects the greater value placed on the skills of pitchers as well as the fact that it would be harder to replace the pitcher. Salary differentials between pro football and pro baseball players may reflect the relative scarcity of baseball skills compared to football skills, the greater value placed on baseball, or more likely, the greater degree of organization and unionization in baseball, which does not have a salary cap as football does.

2. If buyers of grapes or lettuce refuse to purchase the product in large enough numbers, the demand curve for the product shifts to the left, resulting in a lower equilibrium product price. The result is a lower value of the marginal product of the labor curve, and firms respond by hiring fewer units of labor at each wage level.

3. The Wagner Act stated that it was an unfair labor practice for employers to refuse to bargain collectively with unions representing a majority of their workers. It also stated that businesses could not interfere with their workers' right to organize.

4. If unions are able to raise their members' wages by restricting supply or having the high wage itself restrict the number of workers the unionized firms are willing to hire, then the workers who might have otherwise worked for unionized firms are added to the supply of workers at nonunionized firms. This pushes wages down at nonunionized firms. So if there were no unions, the average wage might not change much at all.

Problem Set

1. a.

Marginal product of labor	Value of marginal product (dollars)
2.5	25
2.5	25
2	20
1	10

    b. The wage must be between $10 and $20, because if it were more than $20, the firm would hire only two units of labor and because if it were less than $10, the firm would hire four units of labor.
    c. Three units of labor, because this maximizes its profit.

2. a. $50,000.
    b. 40,000.

3. Two or three.

4. a. *Number of units of labor
           demanded per day*

    2,000
    3,000
    4,000
    5,000

    b. $40.
    c. 4,000 units. 4 units.
    d. $40.
    e. $42.
    f. 3,000 units.

Audio/Text Questions

1. For a given amount of equipment, a firm can produce more and more output only by increasing the amount of labor. As labor is increased, however, each additional worker adds progressively less to output (the law of diminishing marginal returns is part of the short-run production function, see Chapter 15). Therefore, the firm's demand curve for labor slopes downward to the right.

2. Unions can increase wages by restricting the supply of labor in their field; for example, the plumbers union and other craft unions can restrict licensing or try to force employers to hire only union members. Unions may bargain directly for a higher wage and lobby for protection against imports or other competition to increase or maintain the firms' demand for labor.

3. Unions can obstruct the use of new technology or force firms to hire more workers than necessary. They can insist on irrational work rules, create an antagonistic atmosphere that disrupts production, and distort economic efficiency by forcing wages up beyond the "free market" level.

4. By reducing labor turnover and improving morale through better communication, the union can aid productivity growth. Also, if it raises the price of labor, the firm may decide to use more capital per worker to raise productivity (at least temporarily). Unions can improve the quality of work not only by reducing turnover but also through unionized apprenticeship programs.

5. Automation usually means that fewer workers are needed in a particular skills category, but it may slightly increase the demand for higher-paid workers who operate the new machinery. These workers are paid more because their productivity is higher. The New York typographical union, by insisting on an excessive number of highly paid workers for the new technology, inhibited the use of the new technology. The UAW in the 1980s, realizing the value of new technology such as robots, has tried to encourage the use of new technology.

LESSON 23. PROFITS AND INTEREST: WHERE IS THE BEST RETURN?

INTRODUCTION

Suppose you have a $10 bill in your pocket right now. Its real money value, as we discovered in the last chapter, is determined by the amount of goods and services you can exchange it for right now. As all of us are too well aware, the value of money is anything but constant. It changes steadily over time. How much will that same $10 be worth a year from now? Two years from now? To get the most out of that $10, you may decide to buy something with it over the next few days before the value has a chance to decline. Or perhaps you decide that a wiser course is to invest in government bonds, which pay off with interest sometime in the future. How should you go about determining the most profitable sort of investment? As we see in this lesson, your decision depends a great deal on current interest rates.

We usually think of income as wages: the amount of money received in our paychecks. But we can receive income in several other forms: interest, rent, or profit. These three forms of income are known collectively as property income. For example, if you purchase a government bond, you receive interest on your investment. That interest is one form of property income. If you lease 5 acres of farmland, you receive what economists call rent, which is also a form of property income. Perhaps you are a very creative, innovative sort of person. As an entrepreneur, you could find that creativity rewarded in the form of business profits—another sort of property income—resulting from your skill as a manager or your invention of a new product or technique. In this chapter, we take a closer look at these forms of income and the social functions of each.

In addition, we consider the functions of profits and their role in a capitalistic society.

What You Should Learn

By the end of Lesson 23, you should be prepared to

1. Discuss the concepts of *interest, rate of interest,* and *pure rate of interest.*

2. Explain how the *supply curve for loanable funds* and the *demand curve for loanable funds* are derived, and discuss their relation to interest rates.

3. Discuss the ways in which shifting monetary policy or government borrowing projects affect the interest rate.

4. Define the concept of *rent*.

5. Explain the functions of profit in a capitalistic society.

KEY TERMS

rate of interest
pure rate of interest
demand for loanable funds
supply for loanable funds
rate of return
usury
capitalization
land

rent
profit
innovators
risk
surplus value
bond
present value
single-tax movement

VIDEO

Watch

Economics U$A Program 23, "Profits and Interest: Where Is the Best Return?"

Illustrative Events

The scarcity of mortgage money and the historic repeal of Maryland's usury ceilings in the late 1970s, with Maryland State Senator Laurence Levitan and home builder Frank Miano.

The decision by General Motors to build its $3 billion Orion plant rather than refurbish existing facilities, with GM executives and managers.

The remarkable story of the entrepreneurs who launched Apple Computer, turning a garage operation into a billion dollar industry, featuring Steve Wozniak, one of the founders.

After Viewing

Answer the following questions:

1. Usury laws are intended to protect the consumer. Sometimes, however, those very laws can work against consumer interests. Explain.

2. According to economic theory, how do businesses determine whether a particular investment will be profitable?

3. Business entrepreneurs often derive extremely large profits from their adventures. From the economist's perspective, are such profits justified? Why?

Read

Read Chapter 23, "Interest, Rent, and Profit," pages 535–552 in your text. After completing your reading, try the Self-Quiz.

SELF-QUIZ

Multiple Choice

1. Interest, rent, and profit are all forms of

    a. consumer income.
    b. property income.
    c. real income.
    d. derived income.

2. If you invest $100 for a year at an interest rate of 10 percent, and then reinvest your total (principal plus interest) for a second year at the same rate, what will your investment be worth at the end of the second year?

    a. $121
    b. $120
    c. $111
    d. $131

3. Which of the following statements is most accurate?

    a. Everyone who borrows money pays interest on any funds borrowed.
    b. Everyone except the government pays interest on borrowed money.
    c. Consumers and the government pay interest on borrowed money; banks do not.
    d. Banks and the government pay interest on short-term loans only; everyone else pays interest on all money borrowed.

4. The pure rate of interest refers to

    a. the current rate.
    b. interest on government bonds.
    c. the highest rate of interest available to consumers.
    d. interest on a risk-free loan.

5. The demand curve for loanable funds

    a. is horizontal.
    b. is vertical and fixed.
    c. slopes downward and to the right.
    d. slopes upward and to the right.

6. Suppose that firm X has the capability to borrow all the money it wants at the current interest rate. To maximize profits, firm X should accept every investment

    a. it can afford.
    b. that appears relatively risk free.
    c. that promises a return comparable to the pure rate of interest.
    d. for which the projected rate of return exceeds the current interest rate.

7. Under which of the following conditions is the supply curve for loanable funds likely to shift to the left?

    a. The Fed sets a policy of tight money.
    b. Consumers decide to postpone consumption until some future date.
    c. New innovations in technology open up investment possibilities.
    d. Government borrowing increases substantially.

8. Believers in a free market system generally tend to

    a. support anti-usury laws.
    b. support such laws only so long as they do not curb private investment.
    c. oppose anti-usury laws.
    d. feel rather indifferent since antiusury laws have little real impact on investment anyway.

9. As interest rates rise, which of the following kinds of projects would most likely be carried out?

    a. A no-risk project with a relatively low rate of return
    b. A very high-risk project with a moderate rate of return
    c. A moderately risky project with a high rate of return
    d. A very high-risk project with a high rate of return

10. The choice made in question 9 indicates one way that interest rates help ensure

    a. efficient use of resources.
    b. minimal risk with investments.
    c. equitable distribution of funds among all investors.
    d. emphasis on capital investment over private investment.

True-False

_____ 1. If consumers decide to postpone consumption to some future time and very profitable new investment opportunities open up, the interest rate must rise.

_____ 2. If the Fed sets a policy of easy money and profitable investment opportunities open up at the same time, the equilibrium quantity of loanable funds increases.

_____ 3. Most mortgages granted today through commercial banks involve a pure rate of interest.

_____ 4. If the current interest rate is 12 percent, a firm can maximize profits by accepting any investments where the rate of return is equal to or less than 12 percent.

_____ 5. A very large portion of the demand for loanable funds comes from firms' wanting money for investment in capital goods like machinery, buildings, and land.

_____ 6. Interest rates serve a vital function in our economy by allocating the supply of loanable funds.

_____ 7. An asset's rate of return is equivalent to the interest rate earned on investment in the asset.

_____ 8. The lower interest rates fall, the less firms are willing to borrow.

_____ 9. According to Karl Marx, surplus value, which includes what we call profit, is a measure and consequence of the exploitation of labor by the owners of firms.

_____ 10. Profit is the reward for taking risks.

Discussion Questions

1. According to Richard Freeman's calculations, the value of lifetime income (in the 1960s) was about $230,000 for a Ph.D. in electrical engineering but about $208,000 for a B.A. (or B.S.) in electrical engineering. Discuss the relevance of this finding for the decision of whether to do graduate work in electrical engineering.

2. "Money really does not produce anything. You can stick a dollar bill in the earth, and it will not grow. You cannot wear it or eat it. Why should it receive any return? Interest is merely a trick to obtain unearned income for the moneyed classes." Do you agree? Why or why not?

3. What is the relationship between the concept of rent and the concept of opportunity cost?

4. If the government imposes a tax on economic rent, does this affect the supply of resources to the economy? Why or why not?

5. Describe Joseph Schumpeter's concept of profit. How is it related to his view of the process of economic growth? Describe Frank Knight's concept of profit. How does it differ from Schumpeter's?

Problem Set

1. Suppose that you will receive $10,000 in three years. How much is it worth now? (Assume that the interest rate is 6 percent.)

2. Suppose that the demand curve for loanable funds in the United States is as follows:

Interest rate (percent)	Quantity of loanable funds (billions of dollars)
4	60
6	50
8	40
10	30
12	20

    a. Suppose that the existing supply of loanable funds in the United States is $40 billion. What is the equilibrium interest rate, given the data presented here?
    b. If the interest rate is the one indicated in part a and you are considering investing your money in an investment with a rate of return of 7 percent, should you accept the investment? Why or why not?

3. Suppose that the Jones Construction Company can borrow money at 15 percent per year and it is willing to accept only those (riskless) investments that yield 20 percent per year or more. Does this firm maximize profit?

4. Suppose that the Jones Construction Company has the following investment opportunities:

Rate of return (percent)	Amount of money the firm can invest at the given rate of return (millions of dollars)
35	5
30	10
25	8
20	9
17	4

    If it has to pay 15 percent interest, which investment opportunities should it accept?

5. Firm X must choose between investing in machine A and machine B. The machines do exactly the same work, but their purchase prices and maintenance costs differ. The purchase price of machine A is $10,000, while the purchase price of machine B is $5,000. The maintenance cost each year with machine A is $1,000, while the maintenance cost each year with machine B is $1,600. Both machines last so long that it is reasonable to assume (for simplicity) that they last forever.

    a. If the interest rate is 5 percent, which machine should firm X buy? Why?
    b. At what interest rate would firm X be indifferent between the two machines?

LESSON REVIEW

If you had any difficulty with the Self-Quiz or would like additional assistance, read the following lesson review. It should help you to understand the content presented in this lesson.

Interest

Interest is payment for the use of money. Everyone who borrows pays interest, including the government. When you receive interest on a government bond, that is in effect the government's payment to you for the right to borrow your money. The *rate of interest* is the amount of money you must pay for the use of a dollar for one year. If you borrow $100 at an interest rate of 10 percent, you must pay back $110 within the year.

Interest rates vary depending on the financial situation of the borrower (How much confidence can the lender have that the borrower can repay the money?) and the nature of the loan itself. Very high-risk loans entail greater interest. In addition, the cost of bookkeeping and collection is a factor. A firm that makes many small loans and has a hard time collecting must charge a higher rate of interest because it costs such a firm more to lend money.

The *pure rate of interest* is the equilibrium interest rate on a risk-free loan. The closest approximation we have to such a loan is the interest rate on a U.S. government bond. Other rates vary from this rate, depending on relative risk, but the pure rate of interest is a sort of barometer for interest rates in general.

Determination of the Interest Rate

Note that interest is the *price paid for the use of loanable funds*. Like any price, it is determined by demand and supply market forces. The demand curve for loanable funds slopes downward and to the right; this tells us, logically enough, that more loanable funds are demanded at a lower rate of interest than at a higher rate. If you can borrow money at 5 percent interest, you may well borrow considerably more than if you have to pay 15 percent.

Much of the demand for loanable funds comes from firms wanting money for investment in capital: machine tools, buildings, land, and so on. To maximize its profit, a firm borrows money to carry out any investments where the rate of return, adjusted for risk, exceeds the interest rate. Rate of return is the interest rate earned on an investment. For example, suppose an accounting firm calculates it will receive a 20 percent rate of return on an investment in a $15,000 computer system. If the firm does not have the funds to buy the computer, should it borrow them? Yes, provided that the interest rate is less than 20 percent. For then the firm will realize more in its rate of return on the computer than it will give up in interest payments.

The *supply curve* for loanable funds shows the relationship between the quantity of loanable funds supplied and the pure interest rate. The supply comes largely from households and firms that find the available interest rate attractive enough to get them to save. In addition, banks can add to this supply. As we have seen, banks can actually create money when they make loans within limits set by the Fed.

Several factors can influence the demand and supply curves for loanable funds:

1. If people are willing to *postpone consumption* (meaning that they save rather than spend), the supply curve for loanable funds shifts to the right and the interest rate falls.

2. If *new inventions* make investments attractive, the demand curve shifts to the right and the interest rate rises.

3. If the Fed pursues a policy of *easy money,* the supply curve shifts to the right and the interest rate falls in the short run.

4. If the Fed pursues a *tight money* policy, the supply curve shifts to the left and the interest rate rises in the short run.

5. If the *government borrows* heavily, as in wartime, the demand curve shifts to the right and the interest rate rises.

Function of the Interest Rate

Interest rates serve a vital function: They allocate the supply of loanable funds. In so doing, they influence the way in which resources are used.

When funds are scarce, interest rates rise. As a result, only projects with a relatively high rate of return are carried out, for others are not profitable. This generally translates into those projects with the greatest potential and greatest benefit, adjusting for risk. It does not mean that only risk-free projects are undertaken. It does mean, however, that projects promising efficient use of resources are substantially more attractive to investors.

1. *Choosing the most productive projects.* Assuming that firms can borrow all the money they want (at the prevailing interest rate), *they maximize profits by accepting all investment opportunities for which the rate of return exceeds the current interest rate for borrowing.* In determining which projects to invest in, firms use a process called *capital budgeting.* This process involves first estimating the projected rate of return on each potential investment. Then, on the basis of these estimates, the firm accepts all projects for which the projected rate of return exceeds the interest it must pay on money borrowed. What if a firm cannot borrow all it wants? In that case, the firm should accept those investments with the highest rate of return, adjusted for risk. Such estimates are not easy to make, but they provide a sounder basis for managerial decision making than playing hunches.

2. *Capitalization of assets.* Every asset has a market value. How do we determine that value? The market value of any asset depends on the rate of return yielded by that asset and the current interest rate. For example, suppose the current rate of interest is 5 percent. Then, for every $1,000 you invest, you receive a return of

$50. Now suppose you have a chance to purchase a piece of equipment (say, a copy machine) that yields your firm a net return of $1,000 per year. In other words, your firm's profits go up by $1,000 per year, thanks to your new copy machine. How much is the copy machine worth? This is the same as asking, how much would you have to invest in cash to get a comparable $1,000 return? At a 5 percent interest rate, we can conclude that

$$\$1{,}000 = 0.05x,$$

where x = the amount of the investment you would need to realize a return of $1,000 at a 5 percent interest rate. Dividing both sides by 5 percent, we get

$$\$1{,}000/0.05 = x,$$

or

$$x = \$20{,}000.$$

To receive interest of $1,000, you need to invest $20,000. Thus, the machine that yields you a rate of return equal to $1,000 has a market value of $20,000, the equivalent of the required investment. The simple formula for capitalizing an asset (determining its worth) is

$$\$x/r,$$

where x equals the permanent return on the asset and r equals the current interest rate on investments. Interestingly, *as the interest rate declines, the present value of assets goes up*. Why? Because, to earn the same return at lower interest, a greater investment must be made. If the current interest rate is 2 percent instead of 5 percent, the value of the copy machine is

$$\$1{,}000/0.02 = \$50{,}000.$$

Knowing this relationship helps us understand why, in securities markets, *bond prices fall when interest rates rise and rise when interest rates* fall.

Present Value of Future Income

A dollar now is worth more than a dollar later. This seems obvious enough, but in economic terms, what implications does it have for the way we use our money? Suppose you have a rich uncle willing to give you $20,000 in cash. Would you rather take it today or two years from now? Quite aside from the fact that you might be eager to get hold of the money so that you could do what you wanted with it, you would certainly be ahead financially to take the money today. By how much? Again, the answer depends on the interest rates. Keep in mind that no one can say precisely what the value of money will be two years from now; that is, you can only guess to what extent inflation may erode the real purchasing power of money. Assuming the interest rate remains constant, you can be certain that you will lose at least a minimal amount equivalent to that interest rate by delaying your investment.

For example, if the current interest rate is 5 percent, a dollar now is worth $1.05 a year from now and $(1.05)^2$ two years from now. This is assuming that you reinvest the full $1.05 for the second year.

If you do not even receive your money for two years, however, you are delaying this investment. So a dollar you do not receive until two years from now is worth something less than a dollar to you now: It is worth a dollar minus whatever you lose by not investing it. Or, to put it another way, the value of each dollar is the ratio of that dollar to what the value would have been at the current interest rate if the dollar had been invested. Economists use this formula:

A dollar received now is worth $1/(1 + r)^2$ dollars two years from now,

where r = the interest rate.

For our example, the present value of the $20,000 from rich Uncle Fred, if Fred does not give you the money for two years, is

$$\$20,000/(1.05)^2, \quad \text{or} \quad \$20,000/1.1025 = \$18,140.59.$$

This is another way of saying that, if Uncle Fred wanted you to have $20,000 two years from now, considering the current interest rate of 5 percent, he would need to give you $18,140.59 *right now*. This $18,000 plus is the *present value* of the future $20,000.

Nature and Significance of Rent

This chapter deals with three forms of *property income:* interest, rent, and profit. Consider rent for a moment.

To understand the nature of rent, you must realize that economists define both *land* and *rent* somewhat differently from the way to which most of us are probably accustomed. To the economist, *land is any input that is fixed in supply, its limits established by nature.* Land is something that cannot be produced; its quantity is fixed by nature. Even though "rent" is paid on apartments, offices, houses, and cars, these actually fall under the category of capital, not land; their quantity is not fixed. Since apartments, offices, and houses must sit on land, some of the payment we, by convention, call *rent* coincides with what economists define *rent* to be, but the biggest part of these payments are for services the improvements on the land provide.

Income realized from land or from a fixed input is defined as *rent*. Increases and decreases in rent have no affect on the supply since it is fixed. In other words, the supply curve for land is a vertical line, and the price is determined solely by fluctuations in the demand curve. It is important to distinguish between rent and other forms of income because, as noted, fluctuations in rent do not affect the supply. Even if the government imposes a tax on rents, the supply of land to the economy remains the same. This would not be true with taxes on other forms of income; such taxes could greatly affect supply.

Henry George (1839–1897) argued that rents should be taxed away by the government. He believed that landowners received income that was not earned through productive contributions to society. Critics rejoined that land could be improved, providing a worthwhile contribution. Further, they said, many types of income could be unearned, not just land rents. It was unrealistic, they added, to suppose that a tax on rents would be sufficient to raise needed government revenues. Despite these criticisms, George's single-tax movement gained some supporters during the last decades of the nineteenth century and continues to surface occasionally.

Profits

Accountants say that profit is the money a firm's owner has left from total revenue after paying wages, interest, and rent and after allowing for the depreciation of buildings and equipment. The economist takes the position that normal profit must be calculated by also deducting the opportunity costs of the labor, capital, and land contributed by the firm's owner. The economist's view helps explain difference among firms' profit rates, since some owners provide more innovative or efficient management, so that some portion of their "profits" might be viewed as higher corporate salaries to themselves, even though they do not pay themselves directly in this fashion.

Why Do Profits Exist?

Three factors are particularly important: innovation, uncertainty, and monopoly power. We look at each briefly.

Innovations are new products or processes with the potential to increase profits. They are sometimes backed by their inventors, but often by other persons who have the vision and daring to take a risk. According to economists like the late Joseph Schumpeter of Harvard, *profits are the rewards earned by innovators*. Such profits decline with time, of course, as technology spreads throughout an industry or as one innovation is replaced by another. Still, profits from innovations continue to be made.

Backing an innovation requires risk. There are no guarantees that a new investment will in fact be profitable. Most investors therefore avoid risk to the extent possible; therefore, encouraging innovation requires the promise of higher profits. According to Frank Knight of the University of Chicago, *all economic profit is due to uncertainty. And profit is the reward for bearing risk.*

Under perfect competition, there is a tendency in the long run for economic profits to disappear. This is not so under monopoly or oligopoly. For one thing, entry into the market is difficult, not easy as under perfect competition. Thus, competitors cannot readily step in to assume a share of the profits. Moreover, monopoly profits tend to result from contrived scarcities. That is, a monopoly can keep the available supply limited to the extent it wishes, ensuring that demand is always relatively high and profits high.

Functions of Profits

Once we recognize the risks taken by innovators, we can see that profits are not equivalent to receiving "something for nothing." All the same, many people remain somewhat suspicious of profits, believing that they are not always earned, or at least not earned by those who receive them. Karl Marx looked on profits as surplus value, a measure and consequence of exploitation of labor by the owners of firms. Profits and losses are important to the allocation of resources within a capitalistic system, however, for several reasons:

1. Profits and losses are signals to indicate where resources are needed and where they are too abundant. When profits exist, resources flow into an industry; when losses occur (as with the agricultural industry during most of the twentieth century), resources leave.

2. Profits provide important incentives for innovation. If profit did not exist, what would be the motive for taking a risk, for trying something that might not work?

3. Profits are society's reward for efficiency. Without profits, firms have little inducement to use resources wisely and well. Profits also allow for expansion and ventures into new, related fields.

EXTENDED LEARNING

This section of the study guide is specifically designed for the two-semester student.

AUDIO

Listen

Listen to the audiotape that accompanies Lesson 23. There is no additional reading assignment for this lesson.

After Listening

Answer the following questions:

1. What is the difference between the accountant's concept of profits and the economist's? What is the social usefulness of profits in an economist's sense?

2. If all other influences are held constant, the amount of money spent on fixed plant and equipment should fall as interest rates increase. But fixed investment seems to increase whenever the interest rate increases. Does this mean that investment is encouraged by higher interest rates?

3. Say a graduate student has two job offers to work as a research assistant and the student likes both jobs equally, but one pays $2,000 a year for two years while the other pays $3,400 in the first year, $500 in the second. Why should the

market rate of interest affect her choice? Which should she choose if the rate of interest is 5 percent, and which if it is 10 percent?

4. "If the seller of a house also provides the financing for the sale, below market financing rates are likely to be capitalized into the selling price of the house." What is meant by that statement?

ADDITIONAL READINGS

Barrett, Nancy. *The Theory of Microeconomic Policy.* Lexington, MA: D. C. Heath & Company, 1974.

> Pages 261–273 provide a clear discussion of investment criteria, in particular the present value rule, and summarize the positions of Böhm-Bawerk, Fischer, and Keynes. Moderately difficult mathematics and graphs.

Douglas, Evan J. *Managerial Economics,* 3d ed. Englewood Cliffs, NJ: Prentice-Hall, 1987.

> Chapter 15, "Capital Budgeting and Investment Decisions," summarizes the various decision rules that can be used in addition to the present value rule for determining how to allocate investment funds. Moderately difficult mathematics, no graphs.

Hertz, David B. "Risk Analysis in Capital Investment." In *Managerial Economics and Operations Research,* 5th ed., edited by Edwin Mansfield, 164–185. New York: W. W. Norton & Company, 1987.

> An excellent discussion of the problem of risk in deciding on the best type of investment in plant and equipment. Technical discussion, moderately difficult mathematics, simple graphs.

Kirzner, Israel M. "The Primary of Entrepreneurial Discovery." In *Prime Mover of Progress.* Lancing, England: Institute for Economic Affairs, 1980.

> Details the value to society of successful entrepreneurship and analyzes the various factors that tend to discourage or encourage the awareness of opportunity and risk taking. No mathematics or graphs.

ANSWER KEY

Video Questions

1. The case of interest rates in Maryland sheds some light on this issue. According to Maryland law prior to the 1970s, interest rates on consumer loans could not exceed the 10 percent level. During the 1970s, as inflation mounted, this ceiling

meant that banks and other lending institutions could not realize a profit. In fact, they were earning less on their loans than they were paying customers for their savings investments. As a result, banks cut back on available money for lending; the supply simply declined. Money, like other commodities, is subject to laws of supply and demand, and those laws, in the case of money, depend heavily on interest rates. In this situation, the quantity demanded greatly exceeded the quantity supplied at 10 percent interest. The result was a money shortage within the state. Borrowers were forced to go elsewhere, and housing starts were all but preempted. The construction industry was hurt badly. A few consumers were able to borrow at very appealing rates; but others could not secure loans at all, and the whole economy suffered a slowdown as a result. When the usury laws were relaxed and interest rates were allowed to climb, banks made more money available and consumers were granted loans. True, those consumers now had to pay a higher interest rate. But the more significant point here is that the money supply was put in motion again in the state of Maryland, and its economy was allowed to grow again. Low interest rates can benefit consumers only if those rates are sufficiently high to encourage lenders to make money available in the first place.

2. Put in simplest terms, the profitability of any investment depends on a comparison between the expected rate of return on the investment versus the interest charged against the loan required to make the investment. If the current interest rate is higher than the expected rate of return, the investment is not profitable. If it is lower, the investment is profitable. Of course, an entrepreneur must also consider the long-term value of an investment. Take a piece of equipment. Will it last a long time? Will it still be state of the art five years from now or will it need to be replaced long before then? Will one investment require others? For example, will a new piece of equipment require new employees with special training before full use can be made of that equipment? These and similar questions must also be answered. But the key point to remember here is that, once again, interest rates play an important role in determining whether to make a capital investment. The bottom line is that the answer depends on the relative comparison of the interest rate to the expected rate of return.

3. The economist points out that, while profits realized through business adventures are often extremely large, such profits tend to be short lived. They derive from innovation: a combination of cleverness, daring, and creativity. To progress effectively—not only to grow, but to become ever more efficient—an economy must have some way of rewarding such innovation. Profits provide incentive. Each new idea entails some risk. Most new businesses started each year within the United States fail, so there is little reason to suppose at the outset that any new idea will reap large profits. Given that risk, some reward must be given those who persevere against the odds. Then too, within a very short period, most entrepreneurs are faced with stiff competition from those who borrow, refine, or improve their original ideas. As competition increases, profits fall. Therefore, an initial windfall granted to the originator of an idea seems only fair. From the economist's viewpoint, the answer is clear: Windfall profits are fair and just, because without them incentive to progress is lost.

Multiple Choice

1. b Text, 535.
2. a Text, 535.
3. a Text, 535–536.
4. d Text, 536.
5. c Text, 536–537.
6. d Text, 537–538.
7. a Text, 538–539.
8. c Text, 538, Case Study 23.1.
9. c Text, 541.
10. a Text, 541.

True-False

1. False Text, 538–539.
2. True Text, 539.
3. False Text, 536.
4. False Text, 537, 541.
5. True Text, 537–538.
6. True Text, 540–541.
7. True Text, 537.
8. False Text, 537, 541.
9. True Text, 548.
10. True Text, 547.

Discussion Questions

1. In comparing the value of the lifetime income of a Ph.D. in electrical engineering to that of a B.A. (or B.S.) in electrical engineering, Richard Freeman finds a difference of $22,000. Thus, over the life of the engineer, he can expect to earn in present value terms $22,000 more if he has a Ph.D. than he would if he had a B.A. (or B.S.). However, to have a Ph.D., the individual must pay the cost of going to graduate school (the cost of the income forgone while in graduate school has already been included in Freeman's calculation). If the present value cost of going to graduate school is less than $22,000 the individual will find it financially beneficial to attend graduate school. This question overlooks the psychic income the individual receives from the two choices, and it is conceivable that the individual receives great enough psychic income from the Ph.D. to make it worthwhile to earn it even if he does not benefit financially.

2. No, this quote overlooks the fact that it is the resources money commands that provide the return interest represents. If I loan out money, I lose the command of resources that money represents for the time period of the loan. The interest I receive is my compensation for the loss of the use of my money during the time period of the loan.

3. Rent in this chapter refers to the payment an owner of a fixed input receives. The rent is compensation for giving up the use of the resource, and the price or rent should reflect the opportunity cost of the resource to the society.

4. A tax on economic rent as defined in the chapter does not affect the supply of resources in the economy because economic rent is defined as the payment received by resources that are fixed in supply.

5. Schumpeter views profits as the rewards earned by innovators. As such, profits acted as an incentive for innovation. Knight, on the other hand, views profits as the reward for bearing risk. Knight views innovation as inherently risky and sees innovation occurring only if there is the promise of higher profits as a reward for the risk investors face. Schumpeter did not consider the riskiness of innovation, whereas Knight did.

Problem Set

1. Using Table 23.1 in the text, we see that it is worth 0.839 × $10,000, or $8,390. If you use the formula $10,000/(1 + 0.06)³, your answer is $8,396.10.

2. a. 8 percent.
   b. No. Because you can get 8 percent if you lend your money elsewhere.

3. No.

4. All shown in the table.

5. a. If firm X buys machine A rather than machine B, it invests an additional $5,000 now to reduce annual maintenance costs by $600. Therefore, the rate of return on the extra $5,000 investment is $600/$5,000, or 12 percent. Since the interest rate is 5 percent, firm X should make this extra investment; it should buy machine A.
   b. 12 percent. See part a.

Audio/Text Questions

1. Economists use the term *profit* for that part of revenue left over after the direct costs of doing business (wages, interest, leases, etc.) *and* the indirect costs (the opportunity costs of the labor, capital, and land contributed by the owner) have been deducted. Accountants deduct only the direct costs. Profits are useful to society because they signal how resources should be reallocated, they encourage innovation and risk taking, and they promote efficient production methods.

2. Investment expenditures are directly related to the expected stream of returns from a project and inversely related to the interest rate. Normally, interest rates increase when the economy is growing, and at such times the firm's expectations of returns are also going up. If the expectations of returns increase in such a way that the dampening effect of higher interest rates is offset, then investment expenditures increase even though interest rates are increasing.

3. The higher is the interest rate, the more profitable it is for the student to choose the second job, even though the simple sum of the salaries for the two years is less. At a 5 percent interest rate, the present value of the first job is greater; at 10 percent, the present value of the second is greater.

4. If a sale is financed by the seller, the seller gets the same return if he sells at a high price with a low rate of interest on the financing or at a low price with a high rate of interest. If a seller provides a low (below market) rate of interest, he may raise the selling price; this makes up for the low interest rate. The difference between this selling price and what the selling price would have been at the market rate of financing is referred to as *capitalizing the difference* between the interest rates.

LESSON 24. REDUCING POVERTY: WHAT HAVE WE DONE?

INTRODUCTION

Most of us would like to make more money than we do. It is a rare family indeed that does not view increased family income as the vital means to some desired material end: a new house, new car, education, comfortable retirement, travel and recreation—whatever. For some 35 million Americans, however, issues of income are related less to desires for future luxuries than to the necessities of today. These are the Americans who, by the Social Security Administration's definition, live in poverty. By 2003 figures, an urban family of four, with income below $18,400 per year, was classified as poor.

According to statistics for average per-capita incomes worldwide, the United States's poor appear to be rather well off. In India, Indonesia, El Salvador, and much of Africa and Asia, for example, annual per-capita income may average under $2,500. Does this mean we have no real poverty problem here in the United States? Far from it. Some of the United States's poor suffer from malnutrition. Their children lack access to the educational opportunities that might help them escape the cycle of poverty, which is, in many ways, self-perpetuating. And regardless of how one views the relative quality of life experienced by the United States's poor, the fact remains that great income inequality exists in the United States. It has diminished somewhat since the early years of the twentieth century, but the gap between the lifestyles of the rich and poor remains.

Is it realistic to suppose that we can eliminate poverty in the United States? This question has been the center of numerous heated political debates, and a number of public programs have attempted to deal with the problems of poverty. We consider several real and proposed programs and their relative effectiveness. In addition, we look at some of the causes of poverty, including discrimination.

What You Will Need to Learn

By the end of Lesson 24, you should be prepared to

1. Give several potential reasons for income inequality.

2. Explain what is meant by the *trade-off* between income equality and efficiency.

3. Explain how poverty is defined according to the Social Security Administration.

4. Describe our Social Security system and the controversies surrounding it.

5. Describe the characteristics and criticisms of antipoverty programs in the United States, focusing particularly on the Food Stamp program, and Aid to Families with Dependent Children.

6. Discuss arguments for and against the proposed negative income tax program.

7. Explain how economists approach the problem of discrimination by race and sex.

KEY TERMS

income inequality
progressive tax
regressive tax
poverty
structural unemployment
Medicare
unemployment insurance
income distribution
Social Security Act
welfare programs
negative income tax

discrimination
Equal Pay Act of 1963
Title VII of the Civil
   Rights Act of 1964
old age insurance
Medicaid
food stamps
Aid to Families with
   Dependent Children
breakeven income

VIDEO

Watch

Economics U$A Program 24, "Reducing Poverty: What Have We Done?"

Illustrative Events

The birth of Social Security in the midst of the Great Depression; with economist Wilbur Cohen, member of the original Social Security Creation Task Force.

President Nixon's historic effort to consolidate social welfare programs into the Family Assistance Plan, and why neither liberals nor conservatives would buy it; featuring Senator Daniel Patrick Moynihan and William F. Buckley, editor of the *National Review*. Richard Gill analyzes income distribution plans.

How LBJ's Job Corps managed to survive the budget cuts of the early 1980s; featuring Sargent Shriver, former director, Office of Economic Opportunity; Walter Williams, professor of economics, George Mason University; and Job Corps graduates.

After Viewing

Answer the following questions:

1. In what important way did President Franklin Roosevelt's vision of the Social Security system differ from how the system now works in practice?

2. What is the central purpose of the Social Security system, and how successful has the program been in achieving that purpose?

3. What major arguments were posed for and against the Family Assistance Plan during the 1960s?

4. From an economist's point of view, what conclusions can we draw about the relative success of the Job Corps program?

Read

Read Chapter 24, "Poverty, Income Inequality, and Discrimination," pages 553–573 in your text. After completing your reading, try the Self-Quiz.

SELF-QUIZ

Multiple Choice

1. Which of the following statements is probably *most* accurate? Income inequality in the United States is

    a. greater today than at any time in our nation's history.
    b. significant, though less a problem here than in many countries.
    c. gradually declining, as it has each year since 1920.
    d. gradually increasing and is a greater problem here than in most other countries.

2. Which of the following is probably the *least important* factor contributing to income inequality?

    a. Differences in abilities and talents
    b. Luck
    c. Government inefficiency
    d. Monopoly power

3. Which of the following is the *best* example of a regressive tax?

    a. Sales tax
    b. Personal income tax
    c. Gift tax
    d. Estate tax

4. Those who *favor* income inequality are likely to argue that it

   a. restricts capital formation to socially optimal levels.
   b. promotes equal educational opportunity.
   c. provides incentives for greater political participation.
   d. provides needed support for the arts and culture.

5. Consider the following statement: "If we reduce inequality, we may well cut society's total output." Most economists today would probably agree that this statement is

   a. a gross exaggeration.
   b. accurate, though no one can say by how much output would be cut.
   c. a real understatement since the decline in output would be catastrophic.
   d. meaningless since output and income inequality are unrelated.

6. Probably the most widely accepted definition of poverty in the United States today is that developed by the Social Security Administration. Its definition is based on

   a. the cost of a minimally nutritious food plan multiplied by three.
   b. the cost of a minimally nutritious food plan plus the cost of minimal housing.
   c. average per-capita income for families at the bottom 10 percent of the income distribution.
   d. average worldwide per-capita income.

7. According to the definition of poverty posed by the Social Security Administration (question 6), in 2003, how much income would an urban family of four have to have to make it over the poverty line?

   a. $7,000
   b. $10,000
   c. $14,000
   d. $18,000

8. *Most* economists today would probably agree that the primary reasons for poverty are

   a. often beyond the control of poor families.
   b. generally the result of individual differences no one can change.
   c. usually avoidable, given sufficient incentive to work.
   d. nearly all related to inevitable economic and technological expansion.

9. Most observers today would probably agree that social insurance programs, such as Social Security, are

   a. a highly effective means of decreasing poverty at relatively low costs.
   b. remarkably efficient though somewhat costly.
   c. generally worthless and a waste of time and money.
   d. adequate but neither as efficient nor cost effective as one would wish.

10. One criticism of social insurance programs is that they provide no assistance whatever to

   a. women.
   b. children.
   c. the unemployed.
   d. the working poor.

True-False

_____ 1. When people speak of *welfare* programs, they generally refer to programs that provide cash to recipients.

_____ 2. Changes to welfare in 1996 increased federal funding for the food stamp program and Aid to Families with Dependent Children program that were enacted under the Reagan administration.

_____ 3. Under a negative income tax program, families at the breakeven income level would neither pay any tax nor receive any payment from the government.

_____ 4. One effect of racial discrimination is to lower the nation's total output.

_____ 5. There is virtually no evidence to suggest any decline in the effects of racial discrimination on employment practices over the past 20 years.

_____ 6. On the basis of current statistics, we can pretty well conclude that the war on poverty has been won.

_____ 7. Twenty percent of all households in the United States earned less than $17,970 in 2001.

_____ 8. To finance old-age insurance, payroll taxes must be paid by each worker and her or his employer.

_____ 9. A main opposing argument to the negative tax plan is that it generally provides recipients less incentive to work than current social welfare programs.

_____ 10. Suppose the government gave all families of four persons $4,000 per year and then imposed a tax of 25 percent on earned income. If a family's earned income were less than $16,000 per year, its disposable income would be greater than its earned income.

Discussion Questions

1. Suppose that over the next generation or so we have more older people and fewer younger people. How will this alter the Social Security program, both from the cost and benefit sides?

2. What are some salient characteristics of poor families in the United States? What is meant by a negative income tax? Do you favor or oppose such a scheme?

3. Should the prize money at professional tennis tournaments be distributed equally between men and women players? Why might the men be paid more? When should the women be paid more?

Problem Set

1. Suppose that the demand and supply curves for unskilled labor in a perfectly competitive labor market in the land of Canam are as follows:

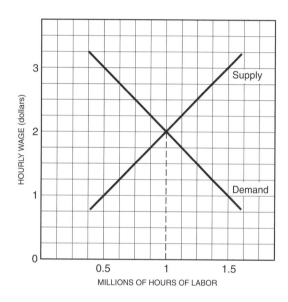

   a. If a minimum wage of $2.50 per hour is established, what is the effect on the total employment of unskilled labor?
   b. What is the effect on the total income received by unskilled workers?

2. Suppose that the amount of tax paid by a person with income equal to X is given by the formula

$$T = 0.3X,$$

   where T is the amount of the tax. Is this progressive or regressive? Why?

3. Nation Z changes its tax system. After the change, the first $5,000 of a person's income is exempted and half of the rest is taxed away. Before the change, the first $2,500 of a person's income was exempted, and a third of the rest was taxed away. John Jameson worked 2,000 hours at a wage rate of $5 per hour before the change.

   a. If he continues to work as much as before the tax change, will his after-tax income change?

b. Assuming that he can vary the number of hours he worked, is an extra hour of leisure worth more or less than $3.35 to him before the change in the tax system? Why or why not?

4. Use this graph to answer the questions about the negative income tax.

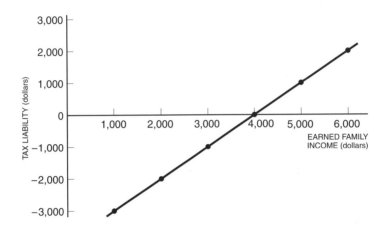

a. What is the breakeven income with this negative income tax?
b. What is the effective tax rate if your income is $5,000?
c. What is the marginal tax rate on the last $1,000 earned if your income is $5,000?
d. How much does a family earning $2,500 receive from the government under this program?

LESSON REVIEW

If you had any difficulty with the Self-Quiz or would like additional assistance, read the following lesson review. It should reinforce and help you understand the content presented in this lesson.

The Nature of Inequality

According to statistics for 2001, about one-fifth of U.S. households at that time were receiving incomes of less than $17,970, while about one-fifth were receiving incomes of $83,500 or more. Income inequality declined substantially between 1920 and the end of World War II, but it has decreased very little since. In fact, by some measures, it increased during the 1980s and 1990s. Why does such inequality exist?

There are several reasons. For one thing, some people possess greater abilities than others. Some receive more training or education; such people must receive greater pay as a result of that training and education, or they would have little incentive to make the sacrifices necessary to acquire it. Another reason for the differences is that some people own large amounts of property. Still others have managed to attain monopoly power. And some have simply been blessed with very good luck.

Effects of the Tax Structure on Income Inequality

A tax is considered *progressive* if the rich pay a higher proportion of their income for the tax than the poor; that is, if the tax rate increases as income level goes up. It is considered *regressive* if the rich pay a smaller proportion of their income for the tax than the poor; that is, if the tax rate is higher for persons at lower income levels. Persons who favor redistribution of income to reduce inequalities tend to favor progressive taxes. Examples of progressive taxes are

- Personal income tax
- Inheritance tax
- Estate tax
- Gift tax

Both estate taxes and personal income taxes can be reduced, of course, through various legal loopholes, so that neither is as progressive as advocates of income equality would wish.

Examples of regressive taxes include

- General sales tax
- Social Security tax

It is hard to say whether the corporate income tax is progressive or regressive, because while the taxes come out of earnings that might otherwise be paid to stockholders, it is also possible that the corporation raises prices, passing on the cost of the tax to the consumer.

Pros and Cons of Income Inequality

Those who favor greater income equality make four main arguments:

1. *Inequality of income lessens total consumer satisfaction.* According to this argument, an extra dollar given to a poor man gives him more extra satisfaction than the loss of that dollar takes away from a rich man. This argument assumes that the rich man and poor man have the same capacity to gain enjoyment from their income; economists deny that consumer satisfaction can be quantified in this manner.

2. *Income inequality is likely to result in unequal educational opportunities for young people.* Children of the poor may be denied an education simply because they cannot afford it. Many of these children are gifted and could make a considerable contribution to society if given the opportunity. Thus, our failure to provide them an education suited to their talents is a great waste of resources.

3. *Income inequality may lead to political inequality.* The rich may have far more political clout and may well have access to better legal counsel.
4. *People who could not predict their position in a society would opt for equality.* That is to say, if people were framing a constitution for a society and could not know in advance what sort of social or economic standing they might inherit, they would want everyone to enjoy equal income. Opponents of this view suggest that this theory has little appeal to persons willing to take a risk, for such persons would prefer to take a chance on receiving a high income rather than settle for a sure thing if that meant accepting a low income.

People who favor income inequality present these four arguments:

1. *Income inequality gives people an incentive to work and create.* If everyone received the same income, what incentive would there be to work harder or try something new? Of course, this argument overlooks the fact that many workers receive satisfaction not just from income but also from doing a job well. But one must counter with another question: At what point do they derive sufficient satisfaction from a job done well to accept lower pay?
2. *Income inequality permits greater savings and greater capital formation.* This argument sounds reasonable enough, but countries with greater inequality of income than the United States have not necessarily had high investment rates.
3. *The rich tend to be patrons of new and high-quality products that benefit society.* There may be social advantages in having a class of people who support the arts and can afford the risks essential in supporting technological advances.
4. *Even if everyone receives the same income, the poor would not be helped very much because there are so many poor and so few very rich.*

Trade-off between Equality and Efficiency

Even if you are an advocate of income equality, it is important to recognize that any measures taken to reduce inequality are also likely to reduce efficiency. If we reduce inequality, we reduce national output. This is so because we would, in effect, remove much of the incentive for achievement. Some egalitarians deny that the effect would be more than minimal (and some go so far as to say there would be no effect whatever), while those who favor income inequality counter that the impact on national output would be extreme. Most economists hold that the truth lies somewhere between these polar positions.

Poverty

In part, poverty is relative. That is to say, we tend to measure it as a function of how one person's income stacks up against another's. What some of us in the United States might regard as poverty, therefore, may seem a relatively high standard of living to persons in parts of Asia and Africa.

Further, we must take care how we define *poverty*. If we say that the poor are "the bottom 10 percent of the income distribution," then by definition we can never wipe out poverty because regardless of how high incomes go, there will also be a bottom 10 percent.

Perhaps the most widely accepted definition of poverty in the United States today is that developed by the Social Security Administration. They determined the cost of a minimal nutritionally sound food plan (as defined by the Department of Agriculture), then multiplied that figure by three, since statistics show that low-income families tend to spend about a third of their earnings on food. Based on these figures, the cutoff in 2003 for an urban family of four was $18,400.

The incidence of poverty in the United States declined after 1947, as one would expect with increases in per-capita income. In 1947, about 30 percent of the U.S. population could be defined as living in poverty; by 1992, that figure had shrunk to about 14 percent. In 2001, 12 percent were still living in poverty. Many observers feel more could and should be done.

Members of all demographic groups live in poverty. Yet, families with certain characteristics are more likely to be poor than others. For example, very large families (seven persons or more) are more likely to be poor. Nonwhite families are also more likely to be poor than white families. And families headed by women are more likely to be poor than families headed by men.

The reasons for poverty are numerous, and many are beyond the control of the poor families. For example, about a third of poor adults have experienced disability or the death of the family breadwinner or family dissolution in some form. Changes in technology sometimes force people temporarily or permanently out of work. Industries may decline as natural resources diminish. Old age can be a factor too; savings sometimes are insufficient to carry people through retirement, particularly if illness occurs, as it does with most older people. Discrimination is a major factor as well; we discuss this further in a later section. Available evidence suggests that poverty tends to be self-perpetuating. That is, children of poor parents are likely themselves to be poor. And in large part, this is due to diminished educational opportunities coupled with a poverty subculture that sustains values which make escape from poverty difficult.

Social Insurance

Until about 70 years ago, the federal government played little or no role in helping the poor. Some private charity was available, but self-reliance was stressed. The poor were expected to fend for themselves.

In 1935, under the Roosevelt administration, the Social Security Act was passed, providing compulsory old-age insurance for workers and the self-employed, as well as unemployment insurance. Every wage earner under Social Security pays a tax; in 2004, this tax amounted to 7.65 percent of the first $87,900 of annual earnings. The employer must match this amount.

Controversies over Social Security

The Social Security program has sparked a number of controversies.

1. *The Social Security tax is regressive.* Those with annual earnings over $87,900 pay a smaller portion of their income in Social Security taxes than those with lower incomes.

2. *Social Security is not an ordinary insurance system.* That is, there is no requirement that the program have sufficient assets to back all its benefits. It is essentially a program for transferring income from the working young and the middle-aged to the retired old. How much will people starting work in the early 2000s receive in benefits? Only time will tell.

3. *Social Security is mandatory for private sector employees.* Some critics charge that it should not be so, that such a system interferes with individual freedom. Supporters of the system argue that under a voluntary Social Security program, few workers would provide adequately for their old age.

4. *Social Security may impede savings and capital formation.* Some economists believe Americans may save less than they otherwise would because they depend on Social Security to take care of them in old age.

Antipoverty Programs

Social insurance programs are generally regarded as useful but inadequate. To supplement these programs, the government has started numerous additional programs specifically designed to help the poor. Some of these programs provide assistance in the form of goods and services; the Food Stamp program is an example. In 1996, it was replaced by the Temporary Assistance for Needy Families program.

In the years leading up to 1996, antipoverty programs had been severely criticized. The cost of such programs had risen enormously, and many experts regarded them as administratively and operationally inefficient. In addition, critics charged that such programs required unnecessary and intrusive meddling into recipients' lives. As an alternative, two leading economists proposed the *negative income tax.*

The negative income tax would have worked this way. Families with incomes below a certain level would receive payment *from* the government rather than paying income tax. Those with incomes above the breakeven level would pay taxes as usual. And those right at the breakeven point would neither pay nor receive payment. This program offered several potential advantages.

1. It would have given people on welfare more incentive to work because they could keep more of their income than under the old system.

2. It would have required no intrusion into recipients' personal lives, and there would have been no penalty if a husband remained with his family (some old welfare programs imposed such a penalty).

3. It might have cost less to administer the negative tax program than the old welfare programs.

Despite these advantages, many persons remained antagonistic to the idea of transferring large portions of income from rich to poor. Given a cutoff of $6,000 (a level below which families would receive income rather than pay tax), about $25 billion would have been transferred to those below the breakeven level. Adjusted for inflation using the CPI, $6,000 represents the same purchasing power in 1970 as around $27,000 does in 2000. And $25 billion in 1970 is about the same as $113 billion in 2000.

Early, limited experiments with the negative income tax suggest that it might have in fact encouraged people to work less, but the results were far from conclusive. In any case, a scaled-down version of the negative income tax was signed into law in 1975. It is called the Earned Income Tax Credit (EITC). It cost $0.808 billion in 1976. The EITC was substantially expanded in 1986, 1990, and 1993. In 2003, it cost $36 billion, which is still significantly less than the inflation-adjusted cost of the 1970 negative income tax proposal. That is mainly because the negative income tax was proposed to replace all welfare programs from Aid to Families with Dependent Children to food stamps whereas EITC was added to them.

Problems of Discrimination

Poverty and discrimination are closely interrelated. And despite evidence of recent declines in discrimination, the fact is that racial discrimination in particular continues to have a large and debilitating effect on per-capita income for nonwhites and on national output as well.

The average income of nonwhites is less than two-thirds that of whites. About one-fourth of the nonwhite population lives below the poverty line (compared to about one-twelfth of the white population). And a smaller percentage of nonwhites than whites are college graduates.

As a result of racial discrimination, nonwhite labor is not allowed to compete with white labor. This is significant because it results in *two different labor markets, one for whites and one for nonwhites*. If this were not the case (that is, if whites and nonwhites competed in one labor market), the wage loss for whites would be very slight in comparison to the wage gain for nonwhites, and the nation's total output would increase substantially because nonwhite labor would be used more productively. As it is, talented nonwhites may be unemployed or underemployed.

Even more widespread than racial discrimination is discrimination against women. Holding age and education constant, women earn less than men. Part of this difference is because women work shorter hours and have less job experience (on the average) than men. However, even adjusting for factors like education and work experience, the difference between earnings remains at about 20 percent.

The government has taken some steps to discourage discrimination toward women. The Equal Pay Act of 1963 requires employers to pay men and women equally for the same work; and Title VII of the Civil Rights Act of 1964 bars discrimination in hiring, firing, and other aspects of employment. Increasingly, women are being appointed to high-ranking jobs in government and the private sector. But these steps, while important, have not eliminated sex-based discrimination, and much remains to be done.

EXTENDED LEARNING

This section of the study guide is specifically designed for the two-semester student.

AUDIO

Listen

Listen to the audiotape that accompanies Lesson 24. There is no additional reading assignment for this lesson.

After Listening

Answer to the following questions:

1. "Since one cannot make interpersonal comparisons of utility (or satisfaction), there is no way to tell whether progressive taxes are really to be preferred over regressive ones." Comment and evaluate.

2. Suppose that the amount paid for a particular tax is related to the income (both in dollars) of the taxpayer in the following way:

Income	Tax
1,000	50
10,000	600
100,000	7,000

   Is this tax progressive or regressive?

3. How has the federal government defined the poverty level? Approximately what percentage of the population is below the poverty level?

4. Is a sales tax progressive or regressive? Why? Is the federal personal income tax progressive or regressive? Why?

ADDITIONAL READINGS

Benenson, Robert. "Federal Jobs Programs." In *America's Economy*, edited by Hoyt Gimlin, 109–132. Washington, DC: Congressional Quarterly, 1983.

> Provides a history of government programs to create jobs, evaluating the effectiveness of the CCC, PWA, and WPA of the 1930s; the recent EDA and CETA

programs; and the programs debated in Congress during the Reagan administration. No mathematics or graphs.

Blinder, Alan. "The Level and Distribution of Economic Well-Being." In *The American Economy in Transition*, edited by Martin Feldstein, 415–479. Chicago: University of Chicago Press, 1980.

> Discusses the problems of measuring equality, Lorenz curves, changes in income and the patterns of consumption, the incidence and causes of poverty, and trends in nonincome aspects of economic welfare for the postwar period. No mathematics, simple graphs.

Danziger, Sheldon, Robert Haveman, and Robert Plotnik. "How Income Transfer Programs Affect Work, Savings, and Income Distribution: A Critical Review." *Journal of Economic Literature* (September 1981).

> Provides an excellent overview of the magnitude of transfer programs, the theoretical issues, and the results of empirical studies of the economic affects of transfer programs. Technical, but no mathematics or graphs.

Okun, Arthur M. *Equality and Efficiency: The Big Tradeoff.* Washington, DC: Brookings Institution, 1975.

> States the problems involved in promoting both a better income distribution and economic growth. The primary points are covered on pages 32–51, 61–75, and 88–106. No mathematics or graphs.

Schultz, George P., and Kenneth W. Dam. *Economic Policy beyond the Headlines.* New York: W. W. Norton & Company, 1977.

> The Nixon administration's attempt to substitute the Family Assistance Plan, which was essentially a negative income tax concept, for a variety of income security and welfare programs is detailed in Chapter 5. The economic rationales for a negative income tax are discussed. No mathematics or graphs.

ANSWER KEY

Video Questions

1. Franklin Roosevelt envisioned Social Security as an insurance program. A worker would pay into the program, her or his payments would accumulate interest as part of a large fund, and the resulting benefits would finance that worker's retirement. In practice, however, the notion of a general fund is largely a myth because payments are transferred immediately to workers who are already retired. Economists regard Social Security as a classic case of a transfer program: Money earned by one worker—and supplemented by that worker's employer—is transferred immediately in the form of Social Security benefits to another worker. The system is based on trust, really. Each generation must feel confident that the succeeding generation will work to cover their

benefits in the same fashion. Roosevelt's initial vision of an insurance program with mandatory participation by employee and employer was designed to protect the program in years to come. Although Social Security may well qualify for classification as a classic transfer program, the fact that it affects virtually everyone makes it far less vulnerable to budgetary cutbacks or elimination.

2. Social Security pays benefits to persons of all ages for a number of different reasons, but its primary purpose has been to provide for the needs of the elderly. Before Social Security, the elderly had nowhere to turn at all. Their needs had to be met by families who often did not have the necessary means of support. Job programs did little to help those who were too old or too sick to work. And most economists would agree that the program has been extremely successful in achieving this objective. Although it can easily be argued that Social Security benefits are insufficient to pay all necessary expenses, they at least offer a consistent and dependable means of easing a serious social and moral problem: poverty among the elderly.

3. The Family Assistance Plan (FAP) was similar in theory to a negative income tax; that is, those who made sufficient income would pay taxes as usual, while those below the poverty line would receive income. The FAP was to replace a host of other welfare programs, simplifying the system and eliminating much bureaucracy. This was a primary argument in its favor. On the other side of this coin were the protests of those welfare program employees who stood to lose their means of livelihood under the new simplified system. Special interest groups from education, medicine, and other fields lobbied heavily to uphold the old, more complex welfare system. Conservatives did not look favorably on the FAP unless it could be a replacement program; they did want to simply add one more payment plan to the pot. Liberals, by contrast, felt that welfare recipients would not receive sufficient income under the FAP, that they might even lose benefits. It was further argued that the FAP treats only the symptoms of poverty but does not get at the causes: lack of training, lack of education, and unemployability. This argument was voiced so strongly in fact that it provided much impetus for the Job Corps (and similar programs) that soon followed.

4. The relative success of the Job Corps program is not easily evaluated, and there is little agreement on this issue among politicians. On the positive side, approximately 90 percent of those who completed the program did eventually find work. Program graduates themselves often are strong advocates, recounting the personal benefits they gained through participation. On the other hand, the training is expensive. Although there is great disagreement about the figures (estimates range from $6,000 to $15,000 per participant), there can be no question that educating and training workers takes time and is therefore costly. The counterargument to the high-cost protest is, of course, that training, however expensive, is inevitably less costly than such alternatives as keeping an individual on welfare or in prison. Certainly the Job Corps, like Social Security, is an example of a transfer program. Those who are working are paying to support those who are not; the difference here is that the payments go toward making those who are not working more eligible to work. This approach is more palatable to many who

dislike the transfer program concept overall, although results of some cost-benefit analyses continue to make many a lukewarm supporter uneasy. Critics also point to the fact that, despite individual success stories, teenage unemployment overall has not declined. Supporters counter that more progress could be made if the program were only bigger. Regardless, the Job Corps has been given a renewed chance to prove itself, and more thorough analyses over the next several years may provide us a better answer to the questions regarding its success.

Multiple Choice

1. b Text, 553–554.
2. c Text, 555.
3. a Text, 556.
4. d Text, 557–558.
5. b Text, 558–559.
6. a Text, 560.
7. d Text, 560.
8. a Text, 561.
9. d Text, 562–563.
10. d Text, 565–566.

True-False

1. True   Text, 566.
2. False Text, 566.
3. True   Text, 566–567.
4. True   Text, 569.
5. False Text, 569.
6. False Text, 560.
7. True   Text, 554.
8. True   Text, 562.
9. False Text, 565–566.
10. True Answer derived from example.

Discussion Questions

1. As the population ages and there are fewer young people relative to older people, we will find fewer workers supporting more retirees. This may result in greater taxation of the workers or a reduction in the benefits the retired population receives. The cost of providing benefits will increase provided the level of benefit paid out to each individual is not altered. Alternatively, the cost will remain the same or fall only if the level of benefits paid out is diminished from its current levels.

2. Nonwhite families are more likely to be poor than white families, and families headed by women are more likely to be poor than families headed by men.

   A negative income tax is a program where families with incomes below a certain level would receive payment from the government instead of paying income taxes. This program was designed to create greater work incentives for poor families since there was less penalty for working than with the welfare system that existed before 1996. This program was designed not to intrude into the personal lives of recipients and it may have had lower administrative costs.

   Whether one favors the negative income tax is a subjective question. Many economists feel there are strong arguments to support the imposition of such a program.

3. It can be argued that men tennis players should receive higher prize money than women because they may play superior tennis. One can also argue that people

are more interested in men's tennis, there is greater demand for this product, and therefore those providing it can receive greater compensation. In contrast to this position, it can be argued that this is inequitable: Men may be able to beat women due to their greater strength and size and not because of any innate skill difference. Cultural reasons may also exist for the difference in prize money for men and women. As we get more accustomed to women's athletics, we may find it as interesting as men's athletics. Finally, the prize money discrepancy may reflect discrimination against women.

Problem Set

1. a. Employment of unskilled labor declines from 1 million person-hours to 0.75 million person-hours.
   b. Income of unskilled workers declines from $2 million to $1.875 million.

2. It is neither regressive nor progressive, since the amount of the tax is proportional to income.

3. a. No, his after-tax income will be $7,500 in either case.
   b. John Jameson was working 2,000 hours a year before the tax change. If he took an extra hour of leisure, he would have worked 1,999 hours. Since he did not take that extra hour of leisure but instead worked that hour, he earned $3.33 in after-tax income. So the extra hour of leisure must be worth less than $3.33 and hence less than $3.35.

4. a. $4,000.
   b. 20 percent.
   c. 100 percent.
   d. $1,500.

Audio/Text Questions

1. From a strict microeconomic theory point of view, the loss in utility from taking a dollar from a rich person cannot be weighed against the gain in utility of giving the dollar to a poor person. The rich person may suffer a greater loss than the poor person gains, there is no objective "proof" one way or the other. However, common sense implies that, for large differences in wealth or income situations, there is a net gain in society's utility if income is transferred from rich to poor.

2. Because the tax represents a greater percentage of income as income increases (5 percent, 6 percent, and 7 percent for the three income categories shown), the tax is progressive.

3. Three times the cost of a minimally nutritionally sound food plan was the initial definition of the poverty level, although now it is based on the Consumer Price Index, not food prices alone. About 13 to 14 percent of the population is below the poverty level.

4. A sales tax on necessities or a general sales tax on everything tends to be regressive because the poor spend a larger fraction of their income both on necessities and in general than do the rich. A sales tax on luxuries could be progressive. The federal personal income tax is progressive in the way the brackets are designed (higher incomes pay a higher percentage tax rate), but deductions against income permit some people with very large incomes a low tax rate.

LESSON 25. ECONOMIC GROWTH: CAN WE KEEP UP THE PACE?

INTRODUCTION

When Thomas Carlyle referred to economics as the "dismal science," he was not expressing concern over an upcoming midterm exam. He was echoing the grave concern of nineteenth-century economists about a future in which the geometric growth of population would outstrip available resources, and the standard of living, bleak though it might be, would be incapable of improvement.

Today, many of us in the United States enjoy a standard of living that would seem to poke a few holes in the grim predictions of earlier times. What Carlyle and his contemporaries failed to take into account is that, while the amount of resources may remain relatively fixed, accessibility can change dramatically. This change occurs through technology that offers us better means of discovering resources, as well as more efficient methods of processing and conserving them.

Since Carlyle's time, economic growth has been particularly striking in the United States. This does not mean that growth is automatic or that it involves no trade-offs. As we shall see, such growth is not easily achieved.

What You Should Learn

By the end of Lesson 25, you should be prepared to

1. Define the concept of *economic growth* in terms of real gross domestic product and real gross domestic product per capita.
2. Explain why small differences in the annual rate of economic growth can make substantial differences in living standards of the future.
3. Describe the significance of the Club of Rome's *The Limits to Growth* report: How does it relate to earlier economic thinking? What evidence exists to validate or discredit the report?
4. Explain the role of *human capital* in increasing economic growth.
5. Describe the role of technological change in influencing economic growth.
6. Discuss the significance of the gap between actual and potential output.

KEY TERMS

- real gross domestic product
- per capita gross domestic product
- marginal product of labor
- corn laws
- capital formation
- marginal product of capital
- economic growth
- per capita
- law of diminishing marginal returns
- innovators
- full-employment GDP
- capital-output ratio
- human capital
- technology
- innovation
- diffusion
- physical capital
- technological change
- endogenous

VIDEO

Watch

Economics U$A Program 25, "Economic Growth: Can We Keep up the Pace?"

Illustrative Events

The development of Henry Ford's assembly line and its contribution to U.S. economic growth in the twentieth century, with historian Stephen Meyer III.

The notable contribution of the telecommunications revolution to U.S. economic growth and how the government spurred progress, with Michael Urkowitz, executive vice president of Chase Manhattan Bank, and Albert Halprin, chief of the Common Carrier Bureau, FCC.

The dire predictions of the 1972 Club of Rome report, *The Limits to Growth,* and the controversy that still rages over our growth potential, with Jay Forrester, professor of economics at MIT; Henry C. Wallich, member of the Federal Reserve Board of Governors; and Edward E. David Jr., president of Exxon Research and Engineering Company.

After Viewing

Answer the following questions:

1. What strategies did Henry Ford use to increase per-capita productivity among workers?

2. Why are Ford's approaches often hailed by economists and others as the "Ford Revolution"?

3. Describe briefly how the space exploration programs begun in the 1950s and 1960s affect our economic and personal lives today.

4. What does the impact of technology imply about the validity of *The Limits to Growth* thesis posed by the Club of Rome?

Read

Read Chapter 25, "Economic Growth," pages 579–601 in your text. After completing your reading, try the Self-Quiz.

SELF-QUIZ

Multiple Choice

1. Prior to the past century, people throughout the civilized world tended to look on poverty as

   a. inevitable.
   b. acceptable and even sanctifying.
   c. the result of economic mismanagement.
   d. none of the above, since poverty was very uncommon until recent decades.

2. Economic growth can *best* be measured by the rate of growth in

   a. an economy's real GDP or potential GDP.
   b. an economy's real GDP or per-capita GDP.
   c. an economy's per-capita GDP divided by population.
   d. all of the above.

3. Measures of economic growth tend to be rather rough approximations of economic *welfare*. This is so, in part, because such measures

   a. are not statistically verifiable.
   b. are based on growth for the nation as a whole, not on per-capita growth.
   c. place too much emphasis on noneconomic changes in the quality of life.
   d. take no account of how available output is distributed.

4. Which of the following statements is *most* accurate? A small difference in the annual rate of economic growth would probably make

   a. no difference at all in future living standards.
   b. a very small difference in future living standards.
   c. a moderate difference in future living standards.
   d. a substantial difference in future living standards.

5. Prior to 1929, the U.S. government

   a. made very little effort to influence the nation's economic growth rate.
   b. influenced the nation's economic growth rate only through capital investment, not through fiscal or monetary policy.

c. was far more concerned than now in influencing the nation's economic growth.
d. worked hard to influence the nation's growth rates through fiscal policy but paid little heed to capital investment.

6. Generally speaking, today's economists tend to believe that a more rapid rate of growth can be achieved only if consumers are willing to

   a. take responsibility for that growth out of the hands of government.
   b. let the economy take its own course without interference.
   c. sacrifice present comforts in favor of future gains.
   d. accept an ever-declining standard of living.

7. Thomas Malthus believed the world's population would tend to grow

   a. mathematically to a limit imposed by available resources.
   b. geometrically and without limit.
   c. mathematically and without limit.
   d. geometrically to a limit imposed by available resources.

8. Between 1940 and 1970, the populations of developing countries grew very rapidly. In part, this increase was because

   a. the theories of Malthus have relatively little implication in developing countries.
   b. technology has brought a transfer of medical advances from developed to developing countries.
   c. increased food supplies in such countries have permitted population increases above earlier levels.
   d. such countries have made a deliberate effort to increase their labor input through population growth.

9. Which of the following *best* summarizes David Ricardo's view of capital formation? Capital investment

   a. increases economic growth without limit.
   b. increases economic growth only up to a point, following which further investment is unproductive.
   c. brings about a decrease in economic growth.
   d. has little or no effect on economic growth.

10. The economic theories of Malthus and Ricardo were limited by the fact that both tended to overlook the

    a. extent to which land would increase in economic value.
    b. many factors, like disease, that naturally curb population growth.
    c. importance of agriculture, even in an industrial economy.
    d. potential growth of future technological change.

True-False

___ 1. Over the past several decades, we have put so much money into new plant and equipment in the United States that investments are no longer so profitable as they once were.

___ 2. The amount by which current investment can increase next year's productive capacity depends on the capital-output ratio.

___ 3. The amount of its output that a country invests in increasing its capital stock has little or nothing to do with its growth rate, everything else being the same.

___ 4. More capital to work with should mean the ability to produce more, but evidence from six large industrial countries during the 1990s seem to indicate that the rate of output growth is inversely related to the percent of output invested.

___ 5. On the whole, the estimated rate of return on a college education was somewhat smaller in the 1970s than it was in the 1950s.

___ 6. Overall, income tends to rise with a person's education.

___ 7. Compared to investment in plant, equipment, and human capital, the rate of technological change is a relatively minor factor in determining a country's economic growth.

___ 8. Once the diffusion process occurs, profits from any given innovation dwindle substantially.

___ 9. A society that respects private property rights is likely to have a higher rate of economic growth than one that does not respect such rights.

___ 10. If strategically applied, monetary and fiscal policies can bring about virtually unlimited increases in economic growth.

Discussion Questions

1. What factors determine a country's rate of economic growth? How can the aggregate production function be used to show the effects of some of these factors?

2. What are the defects in the rate of economic growth as a measure of the rate of increase of economic welfare?

3. "Anyone who prefers more to less should be in favor of economic growth and should vote for government measures to encourage economic growth." Comment and evaluate.

4. What factors determine the rate of technological change and the rate at which changes in technology are applied and spread?

5. To what extent have Malthus's views concerning the effects of population increase on economic growth been confirmed by history? To what extent have

Ricardo's views concerning the effects of capital formation on economic growth been confirmed by history? What factor did both Malthus and Ricardo underestimate?

Problem Set

1. In a highly industrialized economy, suppose that the relationship between hours of labor and production of steel (all amounts in millions) is as follows:

Hours	Tons of steel
1	2
2	4
3	7
4	9
5	10
6	9

   a. At what point does the marginal product of labor decline? At what point does the average product of labor decline?
   b. Suppose that an advance in technology allows this economy to obtain twice as many tons of steel (as shown) for each number of hours of labor. Under these conditions, what is the marginal product of labor when between 4 and 5 million hours of labor are used? What is the average product of labor when 6 million hours are used?

2. a. If the capital-output ratio is 3 in Bangladesh, what effect will $10 million in investment have on Bangladesh's full-employment GDP?
   b. If Bangladesh saves 5 percent of its GDP and its capital-output ratio is 3, what is the rate of growth of its full-employment GDP?

3. The following table shows the output of an economy where various amounts of capital are employed. The amounts of all other resources used are held constant. Fill in the blanks.

Amount of capital (billions of dollars)	Total output	Marginal product of capital	Average product of capital
0	0		___
1	100	___	___
2	210	___	___
3	310	___	___
4	400	___	___
5	480	___	___
6	540	___	___

4. Assume that the capital-output ratio is 2 in a certain developing country and its full-employment GDP is $20 billion. For simplicity, assume that there is no government or foreign trade. The consumption function CC' is plotted in the following graph:

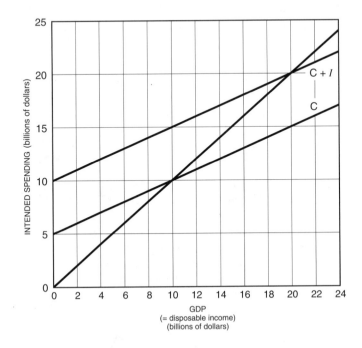

a. How much investment must there be this year if there is full employment?
b. If there is full employment this year, what is the full-employment value of GDP next year?

5. In economy R, investment and consumption are the only components of aggregate demand. The average propensity to consume is 0.8 and the capital-output ratio is 2. Fill in the blanks. Assume that economy R remains at full employment during this period. (All amounts in dollars.)

Year	GDP	Saving	Investment	Change in full-employment GDP
1990	$1 billion	___	___	___
1991	___	___	___	___
1992	___	___	___	___
1993	___	___	___	___

LESSON REVIEW

If you had any difficulty with the Self-Quiz or would like additional assistance, read the following lesson review. It should reinforce and help you understand the content presented in this lesson.

What Is Economic Growth?

Economic growth can be measured in two ways: by the rate of growth of a country's real gross domestic product or net domestic product and by the rate of growth of per-capita GDP. The second provides a more accurate measure of a country's current standard of living.

Per-capita growth, however, has two limitations:

1. It is only a *crude approximation of the rate of increase of economic welfare*. This is because it does not account for leisure, regardless of how highly that may be valued. Nor does it account for improvements in the quality of goods and services or for noneconomic changes in our lifestyles and environment. If manufacturing processes pollute the atmosphere, the costs are not reflected in the GDP. If a certain percentage of land is used for recreation, the benefits are not reflected. Further, per-capita growth rates are only averages. And averages can look much the same whether everyone is getting about the same share of output or most of it is going to a select few.

2. Very small differences in the annual rate of economic growth *can make very substantial differences in living standards a few decades from now*. The differences in average per-capita GDP with only a 1 percent increase in annual growth rate are striking. At the same time, a stable or declining growth rate has ominous implications for changes in lifestyle in years to come.

Thomas Malthus and Population Growth

What effect does population have on economic growth? Clearly, changes in population mean changes in the supply of labor. But at the same time, population growth increases demand and puts pressure on the supply of resources available for production. How do these complex factors work together?

The classic work on the economic effects of population growth was done by the British economist Thomas Malthus. Malthus believed that the population grows at a geometric rate (1, 2, 4, 8, 16, 32, 64, 128, etc.). In contrast, food grows only arithmetically as additional land is brought under cultivation. Through exploration and development, more land could be brought into the market, but the supply itself would be relatively fixed by nature. As a result, Malthus said, the prospect for economic progress was very limited. The standard of living would remain at a minimum subsistence level. If it increased, the population would increase, putting more pressure on resources and driving the standard back down. If it fell below subsistence level, the population would decline because of starvation, and so presumably, resources would become relatively plentiful again, causing the population to increase. Small wonder that historian Thomas Carlyle called economics the *dismal science*.

Malthus could not foresee the explosive growth in technology. Therefore, while Malthusian economics has great relevance to developing countries where technology remains very limited, it is far less relevant today in industrialized countries, where the standard of living has, without exception, improved dramatically. The increased efficiency of agriculture has kept the marginal product of labor from declining, even when more workers are added to the system.

Statistics today suggest little or no relationship between a country's rate of population increase and its rate of economic growth.

David Ricardo and Capital Formation

David Ricardo, an economist, stockbroker, and contemporary of Malthus's, did some interesting pioneer work on capital formation. Other inputs being held constant, a country's output depends on capital investment: The amount of plant and equipment it has and operates. A curve showing the *marginal product of capital* (that is, the extra output resulting from each extra dollar's worth of capital investment) slopes downward and to the right. As more and more capital is accumulated, its marginal product eventually decreases. This is another way of saying that investment is an aid to economic growth up to a point, but there are limits on how much investment can do. On the basis of this theory, Ricardo, like Malthus, believed there were real limits to economic growth, that it would eventually stop.

Like Malthus, however, Ricardo underestimated the effects of technology. For one thing, technology creates new investment opportunities. As rapidly as the impact of investment declines in one area, it grows in another. The effect is to shift the marginal product of capital curve to the right: That is, we are able to invest more capital, thanks to technological change, without any decrease in the marginal product of capital. So long as technology keeps opening new investment opportunities, economic growth continues. And in fact, the rate of return on investment in the United States has fluctuated around a fairly constant level for the past hundred years.

Capital Formation and Economic Growth

Assuming that some level of capital investment occurs, *next year's full-employment GDP will increase because this year's investment will increase the nation's productive capacity*. In other words, investment boosts full-employment GDP, which is another term for potential GDP. How much of an increase will we realize? This depends on the *capital-output ratio,* the number of dollars of investment required to produce one extra dollar of output. For example, if the capital-output ratio is 2, then for every $2 invested, full-employment GDP increases by $1.

What are the implications here? We know that monetary and fiscal policies can affect real GDP, what is actually produced. However, they do not affect potential GDP, what the nation is *capable* of producing under full employment. What this suggests then is that we must strike a balance between investment (our effort to drive up potential

GDP) and fiscal and monetary policies (our effort to increase actual GDP). *So long as the economy sustains noninflationary full employment and the capital-output ratio remains constant, the rate of growth of national output is directly related to the percentage of GDP devoted to investment.*

There is evidence to suggest that investment and economic growth are linked. During the 1970s, the investment rate was higher in Japan than in five other major industrialized countries of the non-Communist world and the growth rate in Japan was higher as well. By contrast, investment rates among those countries studied were lowest in the United States and the United Kingdom, and their growth rates were among the lowest as well. However, during the 1990s, while investment as a percentage of GDP increased in France, Germany, and Japan, their growth rates plummeted, especially Japan's. In the United States and the United Kingdom, on the other hand, the relative level of investment changed little, but their growth rates surged upward.

Other Factors Affecting Economic Growth

A country's rate of economic growth is influenced by several factors in addition to investment in capital. Three of the most significant are investment in human capital, technological change, and sociopolitical environment.

Investment in Human Capital

A society invests in its people, its human capital, through education, on-the-job training, and health programs. Such investment (say, in the form of putting aside money for children's college education) often requires deferring immediate consumption to build future potential.

The United States places a very high value on formal education. The 1987 expenditures for schools at all levels was about $500 billion. Moreover, total investment in education has tended to grow more rapidly than investment in plant and equipment.

To what extent is such investment paying off? Certainly, we are likely to note improvements in lifestyle and greater capacity to develop and enjoy the products of technology. But, on a personal and strictly monetary level, the benefits are more questionable. According to some research, during the 1970s and 1980s, the return to secondary education was 10 to 13 percent and 8 to 10 percent to higher education. But, in addition, differences in income for those who attended college and those who did not seemed to be declining. This trend reversed itself with a vengeance in the late 1980s and the 1990s, and the rate of return for a college education reached as high as an estimated 20 percent by the turn of the century.

Technological Change

The rate of technological change seems to be the most important single determinant of a country's rate of economic growth. Technology provides us new production methods, better marketing and management skills, more efficient ways to use resources, and often the development of new products and resources to replace those that are depleted or inaccessible or prohibitively expensive.

Technology is spurred by innovation. Innovation occurs when changes in technology are applied for the first time by those willing to take the risks associated with a new product or process. Gradually, through *diffusion,* these innovations spread throughout an industry. This diffusion tends to level out competition for a time. But each innovation leads to another and another in a self-renewing cycle that is a major source of economic growth.

Sociopolitical Environment

The economic, social, political, and religious climate of any country influences its rate of growth. Ours is a relatively materialistic society. We place great value, generally, on growth and achievement, on education, on work itself, and on the acquisition of material goods. In addition, our political climate fosters corporate growth and investment. Because of a widespread respect for private property rights, innovation is encouraged and rewarded through both profit and public recognition. Flexibility and openness to change are viewed positively. For more than a hundred years, the United States has enjoyed internal stability, which is in itself conducive to economic growth.

Actual versus Potential Output

Whether the economy operates close to full employment depends on the aggregate demand. If the aggregate demand is too low, the economy experiences considerable unemployment and real output remains far below its potential level. The government can use its monetary and fiscal policies to increase the actual output. However, the efficiency of such policies is limited beyond a certain point because, *once full employment is reached, further growth is achievable only through an increase in the potential GDP.* As we have seen, that potential can be influenced by investment in human resources, technological growth and the capital investment that generally accompanies such growth, and a favorable sociopolitical climate.

EXTENDED LEARNING

This section of the study guide is specifically designed for the two-semester student.

AUDIO

Listen

Listen to the audiotape that accompanies Lesson 25. There is no additional reading assignment for this lesson.

After Listening

Answer the following questions:

1. When the economy is in a recession, it is useful for the government to stimulate personal consumption; this reduces the savings rate. It is often said, however, that the higher is the savings rate, the better off the country will be. Explain the apparent paradox.

2. What are the various ways the price mechanism tends to reduce the adverse consequences of a slowdown in the rate at which new mineral deposits are discovered?

3. What are some of the special circumstances in the United States that favored growth compared to the situation of many developing countries today?

4. How does an educated population make it easier for a country to be economically efficient as technology changes?

5. Will the marginal product of labor tend to change as the country increases the amount of capital relative to the workforce and technology improves? What is likely to happen to per-capita consumption as the marginal product of labor changes?

ADDITIONAL READINGS

Mishan, E. J. *The Economic Growth Debate: An Assessment*. New York: Allen & Unwin, 1977.

> In the first three chapters, Mishan argues that growth is necessary but maintains that a narrow economic approach does not do justice to the growth debate. The effects of growth on social cohesion, the environment, and welfare in general are improperly accounted for and the solutions proposed by economists are too limited. No mathematics or graphs.

Norman, Colin. *The God That Limps: Science and Technology in the Eighties*. New York: W. W. Norton & Company, 1981.

> Chapter 4, "Innovation, Productivity, and Jobs," discusses the various short-run and long-run relationships between technological change and business cycles and growth and compares the potential technological changes of the 1980s with the past. No mathematics or graphs.

Solow, Robert M. "Is the End of the World at Hand?" *Challenge* 16 (March–April 1973): 39–43.

> Discusses the flaws in the Club of Rome *The Limits to Growth* argument. How the price mechanism encourages conservation, substitution, and the development of new sources for minerals; how appropriate policies can avoid unacceptable levels of pollution; and how population may respond to economic development are covered. No mathematics or graphs.

ANSWER KEY

Video Questions

1. Ford was a believer in the "bigger can be better" theory and felt that, by bringing more plant and more workers together, he could increase efficiency. He was right. Part of his secret was simply making more plant and equipment available to each worker, increasing the capital-labor ratio. In addition, Ford attended closely to economies of scale; he realized that, by increasing production, he could reduce costs and prices and thus boost sales, providing additional profits through which to expand further. He paid his workers more than twice what they had been receiving and thereby motivated them to produce more in a shorter period of time. These factors, coupled with the additional available equipment and materials, spelled unprecedented efficiency among Ford's labor force. In addition, Ford standardized. He reasoned that, if parts were all alike, they could be produced faster and cheaper. Therefore, every Model T was like every other Model T. Perhaps most dramatic of all, Ford introduced the assembly line, a novelty (in its time) that increased efficiency by geometric proportions. It brought the product to the worker, rather than the reverse, and brought it faster. It also allowed workers to specialize, each person doing the job at which he or she could be most productive. Given his willingness to try the new and different, Ford was heralded in his own time as well as now as an innovator.

2. The so-called Ford Revolution was eventually felt around the world. Ford's introduction of the assembly line, higher pay for workers, and better capital-labor ratios became models for other manufacturing industries not only throughout the United States but abroad as well. As Ford's methods moved from industry to industry, the whole approach toward efficient production was changed. New methods, attitudes, and philosophies were born. Productivity expanded and prices dropped. More goods became available to a much broader market of consumers, and mass production was well on its way worldwide.

3. From space exploration has come technology that affects our lives in countless ways. Telecommunications are part of virtually every business in the United States today, from education to banking to medicine. Companies actually survive (and expand) on the strength of telecommunications that permit rapid on-the-spot investments and transfer of capital. It is estimated that up to 50 percent of our GDP depends in some way on information use and transfer, made possible through telecommunications. About half our growth in per-capita productivity can be traced to such factors as expansion of labor and population, the other half to improved technology, which has meant more and better education for workers and new knowledge on which to build. It is no exaggeration to say that the technology that first evolved from space research and exploration today touches nearly every aspect of our lives and our current society and economy could not exist without that technology.

4. The Club of Rome doomsayers predicted that the world's high rates of population growth could not continue unchecked. We were in grave danger, they said, of being overrun by growing pollution and depleting our natural resources, given present rates of use and growth. When the price of oil jumped dramatically in the

early 1970s, some observers saw that as evidence that the Club of Rome's predictions were coming true. Our current knowledge of technology tells us, however, that these forecasted global disasters are not inevitable. First, since the earth's crust is some 30 miles thick, we have barely scratched the surface when it comes to uncovering new resources. Some years ago, of course, discovery of those resources was beyond our capabilities; thanks to new technologies, that is no longer the case. As standards of living improve worldwide, the social desirability of smaller families seems to be holding the population more in check than was once predicted. Population growth, for whatever reason, has slowed markedly. Further, as Richard Gill explains, resource shortages trigger responses that benefit society. First, a shortage results in price increases. The immediate result is a scramble to find more of the limited resource, coupled with a desire to conserve. The next step is a development of new technology to uncover alternative resources. Eventually, the shortage is met, and in fact, the need is generally surpassed. What happens is not only that resources are expanded but that the society's capacity to meet its needs is increased through improved technology. Shortages thus become a kind of stimulation toward progress and growth, rather than signposts of doom.

Multiple Choice

1. a Text, 579.
2. b Text, 579–580.
3. d Text, 580.
4. d Text, 580.
5. a Text, 580.
6. c Text, 580.
7. d Text, 581–584.
8. b Text, 583–584.
9. b Text, 587–588.
10. d Text, 588.

True-False

1. False Text, 589.
2. True   Text, 589.
3. False Text, 590–591, Table 25.1.
4. True   Text, 591.
5. True   Text, 592.
6. True   Text, 591–592.
7. False Text, 592.
8. True   Text, 592.
9. True   Text, 595.
10. False Text, 595, 600.

Discussion Questions

1. A country's rate of economic growth is determined by its capital-output ratio, its investment in capital (physical as well as human capital), technological change, and its sociopolitical environment. The aggregate production function can illustrate changes in these variables through changes in the level of potential output.

2. The rate of economic growth does not include the value of leisure, changes in the quality of goods and services, or noneconomic changes in lifestyles or the environment. Furthermore, per-capita figures are just averages, and averages can be misleading because they provide information about only a central tendency and the distribution and range of observations.

3. This quote focuses on more versus less but does not consider the mix of goods being produced or the distribution of these goods. An economy might produce more goods with a total disregard to the environment; not everyone who

advocates economic growth would find this acceptable. An economy might grow very rapidly and reward the top 2 percent of the population with 80 percent of the goods and services produced. Again, growth resulting in this distribution of goods and services might not be acceptable to everyone.

4. The rate of technological change depends on the amount of resources devoted to inventing in a particular field, how profitable the production of inventions seems to be, the demand for products in a particular field, the cost of inputs and the relative stability of input prices (if input prices increase, producers have an incentive to substitute other factors and production processes), and the expected payoff from potential technological improvements. The diffusion of new technology similarly depends on supply and demand, input prices, and the expected profitability of the innovation.

5. Malthus's views about population seem to have been confirmed in developing countries where technology is very limited. They have not been confirmed in countries with rapid technological change. Ricardo's views about the effects of capital formation on economic growth stress that there are real limits to economic growth. Like Malthus, Ricardo grossly underestimated the effects of technology. The prediction of unsustainable economic growth by both Malthus and Ricardo did not adequately consider the impact of technological change on economic growth.

Problem Set

1. a. Beyond 3 million hours of labor, the marginal product falls. The average product of labor increases up to 3 million hours of labor, then falls.
   b. 2 tons of steel per hour of labor. 3 tons of steel per hour of labor.

2. a. It will increase the full-employment GDP by $3.33 million.
   b. 1.67 percent per year.

3.

Marginal product of capital	Average product of capital
	N.A.
100	
	100
110	
	105
100	
	103 1/3
90	
	100
80	
	96
60	
	90

4. a. $5 billion.
   b. $22.5 billion.

5.

GDP	Saving	Investment	Change in full-employment GDP
1 billion	200 million	200 million	100 million
1.1 billion	220 million	220 million	110 million
1.21 billion	242 million	242 million	121 million
1.331 billion	266.2 million	266.2 million	133.1 million

Audio/Text Questions

1. If the economy is fully utilizing its resources, that is, is not in recession, then the higher its saving rate the better off it will be. If the economy dips into recession, it may be necessary to *temporarily* discourage saving and encourage consumption to get close to full employment again. Once close to full employment, however, investment should take over part of the role consumption played in maintaining aggregate demand, and saving should be again encouraged.

2. As a mineral becomes scarce, the price is forced upward. A higher price brings forth new supplies by encouraging the search for new deposits, encouraging conservation, and encouraging the development of new technologies.

3. The United States has had ample natural resources (agricultural land, minerals, navigable rivers, good climate, etc.), a history of political and social stability, massive inflows of investment capital from Europe in its early years, a rate of population growth that did not swamp the availability of land and capital, and a social attitude that encouraged saving, investment, and material growth.

4. Changes in technology require retraining, and the more educated the population is, the more quickly the affected workers can be retrained. The more versatile and adaptable they are, the quicker a new technology can be fully adopted and the less likely growth is reduced through structural unemployment.

5. As the capital-labor ratio increases *and* technology improves, the marginal product of labor increases. This means that more is produced by the workforce, productivity increases, and the level of per-capita consumption can increase.

LESSON 26. PUBLIC GOODS AND RESPONSIBILITIES: HOW FAR SHOULD WE GO?

INTRODUCTION

Throughout each president's administration, we hear considerable discussion about the role of government. How big should government be? How much should we require the government—or allow it—to do for us? And, if we make the role of government too substantial, are we in danger of losing our personal freedom? These and related questions provide part of the focus for Lesson 26.

What You Should Learn

By the end of Lesson 26, you should be prepared to

1. In general terms, contrast the liberal and conservative views of government.

2. Describe the role of government in
    - Establishing and maintaining a legal and social framework.
    - Maintaining competition within markets.
    - Redistributing income.
    - Providing public goods.

3. Explain how government can encourage external economies and discourage external diseconomies and describe their effects on optimal output.

4. Describe the major criticisms made of government by public choice theorists.

5. Discuss the *benefit principle* and *ability-to-pay principle* of taxation, and describe the shortcomings of these principles in establishing an equitable tax structure.

6. Explain, generally, the basis for
    - Personal income tax

- Corporate income tax
- Sales tax
- Property tax

KEY TERMS

mixed capitalist system
conservative
liberal
"rules of the game"
public good
external economy
external diseconomy
special interest group
nonselectivity
property tax
sales tax

benefit principle of
   taxation
ability-to-pay principle
   of taxation
marginal tax rate
tax incidence
externalities
income redistribution
theory of public choice
personal income tax

VIDEO

Watch

Economics U$A Program 26, "Public Goods and Responsibilities: How Far Should We Go?"

Illustrative Events

The stormy birth of the TVA: The project's flood control met the criterion for public good, but its electricity provisions generated as much protest as power; with Alvin Vogtle, retired utilities executive, and the former U.S. senator from West Virginia, William Jennings Randolph. Richard Gill explains the concept of a public good.

The passage of Medicare and Medicaid and their ensuing economic and political troubles, a continuing controversy over public goods, with Dr. James H. Sammons, president of the American Medical Association; economist Henry Aaron, Brookings Institution; and Wilbur Cohen, former undersecretary of the Department of Health, Education, and Welfare.

Howard Jarvis and California's historic Proposition 13 tax revolt: The controversy over its passage and effects; with Howard Jarvis; reporter Ron Sobel, *Los Angeles Times;* and Pat Russell, president of the Los Angeles City Council.

After Viewing

Answer the following questions:

1. When floodwaters destroyed farmland throughout the Tennessee River valley, the TVA offered the promise of relief through flood control. Why was there so much opposition?

2. Why is there a need for government intervention at all in the provision of goods and services?

3. What are the limitations of the free market in ensuring that citizens receive benefits like health care?

4. In the mid-1970s, Proposition 13 passed with an overwhelming margin in California. Yet in 1980, Proposition 9, a similar proposal in many ways, went down in defeat. Why?

Read

Read Chapter 26, "Public Goods and the Role of the Government," pages 602–621 in your text. After completing your reading, try the Self-Quiz.

SELF-QUIZ

Multiple Choice

1. Which of the following statements is *most* accurate? A public good is one that
   a. costs little or nothing to provide.
   b. cannot be provided to one consumer without making it available to others.
   c. entails no external diseconomies.
   d. can never be provided through the private sector.

2. Which of the following is a *major* function of taxes?
   a. To redistribute income
   b. To limit external economies
   c. To curtail the power of special interest groups
   d. To reduce competition in the private sector

3. Which of the following activities is *least likely* to be financed or subsidized by the government?
   a. Research on new pollution control methods
   b. Development of a more powerful automobile engine
   c. Development of new weapons systems
   d. Research on more efficient agricultural methods

4. Which of the following is *not* a public good?

   a. An air raid alert system
   b. A lighthouse
   c. Long-distance telephone service
   d. A national highway system

5. Establishing a legal and social framework within which the price system can operate efficiently is a job for

   a. the government.
   b. the private sector.
   c. the price system itself.
   d. voters.

6. The largest source of revenue for most state governments is the

   a. personal income tax.
   b. corporate income tax.
   c. property tax.
   d. sales tax.

7. Public goods, such as police protection, often seem to be more-efficiently provided by government than through the private sector. The *main* reason for this is that

   a. except in emergencies, there is no real demand for these goods and services.
   b. most public goods are simply too costly to be provided by private industry.
   c. many public goods result in external diseconomies that are best controlled by government.
   d. consumers cannot be excluded from enjoying public goods whether they pay for them or not.

8. Special interest groups tend to lobby in favor of policies and programs that

   a. benefit a small number of people at the expense of a large number of people.
   b. are basically illegal.
   c. result in numerous external diseconomies.
   d. most consumers would support if they had sufficient information.

9. Many observers believe government agencies tend to be less efficient than private firms. One of the *main* reasons for this, say the critics, is that government agencies

   a. care nothing about power and influence.
   b. do not depend on profits to maintain their existence.
   c. are accountable to no one but themselves.
   d. have not had time to develop the same managerial expertise as private industry.

10. Which of the following is probably the *best* example of a tax that relies heavily on the *benefit principle of taxation*?

    a. Personal income tax
    b. Inheritance tax
    c. Gasoline tax
    d. General sales tax

True-False

_____ 1. Suppose your state imposes a tax of 5 percent on all merchandise except food and drugs. The economic incidence of this tax is primarily on the producers and manufacturers of the taxed merchandise.

_____ 2. Only a few states have a sales tax, and for those that do, the rate is usually under 3 percent.

_____ 3. Current federal income tax laws are designed to make the rich carry a larger share of the tax burden than the poor.

_____ 4. Blood donated to the Red Cross is an example of a public good.

_____ 5. The government has considerable power to influence external economies and diseconomies.

_____ 6. Private industry frequently attempts to compete with government in the production of public goods.

_____ 7. The imposition of a sales tax usually means a cut in the sales of the commodities taxed.

_____ 8. Whether a sales tax is absorbed by the seller or passed on to the consumer depends mainly on how sensitive the quantities demanded and supplied are to price.

_____ 9. Suppose a given commodity has an industry demand curve that is almost horizontal. Holding the demand curve constant, a sales tax imposed on that item is likely to increase the price to consumers substantially.

_____ 10. A sales tax on a product like cigarettes tends to increase the equilibrium quantity of that product.

Discussion Questions

1. What are the principle limitations of the price system? It is generally agreed that government must establish the "rules of the game." What does this mean? It is also agreed that the government must see to it that markets remain reasonably competitive. Why?

2. Why are government expenditures so much bigger now than 70 years ago?

3. Former President Ford said that, "A government big enough to give you everything you want is a government big enough to take from you everything you have." Do you agree? Why or why not? How relevant do you think this statement is for the determination of public policy?

4. "The best tax to support government expenditures is the general sales tax because it is very difficult for anyone to evade it and the costs of administering and collecting it are very low." Discuss and evaluate.

5. Suppose that you were given the job of making benefit-cost analyses to determine in which kinds of new energy technologies (such as coal gasification,

coal liquefaction, solar energy, and fusion) the Department of Energy should invest. What are the most important problems you would face?

Problem Set

1. The paper industry has the demand and supply curves that follow:

Price of paper (dollars per ton)	Quantity demanded (millions of tons)	Quantity supplied (millions of tons)
2	80	40
3	70	50
4	60	60
5	50	70

   a. Suppose that this industry results in substantial external diseconomies. What can be said about its optimal output rate?
   b. In the following graph, draw the supply and demand curves for paper. Does the supply curve reflect the true social costs of producing the product? If not, will a supply curve reflecting the true costs lie above or below the supply curve you have drawn?

   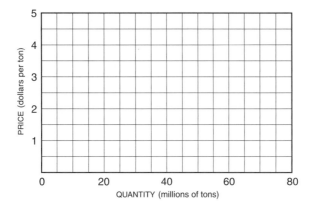

   c. What is the equilibrium price of paper? From the point of view of reflecting the true social costs, is this price the correct one or too low or too high?

2. In the United States, what processes are used to reallocate resources from the private sector (firms and individuals) to the government?

3. The town of Lucretia is faced with a serious smog problem. The smog can be dispelled if an air treatment plant is installed at an annual cost of $1 million. There is no way to clean the air for some but not all of the town's population. Each of the town's families acts independently, and no single family can afford to carry out the project by itself. Why doesn't a private firm build the air treatment plant and sell its services to the town's families (acting individually)?

4. In addition to its smog problem, the town of Lucretia has a transportation problem, which it hopes can be solved by building a new road through the center of

town. Three types of roads can be built, their annual costs and benefits to the townspeople being as follows:

Road length	Total cost (dollars)	Total benefit (dollars)
0 miles	0	0
10 miles	5 million	8 million
20 miles	12 million	16 million
30 miles	20 million	20 million

a. What is the extra annual cost of building a 20-mile road rather than a 10-mile road? The extra benefit?
b. What is the extra annual cost of building a 30-mile road rather than a 20-mile road? The extra benefit?
c. What length of road will maximize net benefits for the town?

5. In the absence of government intervention, the supply curve for soybeans is $P = 2.5Q$, where P is the price (in dollars per bushel) of soybeans and Q is the annual output of soybeans (in billions of bushels).

a. If the government sets a support price for soybeans of $4 per bushel, will farmers produce their full quota of 2.1 billion bushels per year?
b. If the government abandons its price support for soybeans but maintains the output quota of 2.1 billion bushels per year, will the price and output differ from that under a completely free market? If so, how? Illustrate with a diagram. Assume that the demand curve for soybeans is as follows:

Price (dollars per bushel)	Quantity demanded (billions of bushels per year)
4	2.1
5	2.0
6	1.9
7	1.8
8	1.7

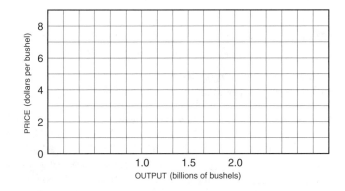

LESSON REVIEW

If you had any difficulty with the Self-Quiz or would like additional assistance, read the following lesson review. It should reinforce and help you understand the content presented in this lesson.

What Functions Should Government Perform?

In part, the expected role of government derives from the fact that the price system suffers from important limitations:

- In the opinion of many people, the distribution of income generated by the price system may be neither the best nor the fairest possible.
- The price system cannot handle public goods adequately.
- External economies or diseconomies can cause too little or too much of certain goods to be produced.

Therefore, the general reasoning has been, if the price system cannot do everything, perhaps government can help take up the slack.

It is generally agreed that government should play an important role in redistributing income in favor of the poor and disabled, providing public goods (such as national defense), and offsetting the effects of external economies and diseconomies. There is little agreement, however, regarding how far government should go in fulfilling this role.

Conservatives are generally skeptical about the ability of government to solve social problems. They tend to question the efficiency of government and worry over the threat that too much government intervention might pose to economic and political freedom.

Liberals, by contrast, believe government serves a vital function in providing goods and services that could not practically or economically be made available through the private sector, road repair, for example. Liberals are less worried than conservatives over the effects of government intervention on personal freedom; in fact, they argue, the price system presents its own threat to freedom by forcing the poor, who cannot always pay market prices, into discomfort and malnutrition.

Establishing "Rules of the Game"

Liberals and conservatives alike agree on some functions of government. The first of these is government's responsibility to establish certain "rules of the game"; that is, the legal, social and competitive framework within which the price system can efficiently function. In maintaining this framework, government must see to it that contracts are honored, private ownership is protected, fraud is prevented. In addition, the government maintains order (through the police) and security (through the military), establishes a monetary system to facilitate trade, and provides standards for quality.

Maintaining a Competitive Framework
The government must also ensure that markets remain reasonably competitive. When markets are dominated by single sellers or a handful of sellers, prices may be kept far above competitive levels and production may be kept far below what is socially optimal.

Distribution of Income
People agree that income should be distributed to the ill, handicapped, old and infirm, disabled, and those who for whatever reason cannot provide for themselves. The idea of welfare is sometimes called a *depression baby* since it first gained popularity and momentum during the Great Depression of the 1930s, a time when many persons might have starved without assistance.

Generally, welfare payments allow the poor to take more from the nation's output than they produce. At the same time, however, it must be recognized that some programs, whether intentionally or not, take from the poor and give to the rich. Certain tax programs, such as the sales tax, also tend to favor the rich, since they spend a much smaller proportion of their income on consumption than do the poor.

Providing Public Goods
We already noted that a major function of government is the provision of public goods: national defense, highway systems, flood control, environmental regulation, public park maintenance, police and fire protection, and a host of other goods and services.

A public good is a socially beneficial product or service that can be consumed by one person without diminishing the amount that can be consumed by others. Once a public good is made available, it is generally impossible to control who will or will not benefit, regardless of who pays the cost. Everyone derives more or less the same benefits from national defense, for example, no matter what percentage of his or her income goes into financing it. And no consumer's benefit detracts from the total amount of defense available.

It is easy to understand why such goods cannot readily be made available through the private sector. It would be very difficult, for example, to market something that was readily available without being able to exclude those who do not pay from consuming it. Further, even if one could control distribution or availability, how could we measure consumption? It is hard to say who benefits most from highways or police protection, for example. As a consequence, public goods are generally funded through taxes. The amount provided is determined through political decision making, which in turn, tends to be greatly influenced through special interest groups.

Externalities

It is generally agreed that government should encourage the production of goods and services that entail external economies and discourage the production of those that entail external diseconomies. This is another way of saying that government should help regulate production in a way that results in the greatest social good for all: the most efficient use of resources, the least damage to the environment, and the optimal production and distribution of desired goods and services.

Effects of External Diseconomies
Suppose an industry's production creates an external diseconomy, through pollution, for example. In that case, the industry's supply curve does not reflect the true social

costs of producing its product. In other words, if the industry had to assume the costs of restoring the environment to its original condition, it would produce *less* of its product at each price level, because its costs would be greater. Its true supply curve, then, lies somewhere to the left of the operational supply curve. And equilibrium output, if social costs are accounted for, would also shift to the left. The government can create a reduction in the industry's output, thus bringing actual production in line with socially optimal production, by imposing a tax on the industry. This tax offsets the cost of the pollution, the external diseconomy.

Effects of External Economies
Suppose an industry conducts research that makes production of several vital products cheaper and more efficient. In this case, the industry's demand curve underestimates the true social benefits of producing this product. In other words, since fewer resources are now required for production, it would be socially desirable to produce more of the product than current market competition may encourage. The government can influence industry output (increase demand) by granting subsidies.

The Theory of Public Choice

Many economists feel that government is induced to make decisions that are not economically efficient. Such decisions may or may not reflect the choices the public would make if given greater control over the decision-making process. And as a result of this tendency toward inefficiency, government services end up costing more than they should. What factors create this situation?

1. *Special interest groups.* Special interest groups can be vocal and financially powerful. Their pressure may persuade politicians to adopt policies that benefit a small number of consumers at the expense of a large number of consumers, each of whom stands to lose only a little. And because members of the large group are giving up, individually, only a small amount, they may be rather indifferent to the whole affair.

2. *Bureaucratic inefficiency.* Many observers believe that government agencies are less efficient than their private sector counterparts. Why should this be so? Some economists suggest that government firms have less incentive than private firms to reduce costs. After all, their competition is less. They are funded by taxes and do not depend on profits to succeed. Further, the power and influence an agency enjoys may be directly related to the size of its budget, inducing the agency to increase costs rather than cut corners. The extent and nature of such inefficiency is hard to document, however, because it is difficult to measure the benefits of, say, pollution control or highway maintenance in any quantified way.

3. *Nonselectivity.* Critics also point to the problem of nonselectivity. A consumer cannot purchase a public program or service the way he or she picks out a briefcase or automobile. Political programs tend to come in packages because, under our representative form of government, we do not always have a chance to vote for programs or policies individually; rather, we vote for a candidate who supports some configuration of programs. Further, it is rare to find a political candidate with whom one agrees fully. As voters, we are forced to make compromises, selecting the candidates with whom we agree most. And the upshot is that most of us, in effect, indirectly vote for programs we would not otherwise endorse.

Principles of Taxation

As already noted, the government acquires most of its money through taxation. Our tax structure is guided by two important principles:

1. *The benefit principle: People who receive more from a certain government service should pay more in taxes to support that service.* Few people would argue with this principle in theory, but in practice it is virtually impossible to apply. Who can say which taxpayers benefit most from flood control? Or police protection? Or road repair?

2. *The ability-to-pay principle: People should pay a higher tax as their income increases.* Generally, this is taken to mean that the rich should pay a larger portion of their income in taxes than the poor. Again, most people agree, but this has proven a difficult principle to uphold since the rich find many ways to avoid taxes.

These two principles are useful guides, but they are too broad, too general to serve as a basis for any specific tax laws. For example, if one person makes $25,000 per year, and another makes $50,000 per year, most people would agree that (assuming equal access to public goods) the second person should pay more in taxes than the first. But how much more? Twice as much? Half again as much? Clearly, many questions remain to be answered.

What we do gain from these principles is a general notion of fairness, a consensus that two people with the same income and approximately the same circumstances (same opportunities to benefit from public services) should pay the same taxes. Such consensus does not eliminate all inequities; nothing can do that. But it does ensure that our tax rates are not based on such arbitrary criteria as political or religious affiliation or whether one's income comes from salary or property investment.

Personal Income Tax

In 1999, the federal government took in about $879 billion in personal income taxes. While taxes increase with income, no one pays over about 40 percent of his or her income in personal income tax. The marginal tax rate (the tax on each extra dollar of income) also goes up as income rises.

The tax system is designed to place the tax burden on those with higher incomes; however, there are many ways people can avoid taxes. Interest on a mortgage is just one example. Any legal measures to lower one's taxes are classified as tax avoidance. In addition, some people may attempt tax evasion, the misreporting of income or any other illegal steps taken to slash taxes.

Corporate Income Tax

Like individuals, corporations must pay income tax. If a corporation's profits exceed $335,000, the corporate income tax equals 34 percent of the profits.

A corporation with profits under $335,000 pays according to a slightly different schedule.

When you are assessed a personal income tax, the burden to pay falls directly on you. But who actually pays the corporate income tax? To the extent that corporations do not reduce dividends or retained earnings, they may pass along the tax burden in the form of price hikes to consumers, or wage cuts for workers. Economists are in great disagreement regarding how much of the tax burden is really shifted in this way.

Property Tax

Local governments gain the bulk of their tax revenue from property tax. Rates are set in this way: Towns or cities estimate how much they need to spend in the next year or two, check the assessed value of all property in the taxable area, and set the rate required to gain the needed income. Suppose Elm City has $100 million in assessed property values and the town needs to raise $2 million to finance its programs and projects for the next year. Then, the property tax rate for Elm City will be $2 million/$100 million, or 2 percent.

Property tax systems have three main problems.

1. Assessed values of personal and real property often differ significantly from actual market values (and usually assessed values are lower).

2. Evasion of personal property taxes is common.

3. Property taxes are not very flexible because assessment rates change so slowly. In other words, a city or town may need to count on the same general amount of revenue for a period of several years or more.

Sales Tax

States derive a large share of their tax revenue through sales tax, which generally adds about 3 to 6 percent to the cost of consumer goods. Only a few states are now without a sales tax. Some states exempt food purchases or medical supplies.

The sales tax puts a greater tax burden on the poor than the rich because the poor must spend a far larger percentage of their income on consumer goods. Recall from Chapter 24 that the poor spend about one-third of their income on food alone.

Who Pays the Taxes?

Who really pays property taxes and sales taxes? If you are a homeowner living in your home, you assume the taxes levied on that property. But if you own a home that you rent, you may ask your tenant to assume part or all of the taxes in the form of a rent increase. In the case of the sales tax, it is generally assumed that the consumer pays the tax in the form of a higher price. That is pretty much the case if the sales tax is general; in other words, if everything is taxed, there is no way to avoid the tax. But if a sales tax applies to only a single commodity or a handful of commodities, the situation could be different because then consumers could substitute other goods or services if they did not like the after-tax prices. Thus, the extent to which the tax can be shifted to the consumer depends on the demand and supply curves for the taxed commodity.

Sensitivity of Demand to Price

Generally, we can say that, holding the supply curve constant, *the less sensitive is the quantity demanded to the price of the good, the bigger the portion of the tax shifted to consumers*. Where the quantity demanded is sensitive to price (as with stereos, for example), the demand curve tends to be relatively horizontal; as prices rise or fall even a bit, the quantity demanded changes, sometimes significantly. Where the quantity demanded is relatively insensitive to price (as with milk, for instance), the demand curve tends to be much more vertical; price changes within a given range have little effect on the quantity demanded. It is much easier for the seller, therefore, to pass on tax costs to the consumer where price insensitivity exists; consumers absorb increased costs with relatively little change in the quantity demanded. For a product that is highly price sensitive, the seller can pass only a small portion of the tax onto consumers without risking a large decline in sales volume.

Sensitivity of Supply to Price

Holding the demand curve constant, *the less sensitive is the quantity supplied to the price of the good, the bigger the portion of the tax absorbed by producers*. Take two markets for beer, market A and market B. In market A, the quantity supplied is more sensitive to price; in other words, producers alter the amount they produce quite a bit as prices change. In market B, the quantity supplied is relatively insensitive to price; that is to say, price changes have less affect on the amount of beer produced. The supply curve for market A would tend to be rather horizontal, that for market B, more vertical. Therefore, a shift in the supply curve in market A affects price much more than a shift in the market B supply curve. This is another way of saying that a tax imposed on beer would mean a bigger price hike for market A consumers than for market B consumers.

As noted, taxes can reduce the equilibrium quantity of the good that is taxed. This is one reason that governments may impose taxes on commodities like liquor and cigarettes, which are considered by some people to be socially undesirable.

EXTENDED LEARNING

This section of the study guide is specifically designed for the two-semester student.

AUDIO

Listen

Listen to the audiotape that accompanies Lesson 26. There is no additional reading assignment for this lesson.

After Listening

Answer the following questions:

1. What principle developed in the lesson helps explain the government's program in 1976 to provide the public with free innoculations against the so-called swine influenza?

2. Does the U.S. government produce goods other than public goods? If so, what nonpublic goods does it produce and why?

3. The supply curve of good Y is a horizontal line. A tax of $1 per unit is imposed on good Y. The increase in the price of good Y due to the tax is

    a. greater if the demand curve is vertical than if it slopes downward.
    b. less if the demand curve is vertical than if it slopes downward.
    c. the same if the demand curve is vertical or slopes downward.
    d. zero.
    e. infinite.

    Explain your answer.

4. In the circumstances described in the previous question, the reduction in the output of good Y due to the tax is

    a. greater if the demand curve is vertical than if it slopes downward.
    b. less if the demand curve is vertical than if it slopes downward.
    c. the same if the demand curve is vertical or slopes downward.
    d. zero.
    e. infinite.

    Explain your answer.

5. It is often argued that excise taxes can be used to discourage the consumption of goods that are socially undesirable (or have negative externalities of consumption). Explain why such a tax would not raise much revenue if it was successful in this sense. What are two common examples of such taxes?

ADDITIONAL READINGS

Break, George. "The Role of Government: Taxes, Transfers, and Spending." In *The American Economy in Transition*, edited by Martin Feldstein, 617–656. Chicago: University of Chicago Press, 1980.

> A thorough analysis of the changes in federal, state, and local expenditures and revenues of the postwar period. The growth of tax transfer programs, the development of intergovernment grants, the greater reliance of the federal government on payroll and income taxes, and the growth of the expenditures of state and local governments are among the topics covered. No mathematics or graphs.

Musgrave, Richard A., and Peggy B. Musgrave. *Public Finance in Theory and Practice,* 4th ed. New York: McGraw-Hill Book Company, 1984.

> Chapter 15, "Tax and Expenditure Incidence: An Overview," describes the concept of incidence and the distribution of expenditure benefits. No mathematics, simple graphs.

Pechman, Joseph A. *Federal Tax Policy,* 5th ed. Washington, DC: Brookings Institution, 1987.

> Chapter 5, "The Corporation Income Tax," describes the arguments about the degree to which the tax is borne by consumers and wage earners, the effect of the tax on investment, as well as some details of the tax regarding inflation accounting, special allowances, and so on. No mathematics or graphs.

Samors, Patricia W., and Sean Sullivan. "Containing Health Care Costs." In *Meeting Human Needs*, edited by Jack A. Meyer, 364–382. Washington, DC: American Enterprise Institute, 1982.

> Describes how the current medical care programs create few incentives to keep medical costs down and discusses how HMOs, PSROs, and other procedures can lead to a more economically efficient provision of care. No mathematics or graphs.

ANSWER KEY

Video Questions

1. The desire for coordinated flood control was very great. Local efforts to achieve flood control had proven largely unsuccessful because resources were limited and there was generally no systematic approach. The question to be answered was this: At what cost would such coordination be achieved? Creation of dams to halt floodwaters also provides a means of generating electricity. Local business people were pleased to have the government in the flood control business but felt threatened at the idea of having the government in the power business. Coal miners, for example, felt that electricity generated through government-subsidized dam projects would cut deeply into their local market and that the government's market might even eventually expand beyond the local area. The general philosophy was that government had a right and an obligation to provide support of flood control but that it did not have a right to make itself a competitor of private industry.

2. Economists have long recognized that certain services must be provided by government or they will not be provided at all. There are several reasons for this. Among them is the simple fact that some ventures are not particularly profit producing, provision of parks and recreational areas, for instance. At the same time, these goods and services are desirable in that they raise the quality of life for all. In addition, it is difficult to determine who would pay for some goods

and services unless all pay through a tax system. Everyone benefits equally from flood control, road repair, national defense, fire prevention, and so on. Were such goods and services to be provided through the free market, who would pay for them? What would be the incentive? If an individual receives the benefits of a service regardless, he or she is unlikely to pay. Moreover, it would be difficult to determine how much each individual should pay. It could be argued, for instance, that the person who benefits the most from road repair is the one who drives the most or perhaps it is the person who must commute each day, the one who lives within city limits, or the one who owns two cars rather than one. Clearly, these are not easy questions to answer. The point is that some goods and services are not efficiently or profitably provided through private industry. When a general indivisible benefit accrues to all, that is generally accepted as a sound reason for the provision of a good or service through government intervention.

3. The free market operates according to its own rules, one of which is that members of an economy tend to reap rewards according to the extents and limits of their own productivity. Generally, this rule offers many benefits relating to the efficient use of resources. It has limitations, however. For the elderly and poor or disabled, for example, such a free market system means that benefits are not distributed equitably. Such persons can contribute in only a limited way to overall economic productivity (although they may, of course, make numerous difficult-to-measure contributions). An unemployed worker who, for example, becomes ill exerts a profound drain on the economy. Not only can she not work and produce, but she requires additional resources because of her illness. In a free market system, without intervention, such a person could not readily receive assistance, except through private charity. Through government intervention, however, a more equitable distribution of benefits like medical care can be achieved, and the cost can be borne relatively equally by everyone. No system is perfect. Government-provided medical benefits can raise medical costs. There is no guarantee of high-quality services. Many critics question the necessity of interfering in doctor-patient relations. Not everyone who needs help receives it. Yet without programs like Medicare and Medicaid, many low-income people would have no provision for medical benefits at all.

4. Proposition 13 limited property taxes in California to 1 percent of appraised value. Had the proposition not passed, there is no doubt that countless fixed-income families would have lost their homes. That fact alone provided extensive support. Beyond that, however, taxpayers pointed to government inefficiency. They did not want further government expansion, did not want more and more services provided through government at ever increasing cost. The general feeling was that a slight cutback in services was a small price to pay for great individual savings. Proposition 9 would have cut state income taxes. This proposition was seen as offering great benefits to private business and persons in upper-income brackets but less benefit to the average taxpayer, who would continue to carry the burden. There may also have been some fear of cutting government-provided services too far. While the doomsayers' predictions about Proposition 13 did not come to pass, there were certainly cutbacks, subtle changes that affected the quality of everyday life for California citizens. Would

more of this type of change be acceptable? What level of government service is desirable? Such questions must be answered on an individual basis, but the collective answer in 1980 was that enough cuts had occurred. It was time to let government provide what public goods it could through the current budget.

Multiple Choice

1. b   Text, 602.
2. a   Text, 609.
3. b   Text, 602–605.
4. c   Text, 602–603.
5. a   Text, 600–601.
6. d   Text, 611.
7. d   Text, 602–603.
8. a   Text, 605–607.
9. b   Text, 607.
10. c   Text, 608–609.

True-False

1. False   Text, 613–615.
2. False   Text, 611.
3. True   Text, 610.
4. False   Text, 602.
5. True   Text, 603–605.
6. False   Text 602–603.
7. True   Text, 604–605, 615.
8. True   Text, 613–615.
9. False   Text, 613–615, Figure 26.3.
10. False Text, 615.

Discussion Questions

1. The price system is limited in that the distribution of income generated by the price system may not be the best distribution nor may it be sufficiently equitable, the provision of public goods is not possible through the price system, and the price system does not correct for external economies or diseconomies.

    The government when it establishes the "rules of the game" creates a legal, social, and competitive framework that allows the price system to perform efficiently. The government must establish law and order, provide for national defense, establish a monetary system, and provide standards for quality.

    Government must also work to maintain reasonably competitive markets because monopolistic markets result in prices that are too high and output levels that are too low from a social point of view.

2. Government expenditures today are much higher than they were 70 years ago in both real and nominal terms. Adjusted for inflation, government expenditures have risen dramatically because the government provides far more goods and services than it did 60 years ago. For example, government provision of assistance to those needing help has increased dramatically as have government expenditures on defense, education, and highways.

3. Whether one agrees with this statement depends on the person's view of the role of government in redistributing income, providing public goods, and correcting for external economies and diseconomies. Liberals believe the government's role in these areas should be extended, while conservatives believe the government's role should be reduced. Public policy as it is enacted tends to reflect the prevailing attitude of the legislature and the public.

4. The general sales tax is extremely difficult to evade and does have low administration and collection costs. However, the general sales tax is thought to be

highly regressive and thus, from an ability-to-pay perspective, is not viewed as a highly equitable tax. Also, a general sales tax does not link the amount of the tax paid by an individual to the benefits that individual receives from government-provided services.

5. The cost of providing energy via the new technologies depends on the cost of inputs, the production processes, and any government-imposed costs or subsidies. The benefits of providing energy via the new technologies depend on the demand for the energy from these new sources. That demand depends on the price of the energy, people's tastes and preferences, people's income, and the prices of related goods. In addition, both the benefit and cost sides would need to consider any external economies or diseconomies. Many of these benefits and costs might prove extremely difficult to quantify.

Problem Set

1. a. It is less than 60 million tons.
   b. The supply curve does not reflect the true social costs. A supply curve reflecting these costs would be above and to the left of the following one.

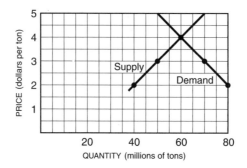

   c. $4. Too low.

2. Levying taxes and borrowing.

3. If any family buys smog-free air, it automatically buys it for others too, regardless of whether the latter pay for it or not. And since no family can afford the cost, so long as families act independently, it is unprofitable for a private firm to carry out this project.

4. a. $7 million. $8 million.
   b. $8 million. $4 million.
   c. 20 miles long.

5. a. If the price is P, $Q = 0.4P$ in the absence of government intervention. Therefore, if $P = 4$, $Q = 1.6$. Consequently, farmers will not produce their full quota of 2.1 billion bushels.

b. The demand and supply curves are as follows:

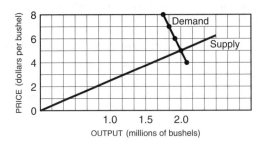

The price will be $5, and the output will be 2.0 billion bushels. Since this is less than the output quota, the free market outcome prevails.

Audio/Text Questions

1. Innoculations against contagious diseases are public goods in the sense that any one person's "consumption" of an innoculation provides benefits to others (in that the likelihood that they would contract the disease is reduced), and there is no way to prevent these people from "consuming" the benefits of the innoculations. This is similar to a positive externality of consumption.

2. The federal government (and state and local governments) produce airports and highways which are not strictly public goods, since those who choose not to pay can be excluded and there are no cases of joint consumption. Providing for good transportation may generate positive externalities, however, and the construction of highways often requires the power of imminent domain.

3. c, because any increase in costs forces the supply curve to move upward by the cost of the tax per unit. Since the supply curve is horizontal, the new equilibrium price is greater by $1 regardless of the characteristics of the demand curve.

4. b, because a vertical demand curve means the same amount is demanded regardless of the price. A downward-sloping demand curve means that less is demanded as the price rises.

5. To discourage consumption, the demand for such goods has to be highly responsive to an increase in the after-tax price. If demand is responsive, an increase in the tax severely curtails the number of units sold, and since excise taxes are levied against the number of units sold, tax collections is very small. Two common examples of taxes that could be supported because they tend to discourage consumption are cigarette and alcohol taxes, although they appear to have only a small effect on total consumption.

LESSON 27. INTERNATIONAL TRADE: FOR WHOSE BENEFIT?

INTRODUCTION

No country can afford to exist as an independent economic entity—no island unto itself. To prosper and to provide a desirable lifestyle for its citizens, it must engage in foreign trade. This applies to the United States as well as any other country.

International trade benefits both the importer and the exporter. Perhaps, at some time, you purchased a Japanese or German car or shoes made in Italy, wine from France, electronic equipment from Japan, dishes or woolens from England, or any of thousands of other imports made available through international trade. If so, then you are already acquainted with some of the personal benefits of free trade. However, that is only part of the story. Trade benefits not only the individual consumer, but the country as a whole, and the entire world market as well. One reason is that trade promotes specialization, which, as already seen, leads to a more-efficient use of resources. Not everyone can or should build automobiles. Not everyone can or should raise grapes for wine. When independent firms are allowed and encouraged to do what they do best, the country as a whole prospers and its economy grows. Similarly, when nations are encouraged to specialize, the international economy benefits.

What determines who specializes in what? And what determines how and when countries establish their trade agreements? We begin exploring these and related questions in Lesson 27.

What You Should Learn

By the end of Lesson 27, you should be prepared to

1. Explain how countries benefit through trade.

2. Discuss what is meant by *absolute advantage*.

3. Discuss *comparative advantage,* contrast it with absolute advantage, and explain the ways in which trade decisions depend on comparative advantage.

4. Describe how the market indicates whether a country has a comparative advantage or disadvantage in production of a given commodity.

5. Discuss the purposes and effects (both economic and social) of quotas and tariffs.

KEY TERMS

exports
imports
absolute advantage
comparative advantage
terms of trade
infant industries

incomplete specialization
tariff
prohibitive tariff
quota
export subsidies
specialization

VIDEO

Watch

Economics U$A Program 27, "International Trade: For Whose Benefit?"

Illustrative Events

The trade advantages brought by President Nixon's historic visit to China, notably the exchange of U.S. technology for Chinese textiles; with Stanley Marcus, president of Nieman Marcus Company, and Don McWhirter, vice president of International LTV Energy Products. Richard Gill explains the concept of comparative advantage.

Voluntary restrictions on imported Japanese cars in the 1970s, bringing protection for U.S. auto industry jobs, but higher auto prices for U.S. consumers; featuring John Dingell, chair of the Commerce Committee, U.S. House of Representatives; Ambassador William Brock, U.S. trade representative; and Robert Crandall, senior fellow of the Brookings Institution.

After Viewing

Answer the following questions:

1. Briefly describe the economic and political circumstances that led up to the Japanese automobile producers voluntarily restricting their exports in the United States in the early 1970s.

2. Economists generally favor free trade, even in times when industries are severely threatened by foreign competition. Explain.

3. In a 1993 debate with Vice President Gore, H. Ross Perot vehemently asserted that passage of the North American Free Trade Agreement (NAFTA) would lead to a "great sucking sound" as jobs in the United States were sent to Mexico. Discuss what actually happened and why.

Read

Read Chapter 27, "International Trade," pages 622–641 in your text. After completing your reading, try the Self-Quiz.

SELF-QUIZ

Multiple Choice

1. In comparison to other countries throughout the world, imports and exports for the United States

   a. are greater, in absolute terms, than those of any other country.
   b. represent a higher percentage of GDP than those of any other country.
   c. are about typical of most industrial countries.
   d. are the lowest of any industrial country.

2. The United States is so well-off, so diverse, so rich in its human talent and natural resources,

   a. that it need not engage in trade with any other country.
   b. that it engages in international trade only as a way to help less fortunate countries.
   c. yet even the United States can benefit from trade because of the gains from specialization.
   d. and it got that way by exploiting other countries, especially the developing countries of Latin America.

3. From an economic perspective, the *main* advantage of trade, both for individuals and for countries, is that it

   a. provides consumers a wider variety of goods and services to choose from.
   b. promotes self-sufficiency.
   c. decreases overdependence on new technology.
   d. permits specialization, thus increasing output.

4. Suppose China can produce a computer using two units of resources, and the United States can produce the same computer using one unit of resources. Similarly, China can produce an automobile using six units of resources, and the United States can produce the same automobile using three units of resources. On the basis of this information, we can conclude that

   a. the United States has an absolute advantage in both computers and automobiles.
   b. the United States has a comparative advantage in both computers and automobiles.
   c. the United States has a comparative advantage in computers but not in automobiles.
   d. neither country has an absolute or comparative advantage in anything.

5. A country tends to *import* those products in which it has

   a. an absolute disadvantage.
   b. an absolute advantage.
   c. a comparative disadvantage.
   d. a comparative advantage.

6. A country's producers know if they have a *comparative advantage* in the production of a given commodity because

   a. worldwide demand for that product is high relative to other products.
   b. consumer demand within their own country is high.
   c. the resources required for the manufacture of the product are readily accessible.
   d. they can realize a profit on the world market.

7. Suppose that the United States imposes a $25 tariff on bicycles tomorrow. The real victim of this tariff is the

   a. government, since it costs more to enforce a tariff than the government takes in.
   b. U.S. consumer, who now pays more for bicycles.
   c. U.S. bicycle manufacturer, who can no longer keep pace with consumer demand.
   d. foreign exporter of bicycles, who now has no market.

8. If the United States establishes a quota on Brazilian rainboots, what effect will that likely have on the price of rainboots here and in Brazil? Prices of rainboots tend to

   a. fall, both here and in Brazil.
   b. rise, both here and in Brazil.
   c. fall here but rise in Brazil.
   d. rise here but fall in Brazil.

9. Which of the following is probably the *most convincing* argument offered in support of tariffs and quotas?

   a. The desirability of maintaining a domestic industry vital to national defense
   b. The need to protect domestic jobs
   c. A desire to encourage and promote the growth of struggling, young industries
   d. Need to improve a country's terms of trade

10. The restrictions imposed on Japanese auto imports in the 1970s illustrated the fact that

    a. overall, quotas have little impact on a well-established domestic industry.
    b. the gains a domestic industry realizes through quotas may be less than the costs to society as a whole.
    c. quotas tend to strengthen an industry's competitive advantage in the long run.
    d. quotas frequently provide the market signals needed to stimulate reallocation of resources.

True-False

_____ 1. Suppose China has an absolute advantage over Japan in the production of virtually every good that might be a basis for trade between the two nations. Then trade between the two nations would be beneficial for Japan but not for China.

_____ 2. A country with a strong comparative advantage in the manufacture of a particular product tends to retain that advantage indefinitely.

_____ 3. Suppose the United States can produce computers with one-half the efficiency of Japan and motorcycles with one-third the efficiency of Japan. Then, we could say that Japan has a comparative disadvantage, relative to the United States, in production of computers.

_____ 4. Currently, exports are relatively unimportant to the U.S. economy, amounting to only 1 or 2 percent of GDP.

_____ 5. Under free trade, a country's overall economic welfare tends to be lower than under a tariff.

_____ 6. An absolute advantage exists any time that one country can produce a good or service using fewer resources than another country, even if the difference in efficiency is very slight.

_____ 7. Quotas can be even more effective than tariffs in keeping foreign goods out of a country.

_____ 8. If country A has more natural resources and human resources than country B, there is probably little mutual advantage to trade between these two countries.

_____ 9. Protecting industries that contribute to national defense is the only justifiable reason for ever imposing a tariff.

_____ 10. A country's terms of trade are likely to change almost constantly.

Discussion Questions

1. Why is it advantageous for a country to trade rather than try to be self-sufficient?

2. Choose an argument used to justify tariffs and then write two statements, one which defends and one which attacks this argument.

3. Is it better to "buy American," because we then have both the goods and the money? Explain.

Problem Set

1. Countries D and E have not traded with each other because of political differences. Suddenly, they reconcile their political differences and begin to trade. Cigars are relatively cheap, but beef is relatively expensive in country D. Beef is relatively cheap, but cigars are relatively expensive in country E.

a. When these countries begin to trade, does the demand for cigars produced in country D increase or decrease? Does the price of cigars increase or decrease in country D?
b. Does the demand for cigars produced in country E increase or decrease? Does the price of cigars increase or decrease in country E?
c. Does the demand for beef produced in country D increase or decrease? Does the price of beef increase or decrease in country D?
d. Does the demand for beef produced in country E increase or decrease? Does the price of beef increase or decrease in country E?
e. Does the demand for the resources used in country D to produce cigars increase or decrease? Does the demand for the resources used in country E to produce beef increase or decrease?
f. Does the demand for the resources used in country E to produce cigars increase or decrease? Does the demand for the resources used in country D to produce beef increase or decrease?

2. Suppose that the demand and supply curves for transistor radios in the United States are as follows:

Price (dollars)	Quantity demanded (millions)	Quantity supplied (millions)
5	5	2
10	4	3
15	3	4
20	2	5

Further, suppose that the demand and supply curves for transistor radios in Japan are:

Price (expressed in dollar equivalent of Japanese price)	Quantity demanded (millions)	Quantity supplied (millions)
5	2.5	1
10	2.0	3
15	1.5	5
20	1.0	7

a. Suppose there is free trade in transistor radios. What is the equilibrium price?
b. Which country exports transistor radios to the other country?
c. How large are the exports?
d. Suppose the United States imposes a tariff of $10 per transistor radio. What happens to exports and imports?

3. Suppose the United States can produce three electronic computers or 3,000 cases of wine with one unit of resources, while France can produce one electronic computer or 5,000 cases of wine with one unit of resources.

a. Will specialization increase world output?
b. Is this an example of absolute or comparative advantage?

4. Suppose that labor is the only input and two countries, Argentina and Brazil, can produce the following amounts of two commodities, bananas and nuts (in pounds), with a day of labor:

	Bananas	Nuts
Argentina	5	3
Brazil	10	4

   a. For both countries to gain from trade, between what limits must the ratio of the prices lie?
   b. Suppose there is free trade and the price of bananas increases relative to the price of nuts. Is this change in the terms of trade to the advantage of Argentina or Brazil?

5. Country G's production possibilities curve follows. So does country H's production possibilities curve. The only goods produced in either country are food and clothing.

	Country G			Country H	
Possibility	Food output	Clothing output	Possibility	Food output	Clothing output
A	0	32	A	0	24
B	5	24	B	4	18
C	10	16	C	8	12
D	15	8	D	12	6
E	20	0	E	16	0

   a. In country G what is the cost of clothing in terms of food?
   b. In country H what is the cost of clothing in terms of food?
   c. If countries G and H engage in trade, which country exports food? Which country exports clothing?
   d. If countries G and H engage in trade, between what limits do the terms of trade lie?

LESSON REVIEW

If you had any difficulty with the Self-Quiz or would like additional assistance, read the following lesson review. It should reinforce and help you understand the content presented in this lesson.

The United States's Foreign Trade

The United States's exports (that is, the things we sell to other countries) amount to about 10 percent of our gross domestic product. In absolute terms (i.e., dollars), our exports and imports exceed those of any other country in the world. What this means, among other things, is that, without foreign trade, our lifestyle would change dramatically.

As a young country, the United States exported primarily raw materials and foodstuffs. Today things are different. More of our exports are manufactured goods. In 1999, around 50 percent of U.S. exports were manufactured goods, around 20 percent were raw materials and food, and around 30 percent were services.

Specialization and Trade

Like individuals, countries trade primarily because it allows them to specialize. This means higher productivity through better and more-efficient use of resources. A country's ability to specialize depends heavily on its resources, both human and nonhuman. Further, the nature of the resources determines the nature of the specialization: A country with rich soil may specialize in agricultural goods, while one with relatively poor soil but much skilled labor may find it profitable to concentrate on high technology. Keep in mind, however, that the bases for specialization do not remain fixed over time. Resources may be depleted or developed; technology may expand.

Overall, specialization increases world output. This is so because, as a country shifts resources from nonspecialty areas into its area of specialization, output per unit of resources increases (assuming the amount of resources required to produce each good to be constant, regardless of production levels). Along with increased productivity comes a rise in the standard of living for each country that engages in trade and uses its resources in this efficient way. Of course, specialization is never complete. Although the United States specializes in wheat, for instance, and Japan specializes in televisions, Japan still grows wheat and the United States still produces televisions.

Absolute Advantage and Comparative Advantage

A country is said to have *absolute advantage* over another when it can produce a commodity using fewer resources. Absolute advantage does not, however, provide the basis for determining specialization. And the reason for this is that a country may have absolute advantage over another without having very much of a competitive edge. The more important question to ask is this: For which commodities does the country have the *greatest* advantage in productive efficiency? These commodities are the candidates for specialization.

As it turns out, even a country with an absolute advantage in several commodities can benefit from specialization and trade, because its advantage is greater for some commodities than others, and it is wise to allocate its resources accordingly.

A country has a *comparative advantage* in those products where its efficiency relative to other countries is highest (higher, that is, than for any other products). Suppose that the United States is 50 percent more efficient in the production of 10 assorted commodities than China. We would say that the United States has an absolute advantage over China in the production of all 10 commodities, but it has a comparative advantage in none because the level of efficiency in comparison to that of China is the same for all 10 commodities. By contrast, to use the textbook's example, say that the United States is 100 percent more efficient than France in the production of computers, but only 25 percent more efficient in the production of wine. Therefore, the United States enjoys a comparatively greater advantage in computer production and can be said to have a comparative disadvantage (comparing computer production to wine production) in wine production. This suggests that the United States is likely to specialize in computers and import wine. France does the opposite. Everyone benefits.

Terms of Trade

The terms of trade are defined as the quantity of domestic goods a country must give up to get a unit of imported goods. To continue with the same example (wine and computers), the United States, by diverting resources from computer production to wine production, could have 2,500 cases of wine for each computer it gives up (recall that the United States can use one unit of resources to produce two computers or 5,000 cases of wine; hence, one unit of resources produces half of either). Similarly, France, by diverting its own resources from wine production to computer production, can have one more computer for every 4,000 cases of wine it gives up. Therefore, the ratio of wine to computers for the United States is 2,500:1, while the ratio of wine to computers for France is 4,000:1. The price ratio is somewhere between 4,000:1 and 2,500:1. This is another way of saying that the terms of trade depend on how many computers can be traded for how many cases of wine. But where does the equilibrium price ratio lie? The answer depends on world supply and demand for the two products. The stronger is the demand for computers (relative to supply) and the weaker the demand for wine (relative to supply), the higher the price ratio. On the other hand, if people begin to drink a lot of wine and go back to scratch pads and paper, the price ratio declines.

International Trade and Individual Markets

How do producers know whether they have a comparative advantage or disadvantage in the production of a given commodity? The answer is that they receive signals directly from the market. Here is how the process works.

First, suppose there is no foreign trade at all. In that case, prices for a given commodity tend to differ greatly from country to country, depending on local markets as well as available resources and production costs. The price within each country is determined by the intersection of that country's supply and demand curves.

Next, imagine what happens if foreign trade is suddenly permitted. At first, because of differing production costs, prices are lower in one country than in another, sometimes dramatically lower. Thus, there is money to be made by exporting the commodity in question to the country where prices are higher. But, as trading continues, prices begin to equalize. Prices in the producing-exporting country go up to induce manufacturers to provide more and more output. At the same time, prices in the importing country gradually fall to induce consumers to buy the additional quantity. When an equilibrium is reached, the *price in the exporting country equals the price in the importing country*. At this point, does trade cease? No, it simply levels off. The equilibrium price represents the level at which the amount of the good one country wants to export equals the amount the other country wants to import. Once the prices have stabilized on the world market and world output of a commodity equals world demand, then a country that can still make a profit by exporting the commodity has a comparative advantage with respect to that commodity and should specialize in it.

Tariffs and Quotas

What is a *tariff*? Free trade has some disadvantages. A struggling firm may be severely threatened by foreign competition. When this happens, the government may choose to impose a tariff, a tax on imports intended to protect domestic industry and its workers. The primary purpose of a tariff is to protect an industry and its workers from foreign competition. In addition, though, tariffs also provide revenue for the government.

If a tariff raises the price of an imported commodity well above the price of a comparable domestic commodity, the effect may be to eradicate trade, unless consumers can be persuaded somehow that the foreign commodity is worth the extra money. (Some consumers may prefer a Swiss-made watch, regardless of whether it is objectively higher in quality than a U.S.-made watch.) Either way, the consumer is the loser. Without foreign competition, domestic producers are free to raise prices. Therefore, the consumer pays more. The advantage is that workers in the relevant industry have more jobs and higher wages than without the tariff, but the protection of their jobs comes at heavy financial and social cost to the society as a whole.

What is a quota? A *quota* is a limit set by the government on the amount of certain commodities that can be imported annually. What is the effect of a quota on free trade?

Suppose the United States imposes a quota on a given commodity, like watches. Because imports are restricted, the quantity demanded exceeds the quantity supplied, and prices go up.

Like tariffs, quotas reduce trade, raise prices, protect domestic industry from foreign competition, and reduce the standard of living for the country as a whole. Overall, however, economists tend to oppose quotas even more than tariffs. This is because there is no way for a foreign exporter to overcome a quota. If the exporter's prices are sufficiently low, it can get around most tariffs. But a quota provides an insurmountable barrier to trade. In isolating domestic industries from foreign competition, the quota, like the tariff, may discourage efficient use of resources in the long run.

Arguments Favoring Tariffs and Quotas

Why do countries impose quotas and tariffs when they are obviously detrimental to society and to free trade as a whole? There are several reasons, some more justifiable than others.

1. *Strengthening national defense.* First, it may be desirable to maintain an industry for purposes of national defense. We could not very well afford to import all missiles, for example, even if some other country could manufacture them far more efficiently. To do so would make our defense system vulnerable to the whims of international politics, potential embargo, as well as the production capabilities of another country. Economists support this reasoning—and many consider the defense argument the most valid of all arguments posed in favor of tariffs—but oppose the use of the defense argument to protect industries with only a tenuous relationship to national security.

2. *Fostering the growth of young industry.* Sometimes it takes a valuable industry several years to become productively proficient. During that critical period, the

industry could well be pushed right out of the market by a more-sophisticated foreign industry. Thus, a tariff or quota may protect a firm during its early growth period. The problem comes when an industry tries to turn a temporary protective measure into something permanent; eventually, the industry should become independently competitive if it is worth preserving.

3. *Protecting domestic jobs and reducing unemployment.* This may seem an important argument in favor of quotas and tariffs, and in the short run it may succeed. In the long run, however, this policy may not work well. If industries cannot successfully compete with foreign producers unaided by government protective policies, it may be that resources within those industries would be more productively shifted elsewhere. This spells a cruel blow to individual workers within such industries, but the country as a whole benefits only when resources are used in the most-efficient possible way.

4. *Preventing a country from depending too heavily on one industry or a handful of industries.* Suppose that under free trade, a country produces one item, umbrellas, and very little else. If rainfall worldwide is fairly light for several years running, exports decline and the country suffers because virtually its total national income depends on the umbrella trade. In this case, quotas or tariffs on other items could motivate production by domestic industries in other areas. (Clearly, in a diverse economy such as ours, this argument carries less weight than it otherwise might.)

5. *Improving a country's terms of trade.* A tariff can reduce domestic demand, thus reducing the equilibrium price of a given commodity in world markets and ultimately increasing the value of other commodities. The net effect is to improve the ratio of import prices to export prices. This effect is likely to be short lived, however, since other countries may retaliate and put everyone, relatively, in about the same position.

EXTENDED LEARNING

This section of the study guide is specifically designed for the two-semester student.

AUDIO

Listen

Listen to the audiotape that accompanies Lesson 27. There is no additional reading assignment for this lesson.

After Listening

Answer the following questions:

1. Technological change increases a country's ability to produce by making labor and machines more productive. Does trade do the same thing?

2. "It is a foolish and dangerous thing for U.S. firms to export their technology since this results in foreign firms' imitating our products and beating us in foreign markets." Discuss and evaluate.

3. Do the gains from trade imply that the expression, "There is no such thing as a free lunch!" is wrong?

4. The concept of comparative advantage is based on the notion of opportunity cost. Explain comparative advantage in terms of opportunity cost.

5. In a study of the effects of quotas on Japanese cars in the early 1980s, an economist concluded that the cost per job saved per year was about $160,000. What would an economist have to take into account to determine a rough estimate of that figure?

ADDITIONAL READINGS

Branson, William H. "Trends in United States International Trade and Investment Since World War II." In *The American Economy in Transition*, edited by Martin Feldstein, 183–257. Chicago: University of Chicago Press, 1980.

> Discusses changes in the U.S. share of world output and trade in manufactures, the composition of U.S. trade, and the causes of changes in U.S. competitiveness and comparative advantage. Patterns of short- and long-term capital flows and the effect of trade and capital flows on exchange rates are also briefly discussed. No mathematics or graphs.

Committee for Economic Development. *Strategy for U.S. Industrial Competitiveness*. New York: CED, 1984.

> Chapter 7, "Unfair International Competition," describes the problems in defining unfair trade practices and the many hidden ways a country can subsidize exports or discourage imports. No mathematics or graphs.

Crandall, Robert W. "What Have Auto-Import Quotas Wrought?" *Challenge* 27 (January–February 1985): 40–47.

> Analyzes the effects of the "voluntary" restraints on Japanese auto imports of the early 1980s. Concludes that the cost per job saved was almost $160,000 per year. No mathematics or graphs.

Kenen, Peter B., and Raymond Lubitz. *International Economics*, 3d ed. Englewood Cliffs, NJ: Prentice-Hall, 1971.

> Chapter 2, "Trade and Resource Allocation," gives a brief but thorough

exposition of the gains from trade, how factor endowments affect comparative advantage, and the way welfare is reduced with tariffs. Simple mathematics, difficult graphs.

Lawrence, Robert Z. "The Myth of U.S. Deindustrialization," *Challenge* 26 (November–December 1983): 12–21.

Argues that U.S. manufacturing is not in a state of massive decline due to more efficient or subsidized foreign competition. Manufacturing employment has held steady, and any problems are due primarily to generally insufficient demand and the overvalued dollar. No mathematics or graphs.

ANSWER KEY

Video Questions

1. At first, when Japanese imported cars hit the U.S. market, there was little interest in the cars. Gas prices were low, and foreign cars seemed to have little to offer against the more luxurious U.S. models. As the gas situation changed, however, interest in small, efficient cars soared; and the U.S. manufacturers had almost nothing with which to compete. Sales of domestic cars slumped. And without incoming revenue, U.S. industries had no capital with which to retool or expand in order to respond to changing market demands. The future looked gloomy indeed. Despite strong theoretical opposition to restrictions on free trade, arguments citing the loss of numerous U.S. jobs gradually grew louder and more persuasive. These arguments were fueled by growing awareness of Japan's barriers against U.S. agricultural products, products the land-rich United States could raise at far less cost than Japan. Ultimately, Congress agreed to pass restrictive legislation aimed at the Japanese car industry. This legislation would go into effect unless the Japanese could be persuaded to engage in voluntary restrictions, to which they eventually agreed. As a result, employment within the auto industry rose. Jobs and businesses were saved. But car prices, for domestics and imports alike, began a steep rise.

2. Economists tend to take a long view. While trade restrictions alleviate a situation in the short run, the long-term effects are often more negative than positive. For example, restrictions may save X number of jobs within a threatened industry, at least for a time. However, such interference generally does little to encourage greater efficiency. Further, it often means significantly higher prices in the market on both imports and the industry's own domestic products. So consumers foot the bill for the restrictions and the saved jobs. For those individuals within the threatened industry whose jobs are saved through restrictions, the results may seem well worth the cost. Economically, there is rarely much of a balance. Normally, because of resulting price increases, it would be cheaper by far to pay industry workers to do nothing than to protect their jobs with trade restrictions.

3. The implication of Perot's assertion was that the unemployment rate in the United States would skyrocket upward, but following the passage of NAFTA in

1993, the U.S. unemployment rate continued to drop for another six years. The prediction of the great "sucking sound" was found to be in error. While NAFTA was not by itself responsible for the economic boom of the 1990s, it did not put a damper on it as predicted. It is true that, when trade barriers are removed, production that can be performed more efficiently elsewhere is moved there. What needs to be recognized though is that this cuts both ways. A given country loses jobs in one place and gains them in another. There were workers, firms, and industries in Mexico that rightly feared the adoption of NAFTA. Most important, it is necessary to keep in mind that free trade benefits consumers by making a wider variety of goods available at lower prices. With the money consumers are able to save because of free trade, they can purchase additional goods and services. This increases the demand for these other goods and services, which in turn leads to increased production of these goods and services and increased employment in the sector of the economy that produces them. This is the market working as it should by allocating resources to where they can by most-efficiently used.

Multiple Choice

1. a   Text, 622.
2. c   Text, 623–624.
3. d   Text, 623–624.
4. a   Text, 624–625.
5. c   Text, 625–627.
6. d   Text, 631.
7. b   Text, 631–632.
8. d   Text, 633–634.
9. a   Text, 634–635.
10. b Text, 637, Case Study 27.1.

True-False

1. False   Text, 625–631.
2. False   Text, 624.
3. True   Text, 627.
4. False   Text, 622.
5. False   Text, 632.
6. True   Text, 624–625.
7. True   Text, 633–634.
8. False   Text, 626, and entire discussion.
9. False   Text, 634–638.
10. True   Text, 627–628.

Discussion Questions

1. Trade benefits a country because it allows it to specialize, thereby increasing the total output of goods and services. This increased production leads to a higher standard of living as well as access to a greater variety of goods and services.

2. In the section "Arguments for Tariffs and Quotas" on pages 636–637 of this lesson, the arguments in favor of restricting trade are discussed. Each of these arguments can be faulted on the grounds that it leads to less specialization and therefore a lower level of total world output. Tariffs and quotas also tend to protect industries from competition: This protection ultimately can lead to higher prices and reduced output for the domestic consumer. Finally, these interventions in the market interfere with the normal signals supply and demand send to the market.

3. No. To "buy American" eliminates the potential gains we as a nation can receive through specialization and international trade. "Buy American" protects U.S.

jobs that no longer reflect a U.S. comparative advantage: As a nation, we are better off producing and exporting those goods where we have a comparative advantage and importing those goods for which we have a comparative disadvantage.

Problem Set

1. a. Increase. Increase.
    b. Decrease. Decrease.
    c. Decrease. Decrease.
    d. Increase. Increase.
    e. Increase. Increase.
    f. Decrease. Decrease.

2. a. $10.
    b. Japan.
    c. 1 million transistor radios.
    d. Exports and imports drop.

3. a. Yes.
    b. The United States has an absolute advantage in computers; France has the same in wine. The United States has a comparative advantage in producing computers, whereas France has a comparative advantage in producing wine. Mutually advantageous trade is based on comparative advantage.

4. a. The price of a pound of bananas must be between 6/10 and 4/10 of the price of a pound of nuts.
    b. Brazil.

5. a. An extra unit of clothing costs 5/8 of a unit of food.
    b. An extra unit of clothing costs 2/3 of a unit of food.
    c. Country H. Country G.
    d. The price of a unit of clothing lies between 5/8 and 2/3 of the price of a unit of food.

Audio/Text Questions

1. Yes, but rather than directly increasing productivity by improving the way something is produced, trade improves productivity by allowing workers and other resources to shift out of areas in which they are relatively unproductive into the sectors of the economy for which this country is relatively more productive. Overall productivity rises.

2. Although the possibility that foreign firms beat us in foreign (or home) markets raises the likelihood of large adjustment costs (workers forced to leave export industry jobs in the affected industry), the more efficient other producers are, the better off the citizens of the United States are in the long run. Better technology means more output for less, so the country is richer and better able to afford those goods in which the United States still has an advantage.

3. Since both sides in the aggregate gain from trade (although there may be an initial adjustment period in which certain individuals are severely harmed by the expansion of trade), trade is in fact a "free lunch."

4. Simply put, the country that has the lowest opportunity cost of producing a good has the comparative advantage in its production even if it does not have the absolute advantage in the good's production. Take the example used in the textbook with the production of computers and wine in the United States and France. The United States has an absolute advantage in producing both goods. France has an absolute disadvantage in producing both goods. The opportunity cost of producing a computer in the United States is 2,500 cases of wine. The opportunity cost of producing a computer in France is 4,000 cases of wine. Obviously, the United States has the lower opportunity cost of producing computers and hence a comparative advantage in their production. The opportunity cost of producing a case of wine in the United States is 1/2,500 computer. In France the opportunity cost of producing a case of wine is 1/4,000 computer. Since 1/4,000 is smaller than 1/2,500, France has a comparative advantage in producing wine even though it has an absolute disadvantage in producing wine. In this simple example, resources are better allocated if the United States stops producing wine, specializes in producing computers, and trades computers for wine from France. And France is better off if it specializes in producing wine and trades wine for computers from the United States. Both countries gain from this specialization and trade. Each country's net consumption increases as a result.

5. The economist would have to determine first how many fewer U.S. cars would have been bought in the absence of quotas and how that would have reduced employment, not only in the auto industry itself but in all the U.S.-based suppliers. Then he or she would have to estimate how much higher prices of both Japanese- *and* U.S.-made cars would be under quotas. The total additional cost to consumers is *roughly* the increase in the average price of a car times the total number of cars sold. Cost per job saved can then be easily calculated.

LESSON 28. EXCHANGE RATES: WHAT IN THE WORLD IS A DOLLAR WORTH?

INTRODUCTION

The emergence of the "superdollar" in the mid-1980s delighted U.S. importers and made this the time to travel abroad. Whether you were traveling in England, Germany, France, or Japan, you were likely to find bargains everywhere: in accommodations, in merchandise, in travel itself. Not all Americans were pleased with the strong dollar, however. For example, U.S. exporters were hurt. And then, by 1990, the dollar had dropped to its lowest level in many years. By 2000, the dollar had regained some of its strength relative to ten years earlier, but it was still much weaker compared to the currencies of Japan and Europe than in 1985.

What causes the dollar to rise or fall as measured against the yen, pound, or euro? To answer this question, we must explore the concepts of exchange rates and balance-of-payments deficits and surpluses. We consider, among other things, the shift from a fixed exchange rate based on the gold standard to a floating exchange rate in which the value of a currency is based, as with any commodity, on market supply and demand. What are the advantages and disadvantages inherent in this shift? We may not have all the answers to that question for some time to come.

What You Should Learn

By the end of Lesson 28, you should be prepared to

1. Describe how international transactions differ from domestic transactions.
2. Explain how the gold standard worked, and how exchange rates were determined under the gold standard.
3. Explain the circumstances under which the gold standard was abandoned.
4. Contrast a system of fixed exchange rates with a system of floating exchange rates, and describe the potential advantages and disadvantages of each.
5. Describe the significance of a country's balance-of-payments accounts.

KEY TERMS

equilibrium level of GNP
foreign trade multiplier effect
exchange rate
gold standard
appreciation
depreciation
fixed exchange rate
purchasing-power parity theory
  of exchange rate determination
devaluation of currency
flexible exchange rate
value of the dollar

overvalued currency
undervalued currency
balance-of-payments
  deficit
balance-of-payments
  surplus
International Monetary
  Fund (IMF)
gold-exchange
  standard
target zones

VIDEO

Watch

Economics U$A Program 28, "Exchange Rates: What in the World Is a Dollar Worth?"

Illustrative Events

The United States's abandonment of the gold standard in 1933, a desperate effort to regain a stable dollar; featuring Edward Bernstein, former principal economist at the U.S. Treasury Department.

The 1944 Bretton Woods Agreement, fixing exchange rates to the dollar instead of gold, an idea that finally failed, featuring economist Edward Bernstein; Joan Spero, senior vice president of American Express; and Marina von Neuman Whitman, former economic adviser to President Nixon.

Abandonment of the Bretton Woods Agreement by President Richard Nixon, leading to continuing controversy over the pros and cons of the "float" for the United States and other countries.

After Viewing

Answer the following questions:

1. What were the immediate and long-term effects of Britain going off the gold standard in the early 1930s?

2. How did dominance of the dollar in world markets "sow the seeds of its own destruction"?

3. What factors encouraged President Nixon to let go of the Bretton Woods Agreement and what was the major impact of that decision?

Read

Read Chapter 28, "Exchange Rates and the Balance of Payments," pages 642–664 in your text. After completing your reading, try the Self-Quiz.

SELF-QUIZ

Multiple Choice

1. Governments during the 1930s worked hard to increase exports and decrease imports. Their *main* motivation for this was to

   a. restore the worldwide balance of trade.
   b. increase each country's national net domestic product.
   c. offset the costs of World War I.
   d. improve international relations.

2. Suppose you purchase a recording of the Beatles' music in England priced at 10 pounds. If the exchange rate of dollars to pounds is 1.5 to 1, what do you pay for the recording in U.S. dollars?

   a. $6.67
   b. $10
   c. $15
   d. $16.67

3. When exchange rates are determined under the gold standard, the value of a country's currency tends to be very

   a. stable and very close to equilibrium value.
   b. stable but not necessarily close to equilibrium value.
   c. unstable yet close to equilibrium value.
   d. unstable and far from the equilibrium value.

4. If the euro appreciates from $0.75 to $1.50, a $240 U.S.-made printer that had sold in Germany for 320 euros now costs Germans

   a. 80 euros.
   b. 160 euros.
   c. 200 euros.
   d. 240 euros.

5. If a country's reserves of foreign currencies and gold have been increasing for a number of years, then it is likely that

   a. its balance of payments have been in deficit.
   b. it is struggling to hold down imports and increase exports.
   c. its currency is currently far above equilibrium level.
   d. its currency is undervalued.

6. To keep the value of its own currency up, a country would probably be *least likely* to
   a. enter the market and buy large sums of its own currency.
   b. increase defense expenditures abroad.
   c. limit the foreign travel of its own citizens.
   d. impose heavy tariffs on imports.

7. The gold standard was abandoned largely because
   a. it kept currency values too low.
   b. it allowed currency values to fluctuate too wildly.
   c. worldwide gold reserves were declining at an alarming rate during the 1940s.
   d. the system did not achieve a sufficiently rapid balance of trade.

8. Under a floating exchange system, exchange rates are determined by
   a. supply and demand.
   b. current market values for gold, sterling, or some other standard.
   c. government regulation.
   d. international agreement.

9. Which of the following would cause the demand curve for the euro to shift upward and to the right?
   a. General Motors decides not to build a plant in Germany.
   b. Europeans demand more U.S. computers.
   c. Americans begin drinking more French wine and German beer.
   d. More Europeans begin traveling in the United States.

10. When a country under the gold standard increases the price of gold, this action is known as
    a. depreciation of currency.
    b. devaluation of currency.
    c. appreciation of currency.
    d. balance-of-payments deficit.

True-False

_____ 1. If there is a run on the dollar, speculators sell dollars in anticipation of a price fall, with the result that the price of the dollar indeed declines.

_____ 2. Under the gold standard, exports and imports tended toward balance because as a country's gold stock declined, its price level fell and it decreased imports, but when its gold stock increased, its price level rose and it increased imports.

_____ 3. When we buy a foreign asset, we get a credit item in our balance-of-payments accounts.

_____ 4. Currency speculators cause volatility in international financial markets.

_____ 5. The overall balance-of-payments accounts *always* balance under flexible exchange rates.

_____ 6. A decline in the U.S. reserve of foreign currencies constitutes a debit item in our balance-of-payments accounts.

_____ 7. With fixed exchange rates, one way in which a country can combat a persistent balance-of-payments deficit is to hold down inflation.

_____ 8. The primary purpose of the International Monetary Fund is to maintain a stable system of fixed exchange rates.

_____ 9. If Americans demand more French wine and cheese, this causes the demand curve for euros to shift to the right.

_____ 10. Most economists today favor an immediate return to a fixed exchange rate, under the auspices of the central banks.

Discussion Questions

1. What does a country's balance-of-payments deficit or surplus measure? What factors were responsible for the chronic deficit in the U.S. balance of payments?

2. The Bretton Woods Agreement established a system of fixed exchange rates. What happened if the amount demanded of a currency did not equal the amount supplied?

3. "Under floating exchange rates, a deficit in our balance of payments is not a measure of pressure on the dollar, as it was under fixed exchange rates." Comment and evaluate.

4. What is the worldwide result of the oil crisis of 1973–74 (and ensuing years) under (a) a gold standard, (b) a fixed exchange rate system, and (c) a floating exchange rate mechanism?

5. "The European Central Bank raised its discount rate to 9.5 percent from 8 percent in a move to bolster the euro." Explain what this statement means, and why this action would have that effect.

Problem Set

1. The supply curve for Japanese radios to the U.S market for two periods of time follows.

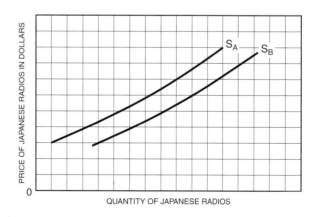

a. One curve is before a depreciation of the dollar relative to the yen; one curve is after it. Which curve is which? Why?

b. What is the effect of the depreciation on the dollar price of Japanese radios?
c. What is the effect on U.S. expenditures (in dollars) for Japanese radios if the demand for them in the United States is price elastic?
d. What is the effect on U.S. expenditures (in dollars) for Japanese radios if the demand for them in the United States is price inelastic?

2. a. Suppose that people in Mexico want to import a product from the United States. If the product costs 5 dollars in the United States, how much will it cost in Mexico if the exchange rate is 9 pesos = 1 dollar?
b. Suppose that the quantity of the product (in part a) demanded in Mexico is related to its price (in pesos) as follows. The table shows the desired expenditure by Mexicans on this product at various levels of the exchange rate. Fill in the blanks.

Exchange rate	Dollar price of good	Mexican price of good (pesos)	Quantity demanded	Total desired expenditure (dollars)
10 pesos = 1 dollar	5	___	500	___
9 pesos = 1 dollar	5	___	1,000	___
8 pesos = 1 dollar	5	___	1,200	___

3. Assume that countries X and Y are both on the gold standard and a unit of country X's currency is worth 1/40 of an ounce of gold, and a unit of country Y's currency is worth 1/8 of an ounce of gold.

a. How much is a unit of country X's currency worth in terms of country Y's currency?
b. How much is a unit of country Y's currency worth in terms of country X's currency?

4. The demand and supply curves for the Swiss franc are as follows:

Price of franc (dollars)	Millions of francs demanded	Millions of francs supplied
0.80	300	400
0.70	320	370
0.60	340	340
0.50	360	310
0.40	380	280

a. What is the equilibrium rate of exchange for the dollar?
b. What is the equilibrium rate of exchange for the Swiss franc?
c. How many dollars are bought in the market?
d. How many Swiss francs are bought in the market?

5. The demand curve for British pounds is as follows:

Price of British pound (dollars)	Millions of pounds demanded
2.00	200
2.10	190
2.20	180
2.30	170
2.40	160
2.50	150

   a. Suppose that the British government sets the exchange rate at $2.40 and the quantity of pounds supplied at this exchange rate is 180 million pounds. Will the British government have to buy or sell pounds? If so, how many?
   b. If the British government has to buy pounds with dollars, where will it get the dollars?

LESSON REVIEW

If you had any difficulty with the Self-Quiz or would like additional assistance, read the following lesson review. It should reinforce and help you to understand the content presented in this lesson.

International Transactions and Exchange Rates

International trade differs from domestic trade because more than one currency is involved. If you purchase a commodity in a foreign country, either you must exchange dollars for the local currency before you make the purchase or the merchant must make the exchange afterward. Either way, exchanging currency is much like buying any sort of commodity; that is, when you trade dollars for marks or pounds, you are actually buying marks or pounds from the bank.

In general, *the exchange rate is simply the number of units of one currency that exchanges for a unit of another currency.* If every Mexican peso you buy costs you $0.10, then the exchange rate between dollars and pesos is 0.10 to 1.

Exchange Rates under the Gold Standard

Before the 1930s, many countries throughout the world were on the gold standard. This meant that *a unit of that country's currency was convertible into a specified amount of gold.* To see how much a country's currency was worth in dollars, you could divide the dollar price of gold by the foreign currency price. For example, if $32 = 1 ounce of gold, and 8 pounds = 1 ounce of gold, then $4 = 1 pound ($32/8 pounds = $4/1 pound).

The gold standard kept the exchange rates fairly constant. Country A would refuse to pay more than the going rate for a foreign currency, because if it had to do so, it would be better off to exchange its currency for gold then convert the gold into the foreign currency. And country B would refuse to sell its currency for less than the going rate, because similarly, it would be better off to exchange its currency for gold and convert it. For example, the price of a pound tended to remain, within a few cents, at right around $4.

The Balance between Exports and Imports

Eighteenth-century philosopher David Hume pointed out that, under the gold standard, a mechanism ensured that trade would be brought into balance. Briefly, this mechanism worked as follows.

If, say, the British bought more from us than we did from them, they would have to give us gold to pay for the difference. As their gold stock declined, their price level would fall (because of a decline in the quantity of money). As our gold stock increased, our price level would rise due to the increase in money. As this occurred, the British would be inclined to purchase less from us (because of higher prices), and we would tend to import more from them (because of lower prices). Gradually, imports and exports would always tend toward a balance.

The Foreign Exchange Market

In reality, the adjustment process forecasted by David Hume simply did not operate fast enough to please either economists or consumers. Wages and prices proved to be relatively inflexible downward. Therefore, when the adjustment mechanism failed to achieve a balance of trade as quickly as desired, the gold standard was abandoned. Britain withdrew in 1930, the United States in 1933. During the next few years, the dollar was allowed to float, that is, to go up and down with the pressures of the market. It took until 1936 to achieve some stabilization of the dollar, the pound, and the franc.

From the 1930s until the early 1970s, exchange rates were fixed by government intervention and international agreement. Then, in 1973, the world began experimenting with flexible exchange rates, a situation in which currency values fluctuate freely on an open market, determined by the intersection of supply and demand, just like the value of any commodity is determined on the open market.

Fixed Exchange Rates

Many economists believe that exchange rates should be allowed to fluctuate freely. However, this was the exception rather than the rule before the early 1970s. From the end of World War II up to 1973, most exchange rates were fixed by government action and international agreement. Governments achieved this by several means. A government can reduce the demand for foreign currencies by

1. Curbing imports from other countries.
2. Controlling capital investment abroad.

3. Limiting the amount citizens can travel abroad.
4. Reducing defense expenditures abroad.

But what happens if a government tries to maintain a fixed exchange rate that is far from the equilibrium rate? This can present great difficulties. For example, if a country's currency is *overvalued* (that is, its fixed price is above the equilibrium price), the quantity supplied of domestic currency exceeds the quantity demanded in the foreign exchange markets. To maintain the inflated value it desires, the government must buy up the extra currency, using its reserves of foreign currency and gold. This action depletes the country's reserves. Things may get worse as speculators predict the reserves will soon run out and begin to sell their shares of overvalued currency as well, causing the deficit to grow even larger. As the reserves run out, the country is forced to devalue its currency.

If a country's currency is *undervalued* (that is, its price is under the equilibrium price), the quantity demanded of its currency exceeds the quantity supplied. To keep the value from climbing, a country needs to exchange some of its currency for foreign currency and gold, building its reserves. Why would a country want to keep the value of its currency down? Because, otherwise, its exports become more expensive to foreign markets and its GDP declines.

Overall, the amount of a country's currency bought must equal the amount sold; hence, the term *balance of payments*. This being the case, we could measure a country's balance-of-payments surplus or deficit by noting the transactions of the country's central bank. The central bank purchases currency if there is a balance-of-payments deficit and sells currency if there is a balance-of-payments surplus. This information is no longer published by the U.S. government, however. Under the system of flexible exchange rates, we can estimate overall deficits or surpluses by noting exchange rates; that is, by noting how the dollar is valued in comparison to other currencies.

Flexible Exchange Rates

To illustrate how a flexible system works, consider the market for European euros. On the *demand* side of the market are

- People who want to import European goods into the United States.
- People who want to travel in Europe (where they need euros to spend).
- People who want to build factories in Europe.
- Anyone who wants to trade dollars for European currency.

On the *supply* side of the market are

- People who want to import U.S. goods into Europe.
- Europeans who want to travel in the United States (where they need dollars).
- People with euros who want to build factories in the United States.
- Anyone who wants to trade euros for dollars.

If Americans decide to buy more German cars or French wine, they cause the demand curve for euros to shift upward and to the right. If Americans decide not to travel in Europe or not to build any U.S. factories there, the demand curve tends to shift downward and to the left.

If the Europeans begin buying more U.S. cars or computers, they shift the supply curve for euros downward and to the right. This is so because the Europeans now supply more euros into the foreign exchange; this causes the value of the euro relative to the dollar to depreciate. If, on the other hand, Europeans stop importing so many U.S. goods, stop traveling in the United States, and decide to build no factories in the United States, the supply curve for euros tends to shift upward and to the left. Now, it takes fewer euros to buy a dollar.

When country A's currency becomes more valuable relative to country B's currency, country A's currency is said to appreciate in value, and country B's currency to depreciate in value. Such a change is possible only under a flexible, open market system; it would not have been possible under the gold standard. For a country to change the value of its currency under the gold standard, it would have to increase the price of gold. This action was called *devaluation of currency.*

Determining Flexible Exchange Rates

We know that flexible exchange rates are determined by supply and demand. But what determines the position of the supply and demand curves? Three factors are particularly important:

1. *Relative price levels.* In the long run, the exchange rate between any two currencies reflects differences in the countries' price levels. In other words, the cost of a given commodity (say, a computer) in one country tends over time to be equivalent to its cost in another country. If country A experiences high inflation then (thus driving prices up), its currency tends to depreciate relative to that of country B (where prices hold steady). This is so because, without such stabilization, consumers on the world market would tend to buy cars only from country B, where prices are better. To illustrate, suppose that a computer in Germany costs 1,000 euros, or the equivalent of, suppose, 900 U.S. dollars. Suddenly, the price of the computer in Germany soars to 2,000 euros. Does this mean that the price on the U.S. market is now $1,800? No. It means, rather, that the value of the euro is depreciating, and the exchange rate is now different. Assuming that the price of the computer in the United States holds constant, the exchange rate is now (dollars to euros) $0.45:1, rather than $0.90:1 as before.

2. *Relative rates of growth.* Of particular importance is that, if one country's economic growth rate is higher than that of the rest of the world, its currency is likely to depreciate. This happens because, when the economy booms, imports increase; consumers have more to spend and demand more variety. When imports grow faster than exports, a country's demand for foreign currency tends to grow faster than the supply of that currency. And as a result, its own currency is likely to depreciate in value.

3. *Relative interest rates.* Investors go where interest rates are highest. So, when interest rates rise and investors are attracted, a country's currency tends to appreciate. Similarly, when interest rates fall, the currency depreciates.

What determines the balance between exports and imports under a flexible exchange rate? The answer is the constant assessment in the rates themselves. If, for example, dollars are currently costly compared to British pounds, the British tend to import less from us and we tend to import more from them. Gradually, this trend begins to reverse as the supply curve for dollars shifts downward and to the right, which causes the price of the dollar to depreciate. Suddenly, British goods are more expensive here than they were, and at the same time, U.S. goods are less expensive for the British. They import more, we import less. And a balance is achieved. The free market thus contains its own mechanism for ensuring a balance of trade, just as under the gold standard.

How Successful Have Floating Exchange Rates Been?

This is not an easy question to answer, in part because not all the evidence is in yet. After all, we lived with fixed rates far longer than we lived with floating rates. But here are a few noted observations thus far:

1. Yes, there has been considerable variation in currency values one day to the next. For example, the exchange rate between the dollar and the mark has varied by 2 percent or more in a day, by 15 percent or more within a period of several months.

2. Rapid variations have made international trade more difficult, and some foreign developers and entrepreneurs may have shied away from building factories or operating businesses in the United States because of the inherent uncertainties of the system.

3. On the other hand, the flexible system has shown remarkable resilience over time, first with the oil crisis of the early 1970s and later with the declining value of the dollar in the late 1970s. The dollar made an impressive comeback in the early 1980s (50 percent increase in value), to the dismay of exporters but the relief of consumers weary of inflation.

Not all votes are in. Some observers want central banks to exert greater control over exchange rates. But many economists still retain faith in the economics of market supply and demand. Therefore, the floating system is likely to prevail for some time to come.

Fixed versus Flexible Exchange Rates

Until 1973, most countries fixed their exchange rates, not allowing them to fluctuate. Why? Partially, it was the fear that flexible rates would vary so erratically that international trade would be threatened. Not only would trade be more difficult to carry out, but the uncertainties involved in shifting values would make many producers less willing to trade in the first place. Further, critics said, speculators could push a currency's exchange rate up or down. And moreover, flexible exchange rates might promote inflation.

On the positive side, many economists supported flexible rates. Why, they asked, shouldn't we trust the free market system to value our currency when we trust it to value other commodities? They argued that countries would have greater autonomy in formulating fiscal and monetary policies if exchange rates were flexible, and they generally dismissed the argument that speculation would cause undue destabilization.

U.S. Balance-of-Payments Deficits, 1950 to 1972

During the period from 1950 to 1972 (the last full year when exchange rates were fixed), the United States showed a chronic deficit in its balance of payments. What factors were responsible?

1. *Postwar recovery of western Europe and Japan.* New technology made Europe and Japan alike tough competitors. Increased efficiency brought their costs down relative to ours and allowed them to undersell us in virtually every market, our own included.

2. *Military and foreign aid.* The United States spent enormous sums on foreign aid and military expenditures, particularly during the Vietnam War. This helped keep our balance of payments in deficit.

3. *Private investment abroad.* Foreign investment skyrocketed during the 1950s and 1960s. The government attempted to restrict such investment during the last of the 1960s, but restrictions were lifted during the 1970s.

4. *Inflation and discrimination against U.S. goods.* Inflation in the United States has made our exports more expensive abroad. To make things worse, foreigners have used various quotas, tariffs, and other measures to keep out U.S. exports.

EXTENDED LEARNING

This section of the study guide is specifically designed for the two-semester student.

AUDIO

Listen

Listen to the audiotape that accompanies Lesson 28. There is no additional reading assignment for this lesson.

After Listening

Answer the following questions:

1. How was the pure gold standard supposed to automatically create payments balances for every country?

2. How do price and wage rigidity and the ability of the country's monetary authorities to create money make the gold standard less workable?

3. What is purchasing power parity and how well does it explain the fluctuations in the value of the dollar?

4. In 1977, when President Carter encouraged the U.S. economy to grow rapidly relative to European economies, the dollar fell in value even though interest rates were higher in the United States. Why did this happen?

5. Why in the United States does a recession born of a tight money policy cause the dollar to rise very high?

ADDITIONAL READINGS

Gill, Richard T. *Economics and the Public Interest,* 4th ed. Santa Monica, CA: Goodyear Publishing Company, 1980.

> Chapter 13, "International Balance of Payments," gives a clear explanation of the relationship between macroeconomic policy and the balance of payments. The gold standard, Bretton Woods, and the floating exchange rate systems are briefly described. Simple mathematics and graphs.

Haberler, Gottfried. *The World Economy, Money, and the Great Depression, 1919–1939.* Washington, DC: American Enterprise Institute, 1976.

> This 44-page essay first summarizes the international monetary events of the interwar period—the restoration of the gold standard in the 1920s, its collapse during the Great Depression, and the attempts to restore monetary stability in the late 1930s—then discusses the various explanations for the monetary and economic problems of the period. Moderately technical, no mathematics or graphs.

Marris, Stephen. "Deficits and the Dollar: The World Economy at Risk." Institute for International Economics, December 1989.

> The summary details how the different macroeconomic policies of the United States and its trading partners caused U.S. real expected interest rates to be high relative to other countries, precipitating a huge capital inflow and an unusually strong dollar. Assesses the likelihood of a crash in the value of the dollar.

Odell, John S. *U.S. International Monetary Policy.* Princeton, NJ: Princeton University Press, 1982.

> Chapter 5, "Farewell to Bretton Woods," describes the evolution of the exchange rate system from Nixon's break from Bretton Woods in 1971, to Volcker's initiation of a tight monetary policy in late 1979. The relationship between political pressures and exchange rate policies are detailed. No mathematics or graphs.

Ritter, Lawrence S., and William L. Silber. *Money,* 5th ed. New York: Basic Books, 1984.

> Part 7, "International Finance," gives a lively account of the exchange rate crisis during the 1960s and early 1970s, describes floating, the extent to which the balance of payments disciplines domestic economies, the role of gold in the past, and the liquidity problem of gold. No mathematics or graphs.

ANSWER KEY

Video Questions

1. The immediate effect was a gold drain. Spurred by fears that the United States would follow suit and also go off the gold standard, foreign countries began exchanging their currency for gold, causing U.S. observers to speculate how long the U.S. economy could withstand this depletion of its reserves. Believing that any resistance would be interpreted as a loss of confidence in the dollar, however, the United States continued to honor requests, despite all fears and reservations about the future of the economy. Eventually, this willingness to honor withdrawal requests stemmed the tide; the drain stopped. The result was renewed confidence in the dollar. At the same time, the Fed raised interest rates to encourage foreign investors to keep their money in U.S. banks. Gradually, the dollar strengthened, to the point where it became overvalued. Thus, the long-term effect was a decline in export trade under the strong dollar and a loss to the U.S. economy. Industries shut down; workers could not find employment. This situation grew steadily worse as the dollar gained strength and U.S. exports grew ever more expensive and unaffordable in foreign markets.

2. Following World War II, it was assumed that the United States would take a lead in reestablishing the economic balance of the world market. And in fact, it seemed to do so by providing economic assistance to countries throughout the world. As a result of the Bretton Woods Conference, the U.S. dollar became the standard for a new fixed rate of exchange. It was a system destined for downfall, however. As countries benefiting from U.S. economic assistance strengthened, they began to manufacture their own goods, becoming ever less dependent on exports from the United States. Economies built by our own strong dollars became effective competitors in the world market, and what had been a trade surplus for the United States rapidly turned into a deficit.

3. The primary factor influencing Nixon's decision was probably the inflexibility of the Bretton Woods Agreement. Over a period of time, the world situation had changed markedly. No longer was the United States the strong economic leader it had been, providing a financial helping hand to struggling economies. Those economies were now in a position to compete effectively against U.S. products. Given our payments deficit, more dollars were going overseas to purchase foreign goods than were coming into the country to pay for U.S. goods. As foreign central banks began exchanging excess dollars for gold, our gold reserves were depleted. With loss of confidence in the dollar, European merchants became reluctant to accept U.S. dollars or travelers checks. Without devaluation, the United States could not regain its competitive status. Yet the Bretton Woods Agreement would not permit such devaluation. Ultimately, Nixon was persuaded to let go of the agreement altogether.

Multiple Choice

1. b Text, 654.
2. c Text, 642–643.
3. b Text, 643–644.
4. b Text, 643.
5. d Text, 643–653.
6. b Text, 644–649.
7. d Text, 655.
8. a Text, 644–649.
9. c Text, 645–646.
10. b Text, 646.

True-False

1. True Text, 651–652.
2. True Text, 644.
3. False Text, 651–653.
4. False Text, 657.
5. True Text, 653.
6. False Text, 651–652.
7. True Text, 661.
8. True Text, 654.
9. True Text, 646.
10. False Text, 658–662, and entire discussion.

Discussion Questions

1. Under a system of fixed exchange rates, a country's balance-of-payments deficit or surplus measures the extent to which a country's currency is overvalued (the situation with a balance-of-payments deficit) or undervalued (the situation with a balance-of-payments surplus). The United States had a deficit in its balance of payments during the period 1950 to 1972 (the last full year when exchange rates were fixed) due to the postwar recovery of Europe and Japan, U.S. expenditures on military and foreign aid, private investment by the United States in foreign countries, inflation in the United States, and discrimination against U.S. goods through the implementation of quotas, tariffs, and other measures by foreign governments.

2. Countries would either buy or sell currency if the demand and supply of the currency was not equal at the fixed exchange rate. When the supply of the currency exceeded the demand for the currency at the fixed exchange rate, the government would purchase the excess using its reserve of foreign currencies. When the supply of the currency was less than the demand for the currency at the fixed exchange rate, the government would sell its currency, thereby increasing its reserve of currencies.

3. Under floating exchange rates, a deficit (or a surplus) in our balance of payments simply reflects differences in the relative price level, relative rate of growth, and relative interest rates between our country and another country, which are resolved in the foreign exchange market by a drop (or a rise) in the value of the dollar.

4. The oil crisis of 1973–74, no matter what the system of international exchange (i.e., gold standard, fixed exchange, or floating exchange), resulted in a redistribution of worldwide income and wealth with the result that oil-exporting countries became relatively richer and oil-importing countries became relatively poorer. Under the gold standard or the fixed-exchange-rate system, there would be no change in the exchange rate; while under the floating-exchange-rate mechanism, the exchange rate could have changed, reflecting changes in the demand for and supply of one country's currency for another.

5. When the ECB increases its discount rate, it leads to appreciation of the euro relative to other currencies because the European interest rate is now relatively more attractive than the interest paid elsewhere.

Problem Set

1. a. The higher curve (S_A) is the one following the depreciation. Because of the depreciation, it takes more dollars to elicit the same supply as before.
    b. It increases the price.
    c. It reduces expenditures.
    d. It increases expenditures.

2. a. 45 pesos.
    b.

Mexican price of good (pesos)	Total desired expenditure (dollars)
50	2,500
45	5,000
40	6,000

3. a. A unit of country X's currency is worth 1/5 as much as a unit of country Y's currency.
    b. A unit of country Y's currency is worth 5 times as much as a unit of country X's currency.

4. a. A dollar sells for 1.67 Swiss francs.
    b. 60 cents.
    c. 340 million francs × 60 cents = 204 million dollars.
    d. 340 million francs.

5. a. Buy. 20 million pounds.
    b. From its reserves.

Audio/Text Questions

1. If a country exported more than it imported, it would be paid in gold. The amount of money (i.e., gold) it circulated in the country would increase, causing prices to rise. The higher prices relative to its trading partners would then cause net exports to ease, because that country's goods would be very expensive. Ultimately the payments would tend to balance.

2. If prices and wages do not fall in the country running a trade deficit or rise in the country with a surplus, the self-equilibrating mechanism does not work. Also, if the gold flows are "sterilized" by central banks (that is, the inflationary impact of a gold inflow is offset by a reduction in the nonspecie money supply), the equilibrating mechanism does not work.

3. According to purchasing power parity, the long-run changes in the values of the dollar in terms of foreign currencies depend on the changes in the relative values of the currencies in their home markets. If the dollar undergoes 10 percent inflation at home and Germany has no inflation, then the value of the dollar vis-à-vis the mark should fall by 10 percent. Purchasing power parity does not take account of capital flows or structural changes in competitiveness, so it is far from an adequate explanation of short-run changes, and it only approximates long-run trends.

4. Growth, inflation, and *nominal* interest rates in the United States were higher. The real interest rate, the nominal interest rate minus expected inflation, was lower than in Europe. Expectations of a decline in the dollar due to a deterioration in the U.S. trade balance made investors even more leery of investing in dollar denominated investments. Therefore, the dollar fell in value.

5. Tight money drives interest rates up and creates an expectation of lower inflation, so the real interest rate becomes very large. This attracts foreign capital, bidding up the value of the dollar. That is in addition to the usual recessionary influences on the dollar. In a recession, net exports increase, so the value of the dollar usually increases.